YASIR ARAFAT

BARRY RUBIN | JUDITH COLP RUBIN

YASIR ARAFAT

A POLITICAL BIOGRAPHY

OXFORD

UNIVERSITY PRESS

2003

OXFORD

UNIVERSITY PRESS

Oxford   New York
Auckland   Bangkok   Buenos Aires   Cape Town   Chennai
Dar es Salaam   Delhi   Hong Kong   Istanbul   Karachi   Kolkata
Kuala Lumpur   Madrid   Melbourne   Mexico City   Mumbai   Nairobi
São Paulo   Shanghai   Taipei   Tokyo   Toronto

Copyright © 2003 by Barry Rubin and Judith Colp Rubin

Published by Oxford University Press, Inc.
198 Madison Avenue, New York, New York 10016

www.oup.com

Oxford is a registered trademark of Oxford University Press

Library of Congress Cataloging-in-Publication Data
Rubin, Barry M.
Yasir Arafat : a political biography / by Barry Rubin and Judith Colp Rubin
p. cm.
Includes bibliographical references and index.
ISBN 0-19-516689-2
1. Arafat, Yasir, 1929– 2. Munaòzòzamat al-Taòhråir
al-Filasòtåinåiyah—Presidents—Biography. 3. Palestinian
Arabs—Biography. 4. Palestinian Arabs—Politics and government—20th
century. 5. Arab-Israeli conflict. I. Rubin, Judith Colp. II. Title.
DS126.6.A67 R83 2003
956.95′3044′092—dc21   2002156587

3 5 7 9 8 6 4 2

Printed in the United States of America
on acid-free paper

This book is dedicated to

Gabriella and Daniel,

our co-authored children

We have tried the utmost of our friends,

Our legions are brim-full, our cause is ripe:

The enemy increaseth every day;

We, at the height, are ready to decline.

There is a tide in the affairs of men,

Which, taken at the flood, leads on to fortune;

Omitted, all the voyage of their life

is bound in shallows and in miseries.

On such a full sea are we now afloat;

And we must take the current when it serves,

Or lose our ventures.

—WILLIAM SHAKESPEARE, *Julius Caesar*

Now is the winter of our discontent...

Our bruised arms hung up for monuments;

Our stern alarums chang'd to merry meetings,

Our dreadful marches to delightful measures.

Grim-visag'd war hath smooth'd his wrinkled front....

But I that am not shap'd for sportive tricks,

Nor made to court an amorous looking-glass...

I that am curtail'd of this fair proportion,

Cheated of feature by dissembling nature....

Why, I, in this weak piping time of peace,

Have no delight to pass away the time.

—WILLIAM SHAKESPEARE, *Richard III*

PREFACE

Writing a biography of anyone is a challenging task, but narrating and analyzing Yasir Arafat's life is a particularly daunting one. Yasir Arafat has occupied the international spotlight for longer than almost any other politician on the planet, yet he remains largely an unknown person. The most basic facts about his background, thoughts, and activities are disputed or unclear. Few leaders evoke such passionate and opposing emotions.

He has succeeded at creating and remaining the leader of the globe's longest-running revolutionary movement. Yet he has failed by not bringing the struggle to a successful conclusion.

He has led his people into more disasters and defeats than any counterpart—no politician in modern history can compare with him in the number of dramatic career ups and downs—yet his standing with them remains high, and his role as the movement's symbol and leader has been relatively unchallenged.

From the time he founded his own political group, Fatah, at age thirty in 1959, and for decades thereafter, Arafat has chosen his historical reputation and his own people's fate to a far greater extent than almost any other human being of his time. In his behavior and personality, Arafat is unique among all of the world's political leaders. He plays by a different set of rules from the others and, as a result, is often misunderstood. Many rulers of states, leading intellectuals, and respected journalists simply have not believed he was doing the things he did, have not understood the meaning of his actions, or have not responded effectively to his behavior.

Arafat poses as the perpetual underdog yet he has been the recipient of many privileges. He has been immune from the harsh and irreversible penalties levied on others who failed to use acceptable methods and as a consequence suffered total defeat. And while his claims of importance on the Middle East stage could seem ridiculously inflated for someone who leads such a relatively tiny group, insignificant in its economic or military power, he has constantly had a disproportionate effect on regional and even world events.

In short, Arafat has been one of the most important, influential, and paradoxical political figures in the twentieth century's second half and beyond. Despite the millions of words spoken by him and written about him, the Arafat phenomenon has remained elusive.

Indeed, the controversy about how to understand Arafat has never been resolved, even after he was finally put to the test. Only when he was offered a Palestinian state on generally reasonable terms in 2000 at Camp David and in the Clinton plan was it possible to conclude whether Arafat was capable of making peace. Would he achieve statehood at last, or had his recurring miscalculations blocked his people's aspirations for decades, actually intensifying their suffering along with that of so many others? Was he capable of peaceful compromise or was only total victory his goal? Would Arafat go down in history as a destructive terrorist buffoon or as a patriotic, even heroic, national liberation fighter and statesman?

This book is the product of decades of study on Yasir Arafat. It is based on a large number of interviews—many of them off the record at the request of those involved—plus archival sources never before cited and printed materials in several languages. We have sought to present a realistic picture that is focused not on the political debates surrounding Arafat but on a genuine effort to understand this unique individual.

Many of those with whom we spoke—including veteran Arafat watchers and those who have worked closely with him—admitted that after many years of experience they still found Arafat to be a mystery. At the end of interviews, the people we were questioning often said they looked forward to reading this book in order to gain a better understanding of this individual who had played a central role in the lives of themselves, their nations, and the world. We hope this book fulfills their expectations.

It should be absolutely clear that this is a biography of Yasir Arafat and thus focuses on him personally. The book is not intended to be a history of the Middle East, of the Arab-Israeli conflict, of Israel, or of any other person, institution, or country. The emphasis is kept on Arafat: his thinking, activities, and those events that most affected him.

Matters that are not discussed or presented adequately have been thoroughly explored in many other books and articles. Exclusion of such matters here has been to let us focus on the book's main subject and not for any other reason.

We wish to thank our agent, Joe Spieler, and our editor, Dedi Felman, both of whom have been an absolute joy to work with at all times. We also benefited from the assistance of researchers Cameron Brown, Caroline Taillander, Joy Pincus, and Amir Ram. Many others also helped by sending us useful material, including Donald Altschiller and Josh Pollack.

Regarding transliteration of words in foreign languages, we have used a system that is consistent, simple for the general audience, and designed to keep familiar spellings of well-known names whenever possible.

On a number of occasions, people were interviewed on background at their request, meaning that their names could not be used. We have identified these in the notes as "Interview" or as an interview with some specific category of person.

CONTENTS

Photo Insert follows page 146

Contents

XIV

YASIR ARAFAT

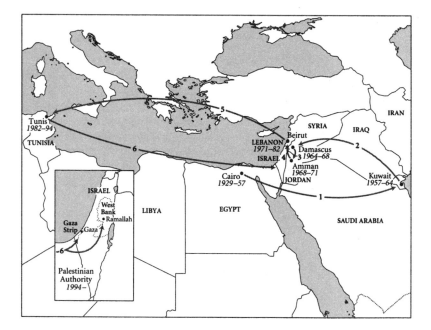

The Odyssey of Yasir Arafat

In the Bunker, 2002

Once again, he was surrounded by the enemy, the sound of gunfire echoing in his ears, the world riveted on his every word. What could be more proper, fulfilling, glorious, or truly revolutionary? No one could call him a sell-out. He had not sacrificed the dream of total victory, even if only a future generation would achieve it. It was far better to be on a battlefield thundering defiance at a besieging foe, professing an eagerness for martyrdom while knowing no one dared to touch you, than merely being sworn in as head of a very small state.

And so, once more, in March (and then again in September) 2002, Yasir Arafat achieved that state of revolutionary nirvana—though not the state of Palestine—just as he had in Amman in 1970, Beirut in 1982, and Tripoli in 1983. What others would have thought to be his worst, most desperate moment seemed to satisfy him far more than when he had to negotiate for peace or administer his near-state in the West Bank and Gaza Strip.

"The more destruction I see," said Arafat, "the stronger I get."[1]

It began on a cloudy night when the Israeli army, responding to a wave of terrorist attacks that had killed 129 of Israel's citizens, advanced into the West Bank town of Ramallah, Arafat's provisional capital for his Palestinian Authority (PA) regime. The army came with a hundred armored personnel carriers, sixty tanks, and twenty-five hundred soldiers. By dawn, soldiers had taken up positions on the main streets, blocking the town's key intersections with ditches and mounds of dirt. Snipers stood atop buildings.

A key target was al-Muqata, Arafat's headquarters. The Israelis knew the buildings well. Before Arafat set up his office there in 1995, the site had been Israel's own military headquarters for governing the West Bank since they had captured it in the 1967 war. The Israelis had turned over the compound, along with all of the West Bank towns, to Arafat's rule. Now, however, with the peace process collapsed and the Palestinians having launched a war of terrorism, the Israeli army was back.

The immediate reason the army was there was due to a lie Arafat had told. The previous October, Israeli cabinet minister Rehavam Zeevi had been assassinated by Palestinian gunmen in Jerusalem. Arafat had assured Israel that the six people responsible had been thrown into prison. In fact, though, he had been protecting them, and when the Israeli army moved in, the perpetrators had even joined Arafat in his compound. The Israelis were determined to see that they were punished.[2]

Israeli troops fired warning shots toward al-Muqata and tanks clanked up to it, ready to shoot if a firefight broke out. Next, armored bulldozers moved in, breaking gaping holes in the compound's wall. Then, squat, tracked armored personnel carriers rolled up. Soldiers emerged from the hatches, some firing stun grenades. Once inside the compound, the soldiers began kicking open doors, moving room to room. They collected ammunition, machine guns, automatic rifles, mortars, and more than forty rocket-propelled grenades. Before leaving the building, they also carted away office files that showed links between Arafat and terrorist attacks against Israel.

But the soldiers were under strict orders to stay away from Arafat and his personal office.[3] The plan was to isolate him there in order to convey an important message: Arafat had lost the war he had unleashed on Israel and should end it. Arafat himself retreated to a windowless room, surrounded by guards and with a submachine gun at the ready.

This siege of Yasir Arafat would last thirty-one days and resemble in all of its major elements many previous events in his life. Once again, Arafat bore the main responsibility for creating the crisis because he did not keep political agreements and promises he made. Once again, he misjudged the balance of forces and attacked an adversary that could easily defeat him. Once again, the Arab states cheered him while lifting no finger to help. Once again, the Israeli enemy did not finish him off, and one more time the United States, a country he often reviled, intervened to rescue him. Once again, he walked away free and unscathed. But once again, too, he had nothing concrete to show for all this turmoil and violence except his own survival.

On the day he was clutching a gun and threatening to make himself into a martyr, he could have been celebrating the independence day of a Palestinian state created by peaceful negotiations. During the year 2000, Arafat had walked away from two major offers that would have given him an independent country and more than $20 billion in international aid. He had promised never to return to violence and then did so. Arafat declared ceasefires and then made no real attempt to implement them. He publicly maintained his non-involvement in terrorism while encouraging, paying salaries, and buying weapons for those who staged attack after attack against Israelis.

Yet despite these developments, Israel had been restrained by international pressure and criticism in fighting the war that Arafat was waging. Previously, Israel's army had attacked buildings and killed leading figures directly involved in making the attacks, but it was reluctant to enter and hold territory governed by Arafat.

That situation changed on March 28, 2002, the first day of Passover, one of the Jewish calendar's holiest days. At the placid Israeli resort town of Netanya, some 250 Israelis gathered at the Park Hotel for the ritual meal. The security man posted at the front door, an example of the intensified efforts to protect civilians since a wave of suicide attacks had begun, left his post for a few moments. The chance was seized by a Palestinian man awaiting such an opportunity. He entered and headed for the hotel's dining room. Guests there were just starting the religious service when he blew himself up, killing 21 and wounding more than 130.

The next day, Arafat told President George W. Bush's envoy, General Anthony Zinni, that he was ready to accept a ceasefire. Zinni had already been in the region for two weeks waiting to hear those words, which were now coming too late. More than once in previous months, Arafat had delayed agreeing to a ceasefire until after a major terrorist attack, in order to forestall Israeli retaliation, and then had done nothing to implement it. Indeed, even as Arafat was speaking with Zinni, a Palestinian gunman attacked a Jewish settlement in the West Bank and killed four Israelis.[4]

The Israeli cabinet met in an all-night emergency meeting to decide on its response. In the end, it launched Operation Defensive Shield, which was designed to do what Arafat would not or could not accomplish: arrest suspected terrorists and seize weapons. Although several cabinet members had argued that Israel should expel Arafat and take its chances with whatever new leadership might emerge, most agreed that such an act would be politically risky and could provoke international condemnation.

But Arafat, ever the master of public relations, gave countless interviews on his cell phone suggesting he was on the verge of being assassinated. "The Israelis want me as a captive, an exile or dead. But I will be a martyr, martyr, martyr," he told *al-Jazira* television. He declared:

> Let those far and near understand: None, among the Palestinian people or the Arab nation, will be willing to bow and surrender. But we ask Allah to grant us martyrdom, to grant us martyrdom. To Jerusalem we march—martyrs by the millions! To Jerusalem we march—martyrs by the millions! To Jerusalem we march—martyrs by the millions! To Jerusalem we march—martyrs by the millions![5]

"Man, don't wish me safety!" he urged an Egyptian TV reporter who had done just that. "Pray for me to attain martyrdom! Is there anything better than being martyred on this holy land? We are all seekers of martyrdom."[6]

At the same time that Arafat was playing the role of heroic martyr, he was appealing to the world to save him from harm. Among the many he telephoned for help on the first day of the siege were UN secretary general Kofi Annan, Lebanese prime minister Rafiq Hariri, and Arab League secretary general Amr Musa. But, once again and ever so ironically, he knew his best chances lay with the Americans.

Arafat said he told the U.S. government, "You must act.... Don't you know this will shake the Middle East?"[7] His solution was for the United States to "order" Israel to withdraw from Ramallah, asking, "Why are [the Americans] quiet despite all that is taking place?"[8] Arafat seemed to have forgotten that the peace plans he had rejected; the ceasefires he had broken; and former president Bill Clinton, whom he had humiliated by that behavior, had all been American, too.

At least at first, the help Arafat cried out for did not come from anyone. The day after the Israelis moved into Ramallah, a suicide bomber blew himself up in a Tel Aviv café. President George Bush, in his first response to Arafat's siege, pointedly did not call for an Israeli pullout from Ramallah. Instead, he said that Arafat and Arab leaders "could do a lot more" to stop Palestinian terror. This step, he made clear, was necessary to achieve peace in the region.[9] The Security Council of the United Nations, always Arafat's ally, did pass a toothless resolution calling for Israel's withdrawal "without delay," and even the United States supported it.[10] But this was only one more paper victory for the Palestinian leader.

No one tried to stop Israel's army as it moved into other towns under Arafat's jurisdiction: Bethlehem, Qalqilya, Tulkarm, Nablus, and Jenin.

It arrested hundreds of suspected terrorists, including members of Fatah, Arafat's political group, and PA security officers, whose job was supposed to be stopping terrorism but who, following Arafat's policy, had instead participated in it. Arafat's forces were in desperate shape. One of his security chiefs, Jibril Rajub, said his men were "forced to surrender because they had no bullets left or even a bottle of water."[11]

Even Marwan Barghouti, Fatah's head in the West Bank and the best-known grassroots leader of the uprising, was captured by Israel on April 15. While no one expected such developments to end the terrorism, they did eventually reduce the number of attacks and put pressure on the Palestinian side to stop the fighting.[12]

Yet, as he often did with his back to the wall, Arafat sought to escalate rather than to calm the situation. He incited his own people and the Arab world with false accusations of Israeli massacres and war crimes. On a broadcast televised throughout the Middle East, he said:

> [Israeli forces] tried to destroy the statue of Mary [inside one of the most sacred Christian sites, the Church of the Nativity in Bethlehem], and today, they are attacking and burning churches and mosques. How could this be acceptable [to] Arabs, Muslims, Christians and the whole world? This is the message we send to the world. . . . Where are you? I have said that before, and I will say it now, I would rather die a martyr, a martyr, a martyr![13]

Asked how he was managing under the difficult conditions, Arafat replied: "I lived in caves while fighting Israeli forces. This is a nation of strong people. I live with a strong people, and I am one of them."[14]

But his personal hardships were not so extreme. Israel was supplying water, food, toothbrushes, and toilet paper to the compound.[15] Although the electricity was cut when the siege began, it was soon turned back on. Arafat and his advisors spent much of their time watching CNN. They also held a "trial" of Zeevi's killers and purportedly sentenced them to prison terms so that Arafat could argue there was no reason for Israel to continue the siege.[16]

Arafat's main worry, however, was the fact that Bush seemed in no hurry to rescue him, especially without some sign of change on Arafat's part. On April 4, Bush had said that Arafat

> has not consistently opposed or confronted terrorists. [In his previous agreements], Chairman Arafat renounced terror as an instrument of his cause, and he agreed to control it. He's not done so. The situation in which he finds himself today is largely of his own making. He's missed his opportunities and thereby betrayed the hopes of the people he is supposed to lead. Given his failure,

the Israeli government feels it must strike at terrorist networks that are killing its citizens.[17]

Bush urged Israel to negotiate with Arafat but in a context that hinted at his hope that Arafat would be replaced:

> As Israel steps back, responsible Palestinian leaders and Israel's Arab neighbors must step forward and show the world that they are truly on the side of peace. The choice and the burden will be theirs. The world expects an immediate ceasefire, immediate resumption of security cooperation with Israel against terrorism, and an immediate order to crack down on terrorist networks. I expect better leadership and I expect results.[18]

Hasan Asfour, one of Arafat's cabinet ministers, expressed his leader's real concern and lack of eagerness for martyrdom when he called Bush's speech "A permit to kill Yasir Arafat."[19] On April 14, the day before Secretary of State Colin Powell was due to visit Arafat at the compound, Arafat's movement called on Palestinians and all Arabs to oppose U.S. policy and threatened that any Arab rulers cooperating with the Americans would be overthrown by their own people.[20]

The tough American stance, however, was only temporary, designed to scare Arafat into behaving better, not to eliminate him. As the siege continued into its second week, the Americans began preparing to save Arafat. Despite strong Israeli disapproval and Arafat's own threats, Powell went to the compound to meet him on April 15. As he did with all Western visitors, Arafat promised that he would stop the terrorist attacks on Israel.[21] Within two weeks, the United States had brokered a deal. Israel would let Arafat leave his compound and, in exchange, the six assassins of Zeevi would be put in a Palestinian Authority jail inspected by American and British wardens to ensure Arafat did not let them out again.

On May 1, Arafat emerged at the compound's door. A bit unsteady, he was held up by aides but managed to make a V-for-victory sign as hundreds of Palestinians cheered and chanted, "God is great!" Immediately, he returned to the verbal offensive, claiming Israel had committed massacres and war crimes and had attempted to burn down the Church of Nativity, which is believed to mark the spot where Jesus was born. But it was Arafat's own men who had seized the church, despite its priests' protests, and fired on Israeli soldiers from its windows.

When Ted Koppel of the ABC television show *Nightline* challenged some of his claims, Arafat, who had never held any military rank, began shouting, "I am a general! You are speaking with Yasir Arafat! You are attacking me? ... You are speaking to General Arafat." The interview ended with a typical Arafatian dramatic flourish as his aides ushered a little girl into the room to sit on his lap. As he hugged and kissed her, Arafat intoned, "We [must not] forget that we have to work hard for the peace for our children and their children."[22]

Nothing could be more appropriately symbolic of Arafat's career than the fact that even after his release he still implemented no ceasefire and again let terrorist leaders take refuge in his compound. After six months of more terrorist attacks, the Israeli army returned to Ramallah in September 2002. Arafat was once more besieged, and the whole process was repeated until the United States again persuaded Israel to pull out.

Once more, Arafat had maneuvered himself into a catastrophic position, dragging his people and many others in the region into crisis. He had again forced a battle and then lost it. True, Arafat found protectors, survived, and largely escaped being blamed for the violence and crises he helped provoke. To credulous audiences, he could still be portrayed as the well-intentioned victim or heroic freedom fighter. In material terms, however, he had produced nothing to defeat his enemy or to benefit his people.

Whole generations, a half-dozen U.S. presidents, and entire regimes have come and gone over the long course of Arafat's career. But Arafat is still there, with three constants always present: he has always survived, has always been in serious trouble, and has never achieved his goals.

How did such a unique leader develop? How has he been able for so long to stride across the global stage as one of the world's most recognizable figures, a man able to shake the Middle East and dominate the attention of governments and the media? And why, given all that, has he been unable to achieve anything lasting beyond the sound and fury of his passage?

The answers make for one of the most fascinating political stories of all time.

1

A Most Unlikely Leader

1929–1967

Everything is controversial when it comes to Yasir Arafat, even the question of where his life began. For many years, his statement that he had been born in Jerusalem was accepted as fact. Certainly, having as his home town the charismatic city sacred to three religions would legitimize his claim to rule a state whose capital would be in Jerusalem.

How, Arafat apparently reasoned, could the man who wanted to be the symbol of Palestine not have been born there? But in fact he was not. Although he has never admitted it, Arafat was really born in Cairo, Egypt, a foreign though Arab land, and spent most of his first three decades there. Even when, years later, he was presented with the irrefutable evidence of his birth certificate from an Egyptian hospital, Arafat continued his denial, insisting that he was born in Jerusalem.

Yet while Egypt is an Arab country, Arafat grew up there as an outsider, one of only forty-five hundred Palestinians at the time of his birth.[1] It was where he attended school, learned about politics, and became a militant activist. Decades afterward, as a compulsive traveler, he expressed an ambivalence toward Egypt that mirrored his sense of homelessness and his understanding of what Arab regimes really thought of him: "[Egypt's leaders] don't want me here. As soon as I arrive they ask: 'When [is he] leaving?' And yet Cairo is the only place where I can have a deep sleep. Everywhere else I sleep with one eye open, but in Cairo I feel secure."[2]

In that city, he was born on August 24, 1929, and was given the name Abd al-Rahman Abd al-Rauf Arafat al-Qudwa al-Husseini. It was a big name, and each part of it was significant. Abd al-Rahman means "slave of Allah the justice-giver," a sign of the family's Islamic piety. Abd al-Rauf was his father's first name, and al-Qudwa was his father's clan and the name Yasir Arafat's own family actually used. But these were the names of his father, a man the young boy never came to love. In contrast, Husseini, the family name of his mother, Zahwa, was that of the most important Palestinian Arab family then in existence. When Arafat was born, during the British mandate of Palestine, a distant relative, Amin al-Husseini, was leading the Arab community there. This prestigious name, however, was that of a powerful clan and high social class to which Arafat did not really belong.

Only Arafat—an important religious site near Mecca in Saudi Arabia—could be said to belong to the child alone. Yasir was his nickname within the family, which means—ironically, given later history—"easy," "no problems." Thus, by ultimately choosing to be known as Yasir Arafat, the future leader was stressing that he was unique, apart, and self-made. He was neither Egyptian, nor an obscure and unimportant Qudwa, nor in the shadow of his father or the aristocratic Husseinis.

Many years later, Arafat would continue to reveal his personal insecurity over that identity even though he had become a globally known leader. When angry or challenged, or if he thought insufficient attention was being paid to his great importance, he would fly into a rage and announce self-righteously: "I am Yasir Arafat!"[3]

Small and chubby, Yasir was the fourth of seven children. Arafat's father had ambitions to become wealthy but remained a small shop-keeper all his life.[4] He had arrived in Egypt from Gaza around 1927 because he had inherited some land there which he thought would be valuable. Yet while he spent his life and used up his money trying to acquire this parcel of real estate, it was tied up in legal problems and he never got control over it, foreshadowing his son's later inability to get full control over the land he devoted his life to obtaining.[5] The family settled in a middle-class area of Cairo whose diverse population included Jews and Lebanese Christians.[6]

But Egyptian nationalism did not welcome the small community of Palestinian Arabs there. They faced discrimination, including being barred from government employment. A Palestinian later wrote that the Egyptian regime feared that their integration would "make the Palestinians forget their homeland" and they would become permanent residents. Thus, they were to be reminded that they were exiles and young Yasir grew up feeling that he was a refugee long before thousands of other Palestinians came to be in that situation.[7]

When Yasir was a little boy, his mother died, perhaps of kidney complications.[8] Left with seven children, his father remarried. The children did not like his father's new wife, and their father did not want all of them around. He sent Yasir and his younger brother, Fathi, to live with a maternal uncle in Jerusalem. Salim Abu Suud and his family were much better off than Yasir's own and lived near the al-Aqsa mosque, the most important one in the country.

At the moment Yasir was born, Arab rioting had erupted against Jews praying at the nearby Western Wall, their Temple's only visible remnant. When he was just two years old, in 1931, an international Islamic conference for the first time focused attention on al-Aqsa as a Muslim site of great political and religious importance.[9] Yasir later made that building a central symbol for his movement. Its picture would adorn his office wall, and control of the mosque would be a key issue in his rejecting the peace offer made at the Camp David summit and launching an uprising seventy years later.

During the mid-1930s, then, Yasir was simultaneously rejected by his own father and offered life in a happier home in Jerusalem than he had in Cairo with his own parents.[10] He had moved from the outermost margin of Palestinian Arab life to the community's religious, political, and intellectual center and to the epicenter of the brewing and passionate political conflict.

In addition to being a critical moment in Yasir's life, it was also a turning point in the Arab-Jewish battle. An Arab general strike in 1936 was followed by a two-year-long nationalist uprising in British-ruled Palestine, which was led by members of the Husseini clan. Although their ostensible targets were the British and Jews, many of the victims were Arabs killed by factional infighting. The young Arafat may have witnessed tumultuous and bloody events. The apparent lessons were that violence was glorious—the best alternative to submission—and that Palestinian civil war was disastrous. At the end of the 1930s, shortly after the revolt petered out, Arafat returned to Cairo.

By this time, Arafat's father had divorced his second wife, but the family was no better off. His father was still squandering time and money on the doomed effort to secure the land he claimed. A third marriage also failed, and Arafat's older sister Inam had to raise the children.

Obviously, Yasir had an unpleasant childhood. Distancing himself from the difficulties around him may have been his first exercise in secretiveness and concealment of facts or feelings. His mother and father had been in conflict, his father's second wife treated the children badly, and the son did not respect the father. He was apparently resentful and felt deprived and sorry for himself. Shoved aside by his father, he seemed to have a deep need to prove his own importance. According to his brother, he never cried and "when he was angry, he would just cast his stare right at us."[11]

Already, the young Arafat was finding solace in politics and religion. At the age of ten, he was organizing neighborhood children and shouting Islamist slogans. His sister recounted years later that he did not want to wear a new suit she had bought him because poorer kids did not have such clothes.

But he was never attracted by social reform. The religious orientation he discovered through pious relatives in Jerusalem, who had sheltered him from his own dysfunctional family, proved a far more important influence. Alone among the entire Palestine Liberation Organization (PLO) or Fatah leadership, who were heavily influenced by Marxism and European-style nationalism, Arafat would fill his talks with quotations from Islamic texts and religious references. This attitude was one key to his world view and broad popular appeal to the more traditionalist masses.[12]

The next period of Arafat's life, during the 1940s, is shrouded in mystery. Determined to be the living embodiment of Palestinian nationalism, Arafat revised his biography accordingly. It would not do for the symbol of Arab Palestine to be born in Cairo, or for the creator of Palestinian nationalism to be an outright Islamist, or for the general commanding Palestinian forces to have never fired a shot during the 1948 war. The alternative life story he created became the pattern for the many false tales he would spin in the future.

Supposedly, according to Arafat himself, the key factor promoting his early political career was a distant relation on his mother's side, Hasan Abu Suud, an important religious official and assistant of Amin al-Husseini, leader of the Palestinian Arabs.[13] After leading the uprising of the late 1930s, Husseini fled arrest by the British and spent World War II in Nazi Germany as a junior ally of Hitler. After the war ended, he was quickly released by his French captors and made his way back to the Middle East to resume his revolutionary activities. Suud, Arafat claims, made him an assistant and a messenger between Husseini's Cairo office and the Arab League headquarters there.

Arafat says that his next mentor was Abd al-Khadar al-Husseini, a nephew of Amin al-Husseini and the main Palestinian military leader. Abd al-Khadar was shot dead in April 1948 when he mistakenly walked into an Israeli army camp outside Jerusalem one night and did not know the password. Arafat at various times claimed to have been Abd al-Khadar's private secretary, a member of one of Abd al-Khadar's units, and the youngest officer in the Palestinian forces. He also told improbable stories of single-handedly stopping an Israeli tank column during the 1948 war and outwitting Zionist agents to obtain weapons left behind on the World War II battlefields of North Africa.

Yet Arafat's claims to such high-level connections are most improbable. Abd al-Khadar died while Arafat was still in Cairo, and Arafat's lack of military training and difficulties in getting to Palestine also demonstrate this fact. And if Arafat was off in North Africa during a war that lasted barely seven months after he claims to have arrived, he certainly did not have time to see any of the fighting.[14]

There is good reason to believe that Arafat did not fight in the 1948 war. He never cited specific battles in which he was involved despite this event's overwhelming importance for Palestinian history and the glory such details would have brought him.

What seems to be true is that around April 1948, Arafat got in touch with Hamid Abu Sitta, an engineering student at Cairo University, who had been organizing demonstrations to encourage students to fight. Arafat volunteered but Abu Sitta told him, "You are not trained. You are very small." Arafat insisted, "I want to fight, really fight. I'm trained and you can depend on me."[15] If Arafat truly had connections with the Husseini leadership, of course, he would not have needed to beg an obscure student to be included in the war, and he was clearly enlisting as a private, not as an officer or on anyone's staff.

Toward the end of April 1948, Arafat, Abu Sitta, and others left by train from Cairo, then rowed in a small boat across the Suez Canal. Arafat later said, "Here we are, three men going to fight Jews . . . with only one weapon. We must be crazy." When they reached the eastern shore, sympathizers drove them to the Egyptian border near Gaza. There, Arafat recounted, an Egyptian officer demanded they turn over all weapons. He ignored their protest and gave Arafat a receipt for his rifle.[16]

The story about the Egyptian officer who looked down on would-be guerrillas and all Palestinian Arabs rings true. It seems to have been Arafat's most important direct experience in the 1948 war and must have been a traumatic one. In effect, Arafat was being told by a professional soldier in a well-pressed uniform to go home like a good little boy and let the real men—and non-Palestinians, too—get on with the job of smashing the Jews. Such an event would have challenged his self-esteem and taught him resentment and distrust of Arab regimes and disdain for the supposed expertise of career officers.

While Arafat was passionate in denouncing how he was kept out of Palestine, he never described how he ever did get there nor provide any evidence for what he did if and when he arrived. On one occasion, he said that he joined a Muslim Brotherhood group and was stationed in the Old City in the Jaffa Gate and Silwan sectors.[17] But if this is true, why did he never mention this story elsewhere? Even in this one case where he did say something specific about his experience, Arafat made a revealing qualification. Asked if he engaged in battle, Arafat replied belligerently, "You are completely ignorant.... The British army was still there.... The main British forces were in Jerusalem."[18]

But the British army had left in May 1948, by the time Arafat supposedly arrived. Most likely, this is a way for Arafat to avoid admitting that Jordan's army, which had many British officers, held East Jerusalem during the 1948 war. In fact, the fighting in that city—one of the few Arab victories in 1948—was won by Jordanian, not Palestinian soldiers, and even Arafat admitted on this occasion that he was not involved in any of it. To make matters worse, he was not even serving in a Palestinian Arab unit.

Whatever the truth of his personal role, the failed Private Arafat of 1948 would demand that he be treated as General Arafat in later decades, although he would more often repeat than avoid the mistakes that had cost the Palestinians so dearly then. By rejecting a compromise peace proposal, the 1947 UN partition plan to establish both a Palestinian and an Israeli state, the Palestinians and the Arab states lost the chance to have a Palestinian state and created the conditions that turned most of the Palestinians into refugees.

By attacking an adversary they underestimated, the Palestinians and Arabs had suffered a terrible military defeat. The leaders had mistakenly believed their own propaganda. Having inflamed their people to passionate militancy, they found this made it impossible for them to compromise or even maneuver politically. Having promised their people a quick, inevitable victory, leaders then had to explain why they had failed so miserably at such an easy task.

The only thing Arafat seems to have learned from the debacle was to blame it on the Arab states rather than on the Palestinians themselves. He complained inaccurately that the Palestinians demanded that the Arab armies advance to victory only to be told they had no orders to do so. Arafat never seemed to consider that the Israelis won the war militarily. Only Arab incompetence or treason could explain why an easy victory was not achieved. He explained, "The Jews could not have captured many of our places if the Arab forces had not withdrawn without a fight. I can tell, for example, that Haifa would not have fallen without a fight if the Arab forces had not opened the way by retreating, according to their orders."[19]

Yet Arafat's account was not accurate. True, Arab forces suffered from poor coordination and bickering commanders—something Arafat would later reproduce by refusing to unify Palestinian groups—but they did not act in a cowardly manner as he implies. The use of Haifa by

Arafat as his main example was particularly telling, a sort of Freudian slip. The Jews did capture Haifa without being threatened by any Arab army, but the Palestinian leadership ordered its people to leave the city in order to avoid the fighting there, which precipitated a large part of the flight that would turn the Palestinian Arabs into refugees. It was not a retreat of Arab forces that ensured a Jewish triumph in Haifa but the flight of the Palestinian population. This was why Palestinians faced humiliating ridicule for years in neighboring Arab states, where they were labeled as cowards who had lost their own country. Arafat attempted to rewrite history to shift the blame for the defeat onto Arab countries rather than accept that an equally significant cause was Palestinian actions.[20]

Arafat's version of what happened in 1948 reveals key themes for his later career. He does not attribute the debacle to a failure to use diplomacy and compromise, nor to an inability to understand that Israel would not be so easily defeated militarily. Instead, he argues that the Arabs could have won if they had not given up. If Palestinians and Arabs kept on fighting and never stopped, no matter how bad the immediate situation seemed, he apparently concluded, they would eventually triumph. This catastrophe also intensified his mistrust of Arab regimes and their professional soldiers. The Palestinians, he concluded, would need their own forces—preferably unlike the regular armies that had failed—if they wanted to win. Finally, since the loss of Palestine was the Arab states' fault, they owed the Palestinians a debt that could never be repaid. It was thus their duty to give Arafat whatever political and military support he demanded.

For Arafat, the core mistake of 1948 was that the Arab side was too moderate. The real "betrayal and treachery," he alleged, was an Arab acceptance of partition. "Why didn't they have the desire and will to continue the war?"[21] To Arafat, losing a war was no excuse for ending it, another policy he would follow in later years.

In addition, while others saw the 1948 defeat and their virtual disappearance from the political scene as proof of the Palestinians' weakness, Arafat would reinterpret this era as proving their strength. The Palestinian issue, he would say later, "was the cause of all the military coups all over the Arab world" during the 1950s. It was their "treason" in not sufficiently supporting the Palestinians that Arafat thought led to the downfall of regimes in Egypt, Syria, and Iraq.[22] Arafat's implication was that this gave the Palestinians tremendous regional leverage: if the Arab states did not do what the Palestinian movement demanded, these governments would be overthrown by their own people.

The Egyptian, Syrian, and Iraqi officers who seized power during those years, however, did not accept Arafat's interpretation. For them,

1948 was most important in domestic terms, by providing another example of the incompetence and corruption in their own countries that had blocked progress. As one of them, Egyptian leader Gamal Abd al-Nasser, wrote in his autobiography, the real battle was at home.[23] This was the reason that these Arab states paid scant attention to the Palestinian issue during the fifteen years following 1948.

Arafat's involvement in any extended military activity in Palestine is also thrown into question by the fact that he was back in Cairo in 1949 applying for college. That fall, he entered King Fuad University in Cairo as a civil engineering student. Later, Arafat would portray this step as part of a predetermined revolutionary march: "I was advanced in mathematics. My specialty was figures and calculations. Engineering was also the most useful subject for me to study. It would not prevent me from continuing with my military march. It would even help me."[24]

But Arafat was not interested in school. Despite bragging about his mathematical ability, he completed his first year with only a pass, had to repeat his second year, and failed math twice.[25] His passion was politics, and he had plenty of company in that regard. Egyptians resented British influence in the country and especially their continuing presence in the Suez Canal zone, where a foreign company controlled one of Egypt's greatest assets. Again, Arafat was not content to say that he was a participant in events but had to cast himself as a hero, insisting he was a major leader of the anti-British resistance.[26] In 1950, he has claimed, he went to the Canal Zone with Muslim Brotherhood units to fight the British. But Hassan Doh, a Muslim Brotherhood activist who gave Arafat military training at the university, said that Arafat never actually did any fighting.[27] Arafat seems to have been a student politician rather than a warrior.

The fact that Arafat went to the Muslim Brotherhood for training— and was close to it politically—was an important factor shaping his identity despite the fact that he did not accept all of its ideology. The Brotherhood, the Arab world's first and largest Islamist group, sought to overthrow Egypt's regime, replace it with an Islamic state, expel Western influences, and destroy Israel. Arafat later sought to play down his connections with the Brotherhood since it posed political problems for him. After all, it was an Egyptian, not Palestinian, group and was Islamist, not nationalist. In later years, too, Arafat wanted good relations with Arab governments that hated and repressed the Muslim Brotherhood and would have been hostile to Arafat if they had identified him with that organization.

But the Brotherhood did inoculate Arafat against other ideologies and gave him a stronger Islamic tinge than any other Palestinian nationalist leader. Arafat was decidedly not a leftist who extolled the

Soviet Union, the importance of ideology, and socialism as the solution to all problems. He also was not a Pan Arab nationalist who followed Nasser or other Arab rulers believing that revolution throughout the Arab world under their leadership was the way to conquer Palestine at a future date.

While he did not become the kind of militant Islamist who later formed groups like Hamas, Arafat's conservative disinterest in transforming society reflects his Islamic perspective. Instead of turning Palestine into a modern socioeconomic paradise, he simply wanted to restore Palestine as Arab and to recreate the traditional society there, a vanished world all the more romanticized by his brief youthful stay in Jerusalem. Thus, he was not inspired by building a new society that would transform refugees into productive citizens, raise the living standards of the people, or create a polity whose success would inspire other Arabs.

His role models did not come from Arab nationalist leaders or thinkers but from the struggle of the early Muslims for whom only total victory over infidels and Crusaders was acceptable. When he later needed an underground alias, Arafat chose the name Abu Ammar to recall Yasir Abu Ammar, whom, Arafat said, had been "captured, tortured to force him to give up his faith and finally put to death by the infidels. [He was] the first martyr of Islam whose name became the symbol of total fidelity to one's faith and beliefs in the Arab world."[28] Such traditionalist and Islam-oriented attitudes made George Habash, leader of the PLO's quasi-Marxist forces, once remark that, if Arafat had his way, a Palestinian state would end up looking like Saudi Arabia.[29]

As a result of this orientation, Arafat had an unusual mix of characteristics compared to other Arabs or Palestinians of that time. Also, unlike other nationalist leaders, Arafat did not see establishment of a state alone—on any borders possible—as a sufficient achievement to justify deep compromises.

First and foremost, Arafat did not exclusively or even primarily seek the creation of a state or a just society but the enemy's destruction and the extermination of his state, even if that interfered with Arafat's other potential goals. While Arafat constantly derided ideology, his highly self-conscious identity as revolutionary and Muslim kept him from being a pragmatist. He expected to win not because he realistically took into account the balance of forces or made constant improvements in his goals and methods based on the lessons of experience but due to the righteousness and even divine sanction for his cause.

At the start, the Palestinian movement was so weak and diverse that such distinctions among strategies or ideas did not matter. Arafat began his political career by joining the Arab Palestine Club and was also elected by the Cairo University engineering school to the Student Union.[30] Arafat and another Palestinian student, Salah Khalaf (later known as Abu Iyad), decided to take over the Palestinian Student Union in 1952. While Abu Iyad was more influenced by leftist views than Arafat, the two men had much in common. "We knew what was damaging for the Palestinian cause. Palestinians could expect nothing from [other] Arabs, who were corrupt or tied to imperialism," Abu Iyad later explained, "and [it was] wrong to bank on the political parties in the region. Palestinians could only rely upon themselves."[31]

Unlike the other student activists—who came from the Muslim Brotherhood; the Ba'th party, an Arab nationalist group; and the Communist party—Arafat and Abu Iyad had no outside political sponsor. This independence was the reason that their ticket won six of the nine seats on the Palestine Student Union's executive committee. Arafat was elected president with a large majority and held that position until he graduated.[32] His activities included organizing debates, campaigning for scholarships for Palestinians, and creating a student magazine.[33]

Aside from the 1948 war, the main event to shape Arafat's political life at the time was the 1952 coup that overthrew Egypt's monarchy and brought to power the Free Officers led by Gamal Abd al-Nasser, who would become the dominant figure not only in Egypt but throughout the Arab world.[34] Nasser was popularly known as *al-ra'is* (the captain), a title Arafat would take for himself forty years later when he became a ruler. Reversing the monarchy's policies and following a Pan-Arab nationalist line, Nasser's government in 1954 gave Palestinians employment rights equal to Egyptian nationals, free hospital treatment and medicine, plus special privileges compared to other foreign Arabs in obtaining commercial licenses.[35]

There then came a period of rapid ups and downs in Arafat's situation as he fell in and out of favor with Egypt's government. At times he might have been in jail; at other moments he may have been a surrogate for that regime, waging a nominally independent armed struggle as a covert agent for Cairo's interests.

Determined to end the British military presence in the Suez Canal zone, the Egyptian government used the Muslim Brotherhood to wage a guerrilla war to force Britain's withdrawal. Arafat claims that he participated as a fighter, but again there is no proof of this. He was still attending university courses, according to his school records.[36]

The next year, 1955, the government clashed with the Muslim Brotherhood. Nasser was speaking to a big rally in Alexandria when gunshots rang out and a lightbulb just above his head exploded. The regime blamed the Brotherhood, and there were mass arrests of its leaders. Arafat claims that he was imprisoned for several weeks. Experience was constantly teaching Arafat the lesson—relatively rare among his contemporaries—that the Arab nationalist rulers were sometimes his allies and sometimes his enemies.[37]

But almost immediately, the Egyptian authorities changed their attitude toward Arafat. They had held the Gaza Strip at the end of the 1948 war but had ruled it like a colony and blocked Palestinian self-government there. Now, however, the Egyptians began to allow and encourage small-scale Palestinian raids into Israel. In February 1955, an Israeli reprisal attack into Gaza caused heavy casualties among Egyptian soldiers. Arafat, trying to make himself sound more important, said that he met with Nasser, who then let him visit Gaza as the head of a student delegation. Actually, though, Arafat and his friends were then protesting against Nasser—who had likely never heard of him—demanding either a war on Israel or his regime's downfall, making this story unlikely.[38]

In response to the escalating fighting and to ensure better control over Palestinian raids into Israel, the Egyptian government established a 700-man Palestinian commando unit in Gaza in April 1955. Its members were trained by Egypt's army and were paid regular wages, including bonuses for completing assigned missions. Many of Fatah's early cadres would later come out of this unit, but Arafat himself did not join it.[39]

Nasser's star was rising everywhere in the Arab world. Not only did he control the limited existing Palestinian activities, but his followers and agents were mobilizing support for his leadership throughout the region. In 1955, he played a leading role in the founding of the Third World nonaligned movement while at the same time he was buying Soviet bloc arms, which allied him to Moscow. In July 1956, he nationalized the Suez Canal company and the British left. But England responded by joining forces with France, which was worried about Nasser's support for the revolutionary forces in its colony of Algeria, and Israel, which expected Nasser to use his new weapons and regional power to launch an attack against itself.

In September, Israel attacked Egypt and, by prior secret agreement, Anglo-French forces came in nominally as "peacemakers" but with the real goal of overthrowing Nasser. Moscow warned that it would use nuclear weapons to defend Egypt's dictator, but Nasser was actually saved by the United States. Washington hoped that rescuing Nasser would earn his gratitude and was worried that the Egyptian regime's fall would bring a much larger, pro-Soviet regional upheaval. The Americans thus acted on this, as on later occasions, from moral qualms and wider strategic considerations. But Arab nationalists interpreted this as a victory over a weak West, which proved their own strategy to be correct.

As a result they kept challenging U.S. interests and confronting the Americans until Washington was forced to oppose them and support their enemies. This would be a mistake Arafat would later make repeatedly.

Arafat, who had just graduated from the university, says that in 1956 he took a three-month course as an officer in Egypt's army. He claims to have participated as a lieutenant in the defense of Port Said, the Sinai peninsula's main town, during the Suez war, and when foreign forces withdrew to have been involved in mine-clearing operations.[40] After the war, he says, he was asked to stay in Egypt's military.

Yet the war began and ended so fast that Arafat's participation, at least in the actual fighting, seems unlikely. Moreover, just before the war began, Arafat was not serving with Egypt's army but was still completely involved in student politics. In August 1956, he and Abu Iyad went to Czechoslovakia to participate in a Communist-sponsored international students' congress. They were invited because they were the Palestinian student movement's leaders and not due to any leftist orientation.[41]

For the same reason, Arafat was then invited to a Western-sponsored student meeting in Ibadan, Nigeria, by the coordinating secretariat of the National Unions of Students, an international organization founded in 1950, which received covert help from the Central Intelligence Agency (CIA) to battle Soviet-sponsored groups. By urging Arafat to join their youth festivals, both sides in the Cold War were now competing for Arafat's favors—and not for the last time either. At Ibadan, Arafat demanded that the Israeli delegation be banned and was supported by other Arab delegates. He rushed from committee to committee trying to influence the meeting's outcome and gave his first interview to journalists. He made an unfavorable impression on Western participants, who noted his rolling eyes, worn and unpolished shoes, baggy pants, and bright red and green tie. When he failed to block admission of the Israelis, Arafat walked out of the meeting room, a tactic he would use many times in the future.[42]

In 1956 Arafat was not quite ready to become a full-time politician or soldier. After receiving his engineering degree with a specialty in sanitation, he took a job with the Egyptian Cement Corporation as an engineer.[43] At this time Arafat was a twenty-seven-year-old man with no previous employment record and—unusual among Arabs—no wife or children. Whatever his connections had been with the Muslim Brotherhood and the Egyptian army or intelligence services, Arafat had no great political prospects either. But aside from his innate talents, he had four particular advantages that would help him to attain the political heights.

First, during these years, he was developing the Arafat persona. Instinctively and through observing Nasser, he grasped the importance of the politician as actor, a man who radiated charisma and embodied his people's hopes.[11] Charisma did not come naturally to Arafat, who was short, ungainly, and no great orator. Yet he was able to develop personal symbols, which would become world famous, to make up for these deficiencies: the stubble of beard, the *kaffiya* (head scarf), and the military uniform among them. He also had a repertoire of behaviors that ranged from intimidating to charming. The result was his embodiment of a combination of roles: fighter, traditional patriarch, and typical Palestinian.

Second, in contrast to almost anyone else, he had the proper world view to become the emerging consensus leader of a Palestinian nationalist movement. He was neither an Islamist nor a leftist, which would in either case have limited his appeal, but was able to learn from the political and revolutionary experience of both camps. Equally important, Arafat was not a Pan Arab nationalist owing allegiance to the leader of some Arab state, dependent on his will and waiting for him to solve the problem. Even in the 1950s he was already grasping the coming trends for Third World revolution, including the glamour of violence and the use of public relations methods, which would only fully emerge a decade later.

Third, Arafat had no real competition in his chosen arena. There was no other serious Palestinian group or leader in the field at the time. Throughout his career, he did encounter personal and institutional rivals, yet none had his will power or staying power. Each challenger either quickly faded away or accepted him as the rightful leader, even if he did not always obey Arafat.

Finally, he had a group of colleagues, some of them quite able, who could balance his shortcomings but who lacked the ambition to seize leadership. Arafat had already worked closely with Abu Iyad, and during his student days he also met another key figure in Fatah's history, Khalil al-Wazir (later known as Abu Jihad), who was studying humanities at Alexandria University. Abu Jihad was seven years younger than Arafat, an age difference that was apparently enough for Arafat to regard him a bit paternalistically. In 1948, his family had left Ramle during the fighting and fled to Gaza.

At age eighteen, Abu Jihad had led a group across the border to attack Israel. On his return, the Egyptians threw him into jail for acting independently, but Egyptian intelligence soon began using him for its own missions. He was a behind-the-scenes figure who, Arafat realized, would never challenge him. He soon became Arafat's personal favorite. Even decades afterward, the late Abu Jihad was the only Palestinian other than Arafat whose picture is allowed to appear widely in the places Arafat controls.[45]

By 1957, however, it was clear that Arafat had done just about all he could without leaving Egypt. Despite his stories about being welcomed into the Egyptian army, the Nasser regime clearly had no more tolerance for his activities. Sounding like a man in trouble with the authorities, he recounted of that time, "Some [people] avoided me, and others seemed to be embarrassed in my presence."[46] When Arafat left Egypt, the government lost no time in dissolving the Palestinian student group he had led.[47]

Many Palestinians had already gone to Kuwait, then a British protectorate, where a combination of an oil boom and a lack of indigenous skilled personnel made them welcome. Abu Iyad also went there as a teacher, and Arafat found a job as a road engineer in Kuwait's Department of Public Works. He would later brag that he made great sums of money in Kuwait and could have become a millionaire many times over if he had chosen to do so. Yet while well paid by contemporary Arab standards, as were all skilled foreign workers in Kuwait, he was a low-level civil service engineer who lived in a small, government-owned bungalow in Kuwait City's Solaybiahat district. The house, with its little garden and high fence, was originally built for a minor British official.[48]

Palestinians, many of them professionals, were invited to Kuwait to help lay the foundation for that country's modern infrastructure. Estimated at about sixty-five thousand people, the community was fairly affluent and regularly sent money to relatives in Jordan, Lebanon, and the Gaza Strip. In those years, Kuwait was the only place in the Arab world where Palestinians arriving from different countries were mixing together, debating openly, and forming groups without interference. For that same reason, only there could an independent national leadership emerge and find funding. In contrast to other Arab governments, Kuwait did not interfere with Palestinian underground activities since it neither sought to control the movement nor felt threatened by it. "Kuwait," wrote Abu Iyad, "was one of the few countries where Palestinians were treated with sympathy and support."[49]

Yet despite their freedom and prosperity, the fact that they were in Kuwait on sufferance, without being allowed to take citizenship or assimilate, heightened the Palestinians' distinct national consciousness. They felt like merely gilded refugees, allowed to stay only as long as Kuwait permitted.[50] Most of the Palestinians working for the Ministry of Public Works—eighteen hundred employees in all—were fired in February 1964. If Arafat had not already embarked on a full-time career as a revolutionary, he might well have become one of the unemployed.[51]

As a result of their situation, the Palestinians did not necessarily feel affection for the Kuwaitis but had to remain silent about their true views. As a U.S. embassy report put it in 1964, Palestinians there viewed themselves as "far superior in education, culture, sophistication and intelligence to the Kuwaitis." They were also bitter that Kuwait enjoyed such fabulous wealth while their own people were suffering.[52] If Arafat shared this resentment, it partly explains why he supported Iraq's seizure of Kuwait in 1990.[53]

In Kuwait, Arafat was reunited with several close Palestinian friends and made some important new ones. Along with Abu Iyad, two other comrades of Arafat and future Fatah leaders, Khalid al-Hasan and Faruq Qaddumi, went to Kuwait about the same time. They were both about Arafat's age, came from well-off families, and grew up in places that had become part of Israel in 1948. The difference between them was that Hasan gravitated first to Islamist politics while Qaddumi joined the Arab nationalist Ba'th party. In later years, Qaddumi continued to follow a more Arab nationalist line and was closely associated with Syria, while Hasan remained more conservative and was close to Kuwait and Saudi Arabia.[54]

These men and about fifteen others, representing perhaps five hundred members of scattered underground groups, came together in a private home on October 10, 1959, to form the group they intended to use to regain Palestine. They chose the name Harakat al-Tahrir al-Filastiniyya (Palestinian Liberation Movement), whose acronym reversed spells Fatah, which means "conquest." Calling Fatah a "movement" rather than a party showed its purpose to be a broad front that would include Palestinians of all ideological and political views.[55] Its basic ideas had been worked out by Arafat and his friends in many years of conversations, and from the earliest days he was the group's leader.[56]

Fatah established a monthly publication, *Filastinuna* (Our Palestine), under Abu Jihad's editorship and with Arafat contributing articles. Several thousand issues were printed in Beirut and circulated throughout the Middle East. Egypt and Syria banned distribution. These regimes wanted to control any Palestinian movement while Fatah's message was that a Palestinian state must be achieved by an independent armed struggle not under the "guardianship" of any Arab state. Of special significance was Fatah's proposed new strategy for the Arab world: instead of the achievement of unity being the only way to reconquer Palestine, fighting for Palestine was the way to obtain Arab unity.[57]

This did not mean that Fatah would win the fight alone. It surmised that Palestinian action would persuade or force the Arab states to go to war. Fatah would appeal to the people over the heads of the governments. "Their people will protect us. We depend on the Arab people," said Abu Iyad.[58] This was inspiring revolutionary rhetoric but a dangerous policy. Not only was it misleading—whatever their attitudes, the Arab masses had never overthrown a single regime—but if Arab regimes concluded that Fatah was trying to overthrow them, they would see it as an enemy to be eliminated.

At the time Fatah was founded and for many years thereafter, most Palestinians did not share Arafat's Palestinian nationalist views. Instead, they expected that Arab states would unite behind Egypt's wildly popular Nasser, not a Palestinian movement and leader, and would launch a conventional war, not a guerrilla or terrorist assault, which would eliminate Israel. Once Israel disappeared, it would be replaced not by a Palestinian state but by the Palestinian province of a much larger Arab country.

This is the reason that the Palestinians failed to revive their identity or seek sovereignty over the West Bank and Gaza during the nineteen years of Egyptian and Jordanian occupation between 1948 and 1967. Ever since 1948, they had been willing to leave the issue in Arab rulers' hands. But while giving lip service to Palestinian rights, Arab states had their own goals and agendas. They used the Palestinian cause to gain domestic legitimacy and further their own interests in inter-Arab rivalries. For example, Jordan had annexed the West Bank in 1950 and offered an alternative loyalty by giving citizenship to Palestinians. Egypt treated the Gaza Strip like a colony and insisted that those who would support the Palestinian cause must back its own conquest of the Arab world.

Thus, while Arafat and Fatah rejected the need to have a political ideology, their need to compete with Nasserism and other doctrines required them to explain why they were the ones best able to achieve victory. The implicit revolutionary doctrine developed by Arafat and Fatah blended Islam, Marxism-Leninism, Arab nationalism, and Third World radicalism. This stance would continue to shape Fatah and the Palestinian movement as a whole for many decades. All of these beliefs argued that victory was certain and, consequently, any compromise short of wiping out Israel would be both treasonous and unnecessary.

On the one hand, in a more traditional vein, they argued that Israel's existence was like the Christian Crusades, a temporary conquest of Palestine doomed to inevitable destruction. Israel was an artificial entity; the Jews were not a nation and had no right to the land. Zionism was the personification of evil, a new version of colonialism, a drive for world conquest. On the other hand, Fatah used quasi-Marxist language to claim that Israel's existence was a product of Western imperialism. It was inconceivable that the Jews, so long despised and quiescent in the

Muslim world, could be the architects of this conquest. Thus, as the Fatah political platform would put it, "The 'Jewish State' was established in order to secure continued imperialist robbery and exploitation of our country."[59]

Therefore, it was extremely hard for any Palestinian movement or the Palestinians themselves to accept any other solution or even have an open debate about this goal without the more moderate side being called traitors. Achieving a Palestinian state was, for all practical purposes, always subordinate to getting all of the land. The Arabs would return and the Jews would disappear or accept a submissive status as they had historically done in the Arab world. If there were a contradiction between these two goals, the harder line would always have the advantage.

Arafat also saw himself as a man of action reacting against years of windy Arab theorizing: "We do not have any ideology—our goal is the liberation of our fatherland by any means necessary." On another occasion he stated, "We have only one motto: Victory or death." Palestine could be recovered only "by blood and iron; and blood and iron have nothing to do with philosophies and theories." He had contempt for politicians: "It is the commandos who will decide the future."[60]

In his opinions and appearance, the young Arafat was a fitting symbol of the new Palestinian generation and its revolutionary tactics. He wore a military uniform and carried a rifle or pistol to make himself seem a fighter fresh from the field who shared the risks and glory of battle directly, rejecting the soft life and endless talk of other Arab leaders. "Our new generation is tired of waiting for something to happen," Arafat said in 1969. "Isn't it better to die bringing down your enemy than to await a slow, miserable death rotting in a tent in the desert?" While Arafat's radical rhetoric and uncouth appearance made him seem unattractive and untrustworthy to Western audiences, their reaction was irrelevant for him. Arafat was cultivating the appearance of a man of the people with his Palestinian *kaffiya* and unshaven stubble.[61]

For Arafat, the Palestinians were guiltless victims entitled to use any means to redress their grievances. Since, in Arafat's words, Israel was "an embodiment of neo-Nazism, . . . intellectual terrorism and racial exploitation," there need be no restraint on Palestinian tactics. The Palestinian public would not only accept such behavior but would cheer it and flock to join those capable of such deeds of revenge.

At least for the first quarter-century or so of Arafat's leadership, whatever public relations–oriented lip service he gave to multicultural solutions, Arafat held on to a chilling idea: the Palestinians had been

A Most Unlikely Leader

victims of political-cultural genocide, and the only possible solution would require another one.[62] "The PLO's aim is not to impose our will on the enemy," said its magazine *Filastin al-Thawra*, "but to destroy him in order to take his place."[63] Thus, the deliberate, premeditated murder of civilians was from the start a central part of Arafat's strategy and not some temporary or easily jettisoned tactic.

There was also an absolute glorification of violence. Arafat himself would often say that struggle, not political organization, held Fatah together. It was an armed force, not a political party, whose job was to lead the masses through battle and not political organization.[64] Arafat told Fatah recruits that having guns would be the most important factor that would make people support and join the movement. In the early days, his slogan was, "People aren't attracted to speeches but to bullets."[65] Armed struggle, Arafat maintained, was the only way to liberate Palestine.[66] He also thought violence had tremendous therapeutic effects: "Armed struggle restores a lost personal and national identity, an identity taken away by force which can only be restored by force. Palestine had been taken away by fire and steel, and it will be recovered by fire and steel."[67]

This approach was a dangerous concept, which Marxists called "militarism" and against which both Vladimir Lenin and Mao Zedong had warned. It was a dogma avoided by virtually all successful national liberation or revolutionary movements and embraced by scores of failed ones. Violence justified as the highest value would become an end in itself whose primacy and justification would dominate the movement, crowding out diplomacy and delegitimizing compromise. Carrying out attacks on Israel was seen as a triumph in itself rather than being assessed on the basis of whether they were leading to some well-defined objective. The chance and imminence of victory was constantly overestimated. Moreover, this was a creed of violence without limit in which any act of terror and any murder could be justified as heroic and beyond criticism.

While it was understandable that Arafat wanted to avoid an ideology that would alienate some and divide the movement, the refusal to articulate a positive goal also made violence and permanent revolution the movement's main tactics and strategy, which would ultimately block any other approach. Hani al-Hasan, one of Arafat's most enduring lieutenants, said that a social revolution would have to wait until after a military victory: "It is nonsense to insist that we wage both revolutions together, because if we do we will lose both."[68]

Nevertheless, many revolutionary and national liberation movements—including a higher proportion of the victorious ones—have taken the opposite position. It could be argued that not waging both revolutions simultaneously is the surest way to lose. But, for example, Arafat never advocated educating young Palestinians so they could make a contribution to a strong future state and never emphasized cultural or economic endeavors as central to a nation-building effort. It was the battlefield, and that alone, that would bring victory.[69]

If there would be no "good society" to look forward to, how could anyone advocate the virtues of compromise or peace leading to material benefits? How could the idea of improving Palestinian living standards or raising a new generation in a state of its own compete with the vision of a glorious endless battle for total victory, no matter what the cost? How could humanitarian values or even tactical limits be introduced into the movement?

Arafat's narrow, almost totally tactical vision did not go far beyond believing that his end justified any means. He told an Arab interviewer:

> I have nothing, for I was banished and dispossessed of my homeland. What meaning does the left or the right have in the struggle for the liberation of my homeland? I want that homeland even if the devil is the one to liberate it for me. Am I in a position to reject the participation or assistance of any man? Can I be asked, for example, to refuse the financial aid of Saudi Arabia with the claim that it belongs to the right? After all, it is with the Saudis' money that I buy arms from China. Are you demanding that I already define the type of government that will rule Palestine after its liberation? If I did so, I could be compared to the man who sells the bear's hide before hunting it down. Must I publish a public statement to proclaim my belief in Marxism? Is this what I am required to do at this stage? Everybody asks what our social views are. Aren't we still in the phase of national liberation? If so, how can people demand that I forbid the whole Palestinian people from participating in the struggle for liberating their homeland?[70]

Yet Arafat never seemed to understand that a willingness to rely on "the devil" to achieve victory could apply to his own strategy, tactics, and other decisions as well as to his choice of external allies. And indeed, according to all major religions, including Islam, the devil is always on the losing side.

With these ideas, though, Arafat started his full-time career as a political revolutionary in 1959. He left his government job and opened a contracting office in Kuwait. "We built roads, highways, bridges. Large construction projects," he later claimed. In 2000 Arafat would tell President Bill Clinton and others at the Camp David summit that he had directed the construction of Saudi Arabia's ports.[71]

But his company apparently only existed to provide a front for his political activities. In Arafat's own version of events, he was a highly successful businessman who later gave it all up for the sake of the cause: "I was once very rich. I used to go to Europe. I visited Greece, Italy, France, Switzerland, Austria.... I had a pocketful of money, like any tourist and I enjoyed.... Yes, I was well on the way to being a millionaire.... I had Chevrolets, and I had a Thunderbird and a Volkswagen."[72]

Arafat did travel, especially often through Lebanon, and owned one Volkswagen. But he was not going places to do business or tourism but to recruit and raise funds among Palestinians. At least one of his trips, in 1964, was to the West Bank to find recruits and plan for future operations. He traveled under the pseudonym of Dr. Abu Muhammad.[73]

The most important of Arafat's trips was his first visit to Algeria after that country gained its independence from France in 1962. Within eight years of starting their revolt, the Algerian guerrillas had defeated the mighty French empire, which had ruled there since 1830. They had done so through a mixture of tactics, including terrorist attacks on the minority population of European colonists. By raising the cost for France in fighting a war of attrition, the revolutionaries had won total victory. France gave up unconditionally and the European settlers had no choice but to leave. It was Arafat's ideal solution to his own issue. "They symbolized the success we dreamed of," said Abu Iyad. Algeria's rulers offered material aid to Fatah. Abu Jihad and his family moved there to open a Palestinian office in 1963. The Algerians also helped Arafat to establish good contacts with the Syrian Ba'thist regime, which took power that year.[74]

But Arafat made a serious error by seeing a parallel between his struggle and the Algerian war. Israel did not have a mother country that would end its existence by withdrawing support. Moreover, Israeli Jews were a majority not a minority, and they had no interest in "returning" to some other place. Arafat could never shake his view that terrorism would be an effective tool against an "artificial" state even though it was disproven by experience time after time over the next forty years, a period many times greater than the Algerians had needed to win their revolution.

In the mid-1960s, though, the Palestinian issue was returning to a major role in Arab politics. At the January 1964 Arab summit, Iraqi leader Abd al-Karim al-Qasem ridiculed his Jordanian and Egyptian rivals. If these states were really Arab patriots, he said, they would support a Palestinian government in Egyptian-ruled Gaza and the Jordanian-ruled West Bank.

Nasser responded to this challenge by sponsoring a new movement, the Palestine Liberation Organization (PLO). In May 1964, four hundred Palestinian delegates from many countries converged at the Intercontinental Hotel in the part of divided Jerusalem that had been annexed to Jordan. This site was carefully chosen. In those days, a border guarded by heavily armed troops went through the center of the city. During the 1948 war, when Israel defeated the invading Arab states and won its independence, the fiercest fighting had been over Jerusalem. When the shooting ended, Israel made the western sector of Jerusalem its capital; Jordan controlled the eastern part. The Palestinians' trauma from that defeat and the effort to reverse it was the central issue shaping the PLO.

Nasser handpicked fifty-seven-year-old Ahmad Shuqeiri as the Palestinian leader. Unlike Arafat, he came from a wealthy Palestinian family and was a professional servant of Arab regimes, including being a Saudi diplomat until he was dismissed in 1963 for taking Egypt's side against Saudi Arabia in a dispute. He was completely dependent on Nasser's backing. The PLO's founding meeting was effectively stage-managed to create exactly the type of movement suited to Egypt's needs. The PLO would have a parliament—the Palestine National Council (PNC)—as well as its own army and treasury. The PLO Charter was adopted as its constitution. But real power resided with Shuqeiri, who followed Nasser's orders. The PLO created in 1964 was incapable of either disputing the policies of Arab states or of fulfilling the Palestinians' desire to destroy Israel and throw out its Jewish population.

Arafat was invited to attend the group's inauguration, but he did not show up, though Abu Jihad and a dozen Fatah members came to complain that the new PLO was poorly led, too subservient to Arab states, and preoccupied with rhetoric rather than action. Arafat and Abu Iyad had known Shuqeiri from their Cairo days, but Arafat was only ready to cooperate with the new PLO as equal partners. This conflicted with Nasser's vision of his PLO controlling all Palestinians and directing them to follow Egypt's policy.[75]

Fatah responded to the new group with a heated internal debate about whether to preempt the PLO's claim to leadership by launching an armed struggle. Some wanted to wait until Fatah was a mass movement before using that tactic, knowing they were poorly equipped and fearing the Arab world would unite against them. Others, in Abu Iyad's words, "took the view that the Palestinian masses had not yet fallen under the sway of Shuqeiri's demagoguery and would be impressed by our dedication and will to act." Fighting would build the movement. Only after a long argument was a consensus reached to launch a war against Israel, beginning December 31, 1964.[76]

A Most Unlikely Leader

That December, Arafat left Kuwait, the beginning of his endless travels. He was using the nom de guerre Abu Muhammad. He says that he gave away all of his cars but the Volkswagen, which he drove into Lebanon, and also left behind some money, which he only recovered years later with help from a member of Kuwait's royal family.[77] By mid-1965, he was in Damascus to set up headquarters there.

The hidden element in this choice of location was that Fatah had successfully allied itself with Syria's new regime.[78] If Nasser had the PLO, Damascus would counter with its own Palestinian group, Fatah. While the PLO only issued threats, Syria would prove its revolutionary credentials by actually sponsoring attacks against Israel. Fatah leaders called Syria their land of sanctuary, and Abu Iyad said that from the beginning Syria was the movement's heart and lungs.[79]

The first training camps for Fatah fighters were opened in Syria, with one hundred volunteers, and Algeria in 1964. Recruits were paid 18 British pounds a month, a good salary in those days. Most of Fatah's money came from wealthy Palestinians living in Kuwait or Saudi Arabia, though Syria probably subsidized it also. Some of its soldiers were veterans of the Egyptian-directed 1955–1956 Gaza attacks.[80]

Syria's role is shown by Fatah's first choice of target: Israel's water system, which used resources Syria wanted for itself. As a result, there had already been a number of border clashes. Fatah was an auxiliary force in that confrontation. But to reduce the danger of Syria being dragged into a war with Israel, Fatah's raids were routed through Lebanon or Jordan.

The first attack—a bomb meant to damage Israel's water system, which did not go off—took place on January 1, 1965. In preparing the attack, Arafat ordered that the explosives be put into the water at a dam, arguing that as an engineer he knew this would increase the force of the explosion.[81] Instead, this decision ensured that the bomb failed to work. So significant did Fatah consider the resort to arms that it set its official founding to coincide with this date, though the organization had begun more than six years earlier. But Fatah issued its first military communiqué under the name al-Asifa (the storm) to be able to avoid involvement if operations failed or brought bad publicity. For Arafat, ensuring he could deny responsibility for terrorist attacks remained an important consideration throughout his career.

From the start, too, the targets of attacks were always primarily civilian, a pattern that persisted in PLO practice. On January 4, 1965, Fatah commandos infiltrated Israel from Jordan and again tried to dynamite the water system. Similar efforts in the following weeks and months were also largely unsuccessful.[82] Israel captured its first Fatah prisoner when his rifle misfired. The first casualty was a Fatah man killed by Jordanian soldiers while returning across the border after an attack on Israel.[83]

Under Arafat's leadership, Fatah staged sixty-one attacks into Israel during its first two years of armed struggle.[84] These were so badly organized and ineffective, however, that when Jordanian and even Syrian officials told British diplomats they had "concrete evidence" that Fatah was an Israeli front, a British diplomat responded, "Indeed the incompetence and ineptitude of many of the attacks could be held to lend weight to these suspicions." But the British did not believe this claim for several reasons, one being precisely the fact that the attacks were so incompetent. "The Israelis would surely put up a better show," the diplomat wrote.[85]

The Jordanian leader Wasfi al-Tal, who later would be assassinated by Fatah, sensed or knew that Fatah was getting lots of help from other Arab states. As a result, he told the British that, in matters of organization and publicity, Fatah was one of the "most efficient" groups in the Middle East.[86] If it seemed to grow quickly, this was apparently due to Syrian help. But the very assistance offered by Damascus also made problems for Arafat in dealing with the other major Arab states: Egypt, Jordan, and Iraq. After all, Fatah was a Syrian client whose purpose was to counter Egypt's strategy of backing the PLO. To make matters worse, Fatah's attacks might embroil those countries in a war with Israel. Why should other Arab regimes help it?

For example, wanting to avoid a military confrontation with Israel, Egyptian military intelligence arrested fifteen Fatah activists who arrived in Gaza planning to use it as a base for attacking Israel in February 1965. Fatah cadres were also jailed in Lebanon. Some Arab states criticized Fatah for not coordinating with them or for "regionalism"—Palestinian rather than Pan Arab nationalism.[87] The pro-Nasser newspaper al-Anwar in Beirut called them CIA agents while the Saudis labeled them as Communists.[88] By mid-1967, some 250 Palestinians suspected of being Fatah's members and sympathizers were in various Arab states' prisons.[89]

Arafat was also directly threatening to overthrow Jordan's government because of its efforts to stop attacks on Israel from its own territory. In the words of one of his communiqués: "The regime of treason and agentry in Amman has imposed itself as the protector and guard of the state of gangsters [Israel]." Fatah appealed to Jordan's soldiers to disobey their government's orders. In December 1966, Fatah claimed, "There is today a comprehensive people's upheaval on both banks of the Jordan," and it urged "armed resistance" to the Jordanian government.[90]

Even the Syrians were suspicious of Fatah. One faction in the ruling junta saw Arafat as an instrument; the other considered him a tool of their enemies. Arafat said he was arrested and held for a day by one

Syrian intelligence agency while transporting dynamite from Lebanon in the trunk of his car just after the head of another service had assured him of its support. Syria's rulers were especially angered by a Fatah plot to blow up the Tapline oil pipeline, which carried Saudi oil through Lebanon to the Mediterranean. The Saudis would not be happy if Syria sabotaged their main source of revenue.[91]

Syria's rival factions thus became patrons of competing leaders within Fatah. After all, while Arafat had assumed the leadership of Fatah and made decisions without consulting colleagues, it was not necessarily inevitable that he would hold the post forever or outrank all the other cofounders. There were still tactical differences and complex debates over both ideology and relations with Arab states. Some already saw Arafat as an autocratic leader. In May 1966, the Fatah Central Committee briefly suspended him for allegedly mishandling funds, ignoring collective decisions, taking unauthorized trips, and making false military reports.[92]

These disputes and Syrian interference made an explosive mix. In 1966, a group of Syrian officers led by Salah Jadid took power by overthrowing fellow Ba'thists. Jadid viewed himself as a revolutionary who would unite the Arab world under his leadership. Yet another general, air force commander Hafiz al-Asad, was already jockeying for power. Jadid viewed Arafat as a protégé, but Asad saw him as a tool of his rival. This was the root of the Asad family's apparently permanent enmity toward Arafat.

The battle began in 1966 as the Asad faction in Syria's regime backed Major Yusuf al-Urabi, a Palestinian officer in Syria's army and close friend of Asad, to be the new Fatah leader. Arafat later claimed that the Syrians planned to assassinate him, but it appears that he or his friends had Urabi killed to eliminate the threat to their leadership. As a result, Arafat, Abu Jihad, and some of their supporters were thrown into the notorious Mezza prison for about six weeks.[93] Asad personally interrogated Abu Jihad about Fatah activities. Whether Jadid saved Arafat or Asad felt he had been sufficiently intimidated, the Palestinians were finally released.[94]

Yet even as Syria became more distant from Arafat, an opportunity was opening for him to take over the PLO. For one thing, everyone was fed up with Shuqeiri's leadership. Ironically, their main complaint was that Shuqeiri made decisions without consulting anyone else, one of Arafat's main characteristics, too. Fatah criticized Shuqeiri for making the PLO a "personal pulpit for himself," while a Jordanian newspaper called him "dictatorial."[95] King Hussein, Jordan's ruler, evenhandedly complained that the PLO was Egypt's instrument while Arafat was Syria's tool.[96]

Relations between the PLO and Jordan steadily worsened. On the morning of November 28, thirty young Palestinians organized by the local PLO office and including Fatah supporters taking military training in Algeria appeared at the door of Jordan's embassy in Algiers, saying they wanted to present a petition. When let in, they bolted the doors, took the embassy staff prisoner for four hours, ransacked the files and offices, and painted anti-Hussein slogans on the walls. Their statement saluted the "popular revolution in Jordan," calling for arming its Palestinian citizens and complete freedom of action for the PLO in Jordan.[97]

Finally, in February 1967, Jordan withdrew recognition of the PLO, saying that Shuqeiri "no longer represents the wishes of the Palestinian people."[98] The king was not the only one who felt that way. The two top PLO army generals openly complained of Shuqeiri's dictatorship after he criticized them in a public speech.[99] Leading Palestinians in East Jerusalem called him an "impossible man" who had lost his following.[100]

The fateful year 1967 changed everything. Ironically, the war represented exactly what Arafat wanted: an Arab military confrontation with Israel. For twenty years, Arab leaders and orators had daily proclaimed such a war to be necessary, inevitable, and certain to end in total Arab victory. In fact, though, the crisis provoked by Syria and Egypt initiated an Israeli preemptive attack, which brought as complete an Arab debacle as was possible. In only six days, Israel first destroyed the air forces of Egypt, Jordan, and Syria, then captured all of the Sinai peninsula, the Gaza Strip, the West Bank, East Jerusalem, and the Golan Heights. Shuqeiri, who had confidently predicted that the Jews would be driven into the sea, was forced to resign in December 1967.

Arafat later recalled, "I was turned completely upside down," but he and Fatah played no role in the great battle.[101] He asserted, "The Palestinians are once again the main victims," a point on which the rulers in Cairo, Amman, and Damascus disagreed.[102] But while the war was a catastrophe for both the Arab regimes and the PLO, it provided Arafat's great opportunity. He had been advocating an alternative strategy of guerrilla war and questioning an exclusive reliance on the Arab states and conventional military forces to destroy Israel. Many now thought that events had proved Arafat to be correct. The defeat would also soon make it possible for him to take over the PLO and install his own men in all key positions.[103]

Fatah's strategy fit well with the Arab states' postwar weakness. It could strike against Israel without Arab regimes having to risk Israeli retaliation or international criticism. For the demoralized masses and governments, this method now seemed to be worth trying. "There must be some group to give an example to the Arab nations," Arafat explained.[104] If all of their costly military equipment and highly trained personnel had been helpless, it was tempting to believe that the power of the masses and the courage of inspired warriors would triumph. This error would remain at the heart of Arafat's strategy into the twenty-first century.

2

The Che Guevara of the Middle East

1967–1971

At a 1970 PLO rally in Amman, Jordan, Arafat told one of his favorite stories. Recalling the ancient battle of Thermopylae, Arafat claimed that the Arabs would help the Palestinians to victory over Israel just as the Greeks had all joined with the brave Spartans to defeat Persia in ancient times. But Arafat got it wrong. In fact, the Greeks did nothing until after Sparta's army fought the Persians alone at the battle of Thermopylae and was wiped out.[1]

It was the true story—not Arafat's more optimistic version—that would typify his relationship to Arab states. A few months after Arafat's speech, the Arab countries, whose help he had assumed, instead deserted the Palestinians as Arafat provoked a confrontation with Jordan and was totally defeated by it.

Arafat was not the only optimistic revolutionary in the 1960s, but he was the most persistent, for many decades pursuing the same strategies long after they had been discredited and abandoned elsewhere. At the time, though, the preferred strategy of those seeking political change throughout the Third World was guerrilla war based on such successful role models as the revolutions led by Cuba's Fidel Castro and China's Mao Zedong. Their strategy was to build rural bases protected by the masses. Gradually, territory would be liberated and a stronger enemy army would be forced on the defensive and defeated.

Arafat, however, was different from his peers who were advocating a "people's war." Arafat said he once told Che Guevara, Castro's right-hand man and the leading advocate of Marxist revolution in the Third World: "each national cause has its own characteristics," which require special doctrines appropriate for each circumstance.[2]

In contrast to most of his foreign colleagues, Arafat's tactics were aimed more at killing the enemy's civilians than at defeating its army. Equally, he lacked any vision of a better society, and rather than mobilizing the peasants or workers, his true constituency was Arab governments, which he expected to ensure his tiny movement's victory. "We are," he said in 1968, "an extension of the hundred million Arabs."[3] Given this approach, he correctly refused the even more suicidal demands by colleagues and rivals to turn the PLO into a regionwide movement seeking to overthrow Arab governments.

Consequently, one of Arafat's most important post-1967 war accomplishments was winning Egypt's support. Defeat in that war had nearly brought down Nasser who, desperate for some success, was ready to forget Egypt's old antagonism toward Arafat as a Muslim Brotherhood sympathizer and Syrian client. So Egypt's leader, the Arab world's most powerful man, invited Arafat for a chat shortly after the war ended. To show he was not intimidated, Arafat brought along his pistol, which he had to be convinced to remove before entering Nasser's office. Nasser remarked sarcastically that he had heard Arafat wanted to kill him.[4] The meeting, however, quickly turned friendlier as Nasser offered to become Arafat's patron to help him take over the PLO and wage war on Israel.[5] Arafat accepted.

With total victory based on Arab states' support as his goal, Arafat first had to help ensure the failure of any effort to bring peace between Arab countries and Israel. On November 22, 1967, the UN Security Council passed Resolution 242 as a basis for future peace negotiations. The proposal called for the return of the territories that Israel had captured in the war accompanied by "a just and lasting peace in which every state in the area can live in security" along with "a just settlement of the refugee problem."[6] All of the Arab states, however, rejected any negotiations, recognition, or peace with Israel. None felt more strongly about this than Arafat himself.

Arafat feared that if Arab states made peace to regain stability and territory lost in the war, his chance to destroy Israel would be forever lost. Even if Israel withdrew from all of the West Bank and Gaza, Fatah explained, "The source of the aggression, . . . the alien Zionist presence in our land" would remain. Arafat objected to Israel's "right to exist" at all.[7]

Instead of seeking a peace settlement, Arafat proposed a dramatic new strategy of going on the offensive by launching a guerrilla war, saying, "A revolution that ceases to act is doomed to extinction."[8] He prevailed over doubtful colleagues by exaggerating the chance for revolution on the West Bank. In August, Arafat led a thirty-man team across the Jordan River and set up headquarters in the West Bank town of Nablus, chosen because of its winding streets and many alleys, which seemed well suited to guerrilla warfare.[9] Growing a beard to change his appearance and taking the alias of Dr. Fawzi al-Husseini—a revealing choice that linked him to his powerful, albeit distant, Husseini cousins—Arafat began organizing underground cells. He traveled by motorcycle to different villages to make contacts, held meetings in cafes and a bookstore, and used runners to transmit messages in order to avoid the less-secure telephone.[10]

Arafat organized sixty-one Fatah military operations in the West Bank between September and December 1967, mostly directed against such Israeli civilian targets as farms, apartment buildings, factories, and a movie theater.[11] By year's end, however, Israel had defeated Arafat's insurgency through a combination of creative military tactics, blocking the Jordanian border, and good intelligence sources among local Palestinians. In one town after another, Fatah activists were wiped out, with a thousand arrested and two hundred killed. Arafat's first attempt at armed struggle was an abysmal failure.

Among Arafat's problems were his sloppy security procedures, a primitive communications system, and a lack of experienced fighters.[12] But the most important shortcoming was Arafat's inability to mobilize local support. West Bank political activists were either pro-Jordanian traditionalists or radical followers of Pan-Arab, Nasserist, Ba'thist, or Communist ideas. Few were Palestinian nationalists, and Arafat's military-oriented doctrine did not put much emphasis on building a popular base.

Making little progress in Nablus, Arafat moved on to Ramallah, where conditions were even less favorable. Ramallah was then an extended village, a hard place for Arafat to hide and build an underground movement. He spent most of his time and energy escaping detection from Israeli forces, which were being aided by Palestinian informants.

Early one December morning, Israeli units raided the three-story villa in Ramallah where Arafat was living. According to one account, he heard the troops surrounding the house, leaped from a window, and hid in a parked car until they left. The Israelis found the mattress to be still warm and the radio next to it was playing Arabic music. Several hours later, Arafat crossed the river into Jordan.[13] The radio was taken as evidence, and when Yakov Peri, an Israeli security officer participating in the raid, realized it belonged to Arafat, he displayed it in his office. When Peri first met Arafat a quarter-century later, he asked if

Arafat wanted the radio back. Arafat laughed gently and said no, but added he hoped that in the future it would play songs of peace.[14]

It would be a long time, however, before Arafat was ready even to talk about peace. Despite all the failures, Arafat used his exploits and escapes in 1967 to mold an image as a daredevil commander risking his life behind enemy lines. As happened so often in his life, despite actual failure, he achieved symbolic success by persuading his followers that they had won a victory.

Arafat drew two major lessons from his time in the West Bank. First, the experience pushed Arafat even further in his counterproductive mistrust of the Palestinian masses. He later remarked, "Without the people to listen to us, we had no sea to swim in."[15] But his solution was not to mobilize them but instead to seek a military victory by heroic warriors as the masses looked on and cheered.

The main Palestinian leaders in the West Bank, however, thought Arafat's all-or-nothing political philosophy made it impossible to better the lot of Palestinians there and delayed any chance for an Israeli withdrawal. When a West Bank Palestinian delegation visited Arafat in Jordan during 1970 to propose declaring a Palestinian state, he angrily threatened them for supporting this "American-Israeli scheme." The idea of a West Bank/Gaza Palestinian state, he added, "is the most dangerous proposal that could be made.... We shall oppose the establishment of this state to the last member of the Palestinian people, for if ever such a state is established it will spell the end of the whole Palestinian cause."[16]

This idea that creating a Palestinian state in the West Bank and Gaza would block the conquest of all Palestine would stay with him a long time. Establishing such an independent state, which most observers later thought to be his real aim and a tempting reward to offer Arafat, always seemed a dangerous notion to him because it would shut the door on total victory. The true goal, Arafat endlessly explained, was the Zionist entity's annihilation and Arab control of all the land. "If we wanted another way than that of liberation, we would have accepted the offers made on numerous occasions to establish a Palestinian entity alongside the Zionist state.... But we have rejected it."[17]

Arafat's second conclusion from his 1967 experience on the West Bank was to make terrorism his main tactic. He believed that the type of guerrilla warfare used in Latin America and elsewhere in the Third World would not work for the Palestinians. Instead, Arafat and his colleagues were certain that terrorizing the Israeli people would induce that society's collapse and surrender while inspiring enthusiastic support from Palestinians and other Arabs.[18] Between 1969 and 1985, PLO groups committed more than eight thousand terrorist acts—mostly in

Israel, though at least 435 abroad—killing more than 650 Israelis, over three-quarters of them civilians, 28 Americans, and dozens of people from other countries.[19]

Whatever his involvement or lack of it in any particular attack, Arafat was the one ordering and justifying this strategy. Violence should be focused against Israeli citizens and their facilities, he explained in 1968, "to create and maintain an atmosphere of strain and anxiety that will force the Zionists to realize that it is impossible for them to live in Israel."[20] Some years later, he added, "The Israelis have one great fear, the fear of casualties." He intended "to exploit the contradictions within Israeli society."[21] Killing enough Israelis would force the country's collapse. It was also the alternative to confronting Israel's army on the battlefield, a contest Arafat knew would be far tougher.[22]

Given his analysis, the terrorist strategy was logical. The PLO's attacks, Arafat said in 1968, were designed "to prevent immigration and encourage emigration,... to destroy tourism, to prevent immigrants becoming attached to the land, to weaken the Israeli economy and to divert the greater part of it to security requirements." By achieving these objectives, the PLO would "inevitably" prevent Israel's consolidation and bring its disintegration. In these early years, Arafat hoped that "a quick blow by the regular armies at the right moment" would then finish Israel off.[23]

In 1968, Arafat was able to implement his ideas. Less than a decade after starting his political group and just three years after initiating armed struggle, Arafat had risen from an obscure engineer with Kuwait's highway department to the leader of the Palestinians and a favored client of several Arab regimes. Jordan, the new base for his war on Israel, certainly seemed perfect for Arafat's purposes. It had a long border with Israel and a population that was largely Palestinian. Jordan was also relatively weak and thus less able than Syria or Egypt to control Fatah. In addition, Fatah's supporters in the Egyptian, Syrian, and Iraqi governments could press Jordan to keep Arafat happy.

At first, Jordan seemed to have regained stability after the 1967 defeat. King Hussein remained quite popular. Within months, however, this changed drastically as the PLO gained support and Arafat quickly became the monarch's rival. Fatah began staging cross-border attacks into Israel, claiming victories when actually it suffered heavy losses.[24] By February 1968, when it became clear that Jordan would not stop Fatah's attacks, Israeli planes bombed areas of the country that were being used as bases by Arafat's men. Israeli and Jordanian artillery shot at each other across the border, and thousands of Jordanian peasants in the fertile Jordan River valley fled the fighting. Whenever Hussein warned that he would crack down, Arafat threatened force, and the king quickly retreated. Arafat promised Hussein that he would coordinate attacks with Jordan's army but then ignored this pledge, putting the country at risk of a full-scale war with its stronger neighbor.[25]

King Hussein felt helpless. Hussein was a man of great dignity, unfailingly courteous, and a bit stiff in dealing with people. The king was proud of not losing his temper or shouting at anyone, and his word was his bond. This put his character in sharp contrast with the mercurial Arafat in every respect. The king knew that the stronger Arafat became, the more he would undermine the monarchy and also that Arafat's patrons, Egypt and Syria, wanted to dominate Jordan. But given foreign Arab pressure and many of his own people's views, the king was reluctant to challenge Arafat. He simply hoped that Arafat would focus on fighting Israel and respect his authority.

But Arafat soon became both more popular and ambitious as a result of another defeat he was able to portray as a victory. His front-line headquarters was in Karama, a Jordan Valley town of seven thousand people, heavily fortified and totally controlled by Fatah. Even the king could not visit without Arafat's permission. In March 1968, Israel's army crossed the river to destroy the main Fatah camp there. Arafat told his troops to fight in the name of the entire Arab world that was defeated by the Jews in 1948. During the battle, Palestinian sources say, Arafat refused to hide inside a ditch, saying that if he had been destined to die, he'd rather die in a battle.[26] Other accounts say that Arafat and Abu Iyad rode away on a motorcycle and left their men to fend for themselves. In the fighting, mostly waged by Jordan's army, Israel lost 21 men while Fatah had 150 killed. The battle was an Israeli victory and the main credit for any resistance belonged to the Jordanians.[27]

Arafat, however, persuaded Palestinians and the Arab world that Karama was a great victory for his forces, making them appear heroic next to the Arab armies' apparent cowardice and incompetence a year earlier. A shattered Israeli tank was dragged around Amman and became a symbol of Palestinian triumph, and the funeral for Fatah's dead turned into a big demonstration. Five thousand men begged to join Fatah. Nasser invited Arafat to Cairo, publicly endorsed him, and gave him a radio station as a gift.[28]

Equally important, Nasser took his new protégé to meet his own Soviet patrons. Up to that moment, Moscow had viewed Fatah, in a Soviet diplomat's words, as "adventurers . . . without an ideology" and "terrorist elements having no contact with the masses."[29] Now, however, Nasser brought Arafat to Moscow as his favorite. In July 1968, Arafat traveled disguised as an Egyptian technician to conceal his new alliance from Israeli or Western intelligence. Still only at the start of a career as the world's most frequent flyer, Arafat had a severe attack of air sickness on the plane. He felt better after the landing, though, and accompanied Nasser to the Kremlin. Nasser urged Moscow to sponsor the PLO and Arafat convinced Soviet leaders Leonid Brezhnev and Aleksei Kosygin that he was friendly to the USSR's interests and hated America.[30] The USSR agreed to supply weapons secretly to Arafat.[31] Afterward, Nasser tirelessly urged Soviet bloc and Third World countries to help Arafat.

With Nasser's backing, Arafat gained a majority over the old, discredited PLO leadership at the July 1968 session of the Palestine National Council (PNC), the PLO's parliamentary body. Arafat also changed the PLO Charter from saying the organization was part of a struggle led by Arab states to stress its own independent, leading role. At the next PNC meeting, in February 1969, Arafat took over completely and became chairman of the PLO's Executive Committee, a post he would hold ever after.[32]

Now, as the PLO's leader, Arafat received even more help from Arab states and the Soviet bloc.[33] The Saudis were especially important because they gave Arafat so much money, partly to ensure he did not become more radical and subvert them, as they would later subsidize Usama bin Ladin to divert his wrath.[34] The Kuwaitis, too, were generous and treated Arafat as a hero during his frequent visits.[35] At the same time, Egypt, Syria, and Iraq were backing Arafat as part of their effort to overthrow moderate regimes in Saudi Arabia and Jordan, chase out the United States, and take over the region. Arafat always made excellent use of that paradox: radical regimes helped him because they saw him as a radical; moderate regimes backed him because they saw him as a moderate. Similarly, Western European states helped Arafat because they hoped to moderate him, while Communist ones sponsored him as a radical who served their regional interests.

Yet Arafat's new status did not mean he no longer needed to worry about Arab states' trying to manipulate or dominate his movement. The PLO's regular military units, the Palestine Liberation Army (PLA) in Syria, Egypt, and Iraq, were controlled by the host Arab states. When Arafat briefly tried to impose his own control over the PLA in 1969, the Syrians arrested his choice for the PLA's chief of staff as he visited Damascus and forced him to resign.[36]

Arafat was also subverted by Arab states ready to sponsor dissident groups within the PLO. During one 1968 PLO meeting, a Fatah member got into an argument with Arafat and walked out, shouting, "I came into this room as a member of Fatah, I'm leaving it as the secretary general of the Action Organization for the Liberation of Palestine!" He collected just seventeen supporters but with Iraqi patronage was soon commanding several hundred men.[37] Arafat knew that any small group

The Che Guevara of the Middle East

or individual he offended could always turn to an Arab government for backing against him.[38]

Syria also promoted its own client groups and cracked down on Arafat's supporters on its territory because it wanted to dominate the Palestinian cause, especially given Asad's personal hatred of Arafat from their earlier conflicts and Fatah's drift toward Egypt.[39] When Saddam Hussein took power in Iraq after a 1968 coup, his regime coined the slogan "All Arabs are Palestinians until Palestine is liberated." But once Iraq created its own Palestinian group, the Arab Liberation Front (ALF) in 1969, it closed down Fatah offices in Baghdad. When Fatah needed Iraqi help in 1970, "revolutionary" Baghdad did nothing as "reactionary" Jordan defeated Arafat.[40]

While these problems explain Arafat's permissiveness toward smaller PLO groups, his weakness in exerting his own authority made his situation far worse. Unlike virtually every successful revolutionary leader, Arafat never tried to impose unity. He preferred decentralization verging on anarchy, an approach that made life for him easier in the short run but would also repeatedly lead him into disaster.[41]

One reason why this was a mistake was that it let smaller groups take stances and actions that were in conflict with Arafat's ostensible strategy. They favored the overthrow of moderate Arab governments as the necessary precondition for liberating Palestine. They favored international terrorism to fight against the West rather than restricting such attacks to Israeli targets.[42]

Arafat had good reasons for rejecting these arguments. For him, the movement's purpose was to destroy Israel. It might sometimes detour by intervening in Arab politics or attacking Western interests but should never stray too far from its path. These ostensible principles let Arafat continue enjoying patronage from conservative Arab rulers while persuading some Western officials that he was moderate and that the real threat was his rivals' revolutionary militancy. At the same time, though, Arafat was often happy to use the smaller groups to further his own ends, thus antagonizing some Arab states and ultimately reducing his chances for getting Western support.

Ironically, despite all of his anti-Western rhetoric, the West was the one part of the world that Arafat did not need to worry about opposing him. On the contrary, many Western states sought to appease Arafat and his movement, trying to avoid attacks on their citizens or property and hoping good relations with the PLO would widen commercial opportunities in the Arab world.

For example, in 1969, the British embassy in Amman began meeting Arafat's representative, a Fatah official named Ahmad Azhari, in response to bomb attacks in London by the Popular Front for the Liberation of Palestine (PFLP).[43] As often happened, a terrorist attack by one PLO group benefited Arafat since it showed his power while he could also disclaim any responsibility for it, despite the fact that he was the PLO's leader. Rather than demand that Arafat try to stop such acts, the British said they "bore no ill will towards Fatah" and thanked it for condemning the attacks even though Azhari said Arafat would do nothing to punish or stop terrorism by those subordinate to him.[44]

Britain's Foreign Ministry was even ready to do public relations work for Arafat. One official urged his government to encourage the British media and security forces "to distinguish between Fatah, which is going out of its way to emphasize its disapproval of wanton terrorism, and the PFLP, a small group which does present a threat." Another British diplomat urged London not to offend Fatah and the PLO since they were powerful and "may one day be a government."[45] One would never guess that at the time Fatah was staging terrorist attacks on Israelis; was the PFLP's close ally; was subverting Jordan's government, Britain's closest Middle East ally; and would within a little more than a year launch a massive international terrorist campaign.[46]

It is not surprising then, that Arafat came to consider terrorism a no-risk strategy and that he had infinite time in which to wage his revolution. In a 1968 interview, he dramatically proclaimed, "Our road is the road of death and sacrifice to win back our homeland. If we cannot do it, our children will, and if they cannot do it, their children will."[47] Similarly, when Nasser asked Arafat how many years he needed to destroy Israel, Arafat responded that a revolution had no time limit.[48] Few could have conceived then just how literally Arafat believed in that answer.

Arafat seemed to share the assessment of most Western observers that he would defeat the king.[49] Not only did Arafat claim leadership over the Palestinian half of Jordan's population, but he also had allies in the Jordanian opposition and agents in the army and intelligence services. His radio station urged non-Palestinian Jordanians to support the revolution. At one point, Arafat said that anyone living in Jordan was a Palestinian.[50]

Many Palestinian leaders viewed Jordan's takeover as an absolute necessity for the conquest of Israel. Arafat did not openly say this but continually subverted the king and behaved as if he were Jordan's ruler.[51] By August 1970, Arafat claimed he had about 37,000 armed men in Jordan, while British and American estimates put the number of PLO soldiers at fewer than 5,000.[52] Abu Jihad later admitted: "Every [local Fatah] commander considered himself God, the intelligence resembled a state, the political organization a state, the military a state, everyone set up a state for himself and did whatever he pleased."[53] The mistaken, but sincerely held, overconfidence of Arafat and his lieutenants seriously misled them, and not for the last time.

But Arafat's comrades trusted his leadership and were so willing to follow him because they were deeply impressed by Arafat's wisdom, cleverness, and bravery. He told his men, "We, the new Fatah leaders, will go forward and cross the river. Whoever wants to can flee to the left [Syria] or flee to the right [Saudi Arabia]." When other Fatah leaders wanted to make Arafat their spokesman, he angrily refused, saying this would limit his scope of activity. Arafat preferred to be a military and underground man rather than a bureaucratic figure.[54]

In contrast to other Arab leaders, Arafat wore a simple army uniform and traditional head scarf, slept with the troops, and ate the same food as they did. Arafat showed them how to clean dishes in the sand since they had no soap. He treated others as equals, made them laugh, and listened to their views. One of Arafat's closest comrades at the time, Abbas Zaki, recalled his own reactions to Arafat: "He is charming. He is witty and quick at grasping things. He is a strategist who knows how to act at the right moment. He seizes opportunities and acts decisively.... He taught his men how a leader should behave. He should be the last one to sleep and the first to awaken; the last one to start eating and the first to finish eating."[55]

Arafat's supporters set up their own institutions independent of the government throughout the country. Fatah ruled the Palestinian refugee camps, which barred Jordanian soldiers, police, or officials from entering. But they also showed their strength nationwide. Large pro-PLO or pro-Fatah posters showing Palestinian guerrillas defeating the Israeli army filled every shop window. Two Fatah men even stuck them up on the U.S. embassy's door, as Jordanian police guards stood by too frightened to intervene. Students went door to door collecting money—the equivalent of twenty-five cents was the minimum recommended donation—and giving receipts that showed a bayonet piercing a map of Palestine.[56] Armed guerrillas drove through Amman's streets or set up roadblocks where they stopped cars, checked Jordanian citizens' papers, and requested or demanded contributions. When the PLO held a demonstration, its own police blocked off streets and directed traffic.[57]

One of the movement's main assets was Arafat's marvelous sense of showmanship. The myths he built did not help him defeat Israel but did ensure that he outmaneuvered Jordan's government and other Palestinian factions. An example of his methods was evident at the General Union of Palestinian Students' 1969 conference in Amman. Arafat made a dramatic appearance at the final session to thunderous applause, upstaging the expensively dressed Jordanian officials present. He entered with an honor guard of four armed commandos and then led the crowd in singing the PLO anthem, "Biladi" (My Country), and a ditty entitled "America, the Head of the Snake." Holding an AK-47 assault rifle, Arafat insisted that armed struggle was the only way to victory. Then he plopped down in a front-row seat next to the obviously embarrassed Jordanian prime minister, Abd al-Munim al-Rifai, who left the hall as soon as he could.[58]

But Arafat also was good at behind-the-scenes infighting. The rival PFLP was popular among students, but Arafat's men kept its delegates out of the convention's sessions. They then quickly adjourned the meeting without passing any resolutions or voting for officers. Afterward, the PLO issued its own list of the meeting's supposed decisions and announced that Arafat's handpicked list of leaders had all been elected.[59]

As long as Arafat appeared the likely winner of the power struggle in Jordan, many climbed on his bandwagon. In the Amman area, large numbers of Palestinians still lived in refugee camps. Thousands of others had moved into neighborhoods where they formed the majority. Anyone recognized as a leader of all these people would be a strong claimant for ruling the entire country.

Yet Arafat's base was much weaker than it seemed. Arafat did not have the total support of Palestinians in Jordan, some of whom backed the monarchy. Others were Arab nationalists, Communists, Islamists, or people whose views were bound up with local clan loyalties.[60] Equally, indigenous Jordanians resented the Palestinian refugees. Palestinians—generally more educated, business oriented, and urbanized—ridiculed Jordanians as primitive nomads, calling them the "barefoot ones."

In turn, Bedouin or village Jordanians, especially those in the army, looked down on the Palestinians as cowards who had lost their own country and now wanted to grab Jordan. A Palestinian returning to Jordan for the first time in ten years said that he knew the soldiers still hated Palestinians and would not follow Arafat because they treated him with their "traditional contempt and willingness to crack him in the head."[61] A senior Jordanian officer told an American counterpart that Jordan's army had lost the 1967 war because its Palestinian soldiers had "run like rabbits." Civilian Jordanians resented the bullying behavior of undisciplined Palestinian gunmen, who often acted like thugs.[62]

The conflict in Jordan steadily escalated throughout 1969 and 1970. Arafat constantly denounced the king as plotting to destroy his movement. Given his priority on unity and perhaps his fear of an internal confrontation, he never tried to impose control on the more important radical Palestinian elements, which were openly calling for a revolution

The Che Guevara of the Middle East

to overthrow the government. Arafat wanted to be treated as the Palestinian leader and commander at the same time that he let anarchy reign and denied responsibility for his subordinates' behavior.[63] Whether Arafat wanted a showdown with the king or saw one as an unnecessary, unwelcome diversion from his goal of destroying Israel, he did nothing to prevent it, apparently believing that violence would do more to help his cause than would negotiating or implementing agreements.

In November 1969, there were particularly bloody clashes between the Jordanian army and Arafat's forces. To reestablish order, the king and Arafat reached an agreement to govern relations between the two armies on Jordan's soil. Palestinian forces were prohibited from carrying guns and wearing uniforms in towns, seizing cars, arresting people, or recruiting Jordanian army deserters. In secret clauses, Arafat promised again not to shell Israeli targets from Jordanian territory and to coordinate any cross-border attacks with local Jordanian commanders. In exchange, Jordan guaranteed the PLO's right to operate in Jordan and to use it as a base for fighting Israel.[64]

Arafat broke the accord within days. Then, in February 1970, fighting broke out once more, and the king again demanded that Arafat respect his authority and order his men to obey Jordanian laws. Arafat refused, calling the king's complaints a U.S.-backed plot to disarm the PLO in preparation for a negotiated deal with Israel. The Palestinian groups quickly formed a united command of their military forces, led by Arafat, to resist the regime, another step showing that Arafat was in a position to control all Palestinian forces in Jordan if he only exerted himself.[65]

Hussein was still not eager for a confrontation and quickly backed down, canceling his decree in exchange for a new agreement with Arafat, which was basically the same as the previous one the PLO leader had failed to implement.[66] The government would leave the PLO alone as long as it maintained discipline and its soldiers did not carry arms in public or appear in uniform.[67] For the next few months, the king followed an appeasement policy toward Arafat, making militant speeches supporting the Palestinian cause and rejecting any political solution with Israel.

Nevertheless, Palestinian forces staged anti-American riots during Assistant Secretary of State Joe Sisco's April visit to Jordan, charging that U.S. policy sought to force Arab submission and liquidate their revolution. In the anti-American atmosphere promoted by Arafat, a U.S. military attaché was murdered—probably by the PFLP—and another was briefly abducted.[68]

After one more clash between Jordan's army and Arafat's forces in June, the king again promised to let the PLO do as it liked in fighting Israel as long as it did not interfere in Jordan's internal affairs. He offered Arafat a government post, which Arafat rejected, saying his only goal was to eliminate Israel. Another agreement was signed, which reiterated the principles that Arafat had accepted and then broken on several previous occasions.[69] The king even accepted a Palestinian demand that he oust from military commands two of his own relatives, whom the PLO accused of plotting with the United States against it, and appointed a government acceptable to Arafat.

At the same time, ten Palestinian commando groups tightened their coordination by forming a twenty-seven-man Central Committee for the Palestinian Armed Struggle Command in Jordan, and elected Arafat as their commander-in-chief. Arafat had disingenuously blamed friction on smaller groups, ignoring the fact that he was supposed to control them as leader of the PLO. "Fatah and I did not commit mistakes," he claimed. "The mistakes were made by other factions that held Marxist banners inside the mosques."[70]

Now was Arafat's opportunity to win a great success. His position within Jordan would have been unassailable if Arafat had lived up to his deal with the king, controlled the smaller PLO groups he commanded, and kept good relations with his Arab state sponsors. But Arafat went too far and lost everything. Not only did Arafat antagonize Jordan's king, army, and many of its people by letting his subordinates menace their country, he also angered Nasser, his main sponsor.

In July, Egypt and Jordan accepted U.S. Secretary of State William Rogers's plan for a military disengagement based on Israeli pullbacks from territory captured in the 1967 war. Arafat denounced the decision and threatened to use force to prevent any political solution with Israel. PLO demonstrators insulted Nasser by carrying posters depicting him as a donkey. Arafat rushed to Cairo, but an angry Nasser refused to embrace him. Nasser warned Arafat that if he provoked the king, Egypt would abandon him, and he would be badly defeated by Jordan's army.[71]

Arafat ignored the advice. At a march of ten thousand PLO supporters in Amman on July 31, he told the crowd, "We reject all peaceful solutions." He was referring to Israel but might just as well have been speaking about his behavior toward Jordan.[72] Sporadic clashes continued between government and PLO forces. Speaking on August 16 at a graduation ceremony for Fatah recruits, Arafat alleged that Hussein was planning to crush the movement and boasted, "We shall turn Jordan into a graveyard for plotters."[73]

The king's patience was reaching its limit. On August 21, he held a meeting of tribal chiefs, warning about PLO ambitions to take over Jordan. He traveled to Cairo and told Nasser that he would not take much more. While Nasser urged patience, Hussein could see that the Egyptian leader would not help Arafat in the event of a confrontation.[74]

Throughout August, fighting gradually escalated, and during the late August PNC meeting in Amman, Arafat called for a mobilization against Jordanian forces and asked Arab states for help against the king. Clearly, he expected assistance from Syria and the seventeen thousand Iraqi troops that were already in Jordan supposedly to protect that country from Israel.[75]

King Hussein, too, sought foreign allies against Arafat. He was so desperate that he asked Britain, his family's patron since the early 1920s, to pass on a request to Israel that it stop any Syrian military intervention against him. The British government refused, favoring Arafat over its old friend and assuming he would take over Jordan. Instead, the king turned to the United States, which saw him as an ally against pro-Soviet forces in the Arab world and a force for stability. It did pass on his request to the Israelis.[76]

Every day, there were new incidents and more deaths. On September 1, a hail of bullets was fired at the king's motorcade in an attempt to assassinate him. Two days later, he went on radio to appeal for peace. But on September 5, the day a ceasefire was supposed to take effect and an Arab League peacekeeping mission arrived, shoot-outs in Amman killed people on both sides.

Then came the worst incident of all. On September 6, three airplanes— two American and one Swiss—and all of their passengers were hijacked by the PFLP. One American plane was taken to Egypt, while the other two were forced to land at an old unused airstrip in Jordan. The PFLP threatened to kill the hostages and blow up the planes unless European governments freed Palestinian terrorists being held in their jails. British prime minister Edward Heath released Leila Khaled, who had just been captured by the Israelis and turned over to the British after she had killed a guard while trying to hijack an El Al airliner in British airspace, and other PFLP terrorists, who had been arrested for earlier attacks, in order to ensure that British hostages were not harmed.[77]

Arafat freed several Western hostages from the hijacking who came into Fatah's hands but did not criticize the hijackings, probably viewing them as strengthening his cause's power and popularity.[78] Jordan, however, saw the hijackings as a challenge to Hussein's authority and as a signal for a revolution to overthrow the king. Jordanian tanks surrounded the airfield, while some officers ordered their troops to march on Amman for a confrontation with the PLO forces, whether their commanders wanted it or not.

At this moment of chaos and bloodshed, Arafat chose to escalate his demands, calling for a national unity government as a precondition for any ceasefire and expressing solidarity with the PFLP as a member of the united forces under his command.[79] Finally, the king decided to move decisively. He declared martial law and demanded that the guerrillas leave Jordan's cities. Arafat called on his troops to be ready and ordered a strike to topple the government.[80]

Yet despite creating the crisis, Arafat did not actually get ready for battle. As Abu Iyad later admitted, "We were totally unprepared."[81] Against lightly armed, untrained, and semidisciplined guerrillas, the Jordanians had 55,000 soldiers, 300 tanks, and an air force. They quickly captured Arafat's Amman headquarters. Rather than seeking peace in this difficult situation, Arafat demanded that the king leave the country, and PLO radio openly called for overthrowing him. As when he faced Israel, Arafat wrongly insisted that the size and weaponry of the opposing military forces were irrelevant because Palestinian motivation and fighting spirit would always prevail.

At 5 A.M. on September 17, the Jordanian army advanced into Amman and attacked PLO forces, firing artillery and mortar shells just as the roosters were crowing. Black and gray smoke covered the city. All communications and power were cut off. An armored column swept past the Intercontinental Hotel, firing at PLO forces as it advanced.[82] The U.S. embassy's outdoor water tanks were riddled by bullets, forcing diplomats to make daring forays into nearby abandoned houses to find something to drink. Thousands of residents fled from their homes, and all of the Palestinian refugee camps were besieged.

At this critical moment, Arafat gave his men no leadership or instructions, though local commanders begged him for orders. For the eleven days of fighting in Amman, Arafat seemed paralyzed. Now was the moment for him either to prove his military ability by leading the fight or his diplomatic skill by ending it. He did neither.

Meanwhile, Jordanian artillery blasted Palestinian refugee camps where PLO forces were based until the fighters were forced into the streets to be gunned down by Jordanian troops. Some PLO men fought bravely and effectively while Jordanian units often performed poorly. Five Palestinian fighters held a Jordanian company at bay all day by moving from house to house. At close range, the Palestinians' rocket-propelled grenades knocked out some of the army's Centurion and M-60 tanks.[83]

The outcome, however, was inevitable. While Arafat himself escaped, Qaddumi and Abu Iyad were captured by the Jordanian army. Arafat's men declared Irbid, Jordan's second-largest city, to be the capital of the Republic of Palestine, showing their goal of taking over the country. But Jordan's army marched into that city, too, and soon Arafat's remaining forces were running toward the mountains of northern Jordan.

Arafat had hoped for Arab states' intervention to save him, but he was wrong again. Certainly, radio broadcasts from Baghdad, Cairo, and Damascus, as well as the pro-PLO Palestinian announcers on the BBC's Arabic service, made it seem like Arab countries were going to fight to save him. Western media coverage, accepting the myths of the militant Arab masses and Arab solidarity with the Palestinians, agreed that Arab states' intervention and a popular uprising would soon ensure Arafat's victory.

Indeed, Arafat's curious relationship with the West served him well on this occasion, as it would on others. While he railed about Western imperialism and anti-PLO plots, no Western state acted directly against the PLO. On September 21, as Jordanian forces were defeating the PLO in Amman's streets, Heath and his cabinet concluded that Hussein might soon fall and that the Arab world would be angry if Britain helped him. They decided to do nothing for that "increasingly precarious" regime and to encourage the United States to let Hussein fall, too.[84] Arafat's ability to get Western powers to appease him—by appearing to be the inevitable victor who enjoyed broad Arab support and would unleash terrorism if angered—at the same moment that he was being defeated was a remarkable talent, which he would use repeatedly.

As so often also happened, though, he was less successful with his Arab counterparts. The Arab world criticized Hussein, but no one intervened militarily. Breaking a promise to help the PLO, Saddam Hussein told Iraqi forces in Jordan to do nothing since he wanted to maintain good relations with the king, whom he thought would be a more important ally than Arafat. On September 20, Syria ordered a force made up of the PLA's Hittin Brigade and elements of the Syrian Fifth Mechanized Division disguised with Palestinian insignias to advance toward the border, but the brigade stopped and soon retreated. While Israel's threat to attack and Jordan's willingness to fight were important factors, so was the decision of Syrian air force commander Asad, who viewed Arafat as an enemy for having sided with a rival Syrian faction, not to cooperate in invading Jordan. A few Jordanian soldiers defected to the PLO, but neither the Jordanian nor the Arab masses rose up to help Arafat.[85]

Finally, on September 22, Nasser called an emergency Arab summit meeting in Cairo. While angry at Arafat, he did not want to see his protégé completely crushed. Nasser worried that the fighting might spread to other Arab states and feared that a total Jordanian victory might lead to stronger U.S. influence in the region and perhaps even an imposed peace with Israel. An Arab League delegation led by Sudanese president Jaafar Numeiry went to Amman to ensure that the Jordanians gave Arafat safe passage to come to the meeting. Arafat promised a ceasefire and called for his forces to leave all cities and towns. Since the Jordanian army hated him so much that it might ignore the king's promise to let him leave freely, Arafat flew out of Amman disguised in Kuwaiti Bedouin robes to appear as a member of Numeiry's delegation.[86]

Arafat and King Hussein both arrived in Cairo wearing pistols. On September 27, the two men made their cases before a tribunal of Arab leaders. The king, wearing an air force uniform, accused Arafat of trying to overthrow him, producing a tape of a PLO radio broadcast as proof. Arafat banged the table and said Hussein was the one conspiring against him. Arafat also falsely claimed that Hussein had massacred thousands of innocent Palestinians.[87] The rulers of Egypt, Kuwait, Lebanon, Libya, Saudi Arabia, and Sudan then sat in judgment of them around a horseshoe-shaped table for six hours, with one break for food, while Hussein and Arafat waited outside like two errant schoolboys.

All of these rulers supported the Palestinian revolution and its goal of destroying Israel, but they urged Arafat to focus on that task and stop destabilizing Jordan. Arafat and Hussein were persuaded to shake hands and sign an agreement. Despite the appearance of accord, the king had emerged the victor. The rulers praised Arafat but would not fight for him and preferred that he make concessions to the king. In addition, Arafat was about to lose his powerful, though increasingly skeptical, patron. Returning from the airport after seeing off some of his guests, Nasser had a heart attack and died.[88]

Nasser's successor, Anwar al-Sadat, wanted to focus on Egypt's internal problems and supported the PLO far less enthusiastically than his predecessor. At his first meeting with Arafat in March 1971, Sadat warned him not to provoke Jordan and said that Egypt regarded the Gaza Strip as its special responsibility, a sharp rebuke to Arafat's position on both issues.[89] Another defeat for Arafat took place in Syria, where his old enemy Asad seized power and held it for the next three decades.[90]

Back in Amman, Hussein forced the PLO out of the city, appointed a tough government, and decreed death for anyone caught with weapons. Arafat tried to hang on in the north, but during 1971 Jordanian forces systematically pushed PLO forces out of these fortified bases, too. By this point, Arafat's men so feared the wrath of Jordanian soldiers that seventy of them preferred to wade the Jordan River and surrender to the Israeli army rather than face their Arab foe.[91]

The Che Guevara of the Middle East

By April 1971, Arafat was hiding in a mountain cave in northern Jordan. While telling his men to fight to the end, Arafat begged the top Palestinian in Jordan's government, Minister of Public Works Munib al-Masri, to rescue him. Masri traveled with the Saudi ambassador to the north and asked Arafat to return to Amman and meet the king. He agreed. But when the car reached the town of Jerash, Arafat asked to be driven across the border to Syria, and from there he made his way to Lebanon.[92]

Even then, Arafat tried to renew his war with Jordan. But when Syria blocked PLO forces from crossing the Syria-Jordan border, continuing the battle was clearly futile. In July, Arafat told the king he was ready to end the war and accept the disarming or expulsion of PLO forces in Jordan.[93] These events set off a great debate within the PLO and Fatah. What had caused this overwhelming, humiliating defeat and to what extent was Arafat responsible? How should the Palestinian movement respond to this situation?

Many PLO and Fatah activists, including Abu Iyad, blamed Arafat for the defeat, complaining he should have tried harder to overthrow Hussein. Others pointed out that not only had Arafat led them to disaster, but he had left them leaderless during the crisis, telling them to fight to the death while he fled.[94] In late 1971, dissident Fatah elements made two assassination attempts on Arafat in Lebanon—one by a package bomb, the other by firing on his car. Outrage increased in December when Arafat returned to Amman, signed an agreement with the government, and even toured Amman's streets with Prime Minister Wasfi al-Tal, whom Palestinians saw as their main enemy. During the visit, some Palestinians booed Arafat.[95]

But Arafat rejected all responsibility for the debacle in Jordan and the calls for reform in his movement. He blamed the defeat on Abu Iyad and Abu Jihad, his two closest allies in the leadership. In a familiar tactic, he walked out of heated debates three times during a November 1971 Fatah meeting in Lebanon.[96] Despite much grumbling, the protests collapsed. Arafat successfully used similar tactics to explain away defeats and ward off demands for reform in later years.

In part, the unwillingness to battle or depose Arafat was due to the successes he could claim. By the end of the 1960s, he had achieved some remarkable feats: awakening Palestinian nationalism, building his own army, initiating war against Israel, working out a consensus program, and taking over the PLO. He had repelled the efforts of Egypt, Syria, and Iraq to control the PLO, made it a state within a state in Jordan, and was doing the same in Lebanon. The PLO enjoyed political support from a growing number of Palestinians as well as leftists, nationalists, and Muslims throughout the Arab world.

None of these successes, of course, canceled out defeat in Jordan, and none was an end in itself. Arafat had far larger ambitions. "Fatah," he said, "will be the leader, the Palestinian people the vanguard, and the Arab masses the supporting base."[9] But he had no reliable Arab support, and the idea that the PLO was a "vanguard" for popular revolution made the regimes even more suspicious of Arafat. Finally, he had led his followers into two big defeats—failure to ignite guerrilla war on the West Bank and defeat in an avoidable war with Jordan—which showed a pattern of serious misjudgment.

A critical element in Arafat's debacle in Jordan was that the confrontation and subsequent defeat seemed completely unnecessary. King Hussein did not want to go up against the Palestinians since it meant possibly challenging his own people and risking confrontation with the Arab world. Hussein could have weathered Israeli retaliation, but it was Arafat's threat to his kingdom's survival that forced Hussein to initiate a civil war. The king had been ready to appease Arafat if he had just helped to maintain domestic peace. But Arafat's ineptness, permissiveness toward radical groups and violent acts, affinity for chaos, and failure to implement his agreements led the PLO to a devastating defeat in Jordan.

3

The Teflon Terrorist

1971–1975

During a May 1973 dinner with Romania's dictator, Nicolae Ceausescu, Arafat bragged about having managed the murder a few weeks earlier of the U.S. ambassador to Sudan. "Be careful," said Ion Gheorghe Maurer, Romania's former prime minister. "No matter how high up you are, you can still be convicted for killing."

"Who, me?" Arafat said, winking mischievously. "I never had anything to do with that operation."[1] Indeed, he was so adept at concealing his links with terrorism and avoiding any penalty for such behavior that Western intelligence officials were beginning to call him the "Teflon terrorist."[2]

In Lebanon, Arafat's new base of operations after the expulsion from Jordan, he repeated many of his old mistakes yet again survived. Soon after arriving there in 1971, he was helping to make Beirut a chaotic copy of what Amman had been like. Arafat created a war zone on Lebanon's border with Israel like the one he had made in the Jordan Valley. His terrorist strategy against Israel, though bloody, still brought no military success. Again, too, although he pledged not to intervene in his host country's politics, Arafat's behavior threatened that country's stability.

Yet Lebanon was an even more pliant host for Arafat than Jordan had been, and his political fortunes continued to prosper despite his failures. True, in Lebanon there were fewer Palestinians than in Jordan and no direct access to the West Bank, but the large Palestinian minority gave

Arafat a support base while areas of the Lebanon-Israel border were excellent for launching attacks. Beirut, then the Arab world's most modern, cosmopolitan city, offered better access to the Western media, which Arafat was learning well how to manipulate, and a more pleasant lifestyle for PLO leaders than had dour Amman.

Most important of all, though, was that Lebanon's central government and its army were weak and thus could not restrict PLO activities. By the same token, the country was less able than Jordan to resist bullying by other Arab states, like Egypt's demand that it give Arafat a free hand to operate in Lebanon. On two occasions, in 1968 and 1973, Lebanon's army clashed with the PLO, trying to curb its power. Each time, though, the Beirut government caved in to the demands of Arafat and his foreign patrons. Yet while Lebanon's deep domestic divisions gave the PLO powerful local allies, once again the prospect of exercising power in his host country seduced Arafat into growing entanglements in local politics, which made him more enemies than friends.

In Beirut, Arafat oversaw the creation of a large political, military, and economic infrastructure, which was well financed by Arab governments' donations and taxes on Palestinians working in Arab states. Illegal methods, which Arafat made no attempt to stop, swelled its treasury and enriched those involved. These included forcing Lebanese businesses that were moving goods through ports to pay protection money to Fatah, whose members also ran large illicit trades in arms, medical supplies, and even drugs. Some robbed stores and turned the loot over to their groups, which then sold it back to the merchants and split the profit with the thieves.[3] Such activities damaged the movement's image among the Lebanese and diverted the PLO from its political goals.

Some of these earnings benefited the Palestinian people, for whom Fatah built hospitals, orphanages, schools, and a police and judicial system. Fatah also had a relief fund for families of those killed in the service of the cause and a network of economic enterprises, including a textile plant and farms, which employed about three thousand people.[4] In the refugee camps, 150,000 Palestinians depended on Fatah for everything, including trade unions, garbage collection, cultural centers, and youth groups. The curriculum in the UN-run refugee camp schools, funded partly by U.S. taxpayers' money, was revised to offer paramilitary training.[5]

Before September 1970, Arafat only had about eight hundred Fatah soldiers in Lebanon, but their numbers tripled as he moved forces from Jordan.[6] They were well paid and given bonuses to ensure that they did not defect to other groups. Supposedly, these troops were for use against

Israel, but Arafat faced anew the dilemmas over intervention in local politics and conflicts among PLO groups.

Rather than concluding that interference in Jordan's internal affairs had been a mistake, PLO and Fatah leaders blamed Arafat for not having tried harder to overthrow the king. They wanted the PLO to become the vanguard of a liberation struggle that would help the masses destroy Arab regimes and fight Western imperialism throughout the Third World. Without transforming the Arab world and expelling U.S. influence from the region, they believed, the PLO could not destroy Israel. Lebanon seemed the ideal place to launch this campaign.

Although Arafat never explicitly accepted this argument, he did not stop subordinates from acting as if they were fomenting a world-wide revolution. In Lebanon, PLO forces trained radicals from many countries, who would later initiate violence in places as far-flung as Turkey, Iran, Nicaragua, and Germany. Only after the PLO was expelled from Lebanon in 1982 did Sudan and later Afghanistan begin to replace the PLO camps as the center for recruiting and training terrorists.[7]

At the same time, Arafat also became involved in subverting several Arab states, especially Jordan and Lebanon. Believing that no Arab regime had a right to control or limit PLO activities, even on its own soil, inevitably brought him into collision with those hosting his movement. Since the Arab states were responsible for Palestinian suffering, they must, in Abu Jihad's words, "be a base for our people" and had no right to limit or control the PLO's choice of timing, methods, or anything else, even if Palestinian activities dragged the host country into war or damaged its vital interests.[8]

Lebanon was especially vulnerable to this strategy. In the past, its unique system for balancing power among its many religiously defined communities had brought stability and prosperity. But this structure had been undermined by radical ideologies and changing population proportions, which produced forces eager to use the PLO to help them seize power.

Arafat heightened the spiraling anarchy in the country in several ways. To strengthen his own hand, he supported Lebanese radical groups that were subverting the country and let PLO member groups fight each other, Lebanon's army, and the militias of Lebanese communities.[9] Obviously, the PLO's presence and Arafat's policies were not the sole causes of Lebanon's breakdown into a destructive, bloody civil war, which eventually brought it under Syrian control, but they were a major factor in accelerating and deepening this tragic process.

The Teflon Terrorist

The first clashes between Fatah forces and the Lebanese army had begun in 1968 and continued sporadically for many months. Arafat demanded unrestricted freedom of action while the government insisted that the PLO not cross the border to attack Israel lest this action force the country into war.[10] The question was settled, in Lebanon as in Jordan, by Nasser, who invited the two sides to Cairo with himself as mediator. On October 28, 1969, the Lebanese delegation arrived. But Arafat refused to come until Lebanon accepted his terms. On November 3, Lebanon accepted an agreement that gave Arafat full freedom of action as long as he respected Lebanon's laws and sovereignty. Arafat promised that he would not launch attacks from Lebanese border villages, shoot at Israel from Lebanese territory, or lay mines along the frontier.[11]

As King Hussein was also discovering, Arafat's pledges on such matters quickly proved useless. Within three weeks, clashes began again in southern Lebanon as PLO forces violated the agreement.[12] Soon Arafat was making speeches urging Lebanon's people to revolt against a government that he accused of being U.S. agents plotting to destroy his movement. Smiling, he told one audience that "the Lebanese people" should punish this behavior.[13] The country's leaders rightfully considered such statements to be inciting revolution. Even Kamal Junblatt, the Druze chief who was Arafat's main Lebanese ally, unsuccessfully urged Arafat to implement the Cairo agreement.[14] As Junblatt had feared, the PLO-initiated border war and Israeli counterattacks made thousands of Lebanese civilians flee from the south.

At the same moment that Arafat was encouraging revolt against Lebanon's government, he was tightening control over his own movement.[15] While tolerant of other PLO groups doing as they pleased, Arafat accepted less pluralism within Fatah itself. In 1971, a group of younger members, who called themselves the Free Officers, attacked Arafat for having lost touch with the membership and creating a "cult of personality."[16] Arafat quickly suppressed them. The same treatment was given the following year to Hamden Ashur, a Syrian-backed leftist who built his own army in Lebanon's Beka'a Valley and claimed Arafat was insufficiently revolutionary, and to Fatah's military commander in eastern Lebanon, Abu Yusuf al-Kayid, who had become too ambitious.[17] Arafat's control over Fatah was ensured. When Arafat thought preserving order was vital for his own interests, he was always able to enforce that.

Yet Arafat did not depend on repression alone to stay in power. He also met the challenge by showing critics that he was a real revolutionary ready to battle Arab regimes and the West. In 1971, he created a covert international terrorist group within Fatah called Black September, a reference to the September 1970 Palestinian defeat in Jordan. The

Black September group was headed by Abu Iyad, staffed by Fatah's intelligence personnel, and used Fatah's facilities and funds. A CIA report concluded that Arafat maintained a "pretense of moderation" but that "the Fatah leadership including Arafat now seems clearly committed to terrorism."[18]

Using terrorism for which he could deny responsibility was another key pattern in Arafat's career. Even though Arafat did not fool either the West or the Arab states, his pretense of non-involvement was sufficient to keep them from retaliating against him. It is understandable why Arafat already thought terrorism to be an easy, appropriate, and successful strategy. He had seen how it mobilized Palestinian and Arab support for the PLO; raised the Palestine issue's international priority; prevented other Palestinians and Arab states from negotiating peace with Israel; and made many Western leaders eager to appease him. The more audacious and horrifying the act was to the outside world, the more admiration it generally received from Arab people and countries. Attacks on Israel did not destroy that country but seemed to show that the struggle was advancing, that revenge was being taken, and that Palestinian action outshone Arab leaders' speeches.[19]

What was distinctive about the era between 1971 and 1974, however, was Arafat's higher priority on attacking Arab governments and the West, an exception to his usual preference for using terrorism only against Israel. Fatah engaged in a wave of plane hijackings, letter bombs, assassinations, and thirteen attacks on Western and Arab embassies.[20] With the failure of the wars launched from the West Bank and Jordan, along with the absence of Arab states' readiness to attack Israel, international terrorism became an attractive alternative. Arafat was also extracting blood revenge on Jordan for the September 1970 war, on other Arabs for doing nothing, and on the West for supposedly encouraging King Hussein to destroy the PLO.[21]

Equally important, an international terrorist campaign let Arafat deflect Palestinian criticism of his responsibility for the defeat in Jordan.[22] By using terrorism, Arafat showed he was waging the revolution and joining his critics, who wanted a harder political line and more revolutionary activity. This would be another pattern that he would repeat in later eras, after other such defeats.[23]

Arafat had one more incentive for such a strategy. In 1971, King Feisal of Saudi Arabia, his main financial backer, secretly urged Arafat to make a deal with King Hussein.[24] Talk of rapprochement with Jordan infuriated Fatah activists, including Arafat's closest comrades. In October, some of these disgruntled forces tried to kill Arafat, and there were demonstrations against him by Palestinians in Lebanon. Some two hundred activists from one refugee camp even temporarily occupied the

PLO offices in Beirut to demand that all talks with Jordan be stopped.[25] By taking the lead in attacking Jordan, Arafat used violence—as he did on later occasions—simultaneously to destroy a negotiating process, to promote unity within his movement, and to stop it from criticizing him.

In April 1971, the U.S. embassy in Beirut was predicting that while Arafat desperately needed a new strategy to handle a "barrage of well-justified" criticisms from Palestinians and retain power, his options were limited. "Unable to match any Arab government in military force [PLO leaders] can only resort to clandestine subversion."[26]

At that moment, Arafat was creating the Black September organization at a Fatah meeting in Dar'a, Syria, near the Jordanian border. He decided to launch a war of sabotage and assassination against Jordan. A few days later, when Jordan's prime minister, Wasfi al-Tal, accused Fatah of planning to kill its officials, the official Voice of Palestine radio station in Cairo broadcast an angry denial. This claim, it said, was a "CIA-Jordanian" attempt to liquidate the revolution. Ironically, though, the indignant response was undercut when the broadcast ended with the words, "Death to the enemies of our revolution and our masses!"[27]

Over the next year, Fatah launched attacks on Jordan that included sabotaging the country's main oil pipeline and its trucks carrying phosphate exports through Lebanon. Even Suleiman al-Nabulsi, the Jordanian politician closest to Arafat, told him that international terrorism would antagonize both the Arab world and the West. Yet Nabulsi admitted that Arafat was not convinced.[28]

On November 28, 1971, Jordanian prime minister Tal was returning from lunch with the Arab League's secretary general when a six-man Black September hit squad shot him down in the lobby of Cairo's high-rise Sheraton Hotel. One assassin lapped Tal's blood. Tal's wife screamed as she stood over the body, "Palestine is finished!" But a few months later, Egypt freed the assassins on low bail and let them leave the country.[29]

Despite the cry of Tal's widow, few, especially in the Arab world, would ever consider Arafat's involvement in terrorism as a reason for not supporting him. The U.S. embassy in Saudi Arabia thought that once the Saudi royal family saw evidence of Arafat's involvement in anti-Jordanian terrorism, King Feisal would "decide that Fatah . . . [has] become the very kind of radical movement . . . which he has most feared." Saudi officials did tell the Americans that if Fatah were implicated in Tal's murder, they would abandon it. Saudi Arabia, they explained, abhorred terrorism and killing.[30] Nevertheless, after being presented with ample evidence, the Saudis only cut off aid to Arafat briefly and always continued to give him political support.

A month after the Tal killing, Black September wounded Jordanian ambassador Zaid al-Rifai in London.[31] The gunman fled to France, which released him. More attacks on Jordanian diplomats ensued. High-ranking Fatah members were captured in Amman as they were about to launch an operation to take Jordan's cabinet as hostages and then attack the U.S. embassy in Amman in 1973.[32] An attempt to kill King Hussein at the October 1974 Rabat Arab summit, planned by Abu Iyad, Arafat's intelligence chief, was also foiled.[33]

Perhaps Black September's most notorious attack was at the 1972 Olympics in Munich, when eight Fatah men, organized by Abu Iyad and dispatched from a Libyan training base, seized the Israeli team's compound, killed two Israeli athletes, and took others as hostages.[34] The West German authorities agreed to give them safe passage out of the country. But as terrorists and hostages were being transferred by bus to the airport, police snipers tried to shoot the kidnappers. The terrorists blew up the bus. In the explosion and firefight, five terrorists and nine more Israeli athletes were killed.

A short time later, Black September terrorists planned to assassinate Israeli prime minister Golda Meir as she took part in a religious service at Bucharest's Chorale Synagogue during a visit to Romania. But Communist Romania, while helping Arafat secretly, did not want a major terrorist attack on its own soil against a foreign leader who was its guest. Government forces seized the four gunmen on a street near the synagogue and then feted them with a lavish dinner—complete with caviar and champagne—before sending them out of the country on a Romanian plane.[35]

Arafat's remarkable ability to escape responsibility for the terrorism he committed was best illustrated by what the CIA would later describe as his personal role in planning the assassination of the U.S. ambassador to Sudan in March 1973.[36]

Starting in 1971, American intelligence had been intercepting and decoding radio transmissions among PLO and Fatah offices. Most messages were routine exchanges of news and the travels of personnel.[37] On February 28, 1973, a radio operator at the secret U.S. navy listening post in Cyprus was monitoring an exchange between the PLO's Beirut and Khartoum, Sudan, offices when, to his astonishment, he heard Arafat and Abu Iyad come on the line in Beirut. At the other end, in Sudan, was Abu Jihad. This was something unusual and significant: the PLO's top three leaders in conversation at once. Their ten-minute meeting was taped, transcribed, and translated. While somewhat cryptic, the talk revolved around whether several operatives had safely arrived in Khartoum and if the equipment was ready. There were also several references to Cold River (Nahr al-Bared), which was a Palestinian refugee camp in Lebanon where a PLO training center had just been hit by Israeli forces. In recent days, Voice of Palestine news programs had often ended with the slogans "Remember Cold River!" and "The martyrs of Cold River will be avenged!"

The senior Arabic linguist at the Cyprus intelligence station immediately contacted James J. Welsh, the analyst responsible for PLO communications at the supersecret National Security Agency (NSA) in Washington, D.C. "This is very unusual," he wrote on the secure teletype connection. The last time Abu Jihad had been so involved in an operation was in preparing the attack on Israel's Olympic team.

Welsh brought in more senior officials for a discussion, and they concluded that the PLO was about to launch a major terrorist operation in Khartoum. They wrote a warning for the State Department to send to Khartoum as a "flash" message, the highest priority. Then they went home for the day, believing they had scored the greatest intelligence coup of their careers.

But when the State Department watch officer called the NSA to check on the message, the analysts were gone, and there was some confusion about the urgency. As a result, the official downgraded the message to a "routine" priority, which would take several days to arrive.

A few hours later, a flash message was sent in the opposite direction— from the U.S. embassy in Khartoum to Washington—reporting that Ambassador Cleo Noel and Deputy Chief of Mission Curtis Moore had gone to a Saudi embassy reception, where they and diplomats from other countries had been taken hostage by a half-dozen Black September terrorists.[38] Their captors' demands were high even by the usual standards: the release of PLO terrorists imprisoned in Germany, Israel, and Jordan and also of Sirhan Sirhan, the Palestinian assassin of presidential candidate Robert Kennedy in 1968. The PLO and Arafat were now even daring to associate themselves with the murderer of one of America's most beloved political figures.

Yet it seemed as if the terrorists knew their demands would not be met and did not care. The captured Arab and East European ambassadors were quickly released, but the kidnappers accused Moore of being behind efforts to stop the "Black September revolution" and of aiding Israel. The Sudanese government offered the terrorists safe passage out of the country, but they refused, making it clear that they were planning to kill the hostages. Instead of trying to stage a rescue raid, incredibly—but not for the last time—a government accepted Arafat's offer to mediate between himself and his own men.

The friendly conversations between Arafat and Abu Iyad, in Beirut, and the kidnappers were intercepted by both the United States and Israel. Abu Iyad and Arafat asked what was happening and then ordered the terrorists to "carry out Cold River." In response, they killed Moore, Noel, and Guy Eid, a Belgian diplomat, who was murdered only because the terrorists mistakenly assumed he was Jewish.[39] A half hour later, Arafat called back to ask, "Have you carried out Cold River? Why didn't I hear about this? Why wasn't it on the news?" The men assured Arafat that they had completed their mission. Some hours later, Arafat told them to surrender.

A captured terrorist admitted that the attack was a PLO operation ordered directly from Arafat's headquarters. The operation had been planned by the director of Fatah's local office, who left the country on a Libyan plane shortly before it began, and had been taken over by Abu Jihad, who was in constant touch with Arafat on what to do next. The terrorists were even driven to the embassy by an official from the Fatah office using its official vehicle. A U.S. State Department report concluded that the terrorists were under the control of PLO headquarters in Beirut and murdered the hostages upon "receiving specific codeword instructions."[40] The PLO's official radio station cheered the killing after it happened.[41]

In an unprecedented speech, Sudanese president Jaafar Numeiry, who had personally rescued Arafat from Jordanian vengeance in September 1970, now condemned his ingratitude and betrayal. Numeiry had let Fatah operate freely in Sudan only to find, among documents seized in the Fatah office after the attack, that Arafat's group was working with Libya and opposition elements to stage a coup against him. He concluded, "The Sudanese people's aid for the liberation of Palestine was being directed to other battles against us."[42] Arafat ignored Numeiry's demand to cooperate in the investigation and return the head of the Fatah office in Sudan for prosecution.

Although it said nothing publicly, the U.S. government was certain that Arafat was behind Black September. "There was little doubt in anyone's mind that the decision [to kill the American diplomats] went right back to Arafat," recalled Harold Saunders, then the National Security Council staffer on the Middle East. "The U.S. government had evidence of his involvement in the go-ahead."[43] Assistant Secretary of State Joseph Sisco wrote at the time, "No significant distinction now can be made between the Black September Organization and Fatah." U.S. intelligence reports described Arafat "as having given approval to the Khartoum operation prior to its inception."[44]

Nevertheless, the U.S. government covered up Arafat's role in the murders to avoid a confrontation with Arafat, which was deemed contrary to U.S. strategic interests, or to hide the bureaucratic mistake that had contributed to the deaths of two American diplomats. As for the gunmen themselves they, like most of their counterparts, were never punished. Two were immediately released by the Sudanese authorities; six others were quickly tried, convicted of murder, then handed over to the PLO and flown out of the country.

But soon another war was shaking up the region and forcing Arafat to reexamine his international terrorist strategy. In March 1973, Sadat had told Arafat during a Cairo meeting that he planned to "light a spark" in the Middle East. But Arafat missed the hint.[45] Seven months later, in October, Egypt and Syria launched a surprise attack that at first stunned Israel, though it soon counterattacked and won the war, capturing additional territory during the three weeks of fighting. The Egyptian army was saved from total defeat only by U.S. diplomatic intervention. Still, many Arabs thought they had regained honor lost in their 1967 defeat.

While Arafat had been urging Arab states to attack Israel for years, he played no role in the new crisis. No Arab leader even consulted Arafat about the war. As always, though, Arafat put the best face on the situation. The 1973 war, he proclaimed, "has given us part of Palestine, and the [next] war will give us Tel Aviv." Now that Israel's "invincibility" had been called into question, Arafat thought—a serious misreading of the military situation—the Arab states would be eager to fight again.[46]

Instead, however, Egypt and Syria made disengagement agreements with Israel in early 1974, trading partial Israeli withdrawals for an easing of tensions. Arafat worried that this would lead to a peace conspiracy in which Arab states would recognize Israel in exchange for getting back the territory Israel had captured in the 1967 war.[47] In that case, Jordan would regain the West Bank; Egypt, the Sinai peninsula; Syria, the Golan Heights; and the PLO would get nothing.

Arafat was determined to stop this from happening. But international terrorism no longer seemed to be a good strategy for doing so. For one thing, Israel was hitting back successfully. On April 10, 1973, Israeli commandos—including a young officer named Ehud Barak—infiltrated Beirut in a daring raid and killed three prominent PLO leaders associated with Black September. Moreover, Arab states were threatening to crack down on the PLO if it continued international terrorist operations. The Saudis were particularly angry at a December 1973 Fatah attack on their embassy in Paris. As a result, Arafat gave an order to stop these types of attacks and to dissolve the Black September group.

Some Fatah members quit in protest to continue their vocation as international terrorists and even to attack the PLO. One of them, Abu Nidal, formed his own group, the Fatah Revolutionary Council, that year. The PLO sentenced him to death for plotting to kill Arafat. He did slay a number of PLO officials in later years, while also murdering more than 300 and injuring 650 other people in many terrorist attacks, two-thirds of them in Western Europe.[48]

It was clear, however, that Arafat was rejecting only international terrorism and not terrorism itself. On May 15, 1974, three terrorists from the Democratic Front for the Liberation of Palestine (DFLP), a PLO member group, entered the Israeli village of Maalot, killed three people in their home, and held more than ninety schoolchildren as hostages, demanding the release of twenty-six imprisoned terrorists. During an Israeli rescue attempt, twenty-one children were killed and sixty-five injured. A similar drama unfolded in Israel's northern city of Kiryat Shemona in December 1974, with fifty-two killed and more than a hundred wounded, mostly women and children. That same month, a bomb went off in Jerusalem's Ben Yehuda street at lunchtime, wounding thirteen. In March 1975, terrorists in two dinghies landed near Tel Aviv, shot at a crowd leaving a theater, and seized ten hostages in the Savoy Hotel. Israeli forces stormed the building. Eleven Israelis and most of the terrorists were killed.

How was all this indiscriminate and murderous bloodshed intended to produce some tangible gains for the PLO? Arafat had always correctly expected that violence would mobilize support among Palestinians and Arabs for his cause while he had incorrectly thought that Israel would collapse from this onslaught. Still, achieving even just the first goal was quite an accomplishment, a point noted years later by Abu Ubeid al-Qurashi, an aide to Usama bin Ladin, who saw the PLO's acts as a model for the September 11, 2001, attacks on the World Trade Center and the Pentagon. While, for example, the PLO's kidnapping of Israel's Olympic team at Munich did not gain the PLO's immediate demands for releasing those involved in past terrorist attacks and even damaged its cause in Western public opinion, Qurashi wrote, "It was the greatest media victory." As a result of this attack, he added, millions of people around the world became familiar with Palestinian claims and demands, "thousands of young Palestinians" joined the PLO, and many new groups arose in the Middle East and elsewhere trying to use terrorism to imitate its political success and publicity.[49]

By the mid-1970s, while generally abandoning international terrorism, Arafat was further expanding his repertoire in several creative ways. First, Arafat learned from the Black September experience that even the flimsiest concealment of his connection to terrorist operations would protect him from being treated as a terrorist. As long as he denied any involvement in attacks, let them be carried out by smaller PLO member groups, or had Fatah members act behind some alias, the Western media and governments as well as Arab leaders would argue publicly that terrorist operations had no proven link to Arafat.[50]

Second, he came to understand that if he adopted even the most transparent, often disproved, pose as a moderate on political issues, many Western policy makers, intellectuals, and reporters were eager to believe him. Few were ready to think that a leader would reject pragmatic compromise when he saw the odds were against him and he had a chance to gain a better life for his people. And if Arafat was not yet moderate, there were many in public life who believed this transformation was inevitable and who wanted to be the one who taught him how to become that way.

Finally, Arafat discovered that not only could terrorism coexist with diplomacy but that even the most horrendous violence could strengthen his international position. Creating a crisis almost always brought foreign leaders running to his door with concessions to convince him to stop it.

To ensure that a strategy based on murdering civilians did not inhibit his diplomatic progress, however, Arafat realized that he had to put his goals in a new and better light. As early as 1969, Arafat had admitted, "Public relations... has not been one of our strong points—we are primarily an action organization. However, we realize that one of the main reasons for Arab failure has been in our inability to match the Zionist propaganda machine and to explain our case to the world."[51] His previous indifference to Western opinion, eagerness to prove himself a revolutionary, and proud insistence that Israel's total destruction was his goal gave way to building a different image in the West.

To counter the PLO's image as a terrorist group seeking the destruction of Israel and its people, Arafat had explained in 1969 that the PLO really wanted to "liberate the Jews from Zionism." In a new program adopted by the 1969 PNC, the PLO promised that after reconquering all of Palestine and destroying Israel, it would "set up a free and democratic society... for all Palestinians, including Muslims, Christians and Jews."[52] Arafat called this "a humanitarian plan which will allow the Jews to live in dignity, as they have always lived, under the aegis of an Arab state and within the framework of an Arab society."[53] There was, however, a massive load of fine print, which defined that state's future citizens in a way that would include few Israeli Jews. The plan also merely offered a people that had gone through a terrible Holocaust and twenty years of conflict with the Arabs a paper promise of limited rights if they surrendered. As if this were not enough, PLO leaders made it clear that Jews would never be allowed to outvote the Arabs.

If Arafat hoped, then, that his strategy would weaken Israel's resolve, it had the opposite effect. It was hardly surprising that such ploys as invitations to join an armed struggle against their own country consisting mainly of killing their fellow citizens made Israelis even more determined to fight and more skeptical about the PLO's ultimate intentions.

Yet it was equally peculiar from the PLO's standpoint that a nationalist movement preferred to promise such a solution—no matter how cynical rather than establish its own exclusively Palestinian nation-state. It was one of many signs over the years that eliminating Israel was a more important priority for Arafat than obtaining a stable and peaceful state of his own.

By February 1974, the PLO came up with another plan that would be the foundation of its long-term strategy. Fearing that Arab states would make peace with Israel in exchange for the return of territories captured by Israel in the 1967 war, Arafat had to do something to ensure that the West Bank did not go back to Jordan and the Gaza Strip to Egypt. Therefore, Arafat proposed a dramatic new policy. The PLO now wanted to "establish a national authority on any lands that can be wrested from Zionist occupation." But he explained this would not mean peace or acceptance of Israel within its pre-1967 borders. Instead, if the Palestinians gained the West Bank and the Gaza Strip, they would be used as a base to advance toward total victory. In this two-stage plan to eliminate Israel, armed struggle, the demand that all Palestinian refugees return to their pre-1948 homes, and the rejection of negotiations with Israel would all continue.[54] In Arafat's words, the strategy was not about peace but about "how the rest of Palestine is to be liberated."[55]

The July 1974 PNC accepted this plan. There was no intention of creating a West Bank/Gaza Palestinian state as a final goal, a homeland where Palestinians could live, prosper, and express their nationhood. It would merely be a liberated zone, another version of Jordan in the late 1960s or southern Lebanon in the early 1970s. But this time the territory would be under total Palestinian control so that no Arab government could interfere, limit the struggle, or take it away from them.

The PNC resolution formulated by Arafat proposed combining armed struggle and a diplomatic effort "to establish the people's national, independent and fighting authority on every part of Palestinian land to be liberated." The main task of this "national authority"—not a state since the Palestinian state could only be built when all of Israel was conquered—would be to continue fighting for full victory. This authority's first duty would be to complete "the liberation of all Palestinian soil."[56]

From a public relations standpoint, this was a stroke of genius. Ever after, Arafat could tell the West that he just sought to regain the territory Israel had captured in 1967 for a Palestinian state. Yet at the same time, the goal of using such an entity as a basis for total victory was the line given to the Arab world and the Palestinians themselves, proving to them that Arafat had not sold out and ensuring that radicals continued to support him.

Each statement could be calibrated to preserve that ambiguity. During the 1970s and 1980s, this was done on a cynical level simply to persuade the West of Arafat's moderation. By the 1990s, however, his attitude toward the 1974 resolution had become more complex. Many Palestinians were interested in a real, lasting, two-state solution, but the brilliance of the 1974 concept let them avoid making a clear choice. During the peace process of the 1990s, Arafat would often justify his policy by referring to that PNC decision, although it was unclear whether he was using the resolution to justify making peace or using a promise of peace to conceal his longer-term goal. The two-stage model continued to compete with the idea of a full and final peace in the minds of Arafat and his followers. When the time for serious decisions came in 2000, he refused to abandon that ambiguity and choose between the alternatives.

The 1974 resolution itself thus provided a remarkably accurate explanation of why the peace process would fail a quarter-century later because Arafat was unable to transcend that strategy or world view. It specified that the PLO would reject an Israeli offer of the West Bank and the Gaza Strip if the price was "recognition, conciliation, [and] secure borders" for Israel or any renunciation of the Palestinian claim to all of Palestine and the demand for a return of all Palestinian refugees to Israel with a right to dissolve the Jewish state.[57] These were the main issues that scuttled negotiations in 2000: Arafat's refusal to end incitement and thus preach conciliation; failure to stop anti-Israel terrorism and thus provide secure borders; rejection of the idea that the treaty would end the conflict and thus renunciation of his claim to all the land; and unwillingness to give up the demand for a full return of the refugees, which would create a situation in which Israel could be subverted and dissolved as a Jewish state.

As part of his new diplomatic strategy in 1974, Arafat also formally ended the Black September era by insisting that the PLO must have good relations with all Arab states, including conservative ones.[58] In response, the October 1974 Arab League summit recognized the PLO—and thus Arafat himself—as the Palestinian people's "sole legitimate representative." For the first time, the Arab leaders invited him to speak at a summit. Afterward, they promised him a large sum in aid money, little of which—a fitting symbol for their relationship—was ever delivered.[59]

Arafat's most important diplomatic breakthrough of all was the UN General Assembly's invitation for him to address it, passed by the lopsided margin of 105–4 with twenty abstentions. This was a remarkable gift to a man who was openly seeking the destruction of a UN member state, deliberately killing its civilians, and who had been recently involved in hijacking airplanes, assassinating diplomats, and attacking the Olympic games. In the face of Arab, Soviet bloc, and Third World support, though, no one considered conditioning the invitation on Arafat's changing his behavior.

Still intent on highlighting his revolutionary credentials and method of operation, Arafat wanted to deliver his November 13, 1974, speech carrying a gun and had to be talked into leaving it behind, though he did wear his empty holster.[60] When Arafat was practicing his speech beforehand, his colleagues urged him to reduce his Egyptian accent, which used a hard "g" sound rather than the soft "j" of Palestinian Arabic. He went too far, saying words like "Nicarajua" and "Anjola."[61] But the speech's six main themes, which had always been central to his world view and would continue to dominate his political line for decades to come, emerged clearly.[62]

First, Arafat claimed that Zionism and Israel were too evil to be allowed to exist. Not only were they "imperialist, colonialist, racist, . . . profoundly reactionary and discriminatory," but they were even anti-semitic and against the interests of Jews as well. His inability to grasp Israel's nature and purpose or accept that it was a real country based on a genuine nationalism showed a lack of the minimal empathy for the other side needed even to understand how to affect it or predict how it would act.

Second, he insisted that the Palestinians were classic Third World victims of oppression, violence, Western imperialism, and racial discrimination. This argument was an attempt to mobilize Third World support while also playing on anti-Western sentiments and Western guilt.

Third, he denied charges of terrorism, trying to divorce the issue completely from any question of the methods he used. Anyone fighting "for the freedom and liberation of his land from the invaders, the settlers and the colonialists cannot possibly be called terrorist," Arafat said. The Palestinians were only acting like the American revolutionaries against the British, the European resistance against the Nazis, or Third World nationalist struggles against the colonizers. In contrast, by waging "war to occupy, colonize and oppress other people," Israelis were innately terrorists and war criminals.

In Arafat's view, quite different from most of the movements he cited, the end justified any means of struggle. Arafat had demonstrated no comprehension of the fact that how a struggle was waged is a relevant consideration. There is a difference between fighting armies and blowing up movie theaters or machine-gunning bus passengers and schoolchildren. The movements whose historic examples he cited deliberately avoided anticivilian terrorism, not merely as a matter

The Teflon Terrorist

of morality but also as a central element in achieving success and protecting the movement from international disdain and internal disorder.[63]

Fourth, Arafat threatened that unless he got his way he would wreak disaster on the region, predicting a new war that would bring "nuclear destruction and cataclysmic annihilation." Arafat frequently repeated such warnings, believing an ability to cause trouble to be his great asset, forcing others to make concessions to stop him from creating a crisis or to persuade him to end one he had begun.

Fifth, he insisted that Palestinian national identity was an established fact whose thirst could be quenched only by total victory. He insisted that always "the Palestinian dreamt of return," and that nothing could change that goal. Yet at the time, Palestinian nationalism was still very much in competition among Palestinians with the Arab nationalist, Marxist, and Islamist approaches. To gain victory for his ideology, Arafat still faced a long, hard, and perhaps even unending struggle.

Finally, he wanted to establish the PLO's irrevocable legitimacy. This was, Arafat explained, based on four pillars: armed struggle, popular support, keeping a broad coalition, and backing from other Arabs. Yet these assets were far less secure than Arafat admitted. He made decisions based on his own—often questionable—interpretation of how to preserve them. He responded to the fragility of the Arab states' backing, the masses' loyalty, and his coalition's unity by using demagoguery and avoiding moderation. And belief that his primacy rested mainly on violence made him fear that the movement would collapse if he pursued a peaceful path or made compromises.

Arafat ended his speech with what became perhaps his most famous line: "I come bearing an olive branch and a freedom-fighter's gun. Do not let the olive branch fall from my hand." It was part of Arafat's mystique that no one noticed the essential contradiction in this statement. Another leader might have said, "Help me to succeed with the olive branch so that I can put down the gun." The United Nations, after all, is an organization that is dedicated to solving disputes peacefully. But Arafat was actually stating his basic belief that diplomacy was not an alternative to violence but only a supplement to it. The idea of implementing a ceasefire in order to negotiate successfully or ordering an end to violence so as to make progress toward peace was usually outside his repertoire.

The behavior of others convinced Arafat that he was right and need not change his tactics. Shortly after his speech—and despite his continued practice of terrorism and his drive to destroy a member state—the United Nations made the PLO an official observer. A year later, the UN General Assembly passed a resolution equating Zionism with racism, endorsing one of his speech's main themes. Other diplomatic successes followed quickly. The PLO gained full membership in the Nonalignment Movement in August 1975, and by the late 1970s, eighty-six countries had recognized the PLO, compared to just seventy-two that recognized Israel.

None of these developments were inhibited by the PLO's continuing campaign of terrorism. In 1975, for example, on the first anniversary of Arafat's UN speech and coinciding with the UN passage of the resolution equating Zionism with racism, Fatah terrorists exploded a twenty-three-pound bomb in front of a coffeehouse in downtown Jerusalem, killing seven people and wounding forty. It was a curious but appropriate symbol of PLO strategy: a massacre to celebrate a diplomatic victory.

To bin Ladin's assistant, Qurashi, a quarter-century later, "the best proof" of terrorism's value as a strategy was that Arafat was an honored guest at the UN General Assembly just eighteen months after his men gunned down athletes at the Olympic games.[64] The lesson Arafat took from these experiences—that terrorism could be a main factor promoting diplomatic success and was no barrier to his receiving rewards—would carry on into the twenty-first century.

Many people and governments told him over the years that continuing violence would damage him politically and leave him a marginal figure. Yet Arafat knew this to be untrue from experience. His ability to cause trouble in the region and to inflict casualties was a measure of his importance and, thus, of his ability to get more benefits and concessions from others. The only two countries boycotting him for his use of terrorism were Israel and the United States, and he had no interest in talking to Israel.

His attitude toward the United States was more complex. Arafat recognized that country's importance but his anti-American radicalism and alliance with the Soviet Union constrained him from trying to improve relations. He sent an aide to Washington in 1972 to open a PLO office, but the U.S. government expelled him due to Black September's exploits.[65] Only later did the PLO succeed in opening even an information center in the United States under Arab League auspices.

Meanwhile, Sadat, Asad, and other Arab leaders were ready to show enough solidarity to urge repeatedly that the United States talk with the PLO.[66] Secretary of State William Rogers seemed to accept this idea, writing President Richard Nixon in a top-secret March 1973 memo that Arafat's group was very able to create instability and undermine peace efforts and might become more radical and terrorist in the future. In contrast to the CIA's more accurate assessment, however, he thought only a "small minority" in the PLO supported or committed terrorism.[67]

In July 1973, a close Arafat associate told a U.S. diplomat in Iran that Arafat was interested in dialogue with the United States. But the message, bizarrely at odds with all of Arafat's previous statements, claimed that he would accept Israel's existence if he were allowed to overthrow King Hussein, take over Jordan, and establish a Palestinian state there. The United States responded by rejecting any interest in subverting Jordan but expressed a willingness to hear how Palestinian goals could be addressed by peaceful negotiations. A second PLO approach came on August 13, when King Hasan of Morocco offered to arrange a U.S.-PLO dialogue.[68]

On October 10, just after the 1973 war began, another secret PLO message to the United States came through Beirut with similar themes. The United States did not want to ignore this approach since, as Secretary of State Henry Kissinger later wrote, "The PLO had potential for causing trouble all over the Arab world; we wanted it to be on its best behavior during the early stages of our approaches to Egypt and while we were seeking Saudi support." Two weeks later, when another message came reiterating Arafat's interest in talks, Kissinger replied that he would send someone for a secret exchange.[69]

One U.S. motive for initiating contacts with Arafat was to avoid more attacks on its own officials. There were credible reports, for example, that Arafat's men were planning to kidnap Rogers during his 1973 visit to the Persian Gulf.[70] Arafat himself was openly threatening such things. In response to "American conspiracies," he told a Baghdad rally in early 1973, the PLO would fight the United States and "turn this region, like Vietnam, into a center of revolutionary radiation [sic] for the entire world."[71]

To defuse such a potential terrorist campaign against the United States, Nixon sent deputy CIA director Vernon Walters to meet PLO officials in Morocco. Walters told Arafat's representatives that the United States sincerely sought a "rapid and comprehensive settlement" of the Arab-Israeli conflict and knew that a solution was only possible if Palestinian interests and aspirations were taken into account. "There are no objective reasons for antagonism between the United States and the Palestinians," he explained. The United States appreciated "the responsible positions" taken by PLO leaders during the 1973 war. But it had no proposals on the Palestinians' future role since the United States "is not so expert in the history of intra-Arab politics and culture that it can invent solutions." Walters also stressed that King Hussein was a friend of the United States, and it would not help Arafat overthrow him. Israel was not mentioned at all.[72]

In return, the PLO promised not to attack Americans directly, and Arafat made Ali Hasan Salama, a key Black September leader and a personal favorite, his liaison to the CIA.[73] The Egyptian, Moroccan, and Lebanese governments continued to urge the United States to meet with Arafat or other PLO officials and offered to arrange it. But Nixon was ready for covert contacts only.[74] Arafat dispatched a personal envoy, Walid Khalidi, a Palestinian intellectual who handled covert PLO academic and informational activities, to meet the U.S. ambassador in Lebanon during early 1974. At the very moment that Arafat was leading a major terrorist campaign against Israel, Khalidi assured the ambassador that Arafat was a moderate who opposed terrorism, wanted to get along with King Hussein, and wanted to participate in negotiations. The immediate goal was to ensure that if Israel left the West Bank and Gaza Strip, these territories would go to the PLO.[75]

But U.S. leaders remained unconvinced. They worried that trying to bring in Arafat would be opposed by both Israel and Jordan while wrecking any hopes for diplomatic progress. Arafat's public statements so contradicted Khalidi's claims of moderation as to make them uncredible. As a result, the contacts went nowhere.[76] The United States refused to deal with Arafat until he really abandoned his radical course. The United States also opposed a UN resolution designating the PLO as the sole representative of the Palestinian people though Kissinger did not try too hard to stop Arafat's 1974 invitation to speak at the General Assembly, telling colleagues that it did not matter.[77]

Arafat did succeed, however, in ensuring that the United States would not attack him or pressure Arab states to crack down on him. While U.S. governments saw the PLO as a hostile, pro-Soviet force engaged in terrorism, they never tried to eliminate it through overt or covert means. Nor did they treat the PLO the same way that they energetically opposed Soviet-backed movements elsewhere in the world. Kissinger merely promised Israeli prime minister Yitzhak Rabin—who also made this Israel's position—that the United States would not deal with the PLO until it abandoned terrorism, accepted UN Resolution 242, and recognized Israel's right to exist. Kissinger did, however, make one exception: the United States could deal with the PLO in any situation where American citizens might be at risk, a recognition of the organization's ability to blackmail Western states through terrorism.[78]

Even these conditions put the initiative in Arafat's hands. Both Israel and the United States left the door open for peaceful compromise whenever he might be ready for one. But Arafat was in no hurry to walk through that door. Instead, he continued a struggle, strategy, and set of goals that would inflict many more defeats on him and more suffering on his people, largely due to his own mistakes.

The Teflon Terrorist

4

Fouling His Own Nest

1975–1983

Yasir Arafat gave a big smile and his fingers formed the V-for-victory sign as if to celebrate one more success. Yet it was hardly Arafat's finest hour as he boarded a ship in Beirut, Lebanon, on August 30, 1982. As had occurred in Jordan, Arafat was being chased out of a country. He had expected to leave Lebanon only for his triumphal return to Palestine. But now he was again fleeing in defeat from a place where he had been so powerful.

To make matters worse, no Arab state would help him stay in Lebanon and none was eager to host him in his newest exile. Arafat had to sail straight out of the Middle East to find temporary refuge in Greece. Able only to find a base two thousand miles from the country he claimed, Arafat moved on to Tunisia, which reluctantly gave him safe haven. Arafat had failed so badly in Lebanon precisely because his strategy against Israel, his behavior toward Lebanon, and that Arab nation's attitude toward him were all contrary to the myth he was creating of Arab support, Palestinian unity, and inevitable victory.[1]

But remarkably, as had happened with his defeat at Karama and expulsion from Jordan, Arafat again persuaded his followers that the flight from Lebanon was a victory. "We were defending an Arab capital, defending Arab honor, standing up before the world for the whole Arab nation," he said just before leaving Beirut.[2]

Lebanon too had suffered from his presence. Arafat and his PLO were major factors in starting and escalating Lebanon's civil war, though the conflict was rooted in Lebanon's communal quarrels and social issues. Hundreds of thousands of Lebanese became refugees or exiles; thousands were killed or wounded. Cities became battlefields, and the once-strong economy collapsed.[3]

While Arafat became one of Lebanon's most powerful figures, his men often acted like glorified street gangs, harassing, robbing, and even arresting its citizens. Many Palestinians used the PLO to get revenge on local residents, who they felt had denied them equality or dignity. The PLO's use of southern Lebanon as a base for attacking Israel, coupled with Israeli reprisal raids, had turned the region into a war zone. The PLO's arbitrary rule and creation of a situation threatening their lives so alienated Lebanese villagers in the south that they turned against the PLO.[4]

Arafat inflamed the conflicts between Lebanese and Palestinians by pretending they did not exist and thus refusing to solve them. A good example of this behavior was that after PLO forces shot one village's independent-minded Islamic cleric, Arafat told the man's son that the Zionists had done it and gave him a pistol so he could take revenge on Israel.[5] But most Lebanese saw through the claim that they and the PLO were brothers and allies. Some sought to use Arafat's power for their own purposes while others resented him.

In Beirut, Fatah and every other PLO group had scores of offices, military bases, social institutions, and business operations.[6] They all competed for power, patronage, and loot with Lebanese Christian and Muslim groups. Beirut's fleshpots also corrupted a group proclaiming to pride itself on a lean revolutionary asceticism. Many of the city's residents called Arafat the mayor of west Beirut, the city's Muslim section, parts of which were dominated by PLO forces in the 1970s. His headquarters was a big building on Corniche Mazraa, which displayed a large PLO emblem. Heavily armed men, many of them carrying AK-47 assault rifles, ran in and out into waiting jeeps, while expensively dressed officials drove down the city's roads at top speed in their Mercedes sedans.[7]

Even the PLO's press spokesman, Rashid Khalidi, later admitted how common was "the spectacle of individual Palestinian officials who had grown rich, or had obtained a luxurious apartment, expensive car, and armed bodyguards" because of their involvement with the PLO.[8] As a result, "a clear majority of Lebanese came to feel that the PLO was using Lebanon for its own ends, without concern for the harm visited on the country in the process."[9]

Arafat did not seek to benefit personally from this greedy pursuit but let it happen in order to raise money for the cause as well as to keep subordinates happy and loyal. In the long term, his behavior allowed the PLO's internal politics and culture to be shaped largely by violence and corruption. In the short term, they made him and his movement unpopular to many Lebanese. The PLO, wrote Lebanese political scientist Ghassan Salama, became merely a machine for its own officials' benefit.[10] It suited their interests if the struggle never came to an end. They could go on forever traveling around the world, being treated as celebrities, and living well on salaries and expense accounts in houses owned by the movement.

Yet this was not the future that Lebanon's leaders preferred. On May 17, 1975, President Suleiman Faranjiyyah invited Arafat for a meeting with the Egyptian and Saudi ambassadors along with several high-ranking Lebanese army officers. Faranjiyyah, nervously chain smoking, told Arafat, "Your behavior is intolerable for the Lebanese population," because of both his own group's deeds and those of leftist Lebanese groups it supported. He blamed the PLO for creating a situation in which Lebanese were now massacring each other. Arafat said that he had done nothing wrong and was the real victim since Christian rightists were preparing a war of extermination against Palestinians. Faranjiyyah lost his temper, yelling, "Proofs! Proofs! Be honest for once and give me documents supporting your allegations!"

Arafat, tears in his eyes, closed his little notebook and snapped back, "I won't tolerate being talked to like that! I am a fighter, and it was as such that I was elected to head the Palestinian movement and not thanks to a one-vote majority in an assembly of notables," a derogatory reference to Faranjiyyah's own election as president of Lebanon.[11]

The meeting ended with more angry exchanges. Arafat had directly and personally challenged the legitimacy of Lebanon's president to rule the country, presenting himself as a higher authority. It was an intolerable insult and a symbol of the threat that Arafat's policies posed to Lebanon's existence. Shortly thereafter, Faranjiyyah told a friend that Arafat was "the biggest liar in the world."[12]

In the early days of the civil war, Arafat and his Lebanese allies— Muslim, Druze, and leftist—had the upper hand over Lebanese Christian forces, which traditionally had been the most powerful community in Lebanon. Arafat even organized his own Lebanese Muslim militia and a revolt in Lebanon's army, encouraging several thousand soldiers to defect and create a pro-Arafat force, the Lebanese Arab Army, in early 1976.

But while Arafat's coalition might have been able to defeat the Lebanese opposition alone, Syria, led by Hafiz al-Asad, was determined to ensure that Arafat and his leftist allies did not take over Lebanon. Not only could Asad use his own army for this purpose, but he also controlled major Palestinian assets: the Syrian-backed al-Sa'iqa was the PLO's second-largest member group with many armed men in Lebanon. Asad also controlled the regular PLO army units stationed in his country.

At a meeting in Damascus with Arafat and Lebanese leaders in October 1975, Asad pounded the table as he blamed Arafat for Lebanon's civil war. "If only you had more sense in the past!" he shouted at Arafat, demanding that the two sides work out a ceasefire.[13] At first, Arafat agreed to stop fighting. But his ceasefires never lasted long and the vicious conflict continued.[14]

Once again, though, Arafat had gone too far. Syria wanted a PLO that fought Israel but not one that dominated Lebanon, a prize Damascus sought for itself. Asad also still hoped to seize control over both the PLO and Israel. "You do not represent the Palestinian[s] more than we do," Asad once told Arafat. "Don't you forget.... There is no Palestinian people and there is no Palestinian entity. There is [only] Syria."[15]

Asad's patience finally reached an end. In June 1976, the Syrian army invaded Lebanon aided by Palestinian and Lebanese client forces. By November, it had conquered almost all of the areas previously held by Arafat and his allies. Arafat raced around the Arab world seeking help, but no country would lift a finger to help him fight Syria nor even press Damascus to stop.

Perhaps Arafat's worst single defeat was the battle for Tal al-Za'tar, one of the largest Palestinian refugee camps, which had been besieged by a Lebanese Christian militia with Syrian military assistance. The situation was hopeless. But Arafat urged his men not to surrender, no matter what the cost in casualties. On August 12, Christian forces finally overran the camp after inflicting heavy casualties. Arafat blamed the defeat on Syria and those "silent Arab regimes" that had not come to his aid.[16]

Yet when Syria and Lebanese Christians agreed to hold talks in September, Arafat escalated his demands. He rejected a ceasefire based on a partial PLO withdrawal from Christian areas and demanded instead that all Syrian troops leave the country. Syria refused, telling Arafat that it had been invited by Lebanon's government. The Syrians did not need to mention that the threat against which Lebanon wanted protection was Arafat and his allies.[17] Given Arafat's intransigence, Syria renewed its offensive, as Arafat futilely begged Arab leaders to save Palestinians "from this new massacre."[18]

Later in 1976, the Arab League finally urged a ceasefire, and even this was on Asad's terms, letting the Syrian army remain to dominate Lebanon. In the June 1977 Shtourah agreement among Syria, Lebanon, and the PLO, Arafat was forced to accept narrow restrictions on what his forces were allowed to do everywhere except in the far south, where they could attack Israel but not interfere in Lebanon. For a while, Abu Iyad and others criticized Arafat for giving up too much and demanded that his power be reduced. But in the end, as always, they stood by him.[19]

Arafat easily withstood these complaints, but his troubles were just beginning. A more pragmatic leader, Egyptian president Anwar al-Sadat had to take into account the heavy burden of permanent war for his country, which had been intensified when it lost its two main revenue sources, the Sinai oil fields and the Suez Canal, in the 1967 war. Sadat viewed the outcome of the 1973 war not as a prelude to new rounds of fighting but as a basis for achieving a compromise peace.

In November 1977, Sadat invited Arafat to a meeting of Egypt's parliament. Listening to Sadat's speech there, Arafat was pleased at first with the lavish praise Egypt's leader showered on him. Then he was shocked as Sadat announced his readiness to go to Israel in order to negotiate peace.[20] Arafat ran from the hall and was heading for his car when Egypt's vice president, Husni Mubarak, persuaded Arafat to come by his house and discuss the matter. But Arafat only stayed a few minutes, complaining that Sadat had made him look like a fool.[21]

Yet, while embarrassing Arafat, Sadat had not intended his initiative—which would lead to the Camp David agreements and a full Egypt-Israel peace in 1979—as an anti-Arafat move. On the contrary, Sadat knew that Arafat's agreement to participate would ensure his plan's success and serve Egypt's interest by creating a stable, peaceful region under its leadership.

Certainly, if Arafat had gone along with Sadat, he would have been criticized by Syria and Iraq, as well as by many within the PLO. But Arafat could also have agreed to be involved in the negotiations with Israel at Camp David or afterward—indeed, he could have insisted on it—and achieved a Palestinian state by the beginning of the 1980s.

The United States, which brokered the Camp David agreements, was also eager to bring Arafat into a peace process if he would end terrorism and recognize Israel. Brokering an Arab-Israeli peace would have been a tremendous U.S. victory in the Cold War. Shortly after Jimmy Carter became president in 1977, his National Security advisor, Zbigniew Brzezinski, had asked Landrum Bolling, a Quaker activist and friend of Arafat, to explore whether Arafat was ready for a real policy change. Brzezinski gave Bolling a list of several phrases, any of which, if uttered by Arafat, would lead to a U.S.-PLO dialogue. Bolling met with Arafat in Beirut to transmit the offer. But when Arafat finally sent a letter to the White House, both Bolling and Brzezinski agreed that it was just Arafat's "same old double talk."[22]

Even after the Camp David agreements were completed, they still provided an opportunity that Arafat could have exploited for his own interests. After all, the accords called for autonomy in the West Bank and Gaza Strip to be followed by talks over their future. Arafat might have used the autonomy provision to organize Palestinians in those territories, control the proposed local self-government bodies, and then demand self-determination at the end of the transition period.

Hoping to gain support for the Camp David agreements, U.S. assistant secretary of state Harold Saunders was sent to meet West Bank Palestinian leaders and brief them on the plan. The local politicians were interested but feared doing anything without Arafat's authorization. Bethlehem mayor Elias Freij threw up his hands and told Saunders, "We are just sheep. We don't lead, we only follow." The next night, Saunders met with West Bank technocrats, who were excited about how the plan could benefit their people and wanted to accept it. Yet they, too, feared Arafat and the militant forces too much to take any action.

Even a few Fatah moderates favored using the chance provided by the Egypt-Israel agreement. Muhammad Zuhdi al-Nashashibi, secretary of the PLO Executive Committee, secretly told an American diplomat in 1979 that he believed that the PLO should support the Camp David agreements if there was a real prospect of self-determination and Israeli withdrawal. The PLO could control the local Palestinians and then step forward and demand to be included directly, he suggested.[23]

But Arafat had no interest in pursuing such a strategy. Instead, he saw the whole Camp David process as a plot to exclude him and eliminate the Palestine issue altogether. He did everything possible to sabotage the Camp David agreements, helping to organize an Arab boycott of Egypt and an alliance of radical forces against them. When Sadat was later assassinated, Arafat remarked, "This is what happens to people who betray the Palestinian cause."[24]

Arafat opposed the Camp David agreements and Egypt's peace policy due to his own beliefs, goals, and self-image. But he was also concerned about being challenged by militant colleagues and Palestinian rivals.[25] In 1978, frustrated at the long series of setbacks, Fatah radicals in Lebanon challenged Arafat's authority. Abu Jihad defeated the rebellion by rallying loyal forces and removing critics from their posts.[26]

Arafat's refusal to work with Egypt also made him dependent on Arab states like Libya, Syria, and Iraq, which were eager to subvert him and interfere in Palestinian politics. Seeking to take over the PLO or render it submissive, Iraq hired the anti-Arafat Palestinian terrorist Abu Nidal to kill its men. Arafat's Fatah responded by shooting Iraqi officials in Britain, France, Pakistan, and Lebanon. At a December 1978 meeting of anti-Sadat forces in Libya, President Muammar al-Qadhafi accused Arafat of conspiring with Sadat. Arafat was so angry that he stomped out of the room, slamming the door. Although Qadhafi cajoled him into returning, Arafat again blew up when Habash, head of the rival PFLP, agreed with Qadhafi's claim. Arafat asked Qadhafi, "Have you invited us here to divide the Palestinians?"[27]

Anti-Americanism was another key part of Arafat's strategy to block progress toward peace. He denounced U.S. policy as "an imperialist plot to liquidate the Palestinian cause."[28] At the November 1979 Arab summit, Arafat urged Arab states to cut off oil supplies to the United States, an idea that had no appeal to Saudi Arabia and other major producers.[29] The virulence of Arafat's anti-Americanism made the U.S. government take seriously the possibility that the PLO might attack American installations. For example, Arafat gave a speech in Lebanon in September 1979 in which he said that Carter's signature on the Camp David agreements "will cost him his interests in the Arab region." The State Department alerted embassies to be on guard against possible PLO terrorist assaults.[30]

But no such attacks actually took place. In practice, Arafat was careful to avoid a direct confrontation with the United States. As part of the secret U.S.-PLO agreement made earlier in Morocco, he had given his assurance that there would be no attacks on American citizens being evacuated from Lebanon in 1974 because of the civil war there.[31] The PLO also gave a little help in the form of low-level information on potential threats against the U.S. embassy from other armed groups since the building was near a PLO-controlled neighborhood whose residents were Lebanese Shia Muslims.[32]

Despite his radical course, militant and anti-American rhetoric, and terrorist activities, Arafat continued to make great strides in his diplomatic standing in Europe. In July 1979, he met Austrian chancellor Bruno Kreisky and Socialist International chairman Willi Brandt in Vienna, then traveled to Lisbon and Madrid for more top-level meetings. Several European states let the PLO open offices; Greece and Austria accepted PLO ambassadors.[33] Some European leaders hoped they would be the one to turn Arafat into a responsible international citizen; others simply wanted to ensure that he did not launch terrorist attacks on their soil.

For Arafat, though, the triumph of Iran's Islamist revolution in 1979 was the best proof that his radical strategy would succeed. If Ayatollah Ruhollah Khomeini could rise from obscurity and exile to conquer a seemingly invincible foe allied to America, Arafat thought he might do so also.

Arafat arrived uninvited in Tehran in February 1979, a few days after the shah fled and Khomeini's forces had taken over. As his plane approached Tehran's Mahrabad airport, Arafat said, "I felt as if I was landing in Jerusalem." His entourage carried Khomeini's picture and chanted, "Today Iran, tomorrow Palestine." He had good reason to expect a friendly reception since many Iranian revolutionaries had been trained at Fatah camps in Lebanon, including Khomeini's own son. Symbolically, the new Iranian government gave the PLO the former Israeli embassy.[34] After more than two decades of struggle, this was the first piece of Israeli real estate Arafat had captured.

Even at this point, Arafat desired no full-scale confrontation with the United States. Although he later exaggerated his role, Arafat did talk, albeit unsuccessfully, with Iranian officials about freeing Americans held hostage at the U.S. embassy in Tehran and supplied Washington with some information about Iran and developments in the hostage crisis. When the Iranians decided in 1980 to release some of the hostages, the PLO tipped off the United States in advance. Given Arafat's penchant for public relations stunts, Assistant Secretary of State Harold Saunders later recalled, "We were afraid that when the hostages got out of Iran and arrived in America, Arafat would come out the plane door leading them by the hand."[35] Such an action would have greatly raised Arafat's popularity in the United States and forced the U.S. government to deal with him.

But Arafat was far more eager to please Tehran rather than Washington. He saw Iran's revolution as offering him the chance to coordinate a new regionwide alliance of Soviet-backed Arabs and Iranians battling against Israel and America. The era of conflict between Arabs and Iranians was at an end, he announced. Iran's revolution had shifted the strategic balance decisively against his enemies. "Iraq can now throw its army fully into the battle against the Zionist enemy. And there is no Persian pressure any more on Saudi Arabia and the Gulf states."[36]

In December 1979, he proclaimed, "We and the Iranian revolution . . . are one revolution led by one man, Imam Khomeini. . . . Tell Imam Khomeini to give the order and we will all obey and move to strike U.S. imperialism and U.S. imperialist interests at any time and in any place."[37] But while Arafat sought economic and political support from Iran, one of his colleagues admitted secretly that the PLO had turned down an Iranian offer to send troops to fight with it, suspicious that Iran wanted to help Islamist forces take over their organization.[38]

Since Iran and Arab regimes—especially Iraq, Syria, and Saudi Arabia—all deeply distrusted each other, Arafat's bigger problem was that friendship with one of them often required enmity with another.

What Abu Iyad said about Qadhafi applied to how all Arab states and Iran, too, dealt with Arafat: "He always wants us to toe his line fully. We must be the friends of his friends and the foes of his foes. . . . What he wants is a [hired] revolution, and he treats us like paid mercenaries."[39]

As always, too, Arafat made some leaders hostile by his own behavior as fast as he soothed others. At an October 1979 meeting of Arab foreign ministers, several of them warned that Arafat's turn toward Iran could make him into a threat to themselves.[40] Yet Khomeini gave the PLO little aid, knowing Arafat did not share his Islamist ideology and had close ties to Iran's Arab rivals. For example, Arafat refused to condemn Moscow's Communist coup and invasion of Afghanistan, instead backing Marxists against the Islamists there.[41] Khomeini called Arafat "the dwarf" and refused to let the PLO open offices outside of Tehran, fearing it might spy for Arab states.[42]

Iraq was the country feeling most immediately threatened by Arafat's pro-Iran policy. Saddam Hussein, preparing for war with Tehran, wanted to ensure that Arafat would be his client. Saddam promised Arafat massive aid and an end to Abu Nidal's assassination attacks on the PLO. Iraq's August 1980 invasion of Iran destroyed Arafat's hope for a broad anti-Israel and anti-American coalition. His attempt to mediate between Baghdad and Tehran angered both sides. Forced to choose, Arafat backed Saddam, a decision that poisoned his relations with Tehran for the next two decades.[43]

Arafat often seemed to spend more time insulting or making up with Arab rulers than he did fighting Israel. He had improved relations with Syria and Iraq—not exactly reliable friends—while antagonizing Egypt, Iran, Libya, and Saudi Arabia. The mercurial Qadhafi, accusing Arafat of abandoning the revolution, closed the PLO's offices in Libya in January 1980.[44] When Arafat came to an April meeting of radical forces that Qadhafi was hosting, Libya's ruler refused to let him enter the conference hall.[45] By promising to be more radical and anti-American, Arafat only temporarily persuaded Qadhafi to keep giving him aid.[46]

In addition, Arafat provoked a potentially dangerous spat with Saudi Arabia when, in June 1981, he publicly complained that the country was not giving him enough money. The Saudis were furious. Arafat quickly went to Saudi Arabia, praised its rulers, and polished his Islamic credentials by making the pilgrimage to Mecca. The Saudis continued sending money but did not forget the insult.[47]

While Saudi Arabia was not interested in making peace with Israel, it wanted to make some diplomatic initiative to ease the regional situation. The Saudis worried that the radical trend in the area, including Arafat's militancy, might threaten themselves.[48] In response, in October 1981, the Saudis presented a peace plan, which they expected Arafat to support since it favored his interests. It demanded that Israel turn the West Bank and Gaza over to the United Nations, which would then give them to Arafat to rule as a Palestinian state. The United Nations would also guarantee the existence of both Israel and Palestine. It was a plan to achieve a peace settlement without any negotiations or compromise with Israel.

Even this idea, however, was too much for Arafat, who rejected the proposal for hinting at recognition of Israel. In vain, the Saudis defended the plan as a public relations effort, intended "not to communicate with the enemy" but rather to persuade the United States and Western Europe to support the Arab cause. Arafat responded that Israel was nothing more than occupied Palestine.[49]

To avoid antagonizing the Saudis even more, however, Arafat cleverly used his skill at sounding flexible while rejecting any real compromise. He welcomed the plan as a "good starting point," then demanded five changes—especially dropping any hint of recognizing Israel—which made the proposal even more one-sided and unacceptable to non-Arabs.[50] Even in this form, Arafat did not like the plan, whose implementation he said would require "two wars" in order to defeat an enemy that wanted to rule "from the Nile to the Euphrates." After being amended to eliminate any hint of recognizing Israel even if it withdrew from all of the West Bank and Gaza, the plan was adopted by the September 1982 Arab summit.[51]

Arafat preferred to put his faith in a combination of hoping Arab states would defeat Israel and trying to do it himself by using terrorism. Yet his military strategy was even more unsuccessful than his shaky alliance system. It was clear that these terrorist operations were not defeating Israel, while periodic Israeli retaliation hit Fatah facilities in Lebanon hard. Arafat's response was to transform his forces in south Lebanon into a regular army of several thousand soldiers supplied with Soviet-made antiaircraft weapons, mortars, artillery, tanks, and rocket launchers.

In the spring of 1981, Fatah launched a new kind of offensive, firing scores of rockets at northern Israel. While few of them hit anything, hundreds of Israeli civilians fled and tensions were high until the United States arranged a ceasefire in July. Arafat saw this as a victory, which showed his ability to intimidate Israel and gain recognition from America. And while Arafat formally observed the ceasefire, he made little attempt to stop PLO member groups from launching more cross-border attacks, continuing to deny any responsibility for their activities.

Within Lebanon itself, the civil war had now raged for seven years, and no solution was in sight. Aside from being harassed by Syria's army, the PLO was also being increasingly challenged by Amal, a Lebanese

Shia Muslim militia, for control of the south. In the spring of 1982, there were fierce Amal-PLO and Lebanese army–PLO clashes. Walid Junblatt, leader of the country's left, warned Arafat that he might lose all local support unless he improved relations with Lebanese groups.[52]

Even the United States tried to help Arafat avoid a ruinous confrontation. The State Department urged Arafat not to provoke Israel as that country might choose to invade Lebanon.[53] But this is precisely what Arafat did by refusing to let Lebanon's army or government or effective UN forces enter the south, since they might restrict attacks on Israel.[54] Meanwhile, smaller PLO groups continued to make their own attacks on Israel. Given this situation, Israeli prime minister Menahem Begin and Defense Minister Ariel Sharon agreed with the main Christian militia to knock the PLO out of south Lebanon and install its head, Bashir Gemayel, as a strong anti-Syrian, anti-PLO president.[55]

On June 6, Israeli forces crossed into Lebanon, shattered the PLO forces, and advanced northward. Some of Arafat's top officers deserted their posts and fled. The PLO was given no help by Syria's army, the USSR, any Arab state, or the Lebanese militias. Lebanese Christians cooperated tacitly with Israel, and many Lebanese in the south welcomed removal of the oppressive PLO presence. Israeli forces besieged Beirut but did not want to enter the city in order to avoid high casualties and an even more adverse international reaction.

According to Arafat, Israel was gunning for him personally, using aerial bombing and booby-trapped cars.[56] In one June incident, he recounted, PLO leaders went for a secret meeting in an apartment building, which only a few security people knew about in advance. An Israeli agent reportedly tracked Arafat there. Just after the meeting began, Arafat later claimed, he shouted, "Get out of the building, now!" He raced to his car and was driven to a deep underground garage as a bomb exploded.[57] A month later, on August 6, a meeting of Arafat and his top lieutenants in another building had just ended when an Israeli aircraft dropped a bomb that destroyed it.[58]

Arafat portrayed the Israeli offensive as a genocidal attack employing demonic weapons and based on a U.S.-led plot. He blamed the attack on the United States, claiming that Secretary of Defense Caspar Weinberger, known in fact for being hostile toward Israel, wanted to test new kinds of weapons on Palestinian civilians.[59] "More than the Zionists themselves," Arafat said, "the United States is principally responsible"[60] for the region's problems. Arafat continued to be a major source of anti-American incitement in the Arab world.

He was equally upset about the refusal of any Arab state to help him. Arafat seemed to have genuinely expected beforehand that the Arab world would go to war against Israel to relieve the pressure on him.[61]

Fouling His Own Nest

Instead, the regimes ignored his plea that a Palestinian defeat would mean "all of us are sunk." Arab rulers were always unmoved by Arafat's accusations that they could easily defeat Israel if they only mobilized the Arab nation's "tremendous human, economic, military and material resources" rather than remain "in a deep sleep" stuck in a "rotten impotent swamp."[62]

For his part, though, Arafat did not appreciate the advice given him by one Arab leader on how he could achieve that mobilization. Since Arafat frequently proclaimed his own willingness to be a martyr, Qadhafi suggested that he commit suicide to protest the situation and glorify the Palestinian cause. Qadhafi claimed, "Your blood will [be] the fuel of the revolution spreading inevitably from the Atlantic Ocean to the Gulf." Arafat declined to sacrifice himself, implying that it would do no good. He responded tartly that he was unaware "of a single demonstration of support . . . in any country 'from the Atlantic to the Gulf.'" Arafat even accused the Arabs of secretly backing "the Israeli-American alliance" against him.[63]

Although this last claim was untrue, Lebanon's leaders were understandably eager for Arafat to leave.[64] They had no interest in seeing the war continued and Beirut destroyed to shield a man and movement that had caused them so much trouble. President Bashir Gemayel told Arafat in a June phone conversation, "It's enough. . . . [You] destroyed the Lebanese army, [you] destroyed the Lebanese state."[65]

Even those far friendlier to Arafat said the same thing.[66] Ironically, it became Saeb Salam's duty to demand that Arafat leave Lebanon. When Salam had been Lebanon's prime minister back in 1971, he had expressed amazement and sorrow about the Jordan-PLO fighting of that time. It should be easy, Salam wrote to Arafat, for him and King Hussein to get along. How, Salam asked, could "the dear blood" of Arabs be shed so wastefully in a civil war? Salam then assured Arafat of his devoted support.[67] But after watching Arafat's behavior close up for a decade and seeing how much Arab blood was shed on Lebanon's soil, Salam better understood the king's viewpoint.

On the afternoon of July 3, 1982, Arafat went to the house of Salam, still a powerful political figure, to meet him and seven other Lebanese Sunni Muslim leaders. Salam first praised Arafat and then got to the point: "The PLO has covered itself in honor and now it is time to leave with honor."[68] Arafat responded that the PLO forces' honor required fighting street by street until they were all killed rather than leave Beirut. After all, he claimed, they had never been defeated by the Israelis before. Salam was so angry that he began shouting. The battle was obviously lost, and there was no sense in sacrificing the people of Beirut.

Arafat asked, "Do you want to push us out? Is that it?"

Salam responded, "With all the sacrifices we have made for your and your cause, you cannot say that about us! It is better for you and for us that you go, with your honor."

Finally, at 5:15, Arafat agreed to think about the Lebanese request, and Salam invited him to dinner. Two hours later, Arafat came back and joined the notables and the Salam family for a meal that included ground meat, cold yogurt, and eggplant. Arafat only ate black olives, then left to perform the evening prayer. On returning to the dining room, Arafat said he had something to deliver, removed a notepad from his pocket, and took out a folded piece of his personal PLO stationery. He put on his glasses and, in a distressed manner, read the following words:

> To our brother, Prime Minister Shafiq al-Wazzan: With reference to the discussions we have had, the Palestinian command has taken the following decision: The PLO does not wish to remain in Lebanon.[69]

On August 21, the French Foreign Legion guarded Beirut's port as more than eleven thousand PLO and PLA soldiers began the process of leaving Lebanon. They shot off weaponry of all calibers in a strange celebration that mixed the obvious fact of their defeat and departure with all the trappings of victory. Men threw rice, women cried and ululated as the soldiers, riding in Lebanese army trucks, passed by offices, buildings, and hotels that had once been Beirut's pride but were now burned-out hulks after so many years of war. In fresh uniforms, they held color photos of Arafat and raised hands in V-for-victory signs. They inched their way through the port's iron gates, where French soldiers and U.S. marines waited to guide them to boats.[70]

The PLO's presence in Lebanon as a $1 billion-a-year enterprise, the country's second-largest employer after the government, and with an army larger than that of its host was at an end. Although he had sworn to be a martyr rather than retreat, Arafat, as always, preferred to survive so as to fight another day. He agreed to leave Beirut if PLO forces and weapons also received safe passage and there was a promise to protect the Palestinians left behind. But he obtained neither binding guarantees for the Palestinian civilians nor any political gains.

Now Arafat worked to recast defeat as a victory, portraying himself as simultaneously victor and victim. On his last night in Beirut, he remarked, "Part of my heart stays here. This is one station. I'm going to another station. The long march continues."[71] In his message to the Palestinian people, Arafat spoke of a "heroic joint struggle" that wrote

> the most glorious pages in the history of our Arab nation.... History stood breathless following the miracle of steadfastness and

heroism . . . written by the valiant civilian sons of Beirut and their brothers, the fighters, defending this city in confronting the most ugly U.S.-Israeli war machine in this modern age. . . . Palestinian and Lebanese revolutionaries rose from this common trench, united under the hell of hundreds of thousands of tons of bombs which fell on us night and day, from the sea, from land, and from the air, for a period of nearly three months.[72]

He referred to the twelve weeks of rather limited fighting with Israel as having produced a "cascade of blood which poured from among the ruins and destruction, . . . massacres and tragedies, . . . caravans of martyrs." That Lebanon had been engulfed for seven long years in a full-scale civil war in which Palestinians and Lebanese had often fired at each other from two separate trenches, creating huge numbers of refugees and massive wreckage, went unmentioned. Even as the United States saved him by securing him safe passage out of Lebanon, Arafat could only express his hatred for the country he held responsible for this "Zionist-U.S. invasion."[73]

On August 30, 1982, the day of his departure, Arafat behaved like a victor. Arriving to meet Prime Minister Wazzan that morning, he joked, "I am changing the PLO's name to PLLO. From now on it is the Palestine and Lebanon Liberation Organization."[74] That phrase gave a good sense of why Arafat was being ushered out of the country. It revealed both his proprietary feeling toward Lebanon and his readiness to call for revolution there.

Although Wazzan told Arafat that he was "overwhelmed by sentiment," he could barely hide his relief that Arafat was going. In what was outwardly a show of support for Arafat but was clearly a litany of complaint, Wazzan called on Arafat to acknowledge all of the sacrifices Lebanon had made for him and insisted that now the "entire Arab world" would have to take up "its responsibilities for the Palestinian cause" and not just "place all the burdens" on Lebanon's shoulders.[75]

At 9:45 A.M., Wazzan, along with Walid Junblatt, accompanied Arafat in his black Mercedes limousine in a speeding motorcade, horns and sirens blaring, which was led by truckloads of French troops. At the port, guarded by U.S. marines and Lebanese soldiers to ensure Arafat's safety, Arafat gave Wazzan a medal and proclaimed that the PLO and Lebanon had defeated Israel and its defense minister, Ariel Sharon, in particular.[76] Not a single representative of any other Arab state came to see Arafat off.

But one of those who did show up to make sure Arafat left was Sharon himself. Israeli soldiers watched Arafat go through their gun sights, but Sharon kept his promise of safe passage. Arafat would claim that Sharon tried to assassinate him thirteen times during the siege of Beirut; Sharon later remarked that he had not tried to kill Arafat but thought in retrospect he should have done so.[77]

The departure ceremony broke down into chaos as crowds of PLO soldiers and foreign journalists surged and shouted. When asked by someone where he was going, Arafat said, "To Palestine, where else? But mind you, wherever I go my heart stays here." Finally, accompanied by an entourage of several dozen aides and amid chants of "Revolution until victory!" and "Palestine is Arab!" Arafat boarded the *Atlantis*, a cruise ship placed at his disposal by the Greek government since Arab regimes were so unwilling to help him.[78]

A fifteen-gun salute boomed out. The *Atlantis* gleamed white in the bright sunlight as it steamed out of the harbor escorted by a French and an American cruiser. Nine other U.S. and French warships maneuvered to guard Arafat in the Mediterranean. Arafat stood on deck wearing his pistol and black-and-white-checked kaffiya, still flashing a V-for-victory sign.

By the next day, when *Atlantis* reached Greece at the Flisvos yacht marina four miles west of Athens, Arafat was in a positively bubbly mood. Four Greek coast guard vessels circled the ship. Hundreds of police, an honor guard of Greek sailors, and a Greek navy band lined the dock to receive Prime Minister Andreas Papandreou's guest. Posters prominently displayed read, "Out with Zionist imperialism from Greece." Arafat came down the gangplank and embraced the Greek leader. A reporter asked Arafat, "Are you defeated?" Arafat replied: "I am with the people and no people can be defeated. With the people of Lebanon and the people of Beirut, we succeeded to protect the city from being invaded and occupied by the Israeli savage, barbarian troops. . . . And we succeeded to prevent their decision to smash the city and carry on with their genocide as they had declared."[79] The man who had helped bring Lebanon to the brink of destruction now took credit for saving it.

The PLO even considered setting up its new headquarters in Greece, said Abu Iyad, "to make the Arab world look silly."[80] Seven Arab states had taken in some PLO men, but the rank and file's mood was typified by a soldier who proclaimed, "Not only Israel is the enemy, but the Arabs—Saudi Arabia, Syria, and all of them. When we get rid of the Arab rulers we will fight [Israel]."[81] For the first time in history, Abu Iyad noted sarcastically, the Arab countries had all agreed on something: to betray the PLO.[82] The snows of mountain peaks, Arafat complained, "were warmer than the hearts of some of the Arab regimes."[83]

Fouling His Own Nest

There was no countervailing gratitude, however, for the United States, which had saved Arafat by finding him a safe refuge when no Arab country wanted to take the PLO. Finally, and not without difficulty, it had persuaded far-off Tunisia to host the PLO's headquarters.[84] Two days after reaching Greece, Arafat flew from Athens to Tunis where, alongside President-for-Life Habib Bourguiba, he rode into town past cheering Tunisians to a luxurious villa in Tunis's northern suburbs which had been placed at his disposal.[85]

Arafat's strategy was to rebuild his organization and hold onto leadership without making any changes or learning any lessons from the Lebanon debacle. Remarkably, he succeeded in these efforts by simply continuing to proclaim himself the victor in Beirut. The PLO, Arafat said, had fought bravely against a U.S.-directed attack, held the city for more than two months, and had yielded only due to a lack of Arab support. Arafat claimed to have won a partial military and total political victory. Khalid al-Hasan even proclaimed, "We should not become arrogant in the future as a result of this victory."[86]

In fact, though, Palestinians were traumatized and isolated. It seemed hard to believe that their situation could be worse. But on the evening of September 16, 1982, the Israeli army, having received reports of armed PLO groups in the Palestinian refugee camps of Sabra and Shatila, let around three hundred Christian militiamen enter from a group commanded by Elie Hobeika, a former close aide of Bashir Gemayel, who had been assassinated by Syria. The Lebanese Christians sought to get revenge for the death of their leader by massacring seven or eight hundred of the camps' residents, many of them Palestinians.[87] The reality was horrible enough but Arafat's response was to exaggerate the casualties and insist he was eager for more battle. "We have lost 5,000 [sic] people at Sabra and Shatila, and we are ready to lose 50,000 people more to free our homeland."[88]

Arafat blamed the United States for not keeping its commitment to protect those Palestinians left behind.[89] Yet as always, the United States saw Arafat's defeat in Lebanon as less a chance to destroy him than as an opportunity to push him toward peace. The September 1982 Reagan plan gave Arafat an opening he could have used to join a political process. It proposed that West Bank and Gaza Palestinians govern themselves for a five-year transition period followed by negotiations, an Israeli withdrawal, and full peace. The projected goal was a Jordanian-Palestinian state, hardly Arafat's preferred outcome.[90]

Yet the elements of Reagan's plan offered Arafat an alternative strategy. As with other peace plans, he could have used its provisions to gain control of the territories during the transition period; win U.S. support; prove himself ruler of the West Bank and Gaza Strip; press for an Israeli withdrawal; and negotiate peace with Israel in exchange for an independent Palestine, perhaps with some minimal, purely formal link to Jordan. It was precisely fear of such an outcome that made Israel's government reject the plan.[91]

Desperate to find some way out of his defeats, Arafat had improved his relations with Jordan to a remarkable extent considering that he had been trying to kill the king just a few years earlier. Arafat had spoken of a possible federation between Jordan and a Palestinian state. But while the PLO refused to negotiate with Israel, it also opposed letting Jordan or West Bank/Gaza Palestinians do so either. Arafat feared that local Palestinian leaders would supplant the PLO or become vassals of Jordan.

Instead, Arafat continued his traditional policy of seeking to destroy Israel through violence. At the February 1983 PNC meeting, Arafat broke the PLO's own bylaws, having himself reelected chairman by acclamation rather than by an Executive Committee vote, where he might face criticism for his leadership style and decisions.[92] Under Arafat's leadership, the PNC rejected the Reagan plan and any deal with Jordan. It echoed Arafat's line that Israel must be eliminated from the map without any compromise.[93] "The confirmation of the legitimate rights of the Palestinian people," said the PLO's magazine in November 1982, "contradicts the existence of the Zionist state."[94]

Isam Sartawi, the PLO's leading moderate, presented a different perspective. Stressing the need for realism, Sartawi noted the positive points in Reagan's proposal, suggested cooperation with the Israeli peace movement, and demanded an investigation of the PLO's poor performance in the Lebanon fighting. He urged the PLO to "wake up" and leave the "path of defeat" that had led to the 1982 debacle. Sartawi realistically but hopelessly ridiculed the wishful thinking that had claimed that war to be a PLO victory. "Another victory such as this," he joked, "and the PLO will find itself in the Fiji Islands."[95]

Yet practical as Sartawi's advice was in the context of the wider world, he won almost no support against Arafat. When Arafat refused to let him speak at the PNC meeting, Sartawi tried to resign. Two months later, on April 10, he was murdered by the Syrian-backed Abu Nidal group.[96]

Ignoring Sartawi's warning, Arafat had ended the PNC meeting by again celebrating the Lebanon war as a PLO success. Rather than acknowledge and try to build on the U.S. role in saving the PLO from complete destruction in Beirut, Arafat claimed the war was a U.S. plot "to destroy the PLO" and that U.S. warships had carried Israeli troops into Lebanon. Some thought Israel's army unbeatable, said Arafat, "but, brothers, by God I have not found it invincible.... I wish all my nation was with me to see the feebleness of this army."[97]

Fouling His Own Nest

King Hussein was ready for one more try to make Arafat moderate his policy. The king insisted that the reluctant Arafat come to Amman for a meeting to see if they could cooperate in entering negotiations. He urged Arafat to accept the Reagan plan as the framework for a peace process. "Arafat's never had to make a decision," Hussein explained. "But this time he's going to have to. I've tightened the screws everywhere as much as I can." The king smiled, "Arafat's veering off in the right direction; he just needs a push."[98]

The king, however, was wrong. After stalling as long as possible, Arafat finally came to Amman in April 1983 for three days of what the king described as "brutal talks." At one point, Arafat told Hussein that by pressing for agreement, "You're asking me to kill myself." But Hussein insisted that Arafat implement a deal before the PLO would be allowed back into Jordan.

Arafat accepted the king's cooperation proposal but pleaded for forty-eight hours to consult a Fatah Central Committee meeting in Kuwait. He promised to return quickly to Amman and close the deal. Hussein agreed, but Arafat did not come back. Instead, five days later, two messengers arrived with his proposal for a totally different agreement. In Arafat's version, the Reagan plan was not mentioned and the idea of the king as mediator was rejected. The next day, April 10, Hussein announced that the talks had failed, blamed Arafat, and proclaimed the Reagan plan dead.[99]

Arafat had cleverly blocked any action rather than seriously seeking an accord. Nevertheless, even the apparent cooperation he had used to achieve his goal horrified more radical Palestinians and Arabs, who took the talks seriously. The furor combined with angry complaints in Fatah and the smaller PLO groups over Arafat's handling of the 1982 war to increase Syrian fears that he might throw in his lot with Jordan and the United States. Syria saw the unrest in the PLO as a chance to try once again to take over the organization, while concern that Arafat would join forces with its enemies gave Damascus another incentive to subvert him.

Arafat's Palestinian critics blamed him for the PLO's expulsion from Jordan and Lebanon. They accused him of betraying the revolution by dealing with Jordan and Egypt and letting Sartawi make secret contacts with Israeli doves. The DFLP and PFLP, both headquartered in Damascus, suspended activity in the PLO to protest Arafat's contacts with the king. Many Fatah men were also outraged that, before the 1982 war, Arafat had promoted officers in Lebanon who were corrupt, inept, and cowardly. In January 1983, Said Musa Muragha (Abu Musa), a senior PLO military officer, castigated Arafat at a high-level Fatah meeting.[100]

Within Fatah itself, these dissatisfied rebels, fed up with incompetence and wary of moderation, joined hands with Syria. Asad saw the PLO's 1982 defeat in Lebanon as his long-awaited chance to take over the organization. He refused to receive Arafat in November 1982 when the Fatah Central Committee met in Damascus. The Syrian media attacked Arafat while Syria encouraged PLO radicals to challenge him. A Syrian leader explained that Arafat defined the Arab states' role as just "supporting him blindly," but Palestine was also an Arab cause "and we have the right—especially after the heavy sacrifices we have made for the cause—to discuss, contest, and even to oppose this or that action of the PLO."[101]

Aware of the danger this criticism posed, Arafat had reinforced his hard-line credentials by rejecting any compromise with Israel, Jordan, or the United States.[102] Even the very militant Qaddumi supported him, assuring a Kuwaiti audience: "Arafat...has been accused of being a moderate. Can you imagine a person who was the first to carry a gun to fight the Israelis being a moderate?"[103] At the same time, Arafat tried to block increased Syrian influence by replacing two commanders in Lebanon—one of them being Abu Musa—who were critical of him with two of his loyalists, Abu Hajim and Haj Ismail. This change was announced on May 7, 1983.

Abu Musa, a man respected for his courage and military ability but not his political sophistication, got revenge for the firing by leading the biggest anti-Arafat revolt that had ever taken place in Fatah. As an officer in Jordan's army, he had graduated from Britain's Sandhurst military academy. After deserting the king during the 1970 civil war, Abu Musa rose in the PLO ranks to become one of its main commanders in Lebanon. Several of his supporters were also ex-Jordanian army officers whose professionalism was offended by the PLO's military incompetence.[104] The dissidents knew that many others supported their views. Abu Musa explained, "We are the conscience of Fatah."[105]

But Arafat had an arsenal of good arguments against the rebels. He had never veered from seeing his movement's whole purpose as the reconquest of all Palestine and could point out that he had rejected every peace initiative. Moreover, he was able to pose as the champion of Palestinian independence from Arab states and preserver of its internal unity. The rebels, after all, were the ones dividing the movement, and they were being encouraged and aided by Syria.

Most Fatah leaders agreed with Arafat. Even though Abu Iyad and Qaddumi accepted some of Abu Musa's arguments, they bitterly condemned his behavior. For them and many others in the organization, corruption and incompetence were preferable to internal conflict and subservience to Arab states. They also knew that Arafat was not infected with moderation.

Thus, Abu Iyad, the man in the best position to challenge Arafat for the leadership and the champion of the radicals in Fatah, called Abu Musa's men "criminals and renegades." There was no need to break with Arafat, he explained, pointing out how the Fatah Central Committee had wrecked the 1983 PLO-Jordan talks.[106] Abu Iyad insisted, "By raising arms against their brothers and shedding Palestinian blood, the dissidents made a big mistake." It was, wrote a Palestinian intellectual, "a Catch-22 situation." The PLO and Fatah leadership had many shortcomings, but changing these leaders would threaten to destroy the movement altogether.[107]

The Palestinian masses agreed with that view. While many of the fighters still in Lebanon joined Abu Musa, Palestinians in Jordan, the West Bank, the Gulf, and elsewhere remained loyal to Arafat. As one Palestinian observer put it, "Arafat is king. If Abu Musa walked through a Palestinian refugee camp [in Jordan], the only people who would follow him would be his own bodyguards."[108] That is why Abu Musa was never able to supplant Arafat.

But Abu Musa had a great deal of support among the Fatah troops in Lebanon, as well as backing from the pro-Syrian PLO groups. On May 9, he announced a revolt against Arafat, who responded by expelling the dissidents from Fatah. Arafat promised reform, an end to corruption, and more democracy. But he rejected the rebels' main demands that he stop engaging in any diplomacy at all and give them half the power in Fatah. The rebels declared that armed struggle, without international political maneuvering, "is the only and inevitable way to revolution."[109]

As the revolt appeared to gain strength, the Syrians became more active participants, helping the rebels seize Fatah's offices and arms warehouses in Damascus. The Syrian media accused Arafat of being "irresponsible, arrogant," and determined to liquidate his opponents.[110] The rebels went on the offensive in Lebanon, defeating the pro-Arafat forces that had remained or returned to Lebanon after the 1982 evacuation. As his men in Lebanon retreated, Arafat offered concessions to the rebels, promising to do just about anything but resign—all to no avail. At the same time, Arafat begged help from other Arab states and from the USSR, while portraying Syria as an American pawn.[111]

Arafat himself sneaked back to Lebanon to deal with the mutiny in September by using an alias, shaving his beard, and wearing a suit and sunglasses.[112] Shortly after arriving in Tripoli, he called a press conference in an olive grove under a tree. Asked about the revolt against him, Arafat took out a gold pen from his pocket, "Asad wants my pen. He wants [control over every] Palestinian decision and I won't give it to him." Now Arafat spoke about making Tripoli, as he had previously done of Amman and Beirut, a city he would see destroyed rather than surrender. An American reporter from Texas asked Arafat if this was like the situation at the Alamo, a great battle in Texas's war of independence against Mexico. Yes, said Arafat, it was the same thing, given the Palestinians' bravery. The reporter then asked if Arafat knew that all the defenders of the Alamo had died. Arafat paused a moment, then said that the Alamo "isn't all that similar" after all.[113]

As Arafat battled openly with Syria, he also may have participated in a covert offensive against the United States. Despite the need to distance himself publicly from Iran in order not to offend Baghdad and Arab public opinion during the Iran-Iraq war, he had secretly kept links to Tehran. On November 18, 1979, shortly after U.S. diplomats were taken hostage in Iran, Arafat had ordered all Fatah cadres to help Iran's revolution. U.S. intelligence discovered that this meant cooperation in terrorist operations.[114]

When Arafat left Beirut in 1982, the many Lebanese who had worked directly for him were now given to the Iranians, who were increasingly promoting Islamist revolution in Lebanon, as their own network there. Perhaps the single most important member of this group was Imad Mughniyah. Born in a poor neighborhood in Beirut's southern suburbs in 1962, Mughniyah had joined Arafat's elite Force 17 security unit as a teenager and rose quickly from rank-and-file gunman to be an important Fatah intelligence figure. After joining forces with Iran, Mughniyah became head of the terrorist apparatus for Hizballah, the radical Lebanese Islamist group which took Americans hostage during the 1980s. In 1983, Lebanese Shia terrorists bombed the U.S. embassy in Beirut and killed sixty-three Americans. Robert Baer, a CIA official who served in Lebanon and later spent years investigating that operation, determined, "The only conclusion a reasonable person could make was that a Fatah cell—with or without Yasir Arafat's knowledge—blew up the American embassy in Beirut on April 18, 1983, in cooperation with Iran and its agents."[115]

Mughniyah was indicted in absentia by a U.S. court for the 1985 hijacking of a TWA plane during which an American navy diver was murdered. For this and other deeds, Mughniyah was put on the FBI's list of the world's twenty-two most-wanted terrorists after the September 11, 2001, terrorist attack on New York and Washington, D.C.[116]

Arafat's men may also have helped carry out the October 1983 attack on the U.S. marine barracks in Beirut, which killed 241 American soldiers. United States intelligence recorded a telephone call at the time in which Iran's ambassador to Lebanon told Tehran how he had obtained bomb material from Fatah for a pro-Iran terrorist group to make the attack.[117] Ironically, some of the marines killed had probably served as Arafat's bodyguards, protecting him when he left the country a year earlier. Nevertheless, the United States took no action against Arafat, the PLO, or, for that matter, anyone else in retaliation for these attacks.

In contrast, the Syrians were determined to chase Arafat and his remaining supporters completely out of Lebanon. On November 3, 1983, Fatah rebels backed by Syrian forces launched a major offensive against Arafat and captured more Palestinian refugee camps. Arafat's last remaining stronghold was Tripoli, which was besieged by Lebanese militia groups and bombarded by Syrian artillery. One day, over a lunch of chicken stew, a smiling Arafat told visitors he was certain that Asad intended to finish him off but hoped the Saudis would save him. His fourth-floor fortress was relatively secure since it was surrounded by taller apartment buildings with Lebanese residents.[118]

Once more, Lebanon and the Lebanese were paying dearly for Arafat's presence, and for a second time, Lebanese politicians demanded that Arafat leave their country. Arafat let himself be persuaded yet again not to become a martyr for his cause. In December 1983, Arafat and four thousand of his men were evacuated from Lebanon, saved, as they had been the previous year, by U.S. and Israeli guarantees of safe passage.

Sailing away from Tripoli in his camouflage uniform, Arafat was at the nadir of his career. Only a daring act could save him. Deprived again of his main base, deserted by many comrades, and attacked by the Arab states leading the anti–Camp David alliance, Arafat felt his only option was to seek help from Egypt, the country he had previously made his worst Arab enemy. Boycotting the moderates, Egypt and Jordan, had made him dependent on Syria. Now he had to turn to Cairo and Amman to save himself from Syria.

On December 22, 1983, Arafat arrived in Cairo to meet President Husni Mubarak. Arafat swallowed the humiliation of unilaterally ending the boycott of Egypt, which he had done so much to create in the first place. But his action stirred lots of criticism in the PLO, with pro-Syrian groups like the PFLP accusing him of treason. Abu Iyad complained that Arafat ignored PLO rules and PNC decisions Another among Arafat's oldest comrades, Khalid al-Hasan, called the contacts with Egypt "political suicide." Even the loyal Abu Jihad approved an official censure of Arafat for violating "the principle of collective leadership."[119]

Once again, though, these leaders complained about Arafat but did nothing to replace him or restrict his power. Responsibility for military defeats did not bring his downfall, and neither did his failures lead to a major strategic change or moderation. The 1979 Egypt-Israel peace, 1982 Lebanon war, and 1983 Syrian-backed split had deprived the PLO of its strongest Arab allies and main bases of operation. Preoccupied by the Iran-Iraq war, the Arab states neglected the PLO even more. The Arab world was so badly disorganized and divided it was incapable of even holding a summit meeting between September 1982 and November 1987.

"I was standing in Tyre, Lebanon, when the Iranian revolution took place [in 1979]," Arafat later recalled, "and I declared that the PLO's strategic depth extends from Tyre all the way to Iran." But with the Iran-Iraq war, the Israeli attack on Lebanon, and the Syrian assault, by 1983 the PLO's strategic depth had "shrunk to . . . a few kilometers."[120]

Unable to win victory and unwilling to seek compromise, Arafat faced an apparent dead end. For the first twenty years of his political career, Arafat had moved up and down, back and forth, east and west, left and right. But he had not really advanced closer to his ultimate goals.

5

Far Away from Home

1984–1991

In February 1991, Yasir Arafat, always sensitive to press reports about him, was being skewered in the Arab media. An Egyptian journalist felt free to write these stinging words: "You are a corrupt war criminal, you clown. You betrayed those who fed you and meanly stabbed those who helped you. You are the clown of every circus.... It is time you retire away from us, you treacherous bloodsucker."[1]

By other people's standards, Arafat had committed many crimes in his lifetime, but among many Arabs his worst deed was backing Iraq's seizure of Kuwait in 1990. How could Arafat do such a thing? Saudi radio asked. "Was Kuwait not the homeland that gave [Arafat] the opportunity to change from an engineer to a leader? Was it not on the land of Kuwait that the first [steps in his] struggle occurred?"[2]

But Arab states were not just angry at Arafat; they also decided to get even with him. With support from Arab governments falling to an all-time low, the PLO faced a serious economic crisis. In March 1991, after a U.S.-led coalition defeated Iraq, Arafat admitted that the PLO had lost $12 million a month from its major sponsors—$6 million from Saudi Arabia, $2 million from Kuwait, and another $4 million Iraq could no longer pay. Kuwait's government expelled more than two hundred thousand Palestinian residents whom it considered collaborators with the Iraqi invaders. Others fled Iraq to escape the war and that country's economic collapse. It was a Palestinian disaster on a scale close to 1948 and 1967.

Things looked bad enough when Arafat first arrived in Tunisia in 1982. Having been kicked from Amman to Beirut and then to Tunis, Arafat's future looked bleak unless he could find some dramatic way out of his dilemma. But escaping from traps into which he had fallen was Arafat's greatest talent. Tunis became the PLO's new headquarters, about as far to the edge of the Arab world as one could go. It was a pleasant but dull city near the ruin of the once-mighty ancient city of Carthage, so flattened by the Romans that nothing remained, a reminder of how history could erase people who lost too many wars.

At times, Arafat did not seem much better off than the Carthaginians. He was fifteen hundred miles away from the place he wanted to conquer and the enemy he wished to destroy. Gone was the international press corps which had constantly buzzed around Arafat in Beirut and provided so much sympathetic coverage. Gone also was the PLO's economic apparatus and any military leverage over its host. The Tunisians had learned from their predecessors' experiences and kept close watch and control over Arafat's activities in their country. The government confiscated arms that PLO men brought from abroad and barred Palestinians from carrying weapons outside of their bases.[3]

But being in Tunis was not without its benefits. With few political restrictions, the PLO was freer there from a political point of view than it would have been anywhere else in the Arab world. Due to the boycott of Cairo following Egypt's peace treaty with Israel, the Arab League had also moved to Tunis, making that city a more important political center.[4] Realizing that their stay there would be prolonged, the PLO built schools and orphanages as its community swelled to about two thousand people.

Not that Arafat spent much time in Tunis. Throughout the 1980s, he flew in what seemed to be perpetual motion, often using his ten-seat jet, which had been donated by Iraq, to visit so many Arab, African, and European capitals that he could eventually claim to have been to every country in the world except Australia.[5] Ever fearful of assassination, Arafat kept a stack of weapons in his plane, and among the passengers was an extra pilot who could take over the cockpit in an emergency.[6]

Some of these trips were required for Arafat to coordinate the PLO's offices and armed units, dispersed across the Arab world by the expulsion from Lebanon. Among the rank and file, morale was low but, ever the optimist, Arafat suggested they were better off distributed among many Arab states so no Arab government could control the PLO. "We have now more bases in the Middle East than the United States," Arafat bragged.[7]

Arafat was always best in adversity, and perhaps that is why he sought out that status so consistently. "As we say in Arabic, ours are tough bones, not easy to crack," Arafat said. "They talk of the Chinese Long March of Mao Zedong. This is our Long March, and it is already more than 6,000 miles long."[8] Many of his colleagues, though, were starting to wonder if their march had been so long because Arafat was leading them in circles. When Algeria and Kuwait, fearful of angering Syria, refused to host the November 1984 PNC meeting, Arafat had to beg his old enemy King Hussein to hold it in Amman. The pro-Syrian Fatah rebels denounced this request, claiming it proved that Arafat was a traitor. The PFLP and DFLP refused to attend.[9]

At this moment of crisis, Arafat called everyone's bluff by threatening to resign at the PNC meeting. The ploy worked. A group of PNC delegates lifted him onto the stage and "forced" him to withdraw his resignation. The PNC even let Arafat reorganize the Executive Committee to ensure his majority and authorized him to cooperate with Egypt and Jordan.[10]

As the PNC's host, King Hussein played an important role in the meeting. His speech embarrassed Arafat, who slouched nervously in his seat as the man he had tried to overthrow and assassinate urged him to cooperate with Jordan. The king bluntly told the PLO that it had underestimated the task of defeating Israel and was deluded to think victory was near. Having demanded that it be recognized as the Palestinians' sole legitimate representative, the king pointed out, the PLO was responsible for the fact that seventeen years after the 1967 war, the West Bank and the Gaza Strip were still under occupation. And, he continued, time was running out for the Arabs; Israel was becoming stronger and the Arabs more divided. Quick diplomatic progress was urgent.

Confronting directly the PLO's rationale for intransigence, Hussein asked, "How long shall we heed those among us who say: 'Leave it for future generations'?" Instead of postponing progress, useless boasting, and endless sloganing, Hussein urged the Palestinians to be flexible and moderate enough to win international support by producing a proposal that Israel might accept. This could only be achieved by Jordanian-Palestinian cooperation and, he hinted, finding a way to recognize Israel. If the PLO backed him, Hussein concluded, he was ready to take the lead in saving the Palestinians from Israeli rule. "However, if you believe that the PLO can proceed alone, we will tell you to go ahead, with God's blessing."[11]

Arafat admitted publicly after the king's speech that his movement was facing many problems and suffered from a lack of Arab state support. Yet his answer to these difficulties, as always, was to invoke the virtue of steadfastness. Ruling out any major policy shift, Arafat quoted an appropriate passage from the Qu'ran: "True to their [covenant] with God...some still wait: But they have never changed their determination in the least."[12]

Yet, having no other Arab ally, Arafat needed at least a temporary rapprochement with Jordan to survive. As a result, on February 11, 1985, Arafat signed an agreement drafted by Jordan that proposed accepting conditions "cited in UN resolutions" in order to win a total Israeli withdrawal from the West Bank and Gaza and establish Palestinian self-determination there in the framework of a Jordanian-Palestinian federation. Exactly how this would be achieved and what such a federation would look like were left open.

As long as he could pursue all paths simultaneously—ordering terrorism while exploring negotiations—and not give any concessions, Arafat felt no need to make a choice. Yet so long as he maintained this ambiguity over his methods and goals, Arafat could make no real diplomatic breakthrough either. King Hussein was well aware of this problem, and so, to avoid a last-minute PLO veto of the deal, as had happened in 1983, he publicly announced the agreement before Arafat submitted it to his Executive Committee.

Hussein's carefully formulated strategy, however, did not maneuver Arafat into accepting and implementing the king's plan. The deal with Jordan implied the PLO's acceptance of UN Resolution 242, which had become a code word for willingness to recognize Israel. But Arafat and his colleagues made clear that this was not true. In Hani al-Hasan's words, "We reject Resolution 242. We rejected it in the past and will reject it in the future." Similarly, the accord with Jordan proposed a Jordan-Palestine federation but the PLO demanded an independent Palestinian state.[13] King Hussein portrayed the use of the phrase "peace for land" in his agreement with Arafat as constituting recognition of Israel. The PLO explicitly rejected that idea.[14]

In addition, while Arafat's agreement with the king accepted a joint Jordanian-Palestinian negotiating team to talk with the United States and with non-PLO Palestinians only, now the PLO insisted on an openly PLO deputation. Abu Jihad affirmed, "Nobody [will] negotiate on our behalf [or] share our representation.... There is no compromise on this whatsoever." Arafat insisted, "I do not conclude agreements to please the United States or to win Israel's acceptance. I conclude agreements with the aim of mobilizing all the Arab resources, including...Jordan and the Palestinians, in order to create a solid base for continuing the struggle."[15] But if Arafat only saw agreements as weapons for battling Israel with no consideration as to whether they were acceptable to the other side, why should Israel make any deals with him? And if Arafat would only implement his agreements as long as they were useful tools for continuing the fight, how could any deal succeed?

On a May 1985 visit to Washington, still hoping to overcome Arafat's backsliding, King Hussein outlined the plan he thought Arafat had originally accepted, including a joint Jordanian-Palestinian delegation with non-PLO Palestinians. But Arafat's proposed list of "non-PLO" Palestinian negotiators consisted almost entirely of PLO officials. When Israeli prime minister Shimon Peres accepted two of those, who were PLO supporters but not active members, Arafat withdrew their names.[16]

These failed efforts showed that Arafat was not ready to negotiate, though he also wanted to ensure that no other Arabs were able to negotiate either. Especially revealing was Arafat's claim that he had secretly written to Ezer Weizman, the Israeli leader most eager for talks with the PLO, and had suggested that Israel be dismantled in favor of a binational Arab-Jewish state. Weizman denied this tale. If Arafat wanted people to believe that this was his proposal to the Israeli leader so ready to compromise with him, it showed how far he was from making any realistic offer.[17]

Armed struggle in the form of terrorism, rather than diplomacy, continued to be Arafat's main tactic. Deprived of the ability to hit Israel from Lebanon, the PLO turned to attacks by sea and operations against Israelis outside the country. Abu Jihad and Arafat's personal bodyguard unit, Force 17, mounted terrorist attacks from Algerian bases. Fatah members also tried to bomb Israeli offices in Frankfurt, Rome, and Madrid. Arafat claimed that attacks on Jewish targets in Europe were actually being "masterminded by the Mossad," which wanted to convince Jews there that they "will never be safe except in the Israeli paradise." He even insisted that Abu Nidal was just "an agent of the Mossad, a simple errand-boy."[18]

Yet there was no doubt that these efforts were being carried out by the PLO and other Palestinian groups. When a Fatah squad blew up four bombs in Jerusalem to coincide with his May 1985 visit to Israel, Secretary of State George Shultz warned Arafat, "Those who perpetrate violence deal themselves out of the peace process." This wave of attacks culminated in a brutal September 25 murder of three Israeli tourists in Cyprus by Force 17. The killers included a British neo-Nazi skinhead working for the PLO, which highlighted Arafat's shadowy connections with the European antisemitic far right; a former member of Arafat's personal bodyguard, who had been an official in the PLO's Athens office; and a Fatah man evacuated from Lebanon with Arafat. PLO denials of involvement thus rang rather hollow.[19]

In October, Israel retaliated with an aerial bombing of PLO offices in Tunisia, including Arafat's personal office. Some seventy-five people were killed. Arafat accused the United States of helping mount the attack in order to intimidate or kill him.[20]

Shortly afterward, but in an operation clearly planned long before, four gunmen from the Palestine Liberation Front, a group led by PLO Executive Committee member Abu al-Abbas, hijacked the *Achille Lauro*, an Italian cruise ship, off Egypt's coast and took its 545 crew members and passengers, including many Americans, hostage. The liner was on an eleven-day trip with stops including Israel, where the terrorists had originally planned to seize it. But they were discovered and decided to act sooner. They shot a sixty-nine-year-old, wheelchair-bound American Jew and threw his body overboard. Rather than denounce this murder, the PLO at first claimed the man had died of natural causes, then Qaddumi suggested with chilling cynicism that his wife must have pushed him overboard to get the insurance money.

Denying any knowledge about the operation, Arafat sent Khalid al-Hasan and Abu al-Abbas to Cairo to negotiate the hijackers' surrender to the Egyptians with an alacrity due to Egypt's warning that U.S. forces were preparing a rescue mission. Intercepted communications between "mediators" and hijackers showed that the two sides were working hand in glove. After being released, some hostages recounted that the hijackers told them: "We came on behalf of Yasir Arafat."[21]

Arafat claimed to be indignant that he did not get the proper credit for ending the hijacking and saving the hostages.[22] But actually his goal was to help the terrorists escape and to conceal their links with the PLO. He persuaded Egypt to smuggle them to Tunis on an Egyptian plane. But U.S. navy fighters intercepted the flight and forced it to land in Italy. The Italian government, however, was so eager to avoid trouble with Arafat that it let Abu al-Abbas escape and soon freed most of the terrorists as well.[23] In the 1980s as in the 1970s, European countries were unwilling to punish terrorists working for Arafat, much less their leader.

Mubarak, who had gone along with Arafat's cover-up, was embarrassed at being shown to have lied to the U.S. government and collaborated in the terrorists' attempted escape. Under his pressure, Arafat issued a promise in November to confine future attacks to Israel and the occupied territories. This was not an abandonment of terrorism but only a promise to limit its territorial dimensions.[24] Arafat also broke this pledge to punish PLO members involved in international terrorism, starting with the *Achille Lauro* perpetrators. After a brief vacation for Abu al-Abbas, Arafat warmly welcomed him back to active participation on the PLO Executive Committee.[25]

For his part, King Hussein had to abandon his peace efforts in February 1986 because he saw Arafat would not keep the promises he made the king about cooperation. The king complained, "We opened all the doors for [the PLO] but they continued to move in empty circles." Political coordination with the PLO leadership would only be possible, said the king, when "their word becomes their bond, characterized by commitment, credibility and constancy."[26]

Jordanian leaders were so frustrated with Arafat's behavior that one top official greeted a foreign diplomat by saying he had a terrible cold and felt miserable. But, he added with a smile, "Tomorrow I'm going to meet Arafat at the airport when he arrives and give him a big kiss on both cheeks to make sure he catches it!"[27]

Trying to reestablish its own influence on the West Bank and develop a local leadership more independent of Arafat, Jordan persuaded four Palestinians to accept office as mayors there.[28] Zafar al-Masri, heir of the most powerful family in Nablus and a man on good terms with Arafat, although not a PLO member, accepted the post only with Arafat's permission. When a PFLP unit murdered Masri in March for taking the job, Arafat swore vengeance, and Masri's funeral turned into a pro-PLO demonstration. But Arafat had no interest in seeing a local, non-PLO leadership in the West Bank. Masri's death was politically convenient for him, and Arafat promptly forgot that pledge. Instead of punishing the PFLP, he renewed his alliance with it. In response, Jordan closed all PLO offices in Jordan and expelled its officials.

Jordan was not the only frustrated Arab country seeking some way around Arafat to foster peace. In October 1986, King Hasan of Morocco invited Israeli prime minister Shimon Peres to visit. While Hasan urged Israel to deal with the PLO, his action signaled a growing unwillingness to let Arafat veto Arab peace moves. Then Tunisia imprisoned one of Arafat's top aides, Colonel Hawari, for preparing terrorist attacks against Morocco from Tunis.[29] Syria was arresting Arafat supporters in Damascus and killing others in Lebanon. Egypt was urging the PLO toward a diplomatic settlement. Arafat could no longer rely on Moscow, as the USSR, undergoing its own political transformation, was also pressuring him to recognize Israel.[30]

On top of everything else, Arafat faced a serious financial crisis. Oil-exporting Arab states, their income slashed by lower prices, cut back on their contributions to the PLO. The PLO did not have large financial reserves, expenses were substantial, and funds were often mishandled.[31] A Jordanian official aptly remarked, "They have to keep Arafat because if he goes, no one will know where the money is."[32] Arafat's personal budget, which he used for bribes, subsidies, bonuses, and special operations, required a constant flow of cash. Income was also sapped by rampant corruption, which Arafat fostered to ensure his hold over his colleagues. All of these factors accelerated the PLO's slide into debt.

Arafat was isolated and battered, yet he chose to move in a militant rather than a moderate direction. He patched up relations with the

Far Away from Home

radical PFLP and DFLP, ignoring their demand for reforms to reduce his authority but pleasing them by formally canceling the 1985 Jordan-PLO accord and criticizing Egypt. Making a dramatic entrance with the PFLP and DFLP leaders, George Habash and Naif Hawatmeh, at the April 1987 PNC, Arafat declared, "We now all stand together, united until the final liberation of Palestine." Abu al-Abbas was reelected to the PLO Executive Committee despite the *Achille Lauro* affair. Even Abu Nidal showed up for a secret, though unproductive, meeting with Arafat. There could be no clearer indication that, for Arafat, Palestinian solidarity took precedence over any flexibility in the PLO's means and goals.[33]

For Arafat, however, no Palestinian who criticized him personally would be protected by such solidarity. Naji al-Ali's mocking cartoons in Arab newspapers, which showed Arafat as an aging bureaucrat giving jobs to cronies and carousing with a woman believed to be Arafat's mistress, apparently went too far. Ali was a fervent Palestinian patriot who created some of the movement's most haunting symbols. Nevertheless, he was assassinated, probably by Arafat's bodyguards, while walking to work in London in July 1987.[34]

Eager to take credit as the leader of the whole Palestinian struggle, Arafat refused to give rival groups credit for operations against Israel. In 1987, two men from the Syrian-backed, anti-Arafat PFLP–General Command Group killed six Israeli soldiers at a training camp before being shot down. When asked about the attack, Arafat first feigned ignorance then implied that his men had carried out the attack, and he threatened an Arab reporter questioning that claim. Expressing his total faith in purely military solutions, Arafat said, "No army . . . can stand against the [fighters] from the Palestinian-Lebanese joint forces. There are no obstacles, resolutions, security forces, or radars that can stand in the face of a [fighter] who has made up his mind to sacrifice his life for his people and nation."[35]

Despite this bravado, though, Arafat knew his fortunes were at a low point in the mid-1980s. "I don't think he has ever been so demoralized," said a friend, or "ever in such a corner." A pro-PLO journalist highlighted the political dilemma: "Arafat . . . finds himself face to face with a simple but almost impossible choice: either to accept [UN Resolution] 242, and thereby betray most of what his 'revolution' once stood for, or to persist in spurning it, thereby denying himself any diplomatic role."[36]

Arafat's response was to postpone having to choose, expecting some new opportunity would inevitably give him an escape route. Asked if he thought he would ever again shake hands with Asad, Arafat grinned widely and shrugged, "Why not? This is the Middle East."[37] Based on his experience, Arafat always believed he would bounce back without making any real concession or irrevocable commitment.

That hope was often fulfilled, and this was certainly true in 1987. The year began as an apparently bad one for Arafat. Asad snubbed him at the Islamic summit conference, and King Hussein did likewise at the Arab summit meeting. The latter gathering focused on the Iran-Iraq war, and the final communiqué omitted the standard reference to the PLO as the Palestinian people's sole legitimate representative. When Arafat saw the document, he snorted, "It is a scandal."[38]

But the Palestinian issue soon forced itself back to center stage, albeit due to Palestinians in the West Bank and Gaza rather than to Arafat. True, the PLO had begun political organizing there some years earlier, but it had continued to put the priority on armed struggle. Now, however, Arafat had nowhere else where he could operate. As Khalid al-Hasan remarked, the residents of those territories "are the only source left to resist."[39]

After twenty years of Israeli presence, Palestinians in the West Bank and the Gaza Strip felt more keenly than those in Tunis the urgency of bringing change whether it involved struggle or compromise. The West Bank middle class, realizing the PLO's prospect for destroying Israel was poor, were more concerned about freeing Nablus and Hebron than about regaining Tel Aviv or Haifa. Fahd Qawasmah, a West Banker active in the PLO, explained this evolution by saying that he had originally expected a total Palestinian victory: "Later, I understood that the Israelis wanted their own flag, they wanted their own state."[40]

Palestinians inside the territories also gained confidence that they knew better than Arafat what needed to be done. The exiles who ran the PLO, Qawasmah remarked, "do not understand the Israeli mentality in the same way as those living in the occupied territories. We have to deal with the Israelis day and night, and we come to understand... the best way to tackle the problem of relations between the Arabs and the Israelis." The local activists were also, unlike Arafat, more attuned to the practical issues of daily life than to the intoxicating rhetoric of revolution. Qawasmah explained, "We must think about the needs of our towns and villages. They need power, water, schools, hospitals, roads.... The first duty of any elected official should be to develop his country, not to develop his arsenal."[41]

Those living in the territories were also dismayed by the PLO's incompetence, infighting, and corruption. "The PLO Must Not Forget the Palestinians" was the appropriate title of an article by West Bank journalist Daoud Kuttab. Arafat, he implied, must start listening to what those in the West Bank and Gaza Strip wanted: a quick solution even if it required compromise with Israel.[42]

A different manifestation of impatience with the PLO was the rise of local Islamist movements, which would eventually become Arafat's main rival. In contrast to the local nationalist activists, radical Islamists responded to Arafat's lack of progress by demanding even more militancy. Reflecting this trend, a top PLO official said, "The leaders can come to any solution they want about a mini-state in confederation with Jordan. The real war will be won when the Islamic people rule all of Palestine with Jerusalem as the undivided capital."[43]

All of these factors came together in a revolt, the Intifada, which was started by the local nationalist and Islamist forces in December 1987. It began with small-scale clashes between Palestinians in Gaza and Israeli forces and then blew up into massive violence, which spread throughout the territories and lasted many months. Arafat and the PLO were caught by surprise. When, in response to the uprising's start, Arafat wanted to request an emergency session of the UN Security Council, the PLO representatives were on vacation in Cuba.[44] Who in the world could have believed or predicted, he asked, that a spontaneous revolt would take place?[45] At first, the Intifada was a strictly local affair, with no sign of Arafat's picture or PLO symbols being carried by those throwing stones at Israeli troops. Palestinian teenagers demonstrated without being told by Fatah to do so, and the most active group was the Islamist Hamas, which was not even a member group in the PLO.

As a result, some Palestinians saw the Intifada as a rejection of the PLO, as did Sufyan al-Khatib, a PFLP member who publicly called Arafat "a clown."[46] But most of the local nationalist leaders urged the PLO to act on the diplomatic front to end Israeli control as quickly as possible. They were loyal to the PLO yet ready to criticize it for reacting so inadequately to a crisis that they sought to transform into a chance to improve their lives. *Al-Fajr*, the Fatah-backed West Bank newspaper, asked the PLO for "clear, specific and straightforward [decisions]. There is no room left for confusing rhetoric."[47]

Arafat's strategy had never focused on mass mobilization in the territories, out of disdain for the residents' abilities and fear that they might take over the movement. Their job was to watch and cheer as his troops defeated Israel. Arafat's constant claims of resistance in the West Bank over the years had hidden the reality that the masses there were passive and that much of the elite collaborated with Israel. Now, however, inhabitants were seizing control of their own fate. They identified with the PLO, but the impotence of Arafat's Tunis headquarters contrasted sharply with the internal residents' newfound energy and power.

Politically, the Intifada was dominated by a split vision. Many Palestinians in the territories saw generating international support and raising the price for continued occupation as a way to gain leverage for making peace with Israel in exchange for a Palestinian state in the West Bank and Gaza. Others focused on mobilizing the Palestinian masses for violence as a step toward destroying Israel. Many individuals held both ideas simultaneously.

As always, Arafat himself did not choose between these alternative goals. Lacking a larger strategic vision for transforming the revolt into Palestinian political gains, Arafat claimed that the uprising would force Israel out of the territories without him having to offer Israel a secure peace and an end to the conflict for doing so through negotiations. At the same time, to undercut local activists, Arafat argued that the main Palestinian tactic should be the PLO's traditional specialty: military operations and rallying Arab states. As a result of Arafat's strategy, there were fewer mass demonstrations and more armed attacks.

To control and direct the rebellion, Arafat made Abu Jihad his chief coordinator. Arafat and Abu Jihad issued orders on how to conduct the Intifada from Tunis through an Amman-based coordinating committee and the PLO's European offices. These were then delivered to the fax machines of PLO-subsidized, activist-staffed East Jerusalem newspapers and tiny trade unions. The people's committees that led the revolt, Arafat said, were established by the PLO "through the support of the Palestinian people" and not the other way around.[48]

Boasting about the PLO's new Japanese-built communication system, Arafat made the Intifada sound like a remote-controlled operation under his constant direction: "When there's fighting, we can send commands to our troops in battle with only a five-minute delay."[49] Arafat ensured that no powerful West Bank figure emerged, and he put none of the local activists deported by Israel for their violent activities into top posts in Tunis. When Israel assassinated Abu Jihad there in April 1988, Arafat personally took over coordinating the Intifada, further centralizing authority and stifling local initiative.[50]

But frustrated West Bank and Gaza activists also began generating their own new ideas. In January 1988, they released a fourteen-point statement which demanded not only Israeli concessions but also local elections and an Israeli-Palestinian peace agreement.[51] The idea of making peace with Israel—rather than defeating it—came from local leaders, not Arafat. Feisal al-Husseini, heir of the most prestigious political clan, emerged as chief among the local leaders who were demanding that Arafat treat them as equals, take a more moderate stance, and develop good relations with the United States in order to enter peace talks with Israel.[52]

Arafat did not listen to them. He neither moderated his policy nor took a dramatic step to make negotiations with Israel possible. He also escalated his anti-American rhetoric. For example, he charged the United States with giving Israel poison gas to use against the Palestinians, blamed it for Abu Jihad's assassination, and claimed that the U.S. government planned to kill more PLO leaders. American policy makers were worried by credible reports that Arafat had ordered attacks on U.S. citizens and facilities.[53]

Still another problem for Arafat was the wide gap between the Arab states' verbal support for the Intifada and their unwillingness to help it. Mubarak urged the PLO to stop the violence and make some concessions to gain Western recognition so that negotiations could proceed. The PLO's "responsibility," he said, "is no longer restricted to adopting protesting or objecting stances. It must take the daring and positive steps which are required for the sake of the Palestinians' future."[54]

The PLO felt abandoned. "We are alone in the struggle," said Abu Iyad. Khalid al-Hasan lamented, "The Arab stand no longer exists. . . . It is now less than zero."[55] Because Arab states gave no funds, Abu Iyad claimed, the Intifada could not be escalated. The June 1988 Arab summit promised little help and delivered even less. Arafat sighed, "I am tired of asking for these commitments to be honored."[56]

Yet an Arab leader's decision was about to save Arafat. In July 1988, King Hussein finally decided to give up Jordan's long-standing claim to the West Bank. For more than twenty years, since losing the territory in 1967, he had subsidized twenty-four thousand public employees and many institutions there. The king now ended this funding, adding to Arafat's financial burden. He was finally implementing the threat he had made three years earlier at the Amman PNC meeting: if the PLO did not want to cooperate with Jordan, it could fend for itself.[57]

Arafat, however, was able to turn an apparent defeat into an opportunity. He had always worried that Jordan and Israel would make a separate deal brokered by the United States. Now that no Arab state claimed either the West Bank or the Gaza Strip, it seemed time to try implementing the 1974 strategy of grabbing any "liberated" piece of land for use as a base against Israel.

A lively debate thus took place in the PLO and among Palestinians on how to respond to Jordan's move and make their own credible bid to rule this territory.[58] Bassam Abu Sharif, an advisor to Arafat, proposed a serious peace effort in a paper he distributed personally at an Arab summit meeting. "The key to a Palestinian-Israeli settlement," he wrote, "lies in talks between the Palestinians and the Israelis."[59] Abu Sharif proposed a dramatic policy shift. The PLO's goal should be the creation of a Palestinian state alongside Israel. The PLO's reason for existing, Abu Sharif claimed, was "not the undoing of Israel, but the salvation of the Palestinian people and their rights."[60]

Maintaining his own ambiguous position, Arafat made no response to Abu Sharif's statement. He did, however, send an envoy to the U.S. government proposing a dialogue.[61] The Americans insisted that he must first reject terrorism and recognize Israel's right to exist. A high-ranking Soviet diplomat made similar suggestions to him in a meeting just a day before Arafat made a major address to the European Parliament in Strasbourg, France. But Arafat disappointed both superpowers by simply repeating all of his old slogans there.

The great majority of PLO leaders, including Arafat, still opposed recognizing Israel or abandoning their traditional goals.[62] But even Fatah radicals like Abu Iyad agreed that something new was needed. "We must admit we do not have all the time in the world," he warned. "We are not capable of war," and Arab regimes would not fight. "We need an initiative to prove to our people that we exist on the political map, so that there will be a goal for the continuation of revolution and struggle."[63]

Arafat then formulated a plan in which the PLO would declare an independent Palestinian state without setting its boundaries, recognizing Israel, stopping terrorism, or foreclosing future options of achieving total victory. As Abu Iyad explained, it would not accept Israel's right to hold "any part of the land of Palestine," as PLO strategy "does not include any concessions."[64] This was the underlying thinking guiding Arafat not only in the late 1980s but in some ways also throughout the peace process of the 1990s.

Certainly, in 1988, Arafat lacked the determination to make a bold, clear change that would transform the PLO's world view and strategy in reality or at least present it in a form more likely to satisfy—or fool—the United States and Israel.[65] But Arafat also knew he needed to launch an initiative to show Palestinians that he was providing leadership and making progress for their cause. A peace offensive could simultaneously appeal to world opinion, isolate Israel, and drive a wedge between that country and the United States.[66] It was a typical Arafat-style solution. By being so ambiguous about his methods and goals, Arafat could hope to convince the West that he was ready for peace and convince his own colleagues that he was determined to continue the struggle. Yet this strategy would inevitably break down when one side or the other forced him to make a clear choice.

Finally, in November, PNC members met to approve the new strategy at Algeria's national conference center, fifteen miles from the capital, Algiers. Arafat's priority was to change U.S. policy by appearing to meet its conditions for dealing with the PLO without actually doing so. Thus, the PNC tried to give the impression of recognizing Israel, while not recognizing Israel; accepting UN Resolution 242, albeit with major qualifications; condemning terrorism, but with loopholes; and declaring a Palestinian state without limiting it to the lands that Israel had captured in 1967.[67]

The last session of the PNC meeting continued long past midnight on November 15 to work out every detail of the final statement. At last, Arafat stood on stage, looked out at the audience of exhausted but excited delegates, and read a declaration of independence: "The Palestine National Council, in the name of God, and in the name of the Palestinian Arab people, hereby proclaims the establishment of the State of Palestine on our Palestinian territory with its capital Jerusalem." The new state, he added, believed in settling disputes peacefully and therefore "rejects the threat or use of force, violence and terrorism" against itself and others. Then an Algerian military band played the Palestinian anthem, "Biladi, Biladi," while a PLA officer slowly raised the tricolor Palestinian flag.[68]

Yet the PNC resolution's actual wording showed that the new policy was, in the words of the *New York Times* correspondent there, "the same old fudge that Yasir Arafat has offered up for years" and "another wasted opportunity."[69] The resolution only mentioned Israel using rhetoric Arafat had employed for decades, defining it as "a fascist, racist, colonialist state based on the usurpation of the Palestinian land and on the annihilation of the Palestinian people." If this were its nature and basis, how could Palestinians recognize this state or make peace with it?[70] Similarly, the PNC only accepted UN Resolution 242 in the context of claiming to endorse all UN resolutions, and even this was conditioned on such principles as demanding that all Palestinian refugees return to Israel. It was more accurate to say, as did one PLO spokesman, that this was "the first time we did not reject 242."[71]

The PNC's specific proposal was also designed to avoid recognizing or making peace with Israel along lines similar to Arafat's modification of the Fahd plan, which had been rejected by Israel and the United States seven years earlier. He now demanded unilateral and immediate Israeli withdrawal from all territories occupied since 1967 including removal of the Jewish settlements established there. These territories would then be placed under UN supervision for a short time after which they would be handed to the PLO. Only then would an international peace conference be convened to produce a peace agreement.

Arafat's "new" strategy, then, was consistent with his old style. The deliberately tricky, ambiguous language was designed to bridge internal differences and to keep open future options. Yet this approach ensured that he would offer too little and make his negotiating partners too suspicious to make a deal possible.

Nevertheless, the United States still wanted to try to engage Arafat in negotiations. President Ronald Reagan's national security advisor, Colin

Powell, sent Arafat a message through a group of American Jewish peace activists, who were meeting with the PLO leader in Stockholm, Sweden, on November 21, 1988. The message was that Reagan would start a dialogue with the PLO if it met U.S. conditions by recognizing Israel, accepting UN Resolution 242, and rejecting terrorism. At the Stockholm meeting, Arafat privately went beyond the PNC resolution, saying he would accept a West Bank/Gaza Palestinian state living peacefully alongside Israel, and he claimed that merely saying so to this delegation had "abrogated" and "nullified" provisions of the PLO Charter.[72]

But this statement was too informal and in no way binding on the PLO. The next day, the State Department denied Arafat a visa to address the United Nations in New York on grounds that he was responsible for having killed at least twenty-one Americans in past attacks and was still ordering terrorism against U.S. citizens.[73] Shultz was not trying to exclude Arafat from negotiations permanently but merely pressing him to meet U.S. conditions. When the UN General Assembly voted to convene a special session in Geneva, Switzerland, just to hear Arafat, the State Department told Arafat it was ready to start a dialogue if he made an appropriate statement in his Geneva speech. Arafat pledged to do so.

Thus, as Arafat mounted the podium on December 13, 1988, the U.S. government expected a breakthrough. Shultz had scheduled a press conference to announce the start of a U.S.-PLO dialogue. State Department officials settled down in front of a television, copies of the agreed language in hand, to watch the performance. But Arafat again broke his promise, making a polemical speech instead of a conciliatory one. Arafat said he condemned "terrorism in all its forms" and then denied that the PLO had ever committed terrorism, claimed that all of its actions were a legitimate part of a liberation struggle, and saluted those "who have been accused by their executioners and the colonialists of being terrorists during the battles for the liberation of their land from the yoke of colonialism."[74]

"We were on the edge of our seats until the end, and when he said 'I, as chairman of the PLO,' we thought he was really going to recognize Israel's right to exist," said a State Department official. "He didn't." Although the State Department noted "some positive developments," the U.S. government was greatly discouraged. Shultz canceled his press conference. One more diplomatic effort was on the brink of failure because Arafat had broken his promise and delivered less than expected at the last minute.[75]

This time, though, to avoid forfeiting the opportunity altogether, Arafat finally gave way at a press conference the next day, December 14.

Even then, he initially tried to keep his statement on the borderline, short of the minimum needed to qualify for a dialogue. Swedish officials had to revise his text, writing changes in the margins. Arafat had some trouble reading the revisions, and Palestinians in the audience whispered, "renounce, renounce," to help him pronounce that word when he came to the point on rejecting terrorism. Finally, resentfully and resisting to the last moment, Arafat said the magic words, "Our desire for peace is strategic and not a temporary tactic. . . . Our state provides salvation for the Palestinians and peace for both the Palestinians and Israelis."[76]

He accepted the "right of all parties concerned with the Middle East conflict to exist in peace and security, including . . . the state of Palestine, Israel, and other neighbors in accordance with Resolutions 242 and 338." Arafat added, "We totally and categorically reject all forms of terrorism, including individual, group, and state terrorism." Clearly under great stress he concluded, "Enough is enough. Enough is enough. Enough is enough. . . . We want peace. . . . We are committed to peace, and we want to live in our Palestinian state and let others live."[77]

A few hours later, Shultz announced that Arafat had met the U.S. conditions. This apparent historical turning point came almost as an anticlimax. For the first time since the PLO's creation a quarter-century earlier, it would be formally engaged in talks with the United States. State Department contact with the PLO had been so strictly prohibited since 1974 that when Arafat was Bourguibah's honored guest at Tunisia's national day celebration, the U.S. ambassador to Tunisia, Robert Pelletreau, had to walk by him on the receiving line as if he did not exist. But soon after Shultz's declaration, Pelletreau telephoned the PLO office and told the secretary who answered, "This is the American ambassador." Then he could hear her running down the hall, yelling excitedly, "The American ambassador! The American ambassador is calling!"[78]

The PLO was eager for the first official meeting with the United States arranged only two days later. While the four PLO officials there spent most of the time airing their historical grievances, the U.S. side stressed the importance of giving up terrorism and pursuing peaceful negotiations.[79] Such one-sided conversations would continue without progress over the next year. Rather than see the dialogue as a chance to prove his readiness for serious negotiation and compromise, Arafat portrayed it as a triumph which had showed that the Intifada was forcing the United States to accept the PLO on its own terms. Events, in the words of Nabil Sha'th, an advisor to Arafat, had "changed the balance in favor of the Palestinian cause." PLO broadcasts falsely boasted, "The U.S. Administration has . . . been forced to cooperate with the PLO as the Palestinian people's sole representative."[80] What the speeches and interviews of Arafat and his colleagues did not do was to tell the masses and activists that there had been any change in PLO policy.

At that time, at least, Arafat was still not ready to follow the good advice given him by Mubarak. The PLO, Egypt's president explained, must be the one to change if it wanted to take advantage of opportunities. Only by being more moderate could it appeal to those who could "influence Israel, such as the United States and European countries." Otherwise, these states would continue to support Israel's policy.[81]

Actually, there had been no U.S. concessions to the PLO. It did not recognize the PLO as either the sole legitimate representative of the Palestinians or as the government of a state. The bilateral exchanges were defined as a constructive dialogue, not as negotiations, and would continue only if the PLO implemented Arafat's pledge in Geneva. Once Arafat proved his moderation, U.S. leaders thought, they would persuade Israel that a deal with Arafat was possible.[82]

Instead, U.S. officials quickly learned how hard it was to deal with Arafat, whose view of America remained that of a highly suspicious anti-imperialist revolutionary. One day, Arafat's key aide at the time, PLO ambassador to Tunisia Hakam Balawi, said Arafat was in a rage. The PLO ambassador to Zambia, Balawi explained, had warned Arafat about some new U.S. plot against him. The State Department replied that the allegation was ridiculous and it was hard to imagine a place less likely than Zambia to discover the truth about U.S. policy toward the PLO. After checking with his boss, Balawi informed his American counterparts that Arafat had decided to believe his man in Zambia rather than the U.S. government.[83]

As had so often happened before, Arafat responded to momentary success with a mixture of arrogance and wishful thinking. The PLO, he claimed, enjoyed great leverage over the United States. "Ninety-nine percent" of the cards were in Arab hands, Arafat said. This was a carefully chosen image. A decade earlier, on the verge of making peace with Israel through U.S. mediation, Anwar al-Sadat had commented that he was doing so because the United States held "ninety-nine percent" of the cards.[84]

Rather than try to persuade the Israelis that they could achieve peace and security by dealing with him, Arafat argued that Israel's decisions were made "in Washington and not in Tel Aviv." He made clear his hope that the United States would order Israel to withdraw from the territories and that the Israelis would comply. Arafat did not just cynically feed false hope to the Palestinian masses; he firmly believed his propaganda and acted accordingly. "Victory," he said in a broadcast to the occupied territories, "requires no more than an hour of patience.... We are in the last quarter-hour of our suffering."[85]

In part, though, Arafat was again correct that he could make diplomatic gains with the merest of verbal gestures and despite continued militant rhetoric and the use of terrorism against Israel. By this time, eighty-four countries had recognized the "State of Palestine." Arafat was received by Spanish president Felipe Gonzalez and King Juan Carlos and held his first official talks ever with European Union representatives, including the foreign ministers of France, Greece, and Spain.[86] Arafat was even added to the select group of famous leaders whose likenesses were displayed at Madame Tussaud's Wax Museum in London.[87]

By endorsing a vaguely worded, double-edged PNC resolution and saying a few words at a press conference, he had brought the PLO further out of isolation and bad repute. Yet when Arafat was actually called on to demonstrate moderation, he would not shake loose from his game of ambiguity, which reinforced Israeli and sometimes American suspicions.

On the verge of his May 1989 gala visit to Paris, for example, the French government told Arafat that it wanted some "new and unequivocal statements" to show that he recognized Israel and renounced terrorism. Arafat responded by dramatically declaring that the PLO Charter, which called for Israel's destruction through armed struggle, was "*caduc.*"[88] By using a vague and archaic French legal term, Arafat let Westerners believe what they wanted while being able to insist to other Arabs that he had not changed anything. After all, the word *caduc* could be defined as "lapsed," "obsolete," "antiquated," "null and void," "decrepit," "broken down," "decayed," or "frail." Asked by reporters to choose the English equivalent, he told them to go and "look it up" in a French dictionary.[89]

When Radio Monte Carlo broadcaster Antoine Nawfal translated *caduc* as "null and void," Arafat said, "Who am I to criticize your translation? Let us say that it [the Charter] has become a thing of the past, superseded, superseded, superseded." Clearly, no one in the PLO regarded the Charter as having been altered. Both Abu Iyad and Arafat's closest aide, Balawi, denied that Arafat's statement meant anything. Abu Iyad rightly pointed out that only the PNC could amend the PLO Charter.[90]

Basking in apparent successes, though, Arafat became prisoner of his own optimistic assessments. While he was running around the world, the Intifada, not Israel, was collapsing. Fewer and fewer Palestinians were participating in demonstrations. With their economic situation very bad, casualties mounting, and no apparent gains being achieved, more and more Palestinians called for an end to the uprising. Dealing with the Intifada only cost 4 percent of Israel's defense budget, said

Israel's defense minister, Yitzhak Rabin, in 1989. Israeli society "has adjusted itself.... What is the choice?"[91]

The Intifada's first full year, 1988, had been marked by big demonstrations, but there was less mass participation in 1989 and 1990 and far more internecine killings of alleged Palestinian collaborators. Israel could not stop the uprising, but neither had months of constant rebellion made any progress toward ending the occupation, obtaining a state, or materially improving the lot of the Palestinians.

It could be argued that the Intifada made Israel more willing to give up the territories and more doubtful about keeping them permanently. But after all, much of Israel's political leadership had always viewed most of this land as a bargaining chip to trade for peace. The question of the last two decades still remained unchanged: was there a Palestinian partner ready to make such a deal? Pressure from the Intifada or international criticism was never sufficient by itself to alter Israel's policy. To get anywhere, the PLO needed to offer Israel an attractive alternative. "What is required from the PLO now is not concessions, but clarity in reaching out to the peace-oriented side of Israel," said former PLO spokesman Rashid Khalidi. "The organization must make it clear that the Palestinians are offering something the Israelis can live with." But Arafat did not even try this method.[92]

By the same token, Arafat did not criticize or challenge his closest colleagues, who continued to deny that the PLO's line had changed toward moderation, compromise, or an abandonment of violence.[93] At Fatah's August 1989 congress in Tunis, the twelve hundred delegates, very much under Arafat's control, passed a resolution full of hard-line language, calling the creation of the "Zionist entity" a crime and demanding intensified armed struggle. There was no word of endorsement for Arafat's Geneva statement, which had made possible the U.S.-PLO dialogue. When the United States criticized the meeting's statement for its "tone of confrontation and violence and its preference for unrealistic principles and solutions," Arafat simply issued a new one without some of the offending phrases.[94]

Arafat had also done nothing to spread his supposed new principles among the rank and file. On the contrary, he and his colleagues acted as if there had never been any recognition of Israel or rejection of terrorism. Instead, Khalid al-Hasan was saying that "whoever historically concedes the rest of Palestine is a traitor."[95] Arafat urged unity and the avoidance of internal conflict. Quoting the Qu'ran, he told his followers to be "strong against unbelievers, [but] compassionate among each other." He explained, "Otherwise we will fall in the trap that our enemy is making for us."[96] By clearly favoring those advocating a hard line and not turning his own Geneva statements into new guidelines, Arafat blocked any serious discussion about shifting from the movement's goal of total victory to a real compromise with Israel which would produce a West Bank/Gaza Palestinian state.

Equally, by acting in this manner, Arafat gave the United States little incentive to push Israel to negotiate or make concessions to him. Since the PLO had not convinced most Israeli voters or even the dovish Labor party—much less the skeptical, conservative Likud party—that it was ready to make peace, no Israeli government would negotiate with it. Thus, the United States proposed a multistage process in the summer of 1989 in which non-PLO Palestinians from the West Bank and Gaza, approved by Arafat, would start contacts with Israel to build mutual confidence and give the PLO more time to prove its credibility.[97]

If Arafat agreed to this plan, the United States promised to support a comprehensive agreement that the Palestinians could accept. Israel was unhappy with the proposal but accepted it in November 1989. Arafat rejected it. By that point, even Mubarak was disgusted with him.[98]

Arafat's diplomatic intransigence was matched by his refusal to stop PLO terrorist attacks. Despite Fatah's relative abstention from terrorism in 1989 and 1990, other PLO groups, part of the organization led by Arafat and on whose behalf he had made the Geneva pledges, continued their attempts to kill Israeli civilians.[99] In no case did Arafat act to stop them beforehand or criticize them afterward.

On the contrary, his threats of punishment were reserved for those who expressed moderate views. When Bethlehem mayor Elias Freij suggested a one-year truce in the Intifada to facilitate negotiations, Arafat warned that anyone saying such things "exposes himself to the bullets of his own people." The State Department complained that this threat fit "very badly" with Arafat's rejection of terrorism.[100] To avoid stopping the dialogue, U.S. State Department diplomats tied themselves in knots to try to explain why attacks on Israel by PLO member groups did not constitute a violation of Arafat's pledge. Their main argument was that since the operations were stopped by Israeli forces killing or driving back the gunmen, no one could prove whom the gunmen would have killed if they had had the chance.[101]

Yet Arafat's closest comrades made no secret of the fact that they viewed continued attacks on Israelis to be completely acceptable. This was quite different from the commitment that the United States thought Arafat had made at Geneva, where he stated that any group engaging in terror "shall be expelled from the PLO ranks." Abu Mazin, one of Fatah's main leaders, explained: "We never declared a freeze on the armed struggle and its cessation. That is a big lie and I do not know who is spreading it."[102] Even Nabil Sha'th said: "The Palestinian side did not and never will accept any decision to end the armed struggle."[103]

As always, Arafat thought that continued violence enhanced his bargaining position when, in fact, it was dangerously counterproductive since such attacks jeopardized the peace process, hardened Israeli positions, and ultimately subverted the U.S.-PLO dialogue. Arafat simply did not understand, then or later, that he could not have both terrorism and a diplomatic option.[104] Equally, Arafat did not make a decisive break with the PLO's historic claim to all of Israel. Even Arafat's personal stationery as president of the "state of Palestine" included a map showing all of Israel as part of his state.

In May 1990, trying to keep the dialogue going, the administration sent Assistant Secretary of State John Kelly to testify in Congress that failed cross-border PLO attacks on Israel could not be defined as terrorism since civilians were not actually killed. One congressman told Kelly that the facts "simply don't support" his claims that the PLO was keeping its commitments. Another bluntly called Kelly's testimony a "pack of lies."[105]

Arafat was about to prove these critics correct. Just a week later, Abu al-Abbas sent a squad from his Palestine Liberation Front (PLF), a member in good standing of the PLO, to shoot civilians on Tel Aviv's beach. Israeli navy gunboats intercepted the attackers at sea and killed or caught all of them. One prisoner, Muhammad Ahmad al-Hamadi Yusuf, the operation's deputy commander, told journalists that the target was Tel Aviv's beachfront hotel district and his orders were: "Don't leave anyone alive. Kill them all . . . children, women, elderly people."[106]

There was ample evidence of Arafat's complicity in the attack. Abbas was a member of the PLO's highest body and a close ally of Arafat. His Tunis office was in the same building as Fatah's, and Arafat was paying much of the group's budget as well.[107] Arafat always stressed that, "while the PLO is comprised of a coalition of 'fronts,' in the military sphere, there is only one command that gives orders to all." He was the head of that one command. A year earlier, the PLO Central Committee had again renewed Arafat's appointment as commander-in-chief of the Palestine revolution forces.[108]

The official PLO radio station carried three PLF communiqués detailing the operation, and both Israeli and U.S. intelligence sources concluded that Arafat had to have known of the attack in advance.[109] Abbas himself declared that the operation had been planned for two years.[110] Nevertheless, Arafat insisted the PLO "had nothing to do with the operation carried out by a Palestinian group off the Palestinian shores occupied by Israel in 1948."[111] Even while asserting his innocence, Arafat had used a phrase that confirmed he still rejected Israel's existence.

Despite all of this evidence, the United States still wanted to find a way to keep the dialogue going. It gave Arafat several ways he could renounce the attack, even in the most ambiguous and superficial way. Yet after two weeks of trying to save Arafat, the U.S. government, left with no choice, broke off the dialogue.[112]

But Arafat, convinced he had a new way to get everything he wanted, was even less interested in making compromises to negotiate with Israel or enjoy U.S. patronage. His new weapon, Iraqi president Saddam Hussein, then seeking Arab leadership, promised Arafat that he would conquer Israel for him. Arafat praised Saddam lavishly as a great hero and once more became intoxicated with dreams of total victory.[113] "I have for Saddam Hussein a limitless admiration and gratitude," explained Arafat.[114] At a March 1990 rally in Baghdad, Arafat told Saddam, "We will enter Jerusalem victorious and will raise our flag on its walls. You will enter with me, riding on your white stallion." Together, Palestinians and Iraqis would fight Israel "with stones, with rifles," and with Saddam's Scud missiles.[115]

During an April meeting in Baghdad, Saddam promised Arafat that he would "liberate" Jerusalem with his missiles or nuclear arms. He told Arafat:

> From now on we shall not need anymore any concessions or political efforts because you and I know that they are useless. They only increase the enemy's haughtiness.... We shall support [the Intifada] by our air force and accurate missiles in order to deal a blow on the enemy and defeat it even without ground fighting.[116]

A few days later, the PLO Executive Committee declared, "Standing by Iraq and putting Arab resources at its disposal is an obligation of the Arab nation."[117] The Intifada would triumph, Arafat told Palestinians in a radio broadcast, because Iraq's missiles have been "presented as a gift from Saddam Hussein, his army, and people to the struggling people of Palestine."[118]

Saddam also started providing more money to the badly indebted PLO, including direct subsidies for Arafat's personal bodyguard, Force 17. There were reports that Arafat was moving large numbers of his forces to Iraq, which was offering them new bases.[119] In early June, the PLO announced that Iraq had given it $25 million in addition to its regular monthly contributions and had doubled the transmission time for the Voice of Palestine's Baghdad service to six hours a day.[120]

Arafat was also reckless in endorsing Saddam's criticisms of Saudi Arabia and Kuwait. He complained that they were not giving him enough aid, though he had previously thanked those two states as the only countries fulfilling their financial pledges to the PLO.[121] Now Arafat argued that Arab oil exporters had more than $250 billion in U.S. banks and should threaten to strangle the world economy if the

Palestinians were not given what they demanded. Then, he added an ominous threat: soon, "as God is my witness," it would be too late for them to repent.[122]

As if to fulfill this prophecy, Saddam seized and annexed Kuwait in August 1990. At the emergency Arab summit called in response, the PLO voted against the resolution demanding Iraq's immediate withdrawal. Two days later, under Egyptian pressure, Arafat endorsed the idea with "reservations."[123] Then, however, Saddam cynically linked any withdrawal of his from Kuwait with an immediate Israeli pull-out from the West Bank and Gaza.[124] The PLO enthusiastically endorsed the initiative, though others realized that this linkage hurt the Palestinian cause by associating it with Saddam's aggression.[125]

Next, Arafat nominated himself to mediate the dispute, proposing a complex plan to give Iraq part of Kuwait and remove all Western troops from the area. If Arafat's plan had been accepted, opposition to Iraq would have collapsed, and Saddam would have become the region's dominant force, able to dictate his terms to everyone else. But Arafat was not just doing Saddam favors. He wanted to ride the Iraqi leader's wave of popularity throughout the Arab world and especially among Palestinians. Asked what would have happened to Arafat if he had sided with Egypt and not with Iraq, Habash claimed: "That would have meant the certain end of Yasir Arafat as the chairman of the PLO."[126]

Whether or not this was true, Arafat's unrestrained enthusiasm for Saddam was leading him toward another disaster as he claimed to be on the verge of his greatest victory: "Among our masses we are at a peak, with the Arab masses, at a peak, with the Muslim nation, we are at a peak, and throughout the Third World." Intoxicated with the Arab states' applause, he proclaimed, "I have gained credibility among my people and the entire Arab nation. Have you seen all the demonstrations...? My picture is being brandished everywhere."[127]

He was hungry for the coming war against Israel, having quickly forgotten any promises to cease terrorism or stop trying to destroy Israel. "Iraq," he declared approvingly, "will...use binary chemicals and anthrax in the war and the first missile will be launched against Israel."[128] He also saw the war as a battle against America. On January 7, 1991, Arafat spoke at a mass rally in Baghdad on the verge of the confrontation and shouted his defiant hatred of the United States. If America "wanted war then I say, 'welcome, welcome, welcome to war! Iraqis and Palestine [will be] together, side by side.'"[129] He arrogantly added that if the West wanted to "have O-I-L then they have to also take P-L-O."[130] The implication was that Saddam would control Saudi Arabia and Kuwait, selling oil only to those who met Arafat's demands as well.

A week later, Abu Iyad, the main critic of Arafat's pro-Iraqi policy, was murdered by the Iraqi-backed group led by Abu Nidal. Saddam had ensured that no one in the Palestinian movement would interfere with his determination to make Arafat his junior partner.[131] Arafat himself took no action and made no protest at the killing of his oldest colleague, a man he had worked alongside so long and so closely.

Abu Iyad had been right in warning that Arafat's decision to back Saddam would lead to one more defeat and disaster. The Arab Gulf states and Egypt were angry at Arafat's betrayal. His support for a country at war with the United States and Europe should have enraged the West. The USSR no longer existed to help him, and the Intifada had already collapsed.

Yet Arafat was correct in an equally important sense. No matter what he did, he would be forgiven.

6

Hero of the Return

1991–1995

In the summer of 1994, Arafat made a telephone call to Israeli prime minister Yitzhak Rabin with a special request. After months of tortuous secret negotiations, which had come close to collapse on many occasions, the two leaders had finally signed the detailed deal on how they would implement the peace process. Arafat was about to return to his ancestral homeland to rule the Gaza Strip and Jericho, starting a transition period that, if all went well, would produce an independent Palestinian state in five years.

First, though, Arafat wanted to request another concession from Israel. In addition to thousands of PLO officials and soldiers about to move from various Arab states to Gaza, he had a special list of "old friends" whom he wanted to bring with him. Rabin knew Arafat was talking about individuals personally involved in many terrorist acts against Israel over the years. When Arafat's list arrived, Rabin sent it to Yakov Peri, head of the Shin Bet, Israel's secret service, asking him to recommend that all but the very worst offenders be allowed into Gaza.[1]

Peri reported that these indeed were people who had been involved in attacks on Israelis, but he reluctantly agreed to admit all but those responsible for the bloodiest ones. When Rabin told him of this decision, however, Arafat was not satisfied. He asked the prime minister to let in even more of those men on the list. Rabin returned to Peri and emphasized the political importance of showing that Israel was being generous with Arafat. So Peri agreed that all but a handful of specific individuals who had committed the worst crimes could come with Arafat. Rabin passed on the good news to Arafat.

Among the few banned from admission were Marduch Nowfel, planner of a 1974 attack on a Ma'alot high school in which twenty-one Israeli teenagers were killed; Nihad Jayousi, a key figure behind the 1972 attack at the Olympic games; Mustafa Liftawi, the main organizer of terrorist attacks for Fatah's Western Sector department; and Jihad Amareen, a Western Sector official who also headed a Fatah-controlled Islamist terrorist group.

On the morning of July 1, 1994, Arafat's motorcade crossed from Egypt into the Gaza Strip. Israeli soldiers at the border were under strict instructions not to touch Arafat's Mercedes or the accompanying cars, which then drove past the Mediterranean coast's sand dunes to Gaza City. At 5 P.M., Arafat ascended a podium at the Square of the Unknown Soldier in front of tens of thousands of people, the biggest crowd ever assembled in Gaza. Millions more watched on television around the world.

One of them was Rabin. But his viewing was interrupted by an urgent phone call from Peri, who insisted that this matter could not wait. Peri had just one thing to tell Rabin: "The bastard brought them in the trunk of his Mercedes." Even after Israel had accepted the return of most of those on Arafat's list, he had still smuggled in Nowfel, Jayousi, Liftawi, and Amareen. An angry Rabin demanded that his aides get Arafat on the phone as soon as possible after the Gaza rally ended. When Rabin finally reached him, Arafat denied the men were in Gaza and insisted that Israel's intelligence was wrong. Unconvinced, Rabin warned, "Mr. Chairman, if you don't take them out, I will give the order to close the [Egypt-Gaza] border." No more PLO officials or police would then be allowed into Gaza.

For the next few days, Arafat continued to insist the men were not there. But Israeli officials were sure they were right. In addition, as Deputy Defense Minister Mordechai Gur put it, "There is no doubt that Yasir Arafat himself was totally involved in this." Once Rabin told Arafat that their presence was confirmed, Arafat conceded that while he had heard rumors that perhaps the men were in Gaza, he could not find them. Rabin now had to decide whether this issue was important enough to jeopardize the entire peace process.[2]

Finally, under serious Israeli pressure, Arafat sent the men back to Egypt. Rabin remarked optimistically, "They have to learn a lesson that they cannot cheat but rather, they should adhere to their commitments." Several weeks later, though, Israeli security discovered that Arafat had smuggled the four men back into Gaza. And there they stayed.

This small incident was a metaphor for everything that happened later. Arafat had shown that his word could not be trusted. Time after time, he begged and demanded concessions from others without ever really giving any himself. Yet a belief repeatedly prevailed that the next time he would do better or that once the two sides made a comprehensive deal, everything would change. If many thought Arafat had finally changed, though, there was also a factual basis for that conclusion. After all, he had crossed a line by negotiating with Israel to reach agreements that seemed likely to lead to a peace treaty.

For Arafat himself, taking that drive into Gaza—which could be portrayed as either a triumphant homecoming or a surrender of all his fondest beliefs—was likely to have been simultaneously the most glorious and most difficult journey in a life filled with constant travel. The fact that this extraordinary shift had been forced on him by inescapable circumstance made it all the more credible. His situation was so desperate that it seemed logical that Arafat was finally facing reality and adopting more limited goals and moderate methods. During the 1990s, the immigration of a million Soviet Jews and America's emergence as the world's sole superpower had strengthened Israel; the collapse of the Intifada, the USSR, and Iraq had weakened Arafat. The demands of many West Bank and Gaza Palestinians that he make a deal, along with the growing support of others for his Hamas rivals, gave Arafat an incentive to seek a quick breakthrough.

Iraq's defeat by a U.S.-led coalition in 1991 had been the last straw. As the Gulf Arabs turned against Arafat for siding with their enemy, his support among Arab states fell to an all-time low. When Arafat tried to embrace Saudi crown prince Abdallah at the 1991 Islamic summit, the Saudi leader drew back and extended his right arm to ward off Arafat.[3] The summit refused to reiterate past pro-PLO resolutions. When Arafat threatened to walk out in protest, the Gulf Arab states called his bluff, and he did not leave.[4]

With no superpower ally, few Arab friends, and near bankruptcy, Arafat seemed to have only one remaining option: to make peace. If that alternative were made attractive enough, Israeli, U.S., and European leaders thought Arafat would make a compromise deal. Rather than using Arafat's dire situation to destroy him, they wanted to moderate Arafat in a way that would benefit both himself and the Palestinian people. Indeed, once Arafat did accept a U.S. plan similar to ones he had rejected in the 1970s and 1980s, he was able to reach the Oslo Agreement with Israel and return to govern the Palestinians in less than three years.

The first step came at the 1991 international peace conference in Madrid following Iraq's defeat where, for the first time, many Arab states sat down to talk with Israel about finding a negotiated solution to the conflict. Arafat was admitted to the victors' camp, as one of those who would be rewarded for helping defeat Iraq's aggression, even though he had supported the losing side in the Kuwait conflict and broken his 1988 pledge of moderation. But since the PLO had not yet clearly or consistently accepted Israel's right to exist or abandoned the use of terrorism, Arafat could only participate by choosing a delegation of non-PLO Palestinians from the West Bank and the Gaza Strip.

This was only a limited sacrifice, since Arafat controlled the delegation from behind the scenes. Nervous about a situation he had been trying to avoid for two decades, Arafat went over the delegates' speeches, demanding that the PLO and his own name be mentioned more often, and sent them detailed orders throughout the conference.[5] He even had the delegation flown to meet him in Tunis or Algiers every weekend. Asked in Madrid where they were going, Nabil Sha'th joked that they were traveling to the Caribbean for a vacation.[6]

When Israel complained that these hardly secret visits to Arafat violated U.S. promises of a public separation between the delegation and the PLO, Secretary of State James Baker replied that Arafat had assured him these meetings would be kept quiet.[7] But soon Arafat was inviting journalists and photographers to watch the "secret" sessions in Tunis. Baker did nothing.

Arafat's constant effort to thrust himself into the limelight was not only intended to establish the PLO's international legitimacy. He wanted to ensure, as always, that residents of the West Bank and Gaza Strip remained obedient to him.[8] "Every Palestinian is a member of the PLO, inside and outside the territories," Arafat said, as if to assuage his own insecurity. "The Palestinian people regard the PLO as their sole and legitimate representative. And they don't accept any kind of alternative!"[9] Arafat let no delegate forget for a moment that he was boss. When Hanan Ashrawi, the delegation's spokesperson, told reporters that she was not a PLO member—which was, after all, a condition of her participation—Arafat snapped at her, "I could bring you back to the West Bank and make you stay at home."[10]

Once the delegation moved to Washington for extended negotiations with Israel, Arafat tightened his control over it further, to the point of wrecking any chance of progress since he had no intention of letting any talks succeed in which he was not a direct participant. The Palestinian delegates were paralyzed with fear that Arafat would use them as scapegoats by letting them make concessions and then portraying them as traitors afterward. In short, he would not let them negotiate, and they were afraid to do so.[11]

The Washington talks also made no progress because of Arafat's great difficulty in deciding whether to abandon two of his most cherished positions. First, rather than make a deal with Israel in order to get the West Bank and Gaza Strip eventually as a state, Arafat maintained the unrealistic demand that he should get full control of all of the territory at the start of the process, before a final agreement was made. Any transitional period of self-rule, he said, was an Israeli idea "that we will not accept, even if the Americans do."[12]

Second, he had still not decided whether he truly wanted to make a compromise deal that would require giving up his claim to all of Palestine and his hope that Israel could be made to disappear. In vowing to continue wearing the PLO insignia, which carried a map showing his definition of Palestine, which included all of Israel too, Arafat said that only after a negotiating process was successfully concluded would he change that goal.[13]

Such attitudes contrasted sharply with the openly conciliatory alternative offered by Feisal al-Husseini, the most important West Bank leader and also a member of the Palestinian negotiating team: "In the past . . . our struggle was for 'pure justice,' for our right to the whole of Palestine—from the Jordan River to the sea. This is no longer the case. We recognize that . . . we must come to a compromise. [We] must set down for once and all: here is Israel with its borders, here is a Palestinian state with its borders."[14] Arafat would rarely, if ever, speak in such terms. A decade later, after many more negotiations and agreements, his insignia, seal of office, and the PLO's emblem would still claim all of the historically disputed land.

During 1992, however, three events did signal the potential opening of a new era in Arafat's life: his marriage, near-death, and the start of his first direct dialogue with Israel. In January, Arafat announced he now had a twenty-eight-year-old Palestinian wife, Suha Tawil. Previously, Arafat had always explained his lack of family life by saying he was married to the revolution.[15] Perhaps this new status indicated Arafat's readiness to settle down and make a transition from revolutionary to head of state. Suha was a controversial choice. While born in Jerusalem and raised in Ramallah, she was far from being a typical Palestinian woman. Her father was a wealthy banker. She was a Catholic, though she converted to Islam for the wedding, who had been educated by nuns and was very much a modern, Westernized woman. Arafat had never shown any interest in women's rights but Suha approvingly quoted her mother, Raymonda Tawil, as saying, "When our women have the chance to get out from under masculine domination, you'll see what they'll do for Palestine." Tawil was a well-known journalist and the leading female Palestinian activist at that time. Young Suha had served tea in her mother's salon to visitors, including many top Palestinian and Israeli leaders.[16]

Arafat was another friend of her mother's, and Suha met him in 1985 on a trip to Amman when she was a student. He later hired her to do public relations for the PLO in Paris, and the two secretly married in July 1990. She claimed the marriage was kept secret for eighteen months because it was inappropriate to celebrate during an uprising in which hundreds of Palestinians were being killed.[17] But this explanation is strange since by that time the Intifada was really over. More likely, the delay was caused by concern over how Palestinians would respond to Suha's Westernized, elite, and Christian background.

Being Mrs. Arafat was a difficult task. "I married a myth," she said. There was no question, Suha explained, of her being admitted into her husband's political life, "a man's world and very closed—like a family with a lot of intermarriages and, well, you know the result of that." She claimed the marriage helped Arafat "step down from his pedestal and become a human being." Yet she later complained that Arafat never listened to anyone. They spent little time together and after the birth of a daughter, Zahwa, at the American Hospital in the posh Paris suburb of Neuilly-sur-Seine on August 27, 1995, Suha spent most of her time in France, and the marriage came to exist in name only.[18]

To many of Arafat's colleagues, who were not exactly advanced on the subject of women's rights, Suha was an embarrassment on two counts. First, she was clearly a member of the Westernized Arab elite, which Arafat had supposedly been fighting all his life. Her expensive clothes, dyed blonde hair, and Parisian shopping trips undercut Arafat's Spartan image as an incorruptible man of the people and pious Muslim.

Second, Suha's tactlessness caused problems in many directions. Her extremist statements—telling First Lady Hilary Clinton that Israel had poisoned Palestinian wells; saying she wished she had a son who would be a suicide bomber—made for bad public relations with the West. But Suha's acerbic remarks about her husband's lieutenants and his regime's shortcomings did not endear her to the Palestinian leadership either.

Shortly after the happy announcement of his wedded status came a sign of Arafat's mortality. In April 1992, en route from Khartoum, Sudan, to Tripoli, Libya, his plane flew into a Libyan desert sandstorm and veered out of control. Arafat prepared himself for his demise. Concerned that he remained dignified even—or perhaps especially—when dead, Arafat stripped off the casual track suit he had been wearing, put on his uniform, arranged his *kaffiya*, and holstered his gun. Then the other passengers wrapped him in blankets and pillows and placed him in the rear of the plane, considered the least dangerous place during a crash.[19]

Arafat would later piously claim that two images went through his head: the Dome of the Rock shrine in Jerusalem and the faces of murdered colleagues Abu Iyad and Abu Jihad. "I knew I will survive this crash. I will live to redeem the sacrifices of all our martyrs. I will continue on this march with my people until we pray in Jerusalem!"[20] Three members of his party were killed in the crash. Arafat had to wait fifteen hours to be rescued and later underwent surgery for a blood clot in his brain.[21] Yet, once again, he had survived.

While awaiting news of her husband's fate, Suha was treated very badly by his associates as she sat for hours alone feeling "dumped, abandoned, already like a widow." But while indifferent to Suha's sufferings, PLO leaders were very worried about what would happen to themselves if she did, indeed, become a widow. Without Arafat, their jobs and possibly the whole movement might disappear. Arafat's miraculous survival reminded them of his indispensability.[22]

After each disaster into which Arafat led the PLO, internal complaints about his leadership temporarily increased but were easily defused by him. The same happened regarding his terrible mistake of supporting Saddam Hussein in 1991. Before the plane crash, leaders complained at the Fatah Revolutionary Committee's March 21, 1992, session that Arafat had too much power over policies, money, and job appointments. Critics claimed that Arafat personally headed thirty-three different offices in the PLO and Fatah. Hani al-Hasan accused Arafat of insulating himself from experienced Fatah veterans to surround himself with young yes-men.[23] But after the crash, at the ninety-two-member PLO Central Council's May 7 meeting, Arafat won total support.[24]

The year's third key event was the June 1992 election of Yitzhak Rabin as Israel's prime minister. Rabin viewed his election as a mandate for talking to the PLO and perhaps even accepting an independent Palestinian state in the West Bank and Gaza. After the election, Arafat said he was pleased that the "the Israeli people had voted for peace" and stressed the need for "an Israeli de Gaulle," who would grant to Palestinians their independence as the French leader had done with Algeria.[25]

What were Arafat's views at this time? There were hints of change mixed with familiar signs of intransigence. In August, he gave an interview to an Israeli newspaper saying he supported a two-state solution and a comprehensive peace that ensured Israel's security. Yet he also insisted that all Palestinian refugees must be repatriated to Israel. His claim that those living in Europe and America would not return concealed the fact that the millions in the Middle East would overwhelm Israel numerically.[26]

Arafat also proposed the quick transfer of all the West Bank and Gaza to his rule after six months, followed by internationally supervised elections leading quickly to the establishment of an independent state.[27] Thus, he accepted a transitional period—albeit a very short one—but saw independence as following quickly, automatically, and under international auspices, rather than depending on proof that he was implementing commitments and on a peace agreement with Israel. All of these points would remain in Arafat's thinking and reemerge to help wreck the peace process later.

One factor clearly pushing him toward a dramatic move was the PLO's critical situation. It was as close to falling apart in the early 1990s as it had ever been. The financial deficit forced employee layoffs and cutbacks in activity. The low morale was further depressed by stories of senior PLO officials' corruption. Arafat could not even pay pensions to the families of casualties from past fighting in Lebanon, some of whom demonstrated outside PLO offices in protest. Unpaid PLO employees seized its embassy in Libya, and one was killed when police threw them out. Palestinian women in Damascus chanted that the PLO leadership had enough money to line its own pockets but not to help starving families.[28] Clearly, as one prominent Palestinian explained, Arafat needed to do something to "break the logjam and create a new political reality."[29]

His response to this crisis would be the momentous Oslo process, and it would start from the smallest of seeds. In late 1991, Ron Pundak and Yair Hirschfeld, Israeli scholars at Hebrew and Haifa universities, respectively, were at Hanan Ashrawi's Ramallah home discussing the future of Israeli-Palestinian economic relations. Ashrawi suggested the two Israelis travel to London in December to meet Ahmad Qurei (Abu Alaa), the PLO's chief economics advisor, who would be visiting there. Ashrawi called Arafat's office in Tunis to clear the idea with him.[30]

This was not just to be a meeting between two Israeli academics and a PLO economist. Abu Mazin later wrote that the key factor in making the PLO pursue this channel was the relationship of Pundak and Hirschfeld through Yossi Beilin, a prominent figure in the Labor party, to Foreign Minister Shimon Peres.[31] The get-together was arranged by Terje Larsen, a Norwegian sociologist who headed the Institute for Applied Social Sciences.[32] That meeting's success soon led to more rounds of secret talks between Israel and the PLO hosted by the Norwegians.

Thus, an alternative, secret negotiating track was created, circumventing the Washington talks and more directly in Arafat's hands. Its first official meeting was held in January 1993, on the grounds of the Borregard paper company in Sarpsbourg, eighty miles from Oslo. To ensure secrecy, Norwegian security agents patrolled the grounds.[33] The Israelis were still limited to Pundak and Hirschfeld. Abu Alaa led the Palestinian team.[34] Born to a wealthy family in Abu Dis, a West Bank village near Jerusalem, he became a math teacher in Kuwait. There he met Arafat and joined Fatah in 1968. Arafat later sent him to Beirut as head of Samed, the PLO's economic arm, which ran thirty-six small factories producing shoes, clothes, furniture, and food.[35]

Abu Alaa had two key skills needed to make a deal: he was a pragmatically oriented technocrat rather than an ideologically oriented revolutionary politician, and he had a strong personal relationship with Arafat. At first, Abu Alaa was so little known to Israelis that when Rabin asked for the Israeli intelligence dossier on him, it was less than five pages long. But they would learn to credit him with a shrewd understanding of details and fierce negotiating skills. He had an endless supply of tasteless jokes and became so emotionally involved in making the talks succeed that once when things were going well he did a frantic, Zorba-like dance of joy. "Without him, Oslo would not have happened," said Uri Savir, who later became the lead Israeli negotiator in the secret talks. "Abu Alaa was there to make a deal," recalled Pundak.[36]

Although, like Arafat, he never attended the talks, Abu Mazin played a key role from Tunis. He was open to making a deal but also ideologically rigid and suspicious of Israel.[37] Born in 1935 in Safed, now in northern Israel, Abu Mazin fled to Syria with his family in 1948. He joined Fatah in 1965 and the PLO Executive Committee in 1980. Chain-smoking from his ebony-and-gold cigarette holder, Abu Mazin spent hours talking by phone to the negotiators. "When we faced difficulties, we went to him," said Amnon Lipkin-Shahak, a member of the Israeli delegation.[38]

But despite Abu Mazin's important role, Arafat was clearly directing the Palestinian position in the Oslo talks. Every point had to be referred to him. He marked up the Palestinian negotiators' reports and drafts of documents in red pen, and he was frequently quoted in the sessions by Abu Alaa and the others.[39]

At the first meeting in Norway, Abu Alaa read remarks approved by Arafat, which bluntly stated that the Palestinians believed they had reached a crossroads, admitted that support for Iraq in the Kuwait crisis had been a mistake, and spoke of a commitment to peace. The two sides agreed to start by discussing the idea of Israeli withdrawal from Gaza and the establishment of Palestinian rule there, building Palestinian economic institutions, and obtaining international aid for a future Palestinian entity.[40] Pundak thought the talks "very pragmatic. . . . We felt we had a partner for negotiations ready to go on to big compromises and make a historical agreement."[41]

As more meetings followed, Arafat made it clear that he authorized the Palestinian delegates to represent the PLO—a point on which the Israelis had some doubts—by sending a personal message to one session, saying: "I'm happy to sign an agreement that would lead gradually to a permanent state, will reach economic development for us and security for Israel." When he heard this, Rabin said, "Because of this message, I will make Oslo work." Later, Arafat sent additional letters of assurance to the Israeli negotiators at key moments and sometimes even spoke with them by telephone.[42]

The talks were upgraded in importance in May with the arrival of Uri Savir, director-general of Israel's Foreign Ministry and the first official representative of Israel's government to participate. Peres moved the talks forward by telling his delegates to ask, "In case we come to an agreement, at what point would Arafat want to come to rule Gaza and Jericho?" This assured Arafat that Israel was not trying to exclude him and make a deal with local leaders. Arafat accepted this step as a first stage in a comprehensive settlement.[43] Arafat announced he would certainly maintain order there, though his citing of his past performance in Lebanon was less than persuasive proof of his ability to do so.[44]

By early July, the two sides had produced a draft agreement, which they sent to their bosses for approval. When talks resumed on July 10 at the Halvorsbole Hotel and Conference Center near Oslo, though, Abu Alaa raised twenty-five new points, including demanding control of a crossing point between Israel and Jordan, letting East Jerusalem candidates run for the Palestinian parliament, and other issues.[45] Arafat and Abu Mazin, Abu Alaa said, could not accept the document. Arafat sent a letter to the Israelis holding forth the prospect of success if only he were given more concessions: "The special negotiations between us are now reaching a serious stage. We have before us a genuine historic chance.... We are both responsible for not losing this opportunity." Arafat urged prompt Israeli withdrawal from Gaza and Jericho and added that the Tunis leadership would arrive as soon as possible to satisfy Palestinian public opinion and counteract "possible actions of extremist groups interested in damaging the new agreement." But a shocked Savir said flatly that Israel could not negotiate with such new conditions. The next night, Arafat sent another message by phone via Abu Alaa, again assuring the Israelis of his intention to reach an agreement.[46]

With both sides still far apart, the Norwegians played a more active role in bridging the gap. On July 13, Foreign Minister Johan Jorgen Holst flew to Tunis to meet Arafat, who spent the first part of the conversation attacking the United States as being biased against him. But when Arafat was alone with Holst, he relaxed and took a different tone. He expressed confidence in the negotiations but was adamant about getting land corridors under Palestinian sovereignty that would connect Gaza and Jericho.

"I want kissing points," Arafat insisted. "Kissing points. Are they on the plan?"

"You mean checkposts?" asked Holst, completely confused.

"No, no, kissing points, like this," Arafat pursed his lips.

When Holst assured Arafat that the plan would include "safe passage" between Gaza and Jericho, Arafat retorted: "I am not Nelson Mandela, I am not Mandela." Holst had no idea why Arafat was referring to the South African leader, though perhaps it was a reference to Mandela's well-known opposition to violence, which Arafat did not share.[47]

While Arafat dropped the demand for a Gaza-Jericho corridor under his control, he insisted in late July that Israel accept all of his other last-minute revisions to the Declaration of Principles.[48] Finally, on August 19, the Oslo process was completed in a marathon seven-hour series of conference calls involving Peres and Holst in Stockholm; Savir in Jerusalem; and Arafat, Abu Alaa, Abu Mazin—all from Fatah—and Yasir Abd Rabbu, a DFLP leader allied with Arafat, in Tunis.

Arafat was at his desk, in front of a picture of Jerusalem. On his desk was a single sharp-edged stone, which symbolized the Intifada, a gift from the boys of a West Bank refugee camp, and a photo of Arafat with Abu Iyad and Abu Jihad. As the conversation progressed, the room became hazy with cigarette smoke. Ashtrays were filled to the brim, and cup after cup of strong Arab coffee was consumed. Holst conveyed the proposals, which Abu Alaa translated for Arafat. After they discussed each issue, Abu Alaa presented the Palestinian response. On the Israeli end, Peres took the lead role. Both sides made some last-minute compromises.

When the deal was completed in the early morning, Arafat told those in his office, "Now we must take our responsibilities seriously, and implement this peace plan. Only we, in this room tonight, know what has been achieved." The next step was to convince the PLO leadership to back the move.[49]

Meanwhile, Peres flew to the United States to brief Secretary of State Warren Christopher. The U.S. government certainly knew about the secret talks but had little idea of how they had evolved since May. One U.S. official long involved in the issue recalled that when he found out about the deal, "I was blown away by what had been produced. We knew there had been channels but didn't know they had turned from discussion to decision making." The United States immediately agreed to help the initiative succeed.[50]

To complete the process, on September 7, Arafat sent a letter to Rabin confirming that the PLO recognized Israel's right to exist in peace and security, accepted UN Security Council Resolutions 242 and 338, and committed itself to resolving the conflict peacefully. In addition, the PLO renounced the use of terrorism and violence, pledging to ensure that all PLO members complied with the agreement. He also stated that those articles of the PLO Charter inconsistent with these commitments were "inoperative and no longer valid," and he promised to order the necessary changes in that document.[51]

In response, Rabin wrote Arafat stating that Israel had decided to "recognize the PLO as a representative of the Palestinian people" and to "commence negotiations with the PLO within a Middle East peace process."[52]

Finally, Arafat had to sell the deal he had made to his comrades. Up to that moment, he had not consulted either local West Bank and Gaza Strip leaders or, except for Abu Mazin, top PLO figures. In June, accusations from PLO leaders against Arafat for poor management and corruption had again produced the usual cycle of events: Arafat threatened to resign and promised to share more power, critics backed down, and Arafat did nothing.[53] In August, three members of the negotiating team in Washington—Feisal al-Husseini, Hanan Ashrawi, and Saeb Arikat—had resigned partly because they discovered the real talks were being conducted behind their backs.[54]

Still, most West Bank and Gaza nationalist activists supported Arafat and his plan. After a brief, timid demand, led by Husseini, for more say in its implementation, they gave up.[55] This signaled the collapse of any independent role for local figures, who might otherwise have formed a moderate, prodemocratic lobby in the Palestinian leadership.

In contrast, Arafat was well aware that most PLO leaders outside of the West Bank and Gaza favored the traditional line and opposed any negotiations with Israel at all. Once the announcement of a deal was made, Iran and Syria encouraged an open anti-Arafat revolt in Lebanon. A Fatah commander, Colonel Munir Maqdah, demanded Arafat's resignation, then quit himself, and was soon paying his men with Iranian funds. Similarly, the Yasir Arafat Social Services Center at Ein al-Hilweh refugee camp was renamed the Imam Khomeini Center.[56]

There were more defections elsewhere. The prominent Palestinian poet Mahmoud Darwish, who lived in Paris, resigned from the Executive Committee on August 21 in opposition to the agreement.[57] The next day, Shafiq al-Hout, veteran director of the PLO office in Beirut, suspended his membership in the Executive Committee as well.[58] Several others took similar action, although Arafat soon won back some dissenters.

At the PLO Executive Committee's August 26–28 meeting, only Arafat and Abu Mazin strongly defended the plan, while almost all of the other members criticized it.[59] Even at the Central Committee meeting of Arafat's own Fatah a week later, six members, including Qaddumi, attacked the accords and accused Arafat of splitting the group. While Arafat announced at a press conference that the meeting had approved his agreement, in fact arguments were so heated that no final statement was issued. Some critics demanded that the PLO Central Council or the PNC be convened to ratify the deal, but Arafat refused, saying the agreement was in line with those institutions' previous decisions.[60]

The final showdown came at the September 8–9 Executive Committee meeting. Arafat submitted the Declaration of Principles and letters of recognition for approval, demanding a quick and total acceptance. Qaddumi, along with the PFLP and DFLP representatives, boycotted the meeting in protest against Arafat's policies and procedures. Three other members resigned. In the end, nine members voted for the approval, with three against and six abstaining or absent.[61] Following the session, another independent member resigned. Despite these disputes, Arafat could accurately claim that the PLO, Fatah, and the masses were behind him.[62]

The stage was now set for the dramatic signing ceremony in Washington, D.C. At first, Rabin did not want to go, viewing direct contact with Arafat as both personally distasteful and politically unwise. At any rate, the two leaders' presence was unnecessary since the document was supposed to be signed by Peres and Abu Mazin. But Arafat would be there, and Rabin concluded that Israel's prime minister must lend his personal presence to such a momentous agreement. The stage was set for a remarkable event.[63]

As he boarded a Boeing 707 jetliner, loaned him by Morocco's government, to fly from Tunis to Washington, a beaming Arafat hailed the agreement as leading to "an independent Palestinian state, with Jerusalem as its capital." When later challenged by a voice in the crowd in Washington saying, "Arafat sold out!" he retorted, "I never stopped anybody from freeing Palestine. If they thought they could do better, why didn't they?"[64]

But even then, there was a last-minute crisis to manage. A few hours before the signing ceremony, Arafat aide Ahmad Tibi went to Peres's hotel room and warned that if he did not substitute the word "PLO" in the document for all references to the Palestinian team or the old Palestinian-Jordanian delegation, Arafat would be on the next plane out of town. The document's text had been initialed in Oslo in August, at a time when Israel did not recognize the PLO. At first, Peres was willing to call his bluff: "Let me know when you're going, because we'll be going, too."

As the time to start the ceremony drew near, Arafat stayed at his hotel, saying he would not sign the accord unless the amendment was made. Only when he heard that Peres had agreed did Arafat go to the White House. But since there had not been time to change the documents, Abu Mazin himself wrote "PLO" before the words "Palestinian delegation" in the preamble. Otherwise, though, there were no direct references to the PLO.[65]

There was also the matter of Arafat's determination to wear his gun at the White House ceremony. Clinton told him, "This is a peace agreement. This isn't a remake of *Rio Bravo*," referring to a 1959 John Wayne movie.[66] On this point, as he had when making his UN speech almost two decades earlier, Arafat gave in.

Rabin, too, made a compromise. When Clinton told Rabin he would have to shake Arafat's hand after the signing, Rabin looked at him and said: "Well, I suppose you don't make peace with your friends." Then he smiled and said, "But no kissing!"[67] Rabin made it clear, though, that he did not want to talk with Arafat before the signing. After everyone else had gone outside, Peres, Clinton, and Arafat remained alone in a White House room. Rabin said something to Clinton; Arafat thought Rabin was talking to him and responded. Clinton jumped in with some small talk. In the end, the two leaders did not exchange a word before, during, or after the ceremony.[68]

This hesitancy arose from Rabin's shy personality but also reflected his view of Arafat. Rabin had fought Arafat for decades and considered him untrustworthy. Even as he made peace with Arafat, he still doubted whether the Palestinian leader had changed.[69] In the words of Rabin's closest aide, Eitan Haber, the prime minister saw Arafat "as a terrorist and murderer, someone who lied even when he didn't need to." Rabin told him, "I prefer to make peace with Queen Elizabeth of England. But we have no alternative. Arafat's the right address. Let's do it."[70]

The moving White House signing ceremony inspired hope that any conflict could be resolved. It almost seemed as if all the barriers so long bedeviling peace and progress in the world had fallen. With Communism so recently collapsed and the seemingly permanent Cold War vanished, many things that had once seemed utopian appeared to be within reach.

And so the two sides signed an agreement atop the 124-year-old walnut table also used at the 1979 Camp David peace accords, when Egypt and Israel had made peace. As applause rang out, Arafat extended his hand to Rabin, Clinton threw his arm over Rabin's shoulder to draw him closer. Rabin visibly hesitated, then grabbed Arafat's hand and shook it. But Rabin, clearly uncomfortable with Arafat, canceled his participation in a planned White House state dinner that evening.[71]

In his speech after the signing, Arafat said that the Palestinians shared with the United States such values as freedom, justice, and human rights. He continued:

> My people are hoping that this agreement which we are signing today marks the beginning of the end of a chapter of pain and suffering which has lasted throughout this century. My people are hoping that this agreement which we are signing today will usher in an age of peace, coexistence and equal rights.... The battle for peace is the most difficult battle of our lives. It deserves our utmost efforts because the land of peace...yearns for a just and comprehensive peace.[72]

Addressing Israel, Arafat stressed the need for "more courage and determination to continue building coexistence and peace." He claimed that Palestinian aspirations would not "violate the rights of their neighbors or infringe on their security."[73]

The U.S. role as host and sponsor was indispensable. One of those most involved in the process, State Department official Aaron Miller, joked, "What we do best is catering for peace."[74] The next day, at an event almost as remarkable as the signing itself, Arafat held a friendly meeting with American senators and congressmen, who promised him financial support as well as the removal of all legal barriers to an official PLO presence in the United States.

It was ironic, and yet profoundly appropriate given Arafat's career, that what could have been his greatest success was the outcome of his consistent failure. After all, Israel was ready to make a deal with Arafat not due to his victories but because his defeats made him seem so weak that he was ready to compromise in order to avoid political oblivion. Yet this was not, as Arafat's militant critics claimed, a plot to force his humiliating capitulation. In exchange for an end to occupation, a real state, and a chance to repatriate refugees to a Palestinian country, Arafat was thought ready to make a full and lasting peace. If Israel had merely wanted to exploit Arafat's weakness, it could have done so far more easily and safely by ignoring or attacking him. Whatever advantage of strength or leverage Israel had over Arafat, it knew that only he could approve a deal and that even his minimum terms would hardly be those of someone surrendering.

Equally, the United States had declared its eagerness to become Arafat's patron and midwife to a Palestinian state. During meetings held with Arafat in the months following the signing, high-ranking U.S.

officials spent hours urging him to create a democratic, honest, and transparent government of which his people could be proud. U.S. officials suggested that Arafat consider George Washington and Nelson Mandela as role models. They told him that if he were to win elections with a 55 percent majority, he would be seen as a credible democratic leader, while a 95 percent majority would make his regime a joke. Two years later, Arafat would get 85 percent of the vote in the Palestinian elections.[75]

Once celebrations ended, the hard work began in a process made necessarily complex by the great mutual mistrust and difficult issues to be resolved. According to the agreement, during the projected five-year transition period, Israel would relinquish territory while retaining control of international borders, overall security, East Jerusalem, and Jewish settlements. Arafat's job was to end Palestinian terrorism against Israel, govern the territories he received, cease hostile propaganda, and build the institutions that would make possible a stable Palestinian state. As Arafat proved his ability to maintain peace and fulfill commitments, more land would be ceded. The hope was that when the time came to make a final agreement, the mutual confidence established would make the ultimate compromises easier to achieve.

During the first stage, whose details were set by a May 1994 agreement signed in Cairo, Israel withdrew from most of the Gaza Strip and the West Bank town of Jericho, which were then fully ruled by Arafat and his Palestinian Authority (PA) government.[76] In stage two, defined by the September 1995 Interim Autonomy Agreement, the PA took over the West Bank's Palestinian-populated areas (September–November 1995), held elections (January 1996), and gained control over most of Hebron (January 1997).[77]

The West Bank would then consist of three zones: Area A, the towns, under full PA control; Area B, the 450 villages, under PA political control but where Israel could intervene for security reasons; and Area C, governed by Israel and including unpopulated areas, key roads, and Jewish settlements. At this point, the PA partly or fully controlled about 30 percent of the West Bank with 99 percent of the population. The October 1998 Wye Plantation Agreement designated another 12 percent of the West Bank to be transferred from Area C to Area B, and 15.2 percent to be moved from Area B to Area A. Thus, the PA was to control about 45 percent of the West Bank.[78]

During the third stage, originally scheduled to begin in May 1996 and to be completed by May 1999 (but which only began at the later date), "final status" negotiations were supposed to produce a treaty resolving all remaining issues. These included the fate of East Jerusalem, refugees, Jewish settlements, security arrangements, and borders.

At each step of the way, this plan faced many delays, barriers, disputes, and shortcomings in implementation. Still, it did advance and, as the authors envisioned—though it took six rather than three years—finally arrived at the take-off point for negotiating a full peace treaty. Judging Arafat's plans and intentions in this period is an extremely difficult task. Was he ready for the kind of real historic compromise needed to ensure the process's success or merely intent on escaping from his latest disaster and gaining a stronger position from which to pursue his old ambitious goals of taking over all of Israel using his traditional methods, such as violence?

There are three important clues for evaluating Arafat's goals and deeds. First, his career showed that he had great difficulty in changing his ways. Everyone knew his history but hoped that a combination of desperation and opportunity would bring personal transformation. A U.S. diplomat recalled, "In 1993 there was no way of knowing Arafat wouldn't be a [fighter turned] statesman like South African leader Nelson Mandela. All over the world, people ready to kill then dramatically changed to make peace."[79] Wouldn't Arafat want to create a state, end his people's suffering, and become a ruler rather than a revolutionary? The fact that this expectation went unfulfilled was the central factor in the peace process's problems and ultimate collapse.

Second, Arafat was acting not so much on the basis of a plan but from his unwillingness to make and implement the firm decisions needed. His obsession with keeping open options, treating weakness as a virtue, and breaking commitments in search of advantage were consistent patterns in his behavior. Refusing to fulfill promises destroyed his credibility; reluctance to constrain radicals sabotaged his progress. Arafat believed that ambiguity and violence would help him gain more in the 1990s. He should have learned from earlier experiences, when such tactics had so often brought defeat.

Third, Arafat's refusal to choose between compromise and pursuing a long-term effort to destroy Israel subverted the process during its seven years' duration and brought it to a dead end at the moment of truth. Ultimately, it did not matter so much whether Arafat's intransigence was based on a trick or a reservation, on personal weakness or ideological stubbornness. His character, behavior, and tactics in the end doomed any chance for peace. Even the lure of a state with its capital in East Jerusalem was insufficient to make him abandon the mirage that he or his successors might one day win everything.

All this lay well in the future during those heady days of late 1993. American and European leaders were convinced that Arafat was eager for peace and would prove a reliable partner. How could the Palestinians not be ready to do everything possible, or at least reasonable, to end the occupation and achieve the cherished goal of independence? In Israel, the Left thought that Arafat would make a reasonable deal and implement it; the Right feared he would make an agreement and then break it once he had a state. None of them expected Arafat would ultimately torpedo an agreement altogether, and some refused to accept this fact even after it happened.

The one group to which Arafat did want to prove his lack of moderation was his own Fatah and PLO colleagues. In October 1993, the PLO Central Council was convened to approve Arafat's policy in accepting the Oslo Agreement. Of 108 members, 26 boycotted the meeting, and Arafat made last-minute appointments to ensure his majority. Rather than defend the agreement as a positive way to achieve a worthwhile goal, he merely insisted it was the best thing possible at the moment, implying that a different situation might mean it could be torn up.

Even his closest comrades gave only lukewarm support. Qaddumi endorsed Arafat's strategy only because he feared an internal conflict would threaten the movement's future. Abu Mazin said the peace plan was too risky and was as likely to strengthen Israel's occupation as it was to produce a Palestinian state. This was ironic since Abu Mazin had been Arafat's closest partner in negotiating and accepting the agreement in the first place. In the end, Arafat won by 63–8 with 11 abstentions. But among the abstainers were three of his most important veteran colleagues, Faruq Qaddumi, Abbas Zaki, and Sakhr Habash, all of whom would have preferred to vote against the measure.[80]

Following Arafat's blueprint, the Central Council next established the PA to govern the areas coming under Palestinian rule. Arafat was named as president and the chair of all twelve of the PA's committees. While Abu Mazin and Abd Rabbu were appointed heads of the team to negotiate with Israel, Arafat ran that also. The only way an angry Abu Mazin could retaliate was by staying away from PLO Executive Committee meetings for a while and delaying his own arrival in Gaza.[81]

"Our democracy," Arafat often bragged, "will be a model which many Arab peoples will want to copy."[82] Palestinians were less impressed by the reality. Arafat rejected a petition signed by 120 prominent figures in the territories, submitted to him in January 1994, which demanded that he discuss with them how to handle the peace process and increase democracy. That was the last time the local leadership challenged him.[83] Promises Arafat did make to his followers—to let a high-level committee oversee talks with Israel, to make appointments based on merit rather than his personal preference, to develop a draft constitution, and to let the PLO Executive Committee make major decisions—were broken.[84]

Despite the expectation of some Palestinians and many Westerners, the task of governing did not force Arafat to listen to others.[85] No one was ready to stand up to him, and he bought off most of his critics by rewards, not threats. Neither critics' threats nor defections, Fatah leaders' demands for power sharing, or even the revelation that Adnan Yasin, a trusted Arafat lieutenant, was an Israeli informant shook Arafat's total power.[86] Whatever the virtues of democracy or collective leadership, though, they would not have assured a successful peace process since there were always far more people criticizing Arafat for being too moderate rather than for being too militant.[87] The problem was that Arafat both preferred and found it easier to appease, use, and imitate the radicals rather than to move his own constituency toward greater flexibility or encourage Palestinian moderates to step forward and organize.

Even with all of the endorsements by key Palestinian institutions in late 1993, however, Arafat was, literally, not home yet. The next step needed was a detailed agreement with Israel, which took several months to negotiate, on precisely how the Gaza-Jericho phase was to be managed.[88] Already, intense suspicion and the desire of extremist forces to block the plan's implementation were apparent. The worst single incident was a February 1994 massacre perpetrated by an American-born Jewish settler, who opened fire at Muslim worshipers in a Hebron mosque, murdering twenty-nine people before being killed himself.

Arafat broke off talks, and they were only renewed on March 20, when a high-level Israeli delegation flew to Tunis on an American military plane to meet Arafat and try to resolve the crisis. They were driven to a modest guesthouse adorned with pictures of Arafat. In the middle of the night, Arafat arrived. He ordered refreshments as the Israelis expressed condolences. All of his colleagues were sleeping, Arafat told them, while he had to do everything by himself. He joked, "We have an upside-down pyramid here. I work and they rest."[89]

Quickly the discussion became more serious. Arafat said he had a stack of letters from Palestinians in Hebron demanding that he stop the peace process. "I'm accused of being a traitor. My people are living in dread of yet another massacre. You must take steps to rebuild our trust. Otherwise the peace process will die."[90]

He tapped his foot and went on in a whisper: "I am definitely interested in moving forward, but I need the trust of my people. You have an elected government, a parliament, and clear laws. Trust is not the only bond between Israelis and their leaders. But it's all there is between my people and me."[91] When Savir suggested bringing in international relief agencies to help Palestinians in Hebron, Arafat exploded: "What do you want to do? Bring in nurses to give people injections? . . . They're burning my portrait in the streets of Hebron, and the Israelis are talking about injections!"[92]

Arafat did eventually agree to return to the negotiations and dropped his demand for immediately removing Jewish settlers from Hebron. That decision stunned even his Palestinian colleagues. But Arafat wanted something else far more important for him: to increase the number of Palestinian police by 400 percent, from the six thousand allowed in the Oslo Agreement to twenty-four thousand. He claimed this was needed because "policing Gaza and the West Bank is one of the toughest jobs on earth. They want us to do all the security work they do now, but with only a token force, although they know a strong Palestinian police force is absolutely necessary to achieve what they want, peace and quiet in Gaza and the West Bank."[93]

Over time, the Israelis did accept this number, and Arafat would secretly equip even more security men than the expanded quota allowed, and with far more sophisticated weapons as well. He would still maintain, however, that this force—the highest ratio of police to population in the world—was insufficient to stop terrorism against Israel. Arafat's real motives were to provide additional jobs for supporters, keep potential rivals in line, and have more troops to fight Israel if or when the peace process broke down.

For the moment, though, the crisis was defused, and the two sides worked out the details for instituting Arafat's rule over Gaza and Jericho. As always with Arafat, talks went down to the last minute and beyond. In early May, the final round was held in Cairo, just down the corridor from Mubarak's office in the presidential palace. Each side was represented by a half dozen people, including Mubarak, Arafat, Rabin, and U.S. secretary of state Warren Christopher.[94]

The tense, exhausting session began in the afternoon and only finished the next morning. When everyone became hungry and found Mubarak's kitchen was closed for the night, two security men were dispatched to a new Pizza Hut nearby, which was open all night. Most of the delegates ate ravenously. Arafat just sat sipping his tea with honey.

The meeting lasted so long because Arafat had three demands on which he would not compromise: to enlarge the Jericho district, get more seacoast in Gaza, and put Palestinian policemen at the Jordan–West Bank and Egypt-Gaza border crossings. Rabin asked for a list of the twenty-four members of the PA's governing council, which was supposed to be included in the agreement. Although this had been requested for months, Arafat insisted it was a new demand. Seeing two Israeli delegates exchange smiles at this statement, Arafat blew up, retorting, "I'm a clown in your eyes, I know it. So go on, gentlemen, laugh."

Rabin replied, "Mr. Chairman, we treat you with the utmost respect. But you're obliged to honor that agreement."

Arafat complained, "You promised me answers about the policemen on the [border]. You promised me an answer about the size of the Jericho sector. Now you're humiliating me with offers of a kilometer here and a kilometer there. You have the upper hand. You decide."

Rabin agreed to make the Jericho area larger, but still Arafat continued to demand more concessions. Mubarak finally had enough. Leaning across the table, he asked Arafat, "Which of these three issues is the most important thing to you?"

After a pause, Arafat replied, "We want more Gaza beachfront."

Mubarak shouted at the Israelis, "Give them some more beachfront!"

The Israelis conferred and proposed a small extension. Then Mubarak said, "Ok! We're finished."

Arafat was startled, "But I have two more issues!"

"We're finished!" Mubarak answered with a withering stare at the Palestinian leader. It was 2 A.M., and the delegates were all eager for sleep.

One delegate from each side stayed behind to do the final drafting. They only completed the maps, showing who would rule where, by 10:30 A.M. on May 4, a half hour before the signing ceremony was supposed to start. The texts were rushed to Cairo's convention center through horrendous traffic jams, arriving moments before Arafat, Rabin, Clinton, and Mubarak came on stage before an audience of twenty-five hundred people and worldwide live television coverage. Shortly thereafter, sitting at the ornate gold-leaf and marble-topped table, Arafat signed the two-hundred-page document first, and it was then passed to Rabin. The Israeli prime minister noticed that Arafat had not initialed any of the six maps annexed to the agreement.

Rabin stood up, approached Arafat, and insisted that he sign them. Arafat refused, saying he believed that the Jericho area to be ruled by the PA was smaller on the map than what had been agreed the previous night.[95] Making such a last-minute scene was a typical way that Arafat demanded more concessions and showed his people that he would fight over every square inch of territory without giving up anything himself.

An angry Rabin threatened to halt the ceremony. In the confusion, Peres and Mubarak began whispering. Meanwhile, Sha'th, who had negotiated the final details, came up to the stage to examine the maps. According to one account, he had fallen asleep after the all-night session and had not had time to give Arafat a last-minute briefing.[96]

Mubarak, the host, was outraged. "Sign, you son of a dog!" he yelled at Arafat. Christopher interposed himself between them. Rabin summoned his motorcade and prepared to leave. Dennis Ross, the chief U.S. negotiator, walked on stage and suggested calling a recess, which was soon announced. The audience was stunned. The feuding leaders walked off stage. During that recess, Arafat asked Rabin for a letter promising to discuss at a future time the three issues Arafat had raised the previous evening. Rabin said he had already agreed to do so and had also accepted the expansion of PA territory in Jericho and Gaza. But if Arafat wanted such a letter, he could have it.[97]

When everyone returned to the stage, Arafat signed the maps with a lengthy note that he was doing so only if Israel would discuss enlarging the Jericho area and stationing Palestinian policemen at the crossing points with Egypt and Jordan. After getting Arafat's note translated, Rabin, too, signed.[98]

It appeared, then, that Arafat had kept alive his chance to get more on all three issues without the slightest concession or equivalent gesture. Yet, clever as his followers might consider such maneuvers, Arafat's readiness to wreck deals by focusing on minor details and making demands that had no chance of being met stirred up so much mistrust and friction with his interlocutors as to be counterproductive. Thus, as often happened with Arafat's management of the peace process, what he actually achieved was to reduce his chances of getting Israeli concessions or international support.

After the signing ceremony, Arafat tried to ease the friction by saying that coexistence was not only possible but inevitable. He concluded, "Our people extend [our] hand to the Israeli people to start this era and end the whirlpool of violence for the sake of our real interests." Arafat's closing speech claimed the agreement had "restored Palestine's name on the Middle East map."[99] His frequent insistence that a Palestinian state already existed and that he was its president showed either a failure to understand the peace process's terms or a refusal to abide by them.[100]

The birth of a state called Palestine was supposed to come at the process's end—and even then only after he made a full peace treaty with Israel—and not at the start. By pretending that Palestine's statehood did not depend on the process's success or on Israel's agreement, Arafat helped delay that state's coming into being. By emphasizing hopes and wishful thinking rather than working effectively on matters of substance like building institutions or a successful economy, Arafat repeatedly fostered friction and mistrust while failing to lay the necessary foundation for resolving the conflict.[101]

Palestine's independence day was also set by such considerations. The celebratory occasion did not take place in either May, when the PA began operations, or July, when Arafat returned to Gaza and was sworn

Arafat at the front line in Jordan, where the PLO staged attacks across the border into Israel, September 25, 1969 (AP/Wide World Photos).

Arafat in Cairo, Egypt, walking with General Emile Boustany (r), commander-in-chief of the Lebanese army, and Mahmoud Riyad, Egyptian foreign minister, after signing the November 1969 Cairo agreement, which allowed PLO military units to attack from south Lebanon near the Israeli border (AFP Photo).

Arafat on August 6, 1970, flashes a V-for-victory sign from PLO headquarters in Amman, Jordan, on the eve of the civil war he will lose (AFP Photo).

Arafat at a ceremony in Cairo, Egypt, to mark the end of forty days of mourning for his patron, President Gamal Abd al-Nasser, on November 6, 1970 (AP/Wide World Photos).

Arafat embraces his ally
Iraqi president Saddam
Hussein on September 25,
1980, during the early days
of the Iran-Iraq war
(AFP Photo).

Arafat is surrounded by
heavy security as he leaves
Beirut at the Lebanese
government's request and
as Israeli forces besiege the
city, August 30, 1982 (AFP
Photo).

Arafat speaking at the opening session of the PNC meeting in Algiers, November 12, 1988. At the conference's end, Arafat declared an independent Palestinian state (AFP Photo).

Arafat walks with Libyan revolutionary committee member Mustafa Kharoubi in Tripoli, Libya, on April 9, 1992, leaving the hospital where he was taken after surviving a plane crash in the Libyan desert (AP/Wide World Photos).

U.S. president Bill Clinton stands between Arafat and Israeli prime minister Yitzhak Rabin as they shake hands on September 13, 1993, on the White House lawn after signing the Oslo Agreement (AFP Photo).

Arafat in Cairo on May 4, 1994, being questioned by (l-r) Israeli foreign minister Shimon Peres, Russian foreign minister Vladimir Kosyrev, Israeli prime minister Yitzhak Rabin, Egyptian foreign minister Amr Musa, and Egyptian president Husni Mubarak after he briefly refused to sign an agreement that would begin his rule over the Gaza Strip and Jericho (AFP Photo).

Arafat on July 1, 1994, as he enters the Gaza Strip to begin his Palestinian Authority government there (AFP Photo).

Arafat dances during the celebration of the sixth anniversary of his Palestinian independence declaration at al-Azhar University in Gaza City on November 16, 1994 (AFP Photo).

Arafat raises his hand during the PNC meeting in Gaza on April 24, 1996, that voted 504–54 to revoke clauses in the PLO Charter calling for the liquidation of Israel. In later years, he would neither discipline nor criticize lieutenants who said that the charter had never been changed (AP/Wide World Photos).

Arafat's wife, Suha, carries the couple's daughter, Zahwa, in the West Bank town of Bethlehem after a ceremony with President Bill Clinton on December 15, 1998 (AFP Photo).

Arafat, Israeli prime minister Ehud Barak, and President Bill Clinton on July 11, 2000, at Camp David, Maryland, the U.S. presidential retreat, during their historic peace talk summit (AFP Photo).

Arafat inspects his damaged headquarters in the West Bank town of Ramallah on June 6, 2002, after Israeli forces ended the siege there. It was twenty years to the day since Israeli forces had begun the attack in Lebanon that drove Arafat out of the country (AP/Wide World Photos).

in as its leader, or even delayed for some future time when a peace treaty would lead to real independence. Instead, the holiday was placed on November 15 to coincide with the PNC's 1988 Declaration of Independence, thus disconnecting that status from the Oslo process.[102]

Equally, Arafat's construction of a Palestinian national identity often seemed deliberately structured to deny the existence of any Jewish history in the land between the Jordan River and the Mediterranean Sea and thus any basis for Israel's existence. Arafat continued to insist that it was the Palestinians who had always lived on the land, built all of its civilizations, and created both Judaism and Christianity there.[103]

In such ways, even at his most apparently conciliatory moments, Arafat made statements which threw into question his intentions. A few days after the Cairo meeting, Arafat went to South Africa for the inauguration of President Nelson Mandela. There, Arafat had his first meeting with Israeli president Ezer Weizman. Arafat and his entourage were heavily armed. Weizman asked, "Why do you need so many pistols?" Arafat replied, "I was warned that there are people in South Africa who are after me and might attempt to assassinate me." South African security denied there had been any such threats. At any rate, the Arafat-Weizman meeting was a cordial one.[104]

A few hours later, however, Arafat delivered a fiery address in a closed meeting at a Johannesburg mosque. A transcript leaked out and was closely perused as a reflection of Arafat's true sentiments on the verge of his return to establish the PA. In the talk, Arafat claimed that "the *jihad* would continue until Jerusalem was liberated." He also compared his agreement with Israel to a treaty Muhammad had made with a Jewish tribe some 1,350 years earlier, which broke down with the result that the Muslims wiped out the Jews.[105]

Arafat's advocacy of *jihad* and his favorable citing of a case where the Muslim side signed a peace agreement at a time of weakness which let them recover and destroy the Jews seemed to hint at his insincerity about peace. To make matters worse, Arafat responded to criticism not only by insisting that *jihad* meant "peace," not holy war, but also accusing Israel of behaving like the ancient Jewish tribe and violating its agreement. Neither the speech nor his defense of what he had said was a promising sign.

Whether or not the speech revealed Arafat's real plans, it certainly reflected his ambiguities. Arafat often referred to the PNC's 1974 strategy as his justification for reaching the Oslo Agreement. Was he using this as a rationale to let him make peace with Israel or as a signal that the two-stage plan to eliminate Israel was still in effect?

Arafat and his top colleagues stopped referring publicly to Israeli cities as part of Palestine and called only for a West Bank/Gaza Palestinian state with its capital in East Jerusalem. But some officials, as well as the PA-controlled media and educational system, continued to talk in traditional terms as if little or nothing had changed. Arafat's strategy of refusing to criticize the radicals or teach moderation ensured that he kept more radical forces, including those within Fatah, in line. But it also made certain that most would consider only hard-line stances to be patriotic and legitimate, as his people were still taught to applaud anti-Israel terrorism and to view moderation as bordering on treason.

He was equally reluctant to decide whether the Palestinian use of violence was a threat endangering the peace process or an asset helping him make Israel yield more. As happened so often in his career, Arafat did not understand that violence was counterproductive. Rabin and Peres, most of Israel's intelligentsia and media, and a majority of its electorate believed him to be ready for peace. To achieve real con-ciliation, they felt it necessary to prove their own sincerity and to avoid demanding more than Arafat could give. But the distrust arising from Arafat's trickiness, ambiguity, and, at best, minimal meeting of obli-gations, undermined these leaders and their claims. In the end, his strategy of violence, high demands, and low compliance failed to win him a state, lost him a tremendous opportunity, and inflicted a high cost on his people.

At the time, though, this all lay in the future. Despite misgivings and Arafat's smuggling in of notorious terrorists, hope still remained high on July 1, 1994, when Arafat returned to Gaza. Israeli forces had pulled out earlier, and the transition went rather peacefully.

Arafat began his trip by leaving Tunis for Cairo on an Air Algerie Mystere-20 jet. He was accompanied by Marwan Kanafani, his media advisor, and Zakaria al-Agha, a veteran activist from the Gaza Strip. These two men's presence indicated Arafat's top priorities. While Kanafani cultivated his image internationally, Agha, his choice to lead Fatah in Gaza, would ensure his total control of the domestic scene. Arafat preferred Agha to the more charismatic, energetic local Fatah leaders precisely because he was colorless, not especially popular, and ready to do whatever Arafat told him. This was to be a model for many of Arafat's other appointments.

They visited Mubarak and then drove to the border. "The last time I left for Gaza it was a secret trip," he told reporters. "Now I'm returning to the first free part of Palestine. You have to imagine how this is moving my head and my heart."[106]

After kissing the ground in Rafia, just inside Gaza's border with Egypt, Arafat bypassed the honor guard and local notables there to welcome him. His motorcade sped off to Gaza City, almost twenty miles north. From the sunroof of his black armor-plated Mercedes,

Arafat emerged briefly to wave to people along the route. Some admirers fired automatic weapons in the air, others waved Palestinian flags or carried Arafat's picture.

His first stop was the Jabilya refugee camp, where the Intifada began in 1987. Thousands of youths cheered Arafat who, in turn, praised them and explained that the agreement with Israel "is the best we can get in the worst situation," about the only justification he ever gave for it to his people. Led by Arafat, the crowd chanted their readiness to sacrifice "blood and spirit" for their leader and the cause, a slogan often associated with violent struggle.[107]

Then he went on to Gaza City to deliver his main speech for the day to a crowd estimated at between fifty and eighty thousand people. Given the occasion's historic nature, Arafat's oration was an almost startling anticlimax, consisting mostly of his standard phrases. He paid tribute to Sheikh Ahmad Yasin, the Hamas leader and his major rival for popularity, vowing to fight for his and all Palestinian prisoners' release from Israeli jails. Other themes included the need for national unity, Jerusalem's importance as the future capital, and a call for "even more courage from [both sides] in order to protect . . . peace."[108] He concluded, "We have lots of work to do to build our Palestinian National Authority and then our free independent Palestinian state."[109]

The PA did indeed have to carry out the staggering job of nation building, for which it had almost no experience. Arafat-the-revolutionary was supposed to become Arafat-the-statesman and Arafat-the-bureaucrat. Arafat's list of the tasks required showed how much there was to be done. The PA had to build "a legal system, infrastructure, job programs, economic production, agriculture, a social security and educational system; finding export markets; attracting capital from abroad for investment; rehabilitating freed prisoners; developing health and childhood and women's projects; and organizing village councils and city government." It also needed to establish a court system and just about every other institution while also performing such day-to-day tasks as making sure the garbage was picked up, mail delivered, and people employed.[110]

Arafat had always seen himself as a political revolutionary but never as a social or economic one. Still, it was one thing for him to have refused to discuss what his state would be like back in the 1960s, when "victory" was a long way off, and something quite different for him to act the same way when he was ruling more than two million people. Aside from his personal disinterest in such matters and concern that building institutions would undermine his full personal control over everything, Arafat also evidently thought that a focus on living standards or social reform would make people less eager to pay the cost of continuing struggle. He was reluctant to do anything to imply that the Palestine emerging from the Oslo Agreement would be a last stop. Impermanence was a symbol that both the immediate and long-term battle was not yet over.

In this context, Arafat had no interest in restructuring Palestinian society. On social issues, he could be profoundly conservative and traditional.[111] At the same time, Arafat's policy was designed to maintain a broad front uniting those PLO officials and soldiers arriving from abroad with both the local Gaza and West Bank residents and those living in refugee camps. "Everybody is building the homeland, hand in hand, because it is the homeland of all Palestinians," he explained.[112]

His conservatism did not extend, however, to a belief in promoting hard work and self-reliance. Arafat never appealed, as did other Third World leaders, to his people to focus on producing wealth or getting a good education. And he never acknowledged that the Oslo process had brought him huge financial assets for helping them, advantages no other Third World state enjoyed in a transition to independence. If he had done so, Arafat would then have had to explain to his people why they received so little benefit from this massive aid. His own policies were the greatest barrier to achieving economic progress or higher living standards.

Instead, Arafat immediately began complaining that international aid was insufficient, too slow in arriving, and too tied up with restrictions.[113] Of course, Arafat's dislike for the donors' constraints was precisely because these were intended to ensure that waste and corruption were minimized and that the aid was spent for the intended purpose. While donors meant for the funds to benefit the Palestinian people and to lay the basis for a strong infrastructure and stable state, Arafat wanted to use the money to ensure his political control, benefit his supporters, and build a strong paramilitary force. He was responsible for the poor use of funds and massive corruption.[114] By the same token, Arafat complained about the economic terms of the agreements with Israel, forgetting that he was the one who had negotiated them.[115]

Arafat was not interested in money for himself. In keeping with his ascetic lifestyle, he chose a modest house in Gaza. Yet he also was less concerned about the state of the economy than about what he called "political money," which could be used secretly to promote PLO influence in East Jerusalem (a violation of the Oslo Agreement) and for various bribes or subsidies for individuals. Foreign aid money given to build apartments in Gaza for poor people was used to construct luxury housing for high-ranking PA officials, including those in Arafat's security services.[116]

Whether in choosing an international telephone service or building a hotel, Arafat wanted to direct each project personally. "I am not an economics theoretician, but I know what to do to make a company and its workers prosperous," he declared.[117] But instead, when he took over one of Gaza's most successful enterprises, a privately owned flour mill, he bankrupted it by bad decisions. When a delegation of Turkish engineers offered to raise money for projects to help Gaza, Arafat replied that he was an engineer, so they could just give him the money and he would spend it properly. The Turks gave up. He refused to set up a tax system because that would lower his popularity.[118]

PA monopolies ensured a flow of cash to Arafat's regime and its officials while stifling private enterprise. Bribes and bureaucratic hold-ups discouraged foreign investment and demoralized Palestinian businesspeople. At the same time, he let crackpots, incompetent engineers, and dishonest businessmen talk him into schemes that were unprofitable, impractical, or criminally corrupt. Much money was wasted, for example, by letting a contractor who personally persuaded Arafat to give him the job of building Gaza port facilities that were washed away by the first storm. Another of Arafat's main Gaza projects was an orange juice canning factory for whose products no export market existed.[119] A Palestinian engineer wailed, "It is hard to imagine how things could be managed more poorly."[120]

Of course, the PA's task of construction was tremendous. "We drink polluted water," Arafat complained, "the electricity grid is inefficient, and the schools operate in three daily shifts with more than 65 pupils in each class."[121] Arafat's domain was hardly an oil kingdom but only part of a tiny land—totaling six thousand square kilometers—with a small population, no heavy industry, and no valuable resources. The gross national product was barely $2.9 billion. Palestinians could not move easily among the PA's cities because of Israeli roadblocks.[122] Their high birth rate—38.1 per thousand people in Gaza—brought additional pressures for creating jobs, income, and facilities.[123]

Coming so comparatively late to state building, a result of Arafat's long refusal to take the necessary steps to enter a peace process, Palestinians found many economic niches already filled by others and the Middle East oil boom long over. The UN Relief and Works Agency (UNRWA), to which the United States was a major contributor, had to reduce educational and welfare services due to declining international contributions to its budget as Arab states gave even less money.[124]

After the 1993 Israel-PLO agreement, nearly $3.5 billion was pledged by donors to the PA in aid and, according to the PA, $2.5 billion of it was disbursed over the next five years. Of this amount, about 50 percent came from European countries, 13 percent from the United States, 13 percent from Japan, and about 5 percent from Western-controlled international lending institutions. Only 8.6 percent—$210 million—came from Arab states (and 60 percent of the Arab donation came from Saudi Arabia alone). Even then, Arab states actually sent less than 45 percent of the amount they had pledged to the PA. In contrast, Norway by itself gave more money than all of the Arab states combined.[125]

According to Toni Verstandig, who handled the peace process's economic aspects as a U.S. assistant secretary of state, Arafat's only economic concern was "money for police salaries and government employees." He complained about there being so much more U.S. investment in Israel than in the PA territories, without considering his need to create an attractive climate for business by stopping violence and moving quickly toward a peace treaty.[126]

Starting in November 1993, Verstandig regularly met with Arafat, urging him to set up pluralist and democratic institutions and to institute better economic policies. But Arafat merely kept repeating, "Miss Toni, I need my money. The Arabs aren't going to give me my money. I have to help my people. Miss Toni, you go to the Saudis." She did. The United States, and to some extent Israel, became Arafat's fundraisers in Europe and the Middle East.[127]

It became clear that, despite their passionate claims of support for the Palestinian cause, Arab leaders were simply not interested in helping and privately expressed contempt and distrust for Arafat. Instead of giving funds to the PA, Iraq, Syria, and Libya bankrolled its Palestinian rivals opposed to the peace process.[128] While giving small amounts to specific projects—especially the United Arab Emirates and Qatar for housing—Gulf Arabs donated far less money than they had before the 1990 Kuwait crisis and only a tiny proportion of what they easily could have provided. Verstandig and other U.S. officials told Gulf Arabs, "You can't expect the United States to do more for the Palestinians than you do." But wealthy Gulf Arab states preferred spending money at home or investing profitably in the West.[129]

When Assistant Secretary of State Robert Pelletreau approached Kuwaiti leaders in 1994 seeking donations, the emir and crown prince complained, "Arafat never apologized to us for his role in supporting Iraq's invasion." Shortly thereafter, Pelletreau met with Arafat and suggested that he make some type of apology to Kuwait in whatever words he chose. Arafat became angry and retorted, referring to his few years as an employee of the Department of Public Works there, "Don't you know? I helped build Kuwait!" It was as if the Kuwaitis were being ungrateful to him personally, regardless of the way he had behaved toward them.[130]

Due to Arafat's decisions and performance, then, the already fragile Palestinian economy was dependent on factors whose support he undermined. Western donors, unhappy with how Arafat handled their money, and wealthy Arabs, angry at his treatment of them, reduced financial support. Meanwhile, as continuing violence brought Israeli border closures and increased feelings of insecurity, Israeli employers laid off or fired their Palestinian workers.[131] The number of Palestinians employed in Israel, where they made double the salary available to them in the West Bank and Gaza Strip, declined from 120,000 in 1993— 33 percent of the PA labor force—to only 30,000 in 1995. After a slight recovery when violence went down and the peace process seemed headed for a successful conclusion in the late 1990s, the number collapsed to near zero after the Palestinians launched a full-scale war in late 2000.[132]

One of the main reasons many had expected the peace process to succeed was the belief that actually governing a territory—being responsible for schools, roads, and garbage collection—would force Arafat to become more pragmatic in order to deliver benefits for his people. In practice, however, Arafat preferred his traditional political style, which depended on tough bargaining, minimal implementation of commitments, appeals for international support, pleas to negotiating partners for unilateral concessions, persuading extremists that he was on their side, and permissiveness toward violence to gain his objectives.

From the beginning, the problem of terrorism—and what Arafat would or could do to stop it—was a particularly important issue in determining whether the peace process would succeed. Dissident Palestinians quickly challenged the new arrangements put in place by the Israel-PLO agreement and discovered that Arafat did not react fully or effectively to stop them. Encouraged by the lack of repression and Arafat's failure to delegitimize their actions or mobilize Palestinian public opinion against them, they escalated their offensive.

On May 20, 1994, in one of the first attacks of the peace process era, Hamas killed two Israeli soldiers in the Gaza Strip. In response, Israel imposed the first of many border closures, demanding that the PA police find the culprits.[133] But although the police failed to catch the killers, Israel soon ended the closure. Rabin and Peres were ready to pressure Arafat to crack down on those responsible for attacks yet also believed that advancing the peace process was the best way to reduce the violence and defeat the terrorists. When the three men met in October at an economic summit in Morocco, their discussion on this issue mirrored many others that Arafat would have with Israeli leaders over the next six years.

While Arafat agreed on the need to "fight the fanatics," he disclaimed his own responsibility by denying they were a local problem and insisting they were directed and financed from abroad. He also did not want Israel to use closures or other methods to pressure him into acting effectively against the terrorists. Instead, Arafat urged Israel to release Yasin, the spiritual leader of Hamas. "He will have an influence on the extremists. I know him. He will call for an end to the violence."

Rabin responded, "We've checked. He's not prepared to do that." Rabin was right. When Yasin was released by Israel two years later, he proved to be a major advocate of increased terrorism. At any rate, Rabin put the emphasis on what Arafat should do: "It's vital that you yourself continue to combat terrorism. That's the key struggle. Public opinion is rebellious in Israel. There are calls among the Jews to kill me."

"Me, too," Arafat said, noting Palestinians might assassinate him.[134]

Arafat also avoided his own need to act decisively by blaming the anti-Israel terrorism on Israel and claiming that Rabin was using security as an excuse to escape its own commitments or even to destroy the PA. In negotiating sessions, Arafat would ask, "Is [the problem here] real security . . . or is it blah, blah [nonsense]?"[135] Arafat complained that Israel "took advantage" of attacks to delay withdrawals and establish new settlements. Arafat described this as "the peace of the siege."[136] And the language he used in 1995 against Rabin at what seemed the peak of a successful peace process was indistinguishable from his accusations against Prime Minister Ariel Sharon in 2002 at the peak of conflict.

Arafat's alternative was for Israel to take greater risks and trust him to reach a political solution which would resolve all problems. Rabin and Peres accepted this argument in the belief that putting up with attacks and casualties would eventually be rewarded when Arafat offered a reasonable deal, conciliation, and full peace.[137]

In the peace process's early years, there were times that Arafat did make reasonable efforts to implement his commitment to stop terrorism. His own men in Fatah were rarely involved in attacks. Arafat periodically tried to get Hamas to stop as well, at times arresting many of its activists and holding them without trial for months.

Arafat also worked with Israel to defuse some crises. For example, in October 1994, Israeli army corporal Nachshon Wachsman was kidnapped by Hamas terrorists who demanded the release of Yasin and two hundred of their comrades imprisoned for previous attacks. Israeli intelligence thought Wachsman was being held in a Gaza area ruled by Arafat, but Arafat insisted to Rabin, "He's not in Gaza, and I don't know where he is. It's not my people who have him."[138] The Israelis later learned that Arafat was right and had ordered his security forces to find Wachsman, who was eventually located in a West Bank town still under Israeli control, though his captors killed him during an Israeli rescue attempt.

Yet there was also much evidence that Arafat was tolerating Hamas and other terrorist groups, making him seem unworthy of trust and likely to take advantage of Israeli concessions to create a more dangerous situation. Basically, he saw the militants' attacks—though not always their timing—as strengthening his position. In addition, he did not want pressure on Hamas to lead to a Palestinian civil war, make him look like an Israeli puppet, or antagonize it so much that it would refuse to become his junior partner.

As Hamas escalated its violence, trying to wreck the peace process in 1995, Arafat's response was complex and contradictory. He had a special incentive to persuade Hamas to stop its offensive because as long as high levels of terrorism continued, Israel would not turn over the West Bank towns to him. One step he took was to establish special military courts to handle "security crimes."[139] These convicted forty-six Palestinians in the 1995–1997 period, giving sentences of up to twelve or fifteen years.[140] Israel charged that while sentences seemed severe, at least eleven of those convicted were soon released, most in exchange for agreeing to join Fatah.[141] Moreover, they were tried for "damaging the Palestinian people's interests," rather than for murder, implying that their real crime was not killing Israelis but doing so at a time or place contrary to Arafat's policy.

While Israeli intelligence officials found Arafat eager to appear helpful when approached with specific requests, he usually did nothing about them. As head of Shin Bet, Israel's equivalent of the FBI, Yakov Peri met Arafat fifteen or twenty times in 1994–1995 on such matters: "We repeatedly gave him the names of those who were preparing or might be preparing terrorist acts. He never said no to these requests. . . . There was a nice atmosphere. The first few times I thought my message was delivered and he would respond. But nothing was done."[142]

"He cheated us a lot," added Carmi Gillon, Peri's successor and a strong supporter of the peace process. When given a list of people Israel said were involved in terrorism, Arafat would reply, "He's not in Gaza," "He's a farmer," or "I checked out your information, and it's not good enough."[143] When asked to do more, Arafat's characteristic responses included: "I can't deliver it," "My people will refuse," "I agree with you. You're 100 percent right, but I can't do it, they will kill me." At other times, he would say, "It's your problem, it's not mine," "Give me intelligence and I'll take care of these people," or "I know better than you how to treat Hamas."[144]

Even to Rabin's face, Arafat untruthfully insisted that Ibrahim Ayyash, the chief Hamas bomb maker, whose creations killed many Israelis in 1994 and 1995, was in Sudan and that no one had seen him in Gaza, where Arafat ruled.[145] He stuck to that story up to the moment Israeli agents killed Ayyash by blowing up his mobile phone as he stood in the middle of a Gaza street.

Arafat also defended his performance by asking how he could be expected to dismantle the Hamas terrorist infrastructure when Israel had failed to do so when it ruled the West Bank and Gaza.[146] But this implied that Arafat failed to understand a central premise of the peace process. If Arafat did a worse job than a direct Israeli presence in stopping violence, what was the advantage of ceding more land to him? If efforts to end the occupation provoked as much violence as maintaining it, what did this tell about Arafat's goals? If Arafat was so unable to stop terrorism, either his competence or his sincerity would have to be questioned.

It was no accident that there had never been a suicide bombing inside Israel before 1994, when Arafat arrived in Gaza, though travel between the territories and Israel had been far more open in those earlier years. Most terrorist attacks on Israel had to come across borders with Arab states, usually Jordan and Lebanon, for a very good reason. By controlling the West Bank and Gaza, Israel was able to stop guns and explosives from coming in or was able to capture them quickly. Terrorists had no safe haven where they could recruit and train men, build bombs, plan operations, or move close to targets in Israel's cities. Those perpetrating attacks could usually be quickly rounded up afterward.

But once Arafat was in the West Bank and Gaza Strip and Israel was gone, staging larger-scale, more frequent attacks in Israel's cities became easier. Smuggling and hiding military equipment was more possible. Terrorist groups could operate openly and even run bomb factories. Terrorist leaders and key personnel were almost immune from arrest, while the PA rounded up those who helped Israel gather intelligence. The idea of the Oslo Agreement was that Israel's departure, the presence of a Palestinian regime, and the expectation of independence in the near future would reduce terrorism. Instead, the level of attacks on Israelis and casualties zoomed upward.

This problem was also related to Arafat's continued exaltation of the culture of armed struggle. Terrorist acts were constantly presented as legitimate and heroic. This was what young Palestinians were taught in their schools and what everyone was told by the PA-controlled media. Rather than explain the dangers of violence, Arafat and his colleagues hardly ever portrayed Israeli measures such as closures or delaying negotiations to their people as inevitable reactions to Palestinian attacks.[147] Only rarely did Arafat speak in a different manner, as at a February 1995 Gaza rally, after Israel had responded to an attack by quarantining the whole area. He asked, "Who is the genius who set out to close off the [Gaza] Strip and deprive its residents of basic staples? Who is the man organizing these conspiracies against Palestinian children, hospitals, and the Gaza Strip industry?"[148]

But Arafat's frequent answer to that question was to create wild theories that Israeli extremists or even the Israeli government itself was behind anti-Israel terrorism. He called Hamas a creation of Israel and at one point accused Israel's chief of staff under Rabin, General Ehud Barak, of planning a coup to stop the peace process.[149] By portraying Hamas as an Israeli puppet—which he knew not to be true—Arafat disclaimed any need to take action in meeting his foremost commitment under the peace agreement and the main criterion by which his role as negotiating partner would be judged.[150]

Arafat made no secret of his view that the threat and practice of violence was his best bargaining chip. He told an Israeli negotiator in the summer of 1995, "I know there are two ways to reach a Palestinian state, through the negotiating table and through a war of independence. We can accept a lot of casualties, thirty thousand martyrs. Can you accept five hundred Israeli soldiers killed?"[151]

Of course, Palestinian suspicion of Israel was understandable, a natural response given the long, bitter conflict and the fact that many within Israel still opposed a Palestinian state. There were many specific Palestinian grievances regarding Israel's implementation of the agreements, including delayed or limited prisoner releases, roadblocks, and real or alleged settlement expansion. But Arafat usually portrayed these things not as individual problems but as proof that the conflict was continuing. This attitude, and its influence on the Palestinian masses, would be something of a self-fulfilling prophecy.

For example, in preparing for the 1995 Middle East economic summit, Israel had good planning sessions with Jordan and Egypt, but no progress was made with the Palestinians. When an Israeli official asked Arafat why, he replied, "I gave the order not to coordinate, I can't be seen to collaborate with you."[152] There were obvious reasons for this concern but, by the same token, why should any Palestinian official or citizen believe cooperation and a compromise agreement would be beneficial when such an example was being set by their leader?

Moreover, as Arafat constantly encouraged mistrust of Israel and the need to struggle against it—quite different from the attitudes of Rabin, Peres, and later Barak (but not Netanyahu) toward him—he also undermined his own ability to make a final agreement that Palestinians would support. In contrast to Arafat's hostility, Rabin and Peres constantly defended Arafat's behavior, sometimes covering up his short-comings on implementation and insisting that he would make a viable agreement at the process's end. Despite temporary closures and post-ponements in response to terrorist attacks, they repeatedly made concessions in order to renew the talks and to ensure they moved forward toward a compromise deal.

Yet reaching a full peace agreement was no favor to Israel but a way of resolving the Palestinians' problems while even raising additional risks for Israel. Once land was turned over and a state established, Israel could not take back its concessions or stop Arafat from violating his commitments. In contrast, for Palestinians, a final agreement, even if it required concessions, would bring an end to occupation, national independence, the departure of Jewish settlers, and the return of ref-ugees to the state of Palestine.

Consequently, it made sense for Arafat to be eager to advance to a full peace agreement, which should have given him an incentive to stop attacks on Israel, prepare his people for a compromise deal, and solve any other problem that stood in the way of completing the process. Often, however, Arafat himself delayed progress by his negotiating tactics and questionable implementation of previous commitments. He seemed to prefer an extended process in which Israel turned over more land but no final agreement was concluded, since this let him receive concessions without having to make a permanent arrangement.

If Arafat was going to expand his domain beyond the Gaza Strip and the tiny town of Jericho, he had to work out an agreement for Israel's withdrawal from West Bank towns. Yet Arafat was a slow and difficult negotiator, whether due to his profound suspicion of Israeli intentions, his desire to prove his iron steadfastness to Palestinians, or his belief that this was a good bargaining technique.

Contrary to the claims of Western observers that he "needed" to show rapid progress, Arafat was, as always, ready to draw out every point, reopen each question, and extend the debate on all issues until he had as close to everything he wanted as was conceivable. And even then he pushed further. The fact that some specific point was already settled in previous agreements made no difference to him. For example, in late 1994, Israel pointed out that the agreements gave it the right to approve any new Palestinian police stations established in areas of shared sovereignty.

"Yes, of course they will coordinate with you," said Arafat.

"No," said one Israeli negotiator, Major General Ilan Biran. "You know the difference. They will have to ask our permission."

Arafat replied, "That's why both sides must coordinate."

Peres repeated Biran's point. According to previous agreements signed by the PA, Israel had principal responsibility for security in the areas under discussion.

Arafat flew out of his chair. "What do you think? That my policemen will be subordinate to yours? That you'll humiliate my security people? That we'll ask your permission to move to a Palestinian village...to deal with a robbery or a family spat? That's not an agreement. I will not be shamed by you. I am not your slave!"

He stormed out of the room and gave the order for the Palestinian team to leave. Israeli negotiator Uri Savir went to Arafat's suite. "You really want to humiliate me," said Arafat. "Well, I prefer that there be no agreement." Peres then agreed to give in to Arafat's demand, despite Biran's opposition.[153] Yet Israeli concessions on this and many other issues never relieved Arafat's relentless pressure for more, never built up any feeling on Arafat's part that he owed reciprocity, or even elicited any positive statements about Israel in Arafat's speeches to Palestinians or by the media he controlled.

While Arafat's toughness with the Israelis slowed progress, the same was true of his handling of his own negotiators. As was his usual practice, Arafat would assign two people the same task and secretly tell them to take conflicting positions on the issue. He would build up a colleague and then quickly tear him down, sometimes in a humiliating fashion.[154] He often lost his temper, once screaming such insults at Sha'th over the telephone that the man collapsed in despair.[155] Sha'th admitted to Americans and Israelis alike that he never knew from one day to the next whether he would be in Arafat's favor or be pushed to the side.[156] The Palestinian negotiators' task was made even harder by the fact that Arafat was uninterested in the actual provisions of agreements and ignored briefings but would become obsessed with a particular detail or complain about the result after having agreed to it earlier.[157]

But since Arafat held all the power among Palestinians, anyone who wanted to remain involved or have any public role had to keep him happy. Demands for Arafat to change always collapsed in the face of this reality. Even Abu Mazin, the second most powerful PLO leader, was completely helpless. Arafat shoved him aside during the May 1994 Cairo talks, and it was Arafat alone who received the Nobel Peace Prize on the Palestinian side while Abu Mazin's counterpart, Peres, shared the honor with Rabin.[158]

In March 1995, almost half of the Fatah Central Committee charged that Arafat made all major decisions by himself. Seven of eighteen members angrily demanded that talks with Israel be suspended until a more representative negotiating team was selected. Yet while some dissatisfied leaders, like Abu Mazin and Abu Alaa, stressed the need for more democracy, others, including Qaddumi, Sakhr Habash, and Abbas Zaki, put the priority on ending the peace process. Arafat easily overcame his divided critics, forcing them to accept both continued negotiations and his monopoly on power.[159]

While Arafat never gave anything to those demanding more democracy, however, he did appease hard-line critics by constantly showing them how tough he was with Israel. He never punished those in Fatah or the media he controlled who expressed views rejecting his peace agreements or a two-state solution. Nor did Arafat ever organize any lobby favoring a deal with Israel. Those holding more moderate views were careful not to express them publicly or push them in high-level meetings. Insisting that Arafat demand more from Israel or demonizing that country carried no penalty; advocating compromise with Israel remained dangerous.

Although it took more than a year to conclude and sometimes involved screaming matches between Arafat and Peres, the two sides finally did reach the next step of the process. Under the Oslo-2 Agreement, Israel would turn over to the PA all of the West Bank towns except for Hebron, which required further negotiations.[160] At last, Arafat would be the undisputed ruler of two million Palestinians, taking another big step toward a peaceful independence.

On September 28, 1995, Arafat and Rabin met again on the White House lawn to sign this new agreement. In his speech, Arafat denounced terrorism, saying that violence was "not only morally reprehensible, but undermine[d] Palestinian aspirations to the realization of peace ... [and their] exercise of political and national options."[161]

For once, these last words proved truly prophetic.

7

There Is a Tide in the Affairs of Men

1995–1999

On January 20, 1996, Arafat won election as head of the Palestinian Authority. This mandate could have been his launching pad for reaching a peace agreement that would make him ruler of a Palestinian state. Within days, however, the peace process faced its greatest crisis. A wave of Palestinian terrorist attacks profoundly shook Israelis' trust in Arafat's intentions and abilities. In response, six weeks after Arafat's triumph at the polls, Israel elected a conservative government far more hostile to Arafat.

The Palestinian elections were a great success for Arafat.[1] The large turnout and relatively fair conduct, by the Arab world's standards, enhanced his legitimacy.[2] His opponent, Samiha Khalil, was a veteran DFLP activist who ran a Ramallah charitable organization and called for rejecting the Oslo Agreement. The PA-controlled media largely ignored her.[3] And since the main opposition group, Hamas, boycotted the election, Arafat easily won 85 percent of the ballots. "I was looking for 51 percent," he joked, knowing a less one-sided victory would have seemed more democratic.[4] He was almost equally successful in the Palestinian Legislative Council (PLC) election, in which Fatah gained two-thirds of the eighty-eight seats.[5]

A central premise of the Oslo Agreement had been that the PA's creation and free elections would ensure Arafat's transformation from a revolutionary using terrorist methods to a politician working hard to build a state. Having his own regime, loyal population, and financing by outside donors who would not interfere politically was supposed to free Arafat to make a compromise peace. By governing an actual population and a specific territory, Arafat would supposedly have to fulfill his citizens' demands for better living standards and aspirations for a state where they could live in peace and freedom. Thus, he would be forced to be pragmatic. Rather than continuing to fight, he would be motivated to abandon the violence that disrupted any chances to create a good school system, job opportunities, and a rapid transition toward independence.

There were several reasons why events belied these assumptions. One factor was that many Palestinians did not believe Israel would ever accept reasonable terms and that the peace process was a trick to ensure their permanent subjugation. While such beliefs were reinforced by specific Israeli actions and by the slow pace of talks, they far exceeded the evidence. To think that Rabin or Peres, and later Barak, wanted to keep control over the West Bank and Gaza Strip permanently was a serious misperception, which continued to have enormous negative consequences for Palestinian interests.

A second problem was that the Palestinian political world view, which had been largely created by Arafat, had a powerful hold on many and intimidated almost everyone else from creating a new one. How could Palestinians put behind them a half-century of hatred and decide to abandon violence against Israel without Arafat leading them in that direction? Why would they abandon the traditional objective of Israel's elimination and replacement by a Palestinian Arab state if Arafat did not tell them that such a goal was futile? Who would advocate ideas that the movement still likened to treason and cowardice? Arafat never really challenged the old principles or tried to replace them with the vision of a Palestinian state whose highest values would be stability, social and economic progress, and the repatriation of refugees to itself.

A third obstacle was Arafat's failure to abandon violence for much of the time. The Oslo Agreement was based on an assumption that Arafat would view anti-Israel violence as threatening his interests because it would delay an end to the occupation and a Palestinian state's birth. Actually, from the spring of 1996 through the summer of 2000, Arafat did work effectively to reduce the level of violence. This effort did encourage an Israeli government to offer him far more concessions in 2000 and made it possible to arrive finally at the point where final negotiations could be conducted then. Yet since Arafat did not dismantle the justifications for terrorism or its infrastructure, this made it easy for him to return to his traditional methods as he rejected those offers.

Finally, Arafat's disinterest in social or economic development and his insistence that such things await the establishment of a state robbed Palestinians of the peace process's immediate benefits. Since they received few interim gains, they had little incentive to protect the process or to believe in the value of compromise.

Yet despite all of these problems, Arafat could still have made peace if he had provided decisive leadership to close a deal with Israel at the process's end. It was reasonable to expect Arafat to act as dozens of other Third World politicians had done all over the world. Scores of nationalist leaders had transformed themselves into presidents of peaceful, if hardly utopian, states. Moreover, the Oslo Agreement only existed because Arafat had acted boldly on that occasion. Why then should he not repeat this feat to make a peace treaty with Israel?

With the establishment of the PA, Arafat was now, more than ever, an undisputed, unconstrained leader. A Palestinian magazine explained: "He holds all the reins, he controls all the money, he takes all the decisions... and he, by and large, is the only law whose authority is respected, established and enforced."[6] Since he shared power with no individuals or institutions, decision making virtually stopped when he was abroad or even away from his office for a day.[7] As one of his PLC critics, Ziyad Abu Amr, put it, "If there is an embodiment of institutionalization, Arafat's style of leadership is the antithesis."[8]

Arafat's political pattern was uniquely his own: a strange mixture of dictatorship and pluralism, repression and conciliation, weakness and tight control. In his pluralistic-conciliatory mode, he sought to avoid confrontation and build a united front. As he had once mollified PLO groups, he now worked to co-opt the Islamist opposition, reconcile former Palestinian exiles with local residents of the West Bank and the Gaza Strip, and bridge gaps between wealthy notables and young activists. As a "weak" leader, he let other groups do as they pleased—as long as they did not challenge his power and generally followed the political line and strategy he advocated.

Clearly, Arafat closely managed every PA decision and appointment. He used secret funds from which, like a traditional village leader, he handed out gifts to supporters.[9] Arafat constantly interfered with the PA bureaucracy's work, undermining its authority and making it afraid to act without his direct approval.[10] He insisted that the Palestinian media always support him. Anyone exposing abuses or questioning maximal Palestinian demands was said to serve Israel's interests, an approach making it acceptable to be more militant but not more moderate regarding the peace process, use of violence, and views of Israel.

This type of paternalistic control and ideological direction was displayed in Arafat's handling of the media. The PA controlled all of the main media outlets by a mix of ownership, licensing, censorship, and intimidation. Arafat wanted to ensure they protected his image and projected his will. He placed his own Gaza office not in the PA government compound, but in the small building housing the Palestine Broadcasting Corporation.[11]

The daily newspapers were quickly tamed. *Al-Quds* editor Mahir al-Alami was jailed in 1995 for putting an item about Palestinian Christian praise for Arafat on page 8 rather than page 1.[12] Arafat let him go after six days with a warning to be more cooperative. Thereafter *al-Quds* avoided displeasing Arafat.[13] Another newspaper, *al-Nahar*, was closed down in 1994 until it took a more pro-Arafat line.[14] No other Palestinian newspaper even reported these incidents.[15] Of the other two main newspapers, one was directly controlled by the PA and the other was edited by one of Arafat's most trusted advisors.

One way that the press served Arafat was to deflect criticisms and conceal information about PA misdeeds while provoking mistrust of the peace process. For instance, the newspapers claimed that Israel was selling spoiled foods in order to poison Palestinians, quoting officials in the PA's Supply Ministry. Unmentioned, however, were detailed PLC reports showing that senior PA officials—including Minister of Supply Abu Ali Shahin, one of Arafat's oldest cronies—were the ones selling such food for their personal profit.[16]

While Arafat controlled all of the newspapers in his domain, the one he most directly supervised was the PA's own *al-Hayat al-Jadida*. Even during the height of the peace process's apparent success, Arafat's official organ seemed to delight in the most provocative anti-Israel, anti-Jewish slurs, including frequent citations from the antisemitic czarist forgery *The Protocols of the Elders of Zion*. "The conflict between the Jews and the Muslims is an eternal and on-going conflict," one of its articles explained. "The fate of the Palestinian people is to struggle against the Jews on behalf of the Arab peoples, the Islamic peoples and the peoples of the entire world." The PA must, Arafat's newspaper told readers, "protect its people and itself from an enemy which bares its Jewish fangs from the four corners of the earth."[17] While other editors were harassed for publishing a single article that displeased Arafat, anti-Israel incitement was never reined in at all.[18]

Similarly, extremists were left alone while Arafat intimidated human rights or democracy advocates, including the Palestinian Independent Commission for Citizens Rights (PICCR), established by him in 1993 to "contribute to the development of democracy in Palestine." Iyad Sarraj, the PICCR leader, was arrested in 1995 and 1996 after accusing the PA of corruption.[19] When a visiting American asked about Sarraj's arrest, Arafat replied in Arabic, and his translator explained that Arafat said it was a regrettable matter and he was looking into it. Arafat angrily interrupted to complain that the translation was inaccurate. What he really had said was that Sarraj had insulted him and would pay for it.[20]

In June 1996, Sarraj was briefly arrested a third time, beaten, and charged with selling drugs and assaulting his interrogator.[21] In 1998, Arafat met with leaders of another human rights group and praised them. But shortly after they left, his police detained them for several hours to demand they stop criticizing the PA's abuses.[22]

Those few individuals appearing to threaten Arafat's regime directly suffered more serious consequences. In July 1996, Mahmoud Jumayyil, a popular Intifada-era leader in Nablus who challenged the local leadership, was killed while in police custody.[23] A PA military court sentenced three police officers to long prison terms for torturing him to death, but there was no investigation of whether high officials ordered his arrest or murder.[24] His funeral turned into an anti-PA demonstration outside the town prison. Police fired into the crowd, killing a Hamas member named Ibrahim Hadaya, who had served eight years in Israeli prisons and had just been released from five months in a PA jail.[25] Arafat lied about what had happened, telling reporters that armed Hamas men had tried to free prisoners and had killed Hadaya by mistake.[26] A PA military court sentenced five demonstrators to prison. In compensation, Arafat made Hadaya a "martyr of the revolution," gave his family a pension, and ordered his brother released from prison. Arafat also appointed a high-level committee to investigate the incident but, as usual, no report was issued or action taken.[27]

Yet the overwhelming majority did accept Arafat's personal rule, and even those who grumbled almost never acted. One reason for Arafat's success in this regard is that although he would not let himself be constrained by laws, courts, or parliament, Arafat was careful to maintain his popularity and consult others in the political elite. Equally, he cultivated top Palestinian figures on an individual basis, substituting for institutions the holding of frequent "leadership" meetings, to which those in his favor were invited.[28] He touched base with each interest group, taking into account the need to balance regions, religions, political affiliations, and even competence.[29] But Arafat could give or take away anyone's authority or position whenever he wanted.

The only institution that might have challenged Arafat was the elected PLC, but Arafat totally outmaneuvered it.[30] Arafat had a clear majority there, at least when he needed to mobilize it, and also claimed to lead that body as well. When attending PLC meetings, he sometimes sat in the speaker's seat to assert this status. Rawiya al-Shawwa, a non-Fatah member from Gaza who sometimes criticized Arafat, explained the prevailing viewpoint that "because he is the president, . . . he is the leader of the [PLC] members."[31] When Arafat resisted the PLC's attempts to demand more power, the legislature always backed down on patriotic and partisan grounds.

There Is a Tide in the Affairs of Men

As PLC member Ziyad Abu Amr, himself a critic of Arafat, recognized, the PLC could never have a showdown with the leader "at a time when the peace process suffers from serious deadlock and deterioration, a situation that compels the Palestinians and the PLC to turn their attention to the external Israeli challenge."[32] Abu Amr admitted, "There is no bloc in the PLC to oppose the [PA] or hold it accountable for its actions."[33] Ashrawi, another member who could be critical, admitted that within the PLC there were merely "different degrees of agreement" with Arafat.[34]

No one was more aware of this fact than Arafat himself. As long as Israel could be presented as a danger and there was no peace treaty, his position as total ruler was sacrosanct. All criticism could be swept away, national unity would be preserved, and demands for a wider distribution of power was always rejected. His real domestic risks would only begin once peace had arrived and a state was created. This gave him less of an incentive to cross that finish line, especially since many PLC members—like others in the PLO and Fatah elites—made it clear that any concession to Israel would be too much for them.

The power struggles between Arafat and the PLC followed a predictable course. The PLC threatened a vote of no-confidence against Arafat's cabinet, then Arafat responded by promising to improve his performance or to obey the courts and PLC decisions, but he never did anything of the sort. After a while, the PLC would do what Arafat wanted without receiving anything in return.

In 1996, for example, key PLC members demanded that Arafat release a thousand Hamas and Islamic Jihad supporters who had been arrested after a bombing campaign against Israeli civilians, in order to get a vote of confidence for his new cabinet.[35] At the June 5–6, 1996, session in Gaza, debate became especially heated. When PLC member Fakhri Turkman ridiculed some of his policies, Arafat angrily warned that critics would have to prove everything they said "or else I will ask the Council to take measures against them."[36] On June 20, the PLC formed a committee to meet with Arafat to demand that he implement PLC resolutions.[37] Arafat did release some prisoners but also went on the offensive.[38] On June 30, the Fatah Central Committee cautioned ten members who opposed a vote of confidence of suspension or expulsion unless they changed their stand.[39] A month later, the PLC approved the cabinet by a 50–24 vote.[40]

Of twenty-eight bills the PLC passed in 1996, Arafat only signed two of them—the Local Committee Councils Law and the Local Committee Councils Election Law. And Arafat did not even implement those two since he never fulfilled his periodic promises to hold local elections. Instead, he merely appointed mayors and other such officials. At the same time, he did not ratify such major legislation as the PLC's draft constitution and the Civil Service Law.[41]

Although a no-confidence motion was submitted to the PLC on November 7, 1996, it was soon dropped.[42] A year later, the PLC again threatened a no-confidence vote unless Arafat changed his cabinet, signed bills it had passed, and answered its corruption charges. On December 28, 1997, Arafat met with about fifty-five PLC members close to Fatah and promised to do better but suggested that the faltering peace process and his need to mobilize international support required national unity. Two days later, the threat of a no-confidence vote once more evaporated.[43]

Arafat controlled the courts as well. When he or his subordinates did not like judicial decisions, they simply ignored them. Even if the PA's Supreme Court ordered prisoners released, security forces held on to them until Arafat personally ordered otherwise.[44] When the Supreme Court's chief justice criticized Arafat, he was forced into retirement, and Arafat waited sixteen months to appoint a successor.[45] Attorney General Fa'iz Abu Rahma resigned in April 1998 to protest the leader's refusal "to respect the judiciary and the sovereignty of the law."[46]

In addition to dominating the PA, the PLC, and the court system, Arafat also controlled two other key Palestinian institutions, Fatah and the PLO. In October 1995, he convened a Fatah congress in Gaza attended by 469 delegates who accepted his policies and nominees to the Central Committee. While Fatah members on the West Bank had held primaries to choose candidates for the PLC elections, Arafat simply ignored the results and named his own slate, most of whom won seats in the general election.

The same was true of the PLO in general. At the April 1996 PNC meeting in Gaza, he added six new members to the Executive Committee and removed anti-Oslo dissidents, ensuring his majority. The next month, Arafat held the first Executive Committee meeting on PA soil and replaced the old secretary, who opposed the Oslo Agreement, with Abu Mazin.[47] Finally, Arafat reaffirmed his control over the PNC by adding to it all eighty-eight PLC members and about a hundred more West Bank and Gaza residents who supported him, thus expanding the PNC to 730 members. Since opponents of the Oslo Agreement boycotted PLO meetings, this weakened the active opposition and ensured Arafat's control.

But one of the PLO's commitments in the agreements with Israel was to abrogate its thirty-year-old Charter, which called for Israel's destruction through armed struggle. This step had enormous symbolic importance for both sides as an irreversible move toward a new, peace-oriented Palestinian world view. As it required a two-thirds vote of PNC

There Is a Tide in the Affairs of Men

members, Israel agreed to admit to Gaza all members of the PNC, scattered across the Arab world, who wanted to attend the session even if they were still involved in violence against it. In the end, Faruq Qaddumi and others still refused to attend at all because of their opposition to the Oslo Agreement.

On April 22, 1996, the PNC convened in Gaza, and Arafat proved himself the master of persuasion, showing he could be an effective advocate of peace when he chose to do so. He insisted that talks with Israel would produce a Palestinian state and demanded that the delegates revise the PLO Charter. "All revolutions end in agreements. Do you think you can get everything you want?" he demanded in an angry exchange with Abd al-Shafi. During a closed session, he warned that those who demanded Israeli concessions before changing the Charter were delaying the creation of a Palestinian state. "Where do you want to be buried, nowhere or in Palestine?" Arafat shouted.[48]

It was the moment when Arafat seemed closest to piloting the movement to a genuine transition. The final vote was 504–54 to remove the Charter's passages contrary to the Palestinians' new commitments and to have the PNC Legal Committee look into composing a new Charter.[49] The Israeli and U.S. governments hailed this action as an important step toward peace. On three different occasions thereafter, Arafat wrote formal letters to President Bill Clinton certifying the abrogation of the Charter's clauses demanding Israel's destruction through violence.

Yet, even here, despite such an apparently ironclad decision, Arafat managed to maintain ambiguity. He carried out no public discussion or educational effort among Palestinians about this apparently huge change in their historic goals. Meanwhile, the PNC's own leader, Salim al-Za'nun, one of Arafat's closest allies, and those in the Fatah hierarchy responsible for ideology denied that the Charter had been changed at all. Arafat did nothing to contradict or discipline them. The media he controlled broadcast material and interviews hinting that the goal was still Israel's elimination. As a result, Israelis critical of the Oslo Agreement insisted that Arafat had shown his true nature.

The same principles applied to Arafat's unwillingness to force radical groups to accept or at least not to violate the agreements he had made as the Palestinians' leader. Despite Arafat's overwhelming power, he did not want to foreclose either his own military option or the possibility of an alliance with Hamas. Israel and the United States had expected that Arafat would force all Palestinians to stop the violence. The more Israel was convinced of Arafat's willingness and ability to guarantee peace, the more concessions it would ultimately give him and the faster the progress toward creating a Palestinian state. Arafat's understanding of this process, however, was different. He implied that he was doing Israel a favor by trying to reduce terrorism rather than serving his own interests.

As a result, in 1995 alone, there had been thirty-three successful Palestinian armed attacks on Israelis that caused casualties. Hundreds more such operations had been foiled by Israeli security forces.[50] Convinced that Rabin was making enormous concessions and that Arafat had no intention of making peace, the Israeli right wing held massive demonstrations. In response, government supporters organized a major demonstration of their own in Tel Aviv just outside city hall. On the warm evening of November 4, 1995, tens of thousands gathered in a festive mood to show their support for the government. The guests of honor were Rabin and Foreign Minister Peres.[51]

After Rabin spoke, a singer cajoled the usually shy prime minister into joining in the chorus of a pro-peace song. Then Rabin and Peres left by the stairs behind the stage. The assassin, Yigal Amir, an extreme right-winger who believed that killing Rabin would stop the peace process, let Peres pass him and then shot Rabin, wounding a bodyguard who tried to save the prime minister.[52] The mortally wounded prime minister died soon after reaching the hospital.

When the U.S. consul general in Jerusalem, Edward Abington, called Arafat at his Gaza home that night to tell him the news, Arafat asked three times whether Rabin was really dead, then broke down in tears. "It had taken more courage to move toward peace with the Palestinians than Jordan and Egypt," he told the American diplomat, "and that is what in fact cost him his life."[53] Perhaps the assassination was also a reminder for Arafat that his own people might kill him for moving toward peace with Israel. King Abdallah of Jordan, President Bashir Gemayel in Lebanon, and President Anwar al-Sadat in Egypt had all suffered that same fate.

In what would be the first trip he would ever make to Israel, Arafat came to the Rabin house near Tel Aviv to offer condolences to the prime minister's widow, Leah Rabin. Demonstrating his respect for Jewish tradition, he even took off his *kaffiya* and put on a hat.[54] Arafat, however, was not permitted to attend the funeral due to security concerns and had to watch it on television from Gaza.

Arafat had professed to admire Rabin because the Israeli prime minister had been a general, a career path Arafat always envied. Ironically, Arafat had less personal regard for Peres, Rabin's successor and a career politician, who was far more positive about dealing with him though often frustrated by that experience.[55] Rabin was a pragmatist who sought peace as benefiting Israel's interests; Peres was a genuine enthusiast who had a vision of a happy Middle East as the result of a successful peace process.

Within Israel, the initial response to Rabin's assassination was a massive outpouring of support for his political legacy. Every poll showed increased backing for a compromise peace with the Palestinians, and a confident Peres decided to hold new elections, which he announced for May 1996. Everyone expected Peres to defeat the Likud party candidate, Benjamin Netanyahu, and to carry forward the peace process vigorously.

Peres, precisely because he was considered much softer on Arafat and security issues than Rabin, authorized the killing of the most effective Hamas terrorist, Yahya Ayyash, nicknamed the "engineer" by the Israeli press. Peres had to act against Ayyash because Arafat had refused to do so. Ayyash had made the bombs for a series of deadly attacks on buses in Israel—including those in July, August, and October 1994—and Israel had information that he was planning more. The Israelis knew Ayyash was in Gaza, but Arafat insisted he was in Sudan. Israel finally took matters into its own hands. In January 1996, Ayyash was killed in Gaza when he answered his cellular telephone, which had been packed with fifty grams of explosives.

Arafat and the PA "claimed he was in Sudan up to the moment when Ayyash was blown up," recalled the head of Israel's security agency, Carmi Gillon. "They did nothing against him, even though we gave [Arafat] intelligence" about Ayyash's activities and whereabouts.[56] While Arafat convened a military court to try some security officials who attended a Hamas memorial rally for Ayyash, he also permitted the PA-controlled media to make Ayyash a hero.[57] Arafat personally paid a condolence call on Hamas leaders to praise Ayyash and called him a "martyr" for the Palestinian cause.[58]

Hamas launched a wave of terrorist attacks in late February and early March 1996, making that the bloodiest month of terrorism in Israel's history. While maintaining publicly that these acts were to revenge Ayyash's death, Hamas had many other motives as well. At Arafat's earlier urging, Hamas had suspended terrorism, although only temporarily, so as not to interfere with Israel's withdrawal from West Bank towns and then the PA elections. These goals having been accomplished, Arafat had less incentive to stop terrorism, and Hamas, eager to return to action, had less reason to believe he would crack down on them. Moreover, since some elements in Hamas seemed ready to make a deal with Arafat, the more militant majority wanted to be sure their organization did not fall under Arafat's control.

These assaults badly shook the peace process. On February 25, a Hamas suicide bomber in Jerusalem blew up a bus, killing twenty-three people and wounding dozens more. The next day, in Ashkelon, a suicide bomber killed himself and an Israeli soldier at a bus stop. On March 3, a Hamas bus bomb in Jerusalem killed nineteen people and wounded ten more. When a March 4 joint Hamas–Islamic Jihad suicide bombing killed twelve people and injured 126 in downtown Tel Aviv, buildings shook for blocks around and the street corner was full of bodies, severed limbs, and blood. Within an hour, anti-Peres demonstrations erupted nearby. The main slogan was "This peace process is killing us."[59]

Belatedly, Arafat began a roundup of Hamas and Islamic Jihad activists. But it was too little, too late. Opposition to Palestinian terrorism in reaction to these attacks replaced sympathy for the peace process in reaction to Rabin's assassination. No one was surprised when Netanyahu defeated Peres in the May balloting.

During the Israeli election campaign, Arafat had repeatedly said that there was nothing to fear from the outcome since the Israeli-Palestinian agreements were "binding on any Israeli government."[60] The Palestinians liked to maintain generally that there were no differences between Israeli leaders and political parties.[61] Once Netanyahu was elected, however, Arafat was said to be in a state of shock, telling a Western diplomat: "The Israeli people have voted against peace. They want peace with Jordanians, they want peace with Egyptians, but they don't want peace with Palestinians."[62] Yet the Israeli vote had not expressed opposition to peace but rather doubts regarding Arafat's capabilities and intentions about delivering on his commitments.

Arafat's refusal or inability to control terrorism was not just a matter of placating Israel but was an absolute necessity if he were to succeed in getting a state through negotiations. Instead, his failure to do so delayed the negotiations' progress, reduced Israel's flexibility, and damaged Palestinians' living standards. Since, for example, in the March 1996 Tel Aviv attack, an Arab truck driver had smuggled the bomber into Israel along with a load of goods from Gaza, Israel's response was to close the frontier between its own and PA-ruled territory, which had a devastating effect on the PA's economy. The United Nations estimated that the PA lost $2.4 million a day in trade and workers' income in Israel.[63]

During this period, the unemployment rate ran as high as 39.2 percent in Gaza and 24.3 percent in the West Bank. Wages and consumption levels fell. Per capita gross national product declined 38.8 percent between 1992 and 1996, from $2,425 to $1,480, also reduced by high population growth rates. By 1998, it had only climbed back to $1,630.[64] Between 1992 and 1996, real GNP declined 22.7 percent, mainly as a result of losing employment in Israel and closures. Things improved markedly during the quieter year of 1997 but worsened each time a round of attacks led to more closures. The ground lost by the PA economy was never really regained.[65]

There Is a Tide in the Affairs of Men

This problem was greatly exacerbated by the fact that Arab states continued to give Arafat little or no material help. The 1996 Arab summit's final communiqué perfectly reflected this attitude. It urged Europe, Japan, and other countries "to continue providing political and economic support to the Palestinian people and their National Authority." But there was absolutely no Arab pledge—not even a nonbinding recommendation—for their own aid program to the Palestinians.[66]

It was hardly surprising that, in a December 1996 poll, only 9 percent of Palestinians said their economic conditions and living standards had improved during the peace process, while almost 48 percent (59 percent in the Gaza Strip) thought they had worsened, and 40 percent (only 29 percent of Gazans) believed they were the same.[67] The following year, when asked the peace process's economic impact, 42.7 percent felt it had been negative, and 27.4 percent felt it had been "very negative."[68] Raji Surani, director of the Palestinian Center for Human Rights, could remark in June 1998, "Today, the living conditions for ordinary Palestinian citizens are no better than they were before the signing of the Oslo Accords."[69] But this fact had far more to do with Arafat's economic policies and his failure to curb terrorism than with the peace process itself.

Arafat was given ample help and encouragement to control terrorism. His forces received training and equipment from European countries and the United States.[70] Even after the U.S.-PLO dialogue ended in 1990, the CIA had continued secret contacts through PLO security officials and the veteran terrorist Amin al-Hindi. The PLO gave the United States information on others involved in terrorism, including Abu Nidal, Sudan, and Hamas, as well as a bit of data on Iran and Yemen.[71]

Once the PA was established, the CIA trained some of its forces, including snipers, police, and intelligence officers. The agency held military exercises with Palestinian units and helped build the West Bank headquarters of the Preventive Security service, the unit responsible for preventing terrorism. It even bought office supplies for Arafat's Preventive Security, ranging from pens to file folders, and gave its members lessons in management, communications, transportation, as well as on how to write reports and evaluate intelligence.[72] Arafat was introduced to CIA officials involved in these activities and was pleased at this further sign of U.S. endorsement for him. The CIA retrained his personal bodyguards. Some high-ranking Palestinian officials visited and took courses at CIA headquarters in Langley, Virginia. But the CIA avoided passing on skills, such as bomb-defusing techniques, which might be used for terrorism.[73]

Responding to the February–March 1996 violence, Clinton organized an antiterrorist meeting of world leaders at Sharm al-Sheikh, Egypt.

Arafat was invited to become a partner in the war on terror. He declared in his speech there:

> We are confronting and will continue to confront terrorism and to uproot it from our land, because our dream of freedom, independence, and self-determination cannot bear fruit and be realized amid a sea of blood and tears, but by perseverance in confronting this terrorism and these extremist and dangerous wings of Hamas and the [Islamic] Jihad.[74]

This was an impressive statement, aimed at the West, but more revealing was what happened behind the scenes. For several months, Clinton had been demanding that Arafat arrest a Palestinian leading many of the terrorist attacks on Israel. Before arriving, Clinton warned that he would refuse to talk to Arafat at the summit unless the man was arrested beforehand. Arafat called Clinton's bluff. He rejected the president's demand, ordered that his plane be warmed up, and threatened to leave the meeting. Faced with the possibility that Arafat would not participate and the summit might fall apart, Clinton backed down. The wanted terrorist was never arrested, and Arafat later allowed him to leave Gaza.[75] As happened so often when Arafat was challenged by superior forces, he won by merely saying "no" until the other side gave in.

Arafat had many tools he could have used to push Palestinians toward a moderate course and to reduce violence, including his popularity; his legitimacy as the national leader; his command of the PLO, Fatah, and the PA; his ability to reward friends with money or jobs; and the threat of punishment. His sizable security forces, which ate up such a large portion of the PA's budget, could also have been employed to ensure that radicals did not block a compromise peace with Israel. But instead he held them back.[76] For him, the security forces' real purpose was to ensure his rule at home, provide jobs for followers, and be an army to fight in a future confrontation with Israel. He thus supported efforts to smuggle in arms and expand his forces to a size forbidden by the agreements he had made.[77]

Precisely because they saw their job as assuring law and order as well as the PA's dominance, many security officers actually wanted to control Hamas and other radical groups. They were restrained mainly by Arafat himself. For example, when Major General Nasir Yusuf arrived in Gaza to run the main police force there in April 1994, he made a one-month agreement in which Hamas promised to stop killing alleged collaborators and to leave such matters to the police, hoping this would be a permanent arrangement.[78]

Soon, however, Hamas returned to its old ways, killing alleged collaborators. Yusuf warned, "Those who attack our people are attacking our rights as a national authority." He demanded that Hamas surrender those responsible or he would catch and punish them even if it cost a hundred police officers' lives. Hamas ridiculed and ignored Yusuf, who was helpless since his leader did not let him take the steps he saw as necessary.[79] Yusuf was frustrated because he knew how much Hamas's terrorism cost the Palestinians in terms of unstable social conditions and economic costs. He told a meeting in Qalqilya when PA forces first entered that town, "We will control the security situation because it has a positive impact" on Palestinians being able to continuing working inside Israel.[80]

The frontline in stopping terrorism was the Preventive Security service, commanded by Colonel Muhammad Dahlan in Gaza and Colonel Jibril Rajub in the West Bank. Both men had been Intifada leaders, who had spent years in Israeli jails but were strong supporters of a successful peace process. Dahlan said that while formerly he had fought Israel, reaching peaceful solutions "was better," though sometimes harder. Rajub added, "I didn't fight for eighteen years to see [Hamas] lead the Palestinian people. I don't believe Palestinians want to live in an Islamic state."[81]

During the 1990s, Fatah and PA security forces rarely engaged themselves in terrorist operations, but this did happen in several cases. For example, one leader of a Hamas cell which had organized suicide bombings in 1997 that killed twenty-one Israelis was Abd al-Rahman Zabin, a Palestinian policeman in Nablus. Zabin and his associates were caught with the help of the PA's Preventive Security service.[82] In violation of agreements with Israel, some Hamas cadres were recruited, sometimes from prison, into the PA security forces. When several of them returned to violent activity, this seriously damaged PA credibility with Israel.

Once the post-March 1996 crackdown had succeeded in quieting the situation, Arafat returned to his usual strategy of trying to co-opt Hamas and other radical, anti-Oslo opposition groups. In February, May, and August 1997, Arafat organized meetings with Hamas, the PFLP, and DFLP to bring them into his coalition. But these exchanges made no progress. The opposition told Arafat that he must end talks with Israel, release its activists from PA jails, and launch a serious anticorruption effort.[83] Rather than make the substantive changes they demanded, Arafat found it easier to let these groups continue their activities, including preparing or sometimes launching attacks on Israel.

But after May 1996, Arafat faced a new challenge in dealing with a truly hostile Israeli prime minister. Netanyahu had opposed the Oslo Agreement and viewed Arafat as a terrorist who had not changed his stripes. True, as Arafat had predicted, Netanyahu had to accept the agreements negotiated by his predecessors. But while Rabin and Peres slowed or suspended talks unwillingly due to terrorist attacks and the difficulties of negotiating with Arafat, Netanyahu was happy to do so.

Second, while Rabin and Peres had accepted the notion that many problems—such as Arafat's oversized security agencies or continued anti-Israel incitement in the Palestinian media—could be deferred until after a full peace agreement was reached, Netanyahu intended to hold Arafat to full compliance with all of his commitments. Finally, while Rabin and Peres looked on Jewish settlements as a problem, Netanyahu and his government backed them.

While this situation presented Arafat with enormous problems, it also gave him an opportunity to gain Western, and especially U.S., support by proving that he was a committed peacemaker compared to an obdurate Netanyahu. Once Netanyahu won the election, Arafat reiterated his own "commitment to peace." He explained, "We have no choice but to adhere to reason, wisdom and courage as well as to the option of peace, based on comprehensiveness, durability and justice." Arafat grasped that his best strategy was to show that the PA was adhering to agreements while claiming Israel was breaking them. Israeli "unilateral measures . . . are liable to destroy the whole peace process," he stated. "Peace and terrorism cannot go hand in hand, [neither can] peace and settlements."[84]

Implementing the PA's commitments, he claimed on another occasion:

> secured for us the respect and trust of the world, in addition to the respect of half [of] Israeli society which voted [for the] Labor [party]. The Netanyahu government, which does not implement agreements, does not enjoy such trust and respect. Thus, we place Israel before world opinion and the world conscience, so that it might feel compelled to implement its side of the agreement. The documents we signed with the Israeli government will prove to be worthless as a peace treaty unless every word in them is implemented.[85]

Whether from fear of Netanyahu's toughness or for other reasons, Arafat tried more energetically to prevent violence after 1996 than he had done before.[86] Shaken by Netanyahu's threat to send his army into PA territory, Arafat reacted decisively, arresting hundreds of Hamas and Islamic Jihad activists, warning Hamas to stop its offensive or face serious retribution, and thus drastically reducing terrorism.[87] Arafat had shown he could certainly stop attacks when he wanted to do so.

On June 27, 1996, the first meeting was held between Netanyahu's aides—Dore Gold and Yitzhak Molcho—and Arafat. It was a surrealistic experience. Dahlan picked them up at the Gaza-Israel border in a black bullet-proofed Mercedes limousine covered with grime and dust. Uniformed PA soldiers had to strain to open the extra-heavy doors with two hands. To Gold's amazement, during the ride to Arafat's residence, their host casually mentioned that he had a picture of Gold's wife, Ofra, the kind of veiled threat usually seen only in spy or gangster movies.[88]

At Arafat's home in Gaza, they were taken to the living room, which was a stifling ninety degrees. Yet Arafat was dressed for cold weather. In addition to the trademark *kaffiya* on his head, he wore another one around his neck like an ascot and a heavy brown army coat. Unlike his guests, though, he never sweated.

Gold gave Arafat a brief five-point message from Netanyahu which insisted that the Palestinian leader control the security situation in the territories but also stressed that the Netanyahu government recognized that it had to work with him. Arafat read the message, puckered his lips like a fish, and stared into space, saying nothing. Molcho reiterated the message but Arafat's only response was to invite his guests to lunch which, he promised them, was kosher. As they gladly moved into the air-conditioned dining room, Arafat joked, telling a pun he often repeated, that the main course was denis, a Mediterranean fish, in honor of U.S. chief negotiator Dennis Ross.

Over the meal, Arafat told fantastic tales about Sadat and former Israeli prime minister Menahem Begin who, Arafat claimed, had offered to let him establish a Palestinian state in Gaza. "Is that a fact?" Molcho asked. Then Arafat described how a Hamas leader and an extreme right-wing Israeli had met on the beach in Gaza to plot a terrorist campaign designed to destroy the peace process. Dahlan smiled to show he thought the story absurd. Then, to his guests' dismay, Arafat suggested they have dessert in the living room. Gold joked that the heat in there would make it easier for Arafat to grill them. Everyone laughed and Dahlan gave Gold a high-five.

Arafat continued the discussion of one of his favorite conspiracy theories—a bizarre topic for his first meeting with a conservative Israeli government—on the alleged alliance between Israel's right wing and Palestinian Islamist radicals. Alluding to a 1995 Hamas bomb attack on a bus stop which had killed twenty-one Israelis, Arafat said that Israeli conspirators had given Hamas false Israeli identity cards so the terrorists could evade security controls. His guests expressed astonishment and doubt at such a claim. "Bring me the box!" Arafat ordered an aide. The man soon returned with a shoebox full of Israeli identity cards.[89]

He then ended the meeting by conveying his good wishes to Netanyahu without ever responding to the issues which had been raised. The whole encounter was a typical blend of Arafat's caginess and bizarre behavior, his control over any agenda, and his assertiveness at the very moment he was at his weakest.

Arafat was cautious at first with the new government. In a July meeting, he told an Israeli visitor regarding the wave of terrorist attacks earlier that year, "I admit . . . our security measures were not sufficient. After those events we took a decision to root out every terrorist act."[90] Indeed, Arafat did crack down. In his first face-to-face talk with Netanyahu on September 4, Arafat declared, "We and Mr. Netanyahu . . . will walk together to advance the peace process." Then, as soon as the meeting ended, Arafat publicly claimed victory, saying that Netanyahu had only gotten together with him because of pro-Arafat international pressure. Now, he added, even the Likud had been forced to recognize the PA and accept the agreements.[91]

Yet Netanyahu was not finished testing Arafat. On November 23, Netanyahu ordered the opening of a tunnel allowing visitors access to the buried portion of the Western Wall of the Jewish Temple in East Jerusalem, now also the al-Aqsa mosque's retaining wall. The Muslims had been given permission to open a new prayer room nearby as part of a deal. But Palestinians, encouraged by the PA-controlled media, spread rumors that the tunnel was a plot to destroy the al-Aqsa mosque itself. In ensuing riots and gun battles between PA and Israeli troops, eighty-six Palestinians and fifteen Israelis were killed and many more wounded. The PA media controlled by Arafat incited violence daily.[92]

The worst incident occurred at Joseph's Tomb in Nablus. Although located in a PA-controlled area, Joseph's Tomb's status as a Jewish holy site and religious school meant that Israeli soldiers were stationed there with the PA's permission. Hundreds of Palestinian policemen and armed demonstrators stormed the site on September 26, killing six soldiers and wounding eight others. An Israeli armored column rushed to the scene but stopped short of entering the PA-ruled area.

One of Netanyahu's aides telephoned Arafat and passed on a message: if the shooting did not stop, Israeli tanks would enter Nablus. Arafat quickly agreed to a ceasefire. Once Arafat decided to end the battle, the PA media immediately began broadcasting soothing messages and urging calm. Netanyahu viewed the crisis's outcome as a victory for himself, having faced down Arafat in a confrontation.[93] Actually, the situation simply returned to one of deadlock. For a time, though, Arafat was forced to be cautious, telling a January 1997 Gaza rally, "We need to find a mechanism . . . to face Israel's refusal to fulfill what has been agreed upon. . . . [But also] we have no choice but to adhere to reason, wisdom and courage as well as to the option of peace."[94]

There Is a Tide in the Affairs of Men

Arafat insisted that the Palestinians would refuse to "change a letter or even a comma" in the previously signed agreements.[95] While Netanyahu spent months renegotiating the deal that Peres had made for security arrangements to allow Israeli redeployment from Hebron—the only West Bank Palestinian city where Jewish settlers lived—in the end he had to sign virtually the same agreement that had previously been made. Abu Mazin took the lead in getting Arafat to agree, though it was clear that Arafat did not understand the complicated arrangements dividing the town into different zones.

In January 1997, the PA took over 80 percent of the city, and Arafat visited Hebron, welcomed by sixty thousand cheering Palestinians. The speech he made on that occasion was one of the peak moments for Arafat's conciliatory tone. "We have made a peace agreement with all the Israeli people" and all of their political parties, he said. "There were eighty-seven votes in the Knesset [in favor of withdrawing from Hebron] for peace . . . and that is something new in the Middle East. . . . Therefore I say that all forces of peace in Israel have voted for this decision and together we will make a just and comprehensive peace in the Middle East."[96]

Perhaps Arafat was conciliatory precisely because he knew that Netanyahu would not be. Indeed, shortly thereafter the Israeli prime minister announced a provocative decision to build sixty-five hundred housing units on Jerusalem's southeastern edge in an area called Har Homa. It was part of a strategy to ring East Jerusalem with Jewish neighborhoods so it could never come under Palestinian rule. This action angered Arafat and raised the level of bilateral friction with Israel, but it also opened the chance for Arafat to move closer than ever to the United States.

While Clinton had been on excellent terms with Rabin and Peres, he knew Netanyahu did not share his views or eagerness for a comprehensive political settlement, which would require major Israeli risks and concessions. When Arafat came to Washington on March 2 for his sixth meeting with Clinton, the president criticized Netanyahu's decision on Har Homa while praising the Palestinian leader.[97] Clinton tried to avoid meeting Netanyahu at all, leading the Israeli prime minister to quip, "The Americans are treating me like Saddam Hussein."[98]

As another reward for Arafat, the United States created a joint U.S.-PA committee to meet regularly to discuss diplomatic, economic, and cultural concerns. This was a framework usually used only with foreign states. Arafat had successful meetings with Congress and officials involved in providing financial aid to the PA. It was a time when, in the words of one U.S. official, the Clinton administration "really rolled out the carpet for Arafat while showing its frustration with the Israeli prime minister."[99] Clinton advised Netanyahu on how to deal with Arafat in words reflecting his own expectations: "You have to know how to talk to him. You can work with him. You can win him over if you're patient."[100]

The U.S. president was staking his Middle East policy as well as the hope for his greatest achievement and legacy on his ability to charm Arafat, who, less than a decade before, had been seen in the White House as the world's leading terrorist. The situation's irony was embodied by the resume of a senior Palestinian official handling U.S. aid at the Ministry of Planning and International Cooperation, which listed his "educational experience" as "explosives engineer."[101] For Arafat, too, the situation was a bizarre reversal. The man who had so long viewed the United States as an enemy, identified himself as part of a world struggle against American imperialism, aligned with the USSR, and murdered U.S. diplomats and citizens was being treated like a favored American client who was being offered a chance to become an ally.

Yet while Arafat did clamp down on terrorism most of the time during this period, he also appeared to hold fast to his belief that violence would increase his leverage in negotiations and strengthen him regarding internal Palestinian politics. On March 21, 1997, a Hamas suicide bombing in a Tel Aviv cafe killed three Israelis and injured forty. The PA condemned the bombing in statements aimed at the West. Netanyahu accused Arafat of giving a green light for terrorism and demanded that the PA crack down on the groups carrying out these attacks, as it had pledged to do in all previous agreements. U.S. secretary of state Madeline Albright responded that Arafat "has condemned the violent acts, but there needs to be some improvement." Privately, U.S. officials conceded that Arafat had apparently changed his tactics as charged.[102]

A wave of Palestinian attacks against Israel culminated in a major bombing in Jerusalem on July 30. In messages directed toward the West, Arafat condemned it and said he would do all he could to prevent future such incidents. But a statement issued by the PA Information Ministry for internal consumption justified the suicide bombings as a response to Israel's policies of "expanding settlements, confiscating Palestinian land, building new settlements, Judaizing Arab Jerusalem, isolating the Palestinian territories, and closing the labor market to Palestinian laborers."[103]

Netanyahu talked frequently about how he would force Arafat to engage in "reciprocity." Israel would make more concessions only if Arafat honored his own commitments. Yet Netanyahu's attempts to pressure Arafat into stricter compliance had no effect. The PA made no serious, consistent effort to collect weapons, break up terror networks, or dismantle bomb factories. When U.S. officials urged Arafat to do more to control terrorism, he would act only temporarily or not at all.

Through a strange twist of events, Netanyahu did give Arafat one interesting opportunity to test out his claims. Arafat had long insisted that he could co-opt Hamas through conciliatory methods. He had campaigned against the extradition of Musa Abu Marzuk, a high-ranking Hamas official, from the United States to Israel.[104] And he had always argued for the release of Hamas's paralyzed spiritual leader, Ahmad Yasin, from an Israeli jail, where he was serving a life sentence for his central role in past attacks. Arafat asserted that a free Yasin would play a moderating role.

In October 1997, Israel released Yasin. Arafat hurried to meet the Hamas leader on his return to Gaza, kissing him several times and in effect claiming credit for his liberty.[105] Arafat gave Yasin a Land Rover car and a PA diplomatic passport. Yasin urged Palestinian unity and praised Arafat. But soon Yasin was attacking Arafat and urging Hamas to continue armed attacks. When permitted to travel abroad to Arab states, Yasin arranged for Hamas to receive large-scale financial support from Saudi Arabia and other countries, which it used to carry on its war against Israel.[106]

Instead of calming the situation, Yasin's release was followed by more attacks, including a November 4 bombing at a Jerusalem mall, which killed four Israeli civilians and wounded 170 and took place just as Israel was starting to lift the restrictions imposed after earlier attacks. The closure was immediately reinstated.[107] Criticized by the United States and threatened by Israel, Arafat again, as he had in March 1996, temporarily arrested Hamas and Islamic Jihad members and closed a Hamas-run newspaper, television station, and charities. Arafat's refusal to restrain Yasin was either a failure of his leadership, a misguided effort to exploit the Islamists, or both.

Troublesome as these periodic confrontations with Israel were, they protected Arafat on the domestic front. Whenever things became quieter, voices were raised about his high-handed rule, monopolization of power, corruption, and incompetence. But when anti-Israel feeling was stirred up or armed clashes occurred, Arafat could successfully argue that the nation must unite behind him. All other considerations became petty, even treasonous, concerns which, by undermining the PA's image and international support, were said to help the enemy.

For example, an internal 1997 PA report disclosed inept or dishonest financial and administrative practices throughout the regime. The highest-ranking officials were implicated, and it was estimated that $326 million in public funds during 1996 alone had been misused or stolen. PLC debates on this issue were ignored in the PA-controlled media, and an independent television station that broadcast them was soon shut down.[108] A PLC report found corruption in virtually every PA department and singled out for particular criticism Planning Minister Nabil Sha'th, Transport Minister Ali Qawasma, and Civil Affairs Minister Jamil Tarifi. The PLC demanded that Arafat dissolve his cabinet within a month and name a new one staffed by honest professionals and experts.[109]

But Arafat refused. Only in January 1998 did he agree to reshuffle the cabinet. Arafat's chief aide, Tayyib Abd al-Rahim, declared that Arafat was now going to fight corruption. The PLC's speaker, Abu Alaa, greeted this statement as "a new beginning." Yet Arafat did nothing at all.[110] When the PLC threatened a no-confidence vote at its June 15, 1998, session, Arafat again promised to act. Only on August 5 did Arafat finally announce his new cabinet. But while adding new ministers from the PLC to buy off his critics, the old ones—including those specifically charged with corruption by the PLC's report—also kept their jobs. The PLC then ratified the new cabinet by a big margin.[111]

He manipulated the Palestinian public with equal skill. By 1998, the PLC had the lowest positive rating in polls of any government institution, at 45 percent, while Arafat had the highest, at 71 percent. When Arafat quarreled with the PA, Palestinians supported Arafat rather than the legislators.[112] It was not that they were unaware of Arafat's arbitrary rule. In a 1999 poll, 71 percent of them—the highest level in history— thought PA corruption was very serious and was not going to improve.[113] But Arafat kept the masses on his side by appealing for militant nationalist unity in the fight against Israel. Instead of complaining about him and the PA, Arafat implied, the PLC should criticize Israel as the source of all the Palestinians' problems.[114] The public saw no alternative and rallied for Arafat whenever relations with Israel deteriorated.

With the end nearing for the five-year transitional period designated by the Oslo accords, Arafat faced the possibility that deadlock might turn the transitional arrangements into a permanent situation. To avoid this outcome, Arafat pledged in April 1998 that he would unilaterally proclaim statehood in 1999 and implied that Palestinians could turn to violence if their demands were not met.[115] Netanyahu immediately warned that such a proclamation would nullify the previous agreements and lead to Israel's annexing parts of the West Bank and Gaza still controlled by Israel.[116]

Arafat never seemed as if he wanted to carry out that threat, however, but used it rather as a way to mobilize Palestinians, gain Arab support, and force a more active U.S. role. And in October 1998, Arafat, Netanyahu, and Clinton held a summit meeting at the Wye Plantation conference center on Maryland's eastern shore. The negotiations centered on Arafat's goal of getting another Israeli withdrawal to give him more land and Netanyahu's objective of getting in exchange some way of ensuring that Arafat would increase his compliance with his earlier unmet commitments.

Almost immediately after the meeting began, Netanyahu took a page from Arafat's playbook and threatened to leave unless Arafat agreed to extradite Palestinians accused of terrorism to Israel and to confirm in a clear way that the PLO Charter had been changed.[117] The Palestinians dismissed this as "political blackmail" and a last-minute tactic to extract more concessions. Then King Hussein flew in from the Mayo Clinic, where he had been receiving chemotherapy treatments for what would prove to be terminal cancer. He spoke plainly, "You all can get over your disagreements and really do something for the children and the grandchildren. Get over whatever your momentary problems are and think about the future." Perhaps the king saved the summit. Like Nasser in 1970, his dying act was to help out Arafat, the man who had tried to unseat and assassinate him in the 1970s and who had sabotaged his own peace initiatives in the 1980s.[118]

On October 23, after nine days of work, Arafat and Netanyahu signed an agreement with a complex timetable of interlocking steps. A U.S.-Israeli-Palestinian security plan was to be drawn up to limit violence. The PA would imprison thirty murderers on Israel's wanted list—Netanyahu dropped his demand for extradition—and collect the radical groups' weapons. The PLO's highest bodies would confirm the Charter's change; and an Israel-PA anti-incitement committee would seek to reduce media encouragement of violence and terrorism. The Palestinians would receive their own Gaza–West Bank safe passage route, airport, and seaport. The agreement accepted the PA's violation of earlier commitments to build a 30,000-strong security force and set that number as the new limit. Israel would make three redeployments to turn more West Bank territory over to the PA and release 750 Palestinian prisoners involved in past violence.[119]

In his speech at the signing ceremony, Arafat said the Palestinians had permanently rejected violence:

> We will never leave the peace process, and we will never go back to violence and confrontation. . . . I would like to assert in honesty and sincerity that we are fully committed to whatever is required from us in order to achieve real security and constant peace for every Israeli person and for the Israeli people. We will not forget our duties as we underline our rights. I am quite confident that I'm talking in the name of all Palestinians when I assure you that we are all committed to the security of every child, woman and man in Israel.[120]

Israel's Knesset approved the Wye agreement, but the right wing of Netanyahu's coalition rebelled against his concessions, and he was forced to call new elections for May 1999. Israel released 250 Palestinian prisoners and made its first redeployment on the northern West Bank. Later, the PA would get its airport and seaport. But there was no change in the Palestinian media's tone, no collection of weapons, and no long-term imprisonment of terrorists. The security plan never materialized either.

Instead of cracking down on incitement against Israel in PA institutions, Arafat used the Wye agreement's anti-incitement clauses to block Palestinian criticism of his own policies or officials, then blamed these measures on alleged Israeli demands.[121] Yasir was not the only Arafat involved in incitement. When First Lady Hillary Clinton visited Ramallah to open a U.S.-funded health program, Suha Arafat falsely told her that a major health problem was the "intensive daily use of poison gas by Israeli forces [which is producing] increased cancer cases among Palestinian women and children."[122]

But the Clintons were doing everything possible to help the Arafats get a state of their own. To encourage Arafat to advance toward a peace treaty with Israel, Clinton went to Gaza in December 1998 and made a stirring speech to five hundred Palestinian leaders assembled at the Rashad al-Shawwa Center, expressing understanding for Palestinian grievances and explaining why a compromise peace with Israel was the best way to resolve them.[123] To ensure that Arafat did not embarrass Clinton or resort to his usual ambiguity, Clinton's Middle East coordinator, Dennis Ross, wrote Arafat's remarks for the meeting.[124] Arafat called for a show of hands of those supporting the repeal of key passages of the Charter. The crowd responded favorably. It was understandable that Clinton could leave Gaza believing that conciliation was inevitable.

Arafat saw Clinton's visit as a big success for himself, and another event soon gave Arafat the greatest opportunity of his career to bring a Palestinian state within reach. On May 17, 1999, the Israelis elected as prime minister Ehud Barak, a man who had promised to make a deal with Arafat even if it required big Israeli concessions. Arafat should have been elated. The man who did not want to deal with him was gone; the new prime minister was ready for serious compromise. To make matters better, Barak's colleagues included the Oslo Agreement's creators. It was a government eager to cooperate with Arafat, give him concessions, and conclude a deal.

Finally, in September, the final status talks formally opened. At last, the two sides were discussing the issues that they had to resolve if there was to be real peace. Israeli foreign minister David Levy and Abu Mazin launched this new stage in a ceremony at the Erez checkpoint between Gaza and Israel. But Arafat delayed appointing his delegation for several days, hoping that opposition groups would join. Finally, he appointed the hardliner Yasir Abd Rabbu rather than Abu Mazin or Abu Alaa to head his negotiating team, a choice signaling that Arafat did not want or expect any progress.[125]

Barak thought he might reach an agreement faster with Syria. The resumption of Israeli-Syrian negotiations in December 1999, though outwardly welcomed by the PA, evoked fear among Palestinians that they would be, in the words of one journalist, "left alone at the station, waiting for a final settlement, [while] the train speeds off with the last passengers in Damascus and Beirut."[126]

When Barak was elected, Palestinian backing for the peace process had been relatively high: 70 percent supported it—apparently believing an acceptable agreement could be reached with Israel—against only 27 percent opposition. At the same time, though, like Arafat, many Palestinians thought armed attacks on Israelis did not undermine negotiations, and two-thirds distrusted the intentions of Israelis in general and Barak in particular on the peace process. While their skepticism was based on experiences, it was also reinforced by what their leaders and the PA-controlled media told them. Still, if Arafat had wanted to promote a deal, public opinion data suggest that he now had a good chance to mobilize massive support for one.[127]

Moreover, Arafat remained the Palestinians' unchallenged leader, the only man capable of making a deal and persuading his people to accept it. In a June 1999 poll, for example, he had four times as much support as the potential candidates of Hamas or the Left.[128] Thus, Arafat dominated every aspect of Palestinian society, politics, and the economy. The PLO, Fatah, PNC, PLC, PA, court system, and security agencies all obeyed him. The masses supported him. And the armed opposition knew that it could not fight him directly. Arafat showed his ability to minimize violence during most of Netanyahu's term, surely the toughest test of all if it was true that the main cause of terrorism was Palestinian frustration over a deadlocked peace process.

Arafat had been complaining that Israel's leader Netanyahu did not want to implement the agreements. Now, he had a counterpart who staked his whole political career on doing so. Arafat had been the one insisting on arriving at an agreement that would bring the creation of a Palestinian state. Now, he had an Israeli leader ready to accept that outcome. Arafat had repeatedly demanded a larger U.S. role in the negotiations. Now, he had a U.S. president willing to devote all his energy to this issue and convinced that the moment of decision would soon be at hand.

In the year 2000, Arafat would get his way on all these points and the best chance ever to reach his expressed goals.

8

The Moment of Truth

2000

The pivotal moment of Yasir Arafat's life may have taken place on July 24, 2000, at the U.S. presidential retreat of Camp David in Maryland. A few days earlier, Arafat had rejected, even as a framework for further negotiations, a plan that would have given him an independent state with its capital in Jerusalem. Enraged by Arafat's response to the peace proposal that had been the culmination of years of negotiations between Israelis and Palestinians, Clinton banged on the table and said, "You are leading your people and the region to a catastrophe."[1]

Now Clinton tried one last time, coming up with some additional concessions that might persuade the Palestinian leader to change his mind. Expecting Arafat to say no once again, American delegates begged their Palestinian counterparts to reconsider. At the last minute, Clinton sent one of his officials, who had a particularly good relationship with Arafat, to speak with him directly. The envoy made an impassioned plea: make a deal, get a state, help your people, and do not lose the best opportunity for the Palestinians since 1948. Arafat simply replied, "I can't."

A few hours later, the Palestinians read Clinton their formal rejection of the proposals. The thirteen-day summit came to an end. While the decision to reject the Camp David effort as a basis for negotiation was a fateful one, Arafat was afterward offered by Clinton even better terms to change his mind and his course. He did not do so. Within weeks after his decision at Camp David, Palestinians began a new uprising under

Arafat's leadership. Hundreds died on both sides, and the Middle East was once again plunged into bitter conflict.

Earlier in the momentous year 2000, peace had still seemed very possible, even inevitable. The projected five-year deadline for completing the Oslo Agreement had passed in 1999, and Arafat was threatening to declare a state unilaterally. But this impatience seemed a positive omen, suggesting that Arafat was eager to conclude a peace treaty.

Shortly after starting his term of office, Barak had put the priority on working out a peace agreement with Syria. The Palestinians both feared and resented this choice. In December 1999, Arafat told a visitor, "Barak should not take me for granted."[2] And when, several months later, President Asad rejected the peace proposal, Arafat knew that Barak had lost any leverage or alternative, strengthening Arafat's own hand in the bargaining process.

Still, Israel and the Palestinians had agreed to produce a basic outline of what a peace treaty between them would look like, a technique favored by Barak based on the successful Egypt-Israel negotiations at Camp David in 1978.[3] Moreover, he wanted to see if Arafat would commit himself to anything. Barak worried that continuing the step-by-step approach, in which a series of partial agreements would be made over a long period of time, meant that Israel would keep turning over more West Bank land without the Palestinian side making any compromises for a final settlement or even implementing its earlier pledges.[4]

So Barak preferred, as Arafat said he also did and as the Oslo plan mandated, to move quickly and steadily toward a comprehensive peace treaty. By the spring of 2000, the time seemed ripe for a big push. Dennis Ross, the chief U.S. diplomat on the peace process, urged that a back channel be opened as the best way to achieve progress. Secret, informal meetings would let negotiators try out new ideas and possible concessions outside the constraints and pressures of media coverage and irrevocable offers. After all, this had been how the Oslo Agreement was successfully created in the first place.

Starting in April 2000, a series of secret meetings was held, some in the Israeli Arab village of Abu Ghosh near the Jerusalem–Tel Aviv highway. In May and June, the talks moved to Sweden. There were fifteen sessions over two long weekends and another weekend meeting in Tel Aviv. Representing Israel was Foreign Minister Shlomo Ben-Ami and Gilad Sher, a lawyer. Abu Alaa and Hasan Asfour, both Oslo veterans, were the Palestinian delegates.

At first, the Palestinians did not respond to Israeli suggestions for solving problems with ideas of their own. This fed the Israelis' fear that they would make concessions and the Palestinians would demand more without reciprocating. In a telephone conversation, Ross reminded

Abu Alaa that the channel's purpose was not to repeat long-held positions but to try for something new. "We're looking forward to your getting here," said Abu Alaa. While both sides invited Ross to join them in Sweden, he worried that his presence might wreck any chance for success since negotiators would spend the time trying to persuade him they were right rather than working things out with each other. Instead, he offered to come only at the end.[5]

This seemed to have been a correct assessment because as time ran out on the meeting, Abu Alaa went into action. He began to propose compromises, including for the first time a territorial swap, which would allow some Jewish settlements to be incorporated into Israel. "No one's a better negotiator for the Palestinians" than Abu Alaa, Ross later remarked. He was able to protect Palestinian positions while also being creative in finding solutions.[6]

In the secret channel, recalled Sher, "There was a readiness to explore far-reaching ideas, solutions and schemes." They talked about how a Palestinian state might be created in exchange for Israel annexing a small portion of the West Bank, which would include a large proportion of Jewish settlers and would help Barak build the national coalition he needed to make other concessions. In retrospect, it was a rehearsal for Camp David.[7]

At this point, Sher was relatively optimistic even though the Palestinians were not ready to talk about more details or draw up maps. The Palestinian negotiators were acting as if they were fully authorized by Arafat to discuss everything. Sher and Abu Alaa were even able to draft a seven-page unofficial paper outlining a basis for agreement on several issues. This was, Sher later said, "the closest we ever got to a reasonable text, taking care of all the main issues that needed to be concluded, excluding Jerusalem. It was the best any negotiator could do."[8]

Only the national leaders could close the gaps, confirm the proposed solutions, and complete them. "A historic decision had to be taken by the leadership" on both sides, said Sher. But there were signs that Arafat was not really behind his negotiators. One of them was Arafat's unwillingness to stop violence back home during that year's commemoration of Nakba (Catastrophe) Day. To coincide with Israel's Independence Day each May, Arafat had initiated a new Palestinian observance, Nakba Day, which mourned Israel's creation in 1948. Organizing an exercise to show that Palestinians saw Israel's existence as contrary to their interests and feelings was a most peculiar step for someone supposedly engaged in a peace process aimed at conciliation, which included Arafat's promise to end incitement against Israel.

Knowing that this would be a tense time, Ross, in Stockholm observing the talks, drafted a message for Clinton to send to Arafat, urging him to maintain the peace that day as a clear sign that he wanted the secret talks to succeed. Instead, Arafat stood aside as Palestinian rioting led to eight days of heavy clashes, the worst violence in four years. Ross worried that this was an indication of Arafat's real attitude toward the negotiations.[9]

To make matters worse, Arafat's behavior implied that he would not support the kind of flexibility his negotiators had shown in the back channels. The Palestinian negotiators told the Israelis that they were afraid to tell Arafat the truth about concessions they had suggested in Stockholm and what they knew was necessary to reach an agreement. Ross's concern was deepened when he personally briefed Arafat about the back channel talks. Arafat professed himself unfamiliar with what was happening there. In contrast to the Oslo negotiations, Ross noticed, "He didn't engage and didn't respond at all. It showed me he was distancing himself from the talks."[10]

When Sher briefed Arafat about the meetings, he also concluded that Arafat was so uninterested in supporting the efforts there that the secret talks might be called a "bad channel" instead of a back channel. By claiming to authorize his negotiators to make serious offers but then withholding his backing, Sher concluded, Arafat sought to garner Israeli concessions and then disown his own delegates' proposals used to obtain them in the first place.[11]

By this point, though, the Israelis and Americans had reached two conclusions. First, the secret talks had shown that an agreement was possible but that the negotiators had reached their limit. Only a meeting of top leaders could show whether Arafat would endorse the ideas developed there. Second, the threat of growing violence also showed that a summit meeting was needed. For the Americans, the unrest proved the need for quick progress toward a negotiated settlement. Ami Ayalon, head of Israel's security service, told Ross that violence would increase in the future if an agreement was not reached.

Barak especially wanted to move toward a summit, to discover once and for all if Arafat was capable of making a deal. Otherwise, each side would just dig in and refuse to put forward its ultimate bargaining positions until such a meeting did take place. Clinton, too, was eager to have a summit as soon as possible. For Clinton, the deadline was not January 2001, when he would leave office, or even November 2000, when the U.S. presidential election would take place, but August 2000, when the campaign began in earnest. He did not want to be accused of unfairly using the presidency's power to ensure the victory of his vice president, Al Gore.[12]

Clinton and Barak had good reason to believe that if they did not go to a summit, the whole peace process would be lost. After all, Barak's government was in serious trouble while Clinton's time was limited. To postpone the summit was to risk that it would never happen or be put off for years. Barak had won election on the basis of his promise to achieve peace with the Palestinians. Clinton still hoped to end his political career with a fabulous achievement and guarantee his place in the history books as a great statesman.

In theory, Arafat, who had been long complaining about the pace of negotiations and insisting he wanted a state as soon as possible, should also have been eager for a summit. Yet he was reluctant to go to any meeting unless he knew in advance that all his demands would be met. "I need more time," Arafat told Secretary of State Madeline Albright when she met him in Ramallah in early June to discuss organizing a summit.[13] To Ross, Arafat remarked, "We can't go to a summit because it's our last hope. If we go to a summit and it fails, we're lost."[14]

At one point, Arafat proposed two weeks of continuous lower-level talks to start at the end of June. If these talks were unsuccessful, he suggested, they could then be followed by a summit. Barak declined this offer, believing that these exchanges would be leaked and hurt him politically without bringing any diplomatic progress.[15] Equally, if preliminary talks failed, that would make it even harder to have a successful summit.

Arafat's attempts to avoid the summit were peculiar given his supposed eagerness to end the occupation and obtain a state, as well as his frequent calls to speed up the negotiations. Indeed, two weeks before the summit, when Ben-Ami and Sher met with Arafat in Nablus to discuss the issues that would be raised, Ben-Ami proposed postponing a decision on Jerusalem's future for two years. Arafat responded, "Not even for two hours!"[16]

Arafat claimed that the sides needed more preparation. Abu Alaa later remarked, "We told [Barak that] without preparation it would be a catastrophe, and now we are living the catastrophe."[17] But Arafat was long familiar with the issues on the table—borders, refugees, Jerusalem—had already explored them in the secret channel, and had many years to prepare his positions. As for Palestinian public opinion, Arafat, by his own decision, had never tried to prepare his people for the type of compromises and psychological adjustments required if a deal were to be made.

Barak later remarked that the idea of needing more time before having a summit meeting was incomprehensible:

It had been nine years since the Madrid conference, seven years since the signing of the Oslo Agreement, three years beyond the deadline for opening final negotiations, and a year after the deadline for finishing them. Tons of paper had been prepared [analyzing the problems and options]. We had spent a lifetime on these issues and knew them well. It's ridiculous. Even in my one year in office I had spent hundreds of hours in negotiation.[18]

Abu Mazin, who did not like the idea of going to a summit but was resigned to it, made an interesting suggestion as to what was really bothering Arafat: "The Israelis thought that if we go directly to the summit, it would be possible [for them] to get Palestinian concessions."[19] And this was what Arafat did not want to do. Equally, he was reluctant to make any final decisions at all. As Ross noted, Arafat "was constantly avoiding getting into any discussion about the terms of a permanent peace agreement as a tactic to avoid facing up to his own responsibility, never having to prepare himself, never having to decide."[20]

Yet Arafat also hinted that a summit to reach a full peace agreement might succeed if it offered him something new. At times, according to Palestinian sources, Arafat suggested that he might match Israeli concessions on one issue by offering his own compromises on others. This gave the Americans and Israelis hope that the summit actually might succeed. At one point, Arafat told Clinton that if he were given a reasonable deal on the refugee question, he would try "to present it as not betraying the right of return."[21] At another point, Arafat sent Clinton a letter stating that if the United States offered him all Jerusalem, he would accept its suggestions on borders.[22]

So Clinton made plans to go ahead with the summit. As an incentive to get Arafat to go to Camp David, Clinton promised Arafat not to blame him if the summit failed.[23] During the preparatory meetings held at Andrews Air Force Base in Washington in mid-June, however, the Palestinians retreated from their statements in Stockholm and simply presented their traditional positions. Without Arafat's full backing, Abu Alaa could not develop a deal the way he had done at Oslo when authorized to do so. He was certainly not going to say anything that risked Arafat or others accusing him of betrayal.[24]

Given the constant competition, mistrust, and demands for militancy among Palestinian leaders, Abu Alaa had to protect himself by showing that he was as intransigent about claimed Palestinian rights as everyone else. Abu Mazin, already less flexible, made a similar decision. As Ross put it, "These were the two people on the Palestinian side who understood Arafat the best. They knew that he wasn't ready [to make a deal] and so they basically stepped back."[25]

But would Arafat be ready when given a specific offer in the most serious possible circumstances? Israeli leaders thought the effort was both necessary and worthwhile. Said Danny Yatom, Barak's chief of staff, "We went to Camp David because it was clear that that was the only way to find out if there was the possibility to strike a deal. . . . There was no value to continuing talks with representatives." Only talking to Arafat could answer that question.[26] Barak also hoped that "Arafat would rise to the occasion and display something of greatness, like Sadat and [King] Hussein, at the moment of truth. They did not wait for a consensus [among their people], they decided to lead."[27]

Clinton, too, knew the difficulties and risks involved. Yet, he felt, the alternative to not trying would be a complete failure. When Clinton asked each of his top advisors at a meeting for an assessment of what he should do, they unanimously responded that he must hold the meeting. If he failed to do so, each one insisted, violence would break out and he would be blamed for inaction.[28] Moreover, he believed in his own persuasiveness. He had succeeded with Arafat at the Wye talks, had gone to Gaza to express his sympathy for the Palestinian people's suffering, and had confronted Netanyahu. While Clinton knew that Arafat always waited until the last possible moment in order to extract maximum concessions, he was confident that he could make Arafat understand that this summit was indeed that moment and that the deal being offered was the best one possible.[29]

"Arafat," said Ross, "always moves only at one minute to midnight." As leaders gathered at Camp David, the bell was close to chiming those dozen strokes. Ross was worried that this time Arafat "was misreading the clock."[30]

At 1 A.M. on July 11, Arafat stepped from the door of a presidential helicopter, loaned by Clinton for the occasion, to be greeted on the grounds of Camp David by Secretary of State Madeline Albright. During the next ten days, the personality, goals, and world view of Yasir Arafat were put to the test. One Palestinian negotiator told an American counterpart, "If we can't do an agreement under these circumstances, we ought to be fired."[31]

The summit was held amid the utmost secrecy and tightest media blackout that Clinton could manage. Nothing was put on paper and no other countries were briefed by the United States on the details of the discussion. The reason for this approach was that Barak was about to make major concessions, including giving up almost all of East Jerusalem, a step that would provoke great criticism of him in Israel unless he could show he had received real gains from Arafat for doing so. Ironically, the secrecy at Camp David ultimately harmed Barak more than anyone else by making possible the circulation of misleading accounts of what had happened there. Barak had feared his concessions would be exaggerated in Israel. Instead, they were often minimized in the West and in the Arab world.[32]

But all that was truly important lay in what happened at the actual meeting, not in the speculative coverage about it during or since the event. The first step at Camp David was the creation of four committees to deal with the main issues: refugees, borders and settlements, security, and Jerusalem. American, Israeli, and Palestinian delegates were assigned to each group. Arafat and Barak stayed out of the meetings, but each repeatedly met separately with Clinton. Periodically, sessions would adjourn while delegates met with their respective leader to brief him and get instructions.

The Americans, great believers in diplomacy based on personal warmth, tried to build friendship among the two sides. They invited the delegations to play basketball, but when no Palestinians showed up, the Israelis played the U.S. Marines guarding the compound.[33] At meals, delegates were seated across from those on the same committee so that they could continue their discussions.[34]

Clinton and his staff had designed the meeting so as to maximize the chance of getting Arafat to take a flexible position by letting Arafat postpone his decision to the last possible moment when it was clear how much he could obtain by making peace. First, Barak and Arafat were supposed to authorize their delegates to go as far as possible to reach agreement. Only then would the top leaders come together to close the gaps and try to conclude a deal. Barak thought that if this encounter were held too soon, they would end up arguing and repeating traditional positions rather than developing new ones. He also feared, as Ross put it later, "that everything he would say would be committing himself, and Arafat would say nothing at all."[35]

Certainly, Barak's intellectual power was more impressive than his social graces. "He's not good at cross-cultural communication. He tells everyone the same thing in the same way," noted Ben-Ami.[36] Barak had a background in science, and one U.S. official recalled, "He sat there with his yellow pad as if he were mapping out lab experiments in which he could control all the elements."[37] Ross remarked that while Barak was courageous and a fine strategic thinker, "He alienated everybody around him. . . . He is someone who felt he knew best, that if he thought something was reasonable, ipso facto it was."[38] Yet this shortcoming provided another reason to avoid pushing Barak and Arafat together into direct conversation, depending instead on the highly charming Clinton, whose task would be to bridge any differences and propose ways of achieving both sides' main goals.

This was also how the first Camp David summit and the Oslo negotiations had been conducted, with the two sides' leaders never meeting until the very end. Begin and Rabin both succeeded in their negotiations though neither was known for his charm or social skills.

Barak and Arafat did engage in small talk during social periods at Camp David, and on one occasion Barak visited Arafat's cabin for two hours. But Barak maintained, "The right time for a meeting between us was when things were ready for a decision by the leaders."[39]

At any rate, Arafat had never been swayed earlier by his like or dislike of negotiating partners. His behavior at Camp David was completely in line with his previous performance patterns and political positions. Arafat complained that Barak did not treat him with proper respect. "What does he think, I'm his slave?" he asked angrily.[40] But this was always Arafat's response when challenged or pushed into a corner. He had spoken in similar terms of Rabin and Peres.

Arafat himself was not an easy man to deal with at Camp David. He was in a foul temper throughout the meeting, angry, yelling, and insulting his own negotiators. There was nothing for him to do, being stuck in his cabin all day. He read Arab newspapers, underlining the articles which agreed with him and complaining of those that denounced him, "They could at least have postponed their slander until the end of the summit." Like a caged animal, he paced furiously back and forth. Clinton handled Arafat about as well as possible, knowing how to show him respect without being manipulated by him. When Arafat told Clinton, for example, that Rabin had promised him all sorts of things, the president merely responded, "Cut the bull. He never promised you that."[41]

Yet despite all these personal factors, this was, after all, a meeting involving the entire future of two peoples. It was "ridiculous," as Barak asserted, to ignore the whole history and nature of the issues—and especially Arafat's long record of opting for militancy and avoiding decisions—to accept a soap opera version of events. Did Arafat pass up an opportunity to end a half-century-long conflict because he did not like how Barak behaved during the talks?

What ultimately and most basically killed any chance of progress at Camp David was Arafat's rigid stance. He instructed his delegates to develop no original proposals, introduce no counteroffers, and suggest no compromises. He would agree on procedural matters, including the holding of an all-night bargaining session, but that was the extent of his flexibility. The Palestinian delegates were thus reduced to repeating slogans and decades-old speeches.

Real differences within the Palestinian delegation existed, and Arafat encouraged the harder-line members to attack their more moderate colleagues.[42] The two most senior Palestinians, Abu Alaa and Abu Mazin, were personally open to making a deal, while two of their colleagues—Muhammad Dahlan, Arafat's protégé and commander of the Preventive Security force in Gaza, and Muhammad Rashid, Arafat's financial advisor—even went privately to the Israelis and Americans to propose some possible mutual concessions. They admitted that they could not persuade Arafat to show flexibility and asked the other two delegations to do it for them during the summit, complaining that the older Palestinian leaders were "backing away and dodging responsibility."[43]

Ultimately, though, no one would challenge Arafat. Concluding that nothing would be accomplished there, Abu Mazin left the summit early on family business and never returned.[44] Later, he would protect his position by publicly criticizing some Palestinian delegates who wanted to make a deal at Camp David. He warned that anyone saying the Palestinians missed an opportunity at the summit or that there was anything good about the deal offered there "weakens the Palestinian position."[45]

At any rate, Arafat's strategy and the resulting lack of serious discussions in the committees infuriated Clinton. On the third day of talks, Israeli delegates in the border committee spoke about how a small part of the West Bank could be yielded to Israeli sovereignty while the rest would become part of a Palestinian state. Abu Alaa insisted that the Palestinians were entitled to all the West Bank. Clinton lost his temper: "Don't simply say to the Israelis that their [proposal] is no good. Give me something better!"

Abu Alaa said he replied, "Mr. President, I don't have proposals. My proposal is the 1967 borders."

Clinton said, "But you should offer a proposal."

"Mr. President, I cannot take my hand, part of my body, and give it to somebody else."

Clinton became angry and said, "Sir, you hold personally the responsibility for the failure of the summit. If you want to address speeches, go to the UN Security Council, address speeches there. Don't waste my time here."[46]

Another Palestinian delegate said that they did not have to make a counteroffer since they had nothing left to give. Why should they show "flexibility" or make "concessions" to match Israel since, "The Palestinians are the victims of Israeli aggression and . . . the land the Israelis are offering to 'give up' is Palestinian land occupied by military force."[47]

Clinton was frustrated not only by Arafat and the Palestinians. While the Israeli delegates proposed various ideas in the committees, Barak was not yet ready to reveal his own comprehensive plan. On the summit's fourth day, Ross told him, "Your whole argument for coming to Camp David was that neither side could negotiate outside of the isolation of this kind of place. Now here we come and you still won't reveal yourself."[48]

Eventually Barak did reveal what he was willing to accept, which went far beyond any previous Israeli offer. He worked out the details with Clinton, who made additional suggestions and encouraged him to go even further in order to try to gain Palestinian acceptance. Thus, in the end, Clinton's contribution made the Barak plan his own Clinton plan.

Clinton presented the proposal to Arafat on July 19, twenty-four hours before he was due to fly to Okinawa, Japan, for a summit of industrialized nations. While the exact contents of the offer have been distorted by some accounts, the vast majority of those present agree precisely on the basic terms.[49] On borders, the Palestinians would receive an independent state whose territory would include all the Gaza Strip, the equivalent of 92 percent of the West Bank (including a 1 percent trade of land with Israel), and most of East Jerusalem. The state would be demilitarized, though it is worth noting that Arafat's PA was already defined as demilitarized since it had huge security agencies but no formal armed forces.

According to this plan, settlements on the 9 percent of West Bank land to be annexed by Israel would remain while Jewish settlers would leave those areas becoming part of the Palestinian state. During the refugee committee meetings, Israeli delegates had even raised the idea that the buildings and other assets of Jewish settlements would be turned over as part of the compensation for Palestinian refugees, who could either live in those places or sell them.

On East Jerusalem, Barak took a step hitherto unthinkable for any Israeli prime minister by proposing that the Palestinian state include seven or eight of the nine Arab neighborhoods in the city, plus the Muslim and Christian quarters of Jerusalem's Old City. Israel would annex the Jewish quarter and also the tiny Armenian quarter, which mainly consisted of Christian religious buildings with few residents. This area was needed to provide access to the Jewish quarter from Israeli territory, which even then would comprise a corridor only a few yards wide. There would be some shared security control in several other neighborhoods under Palestinian control.

As for the most controversial place, the mount containing the remains of the Jewish Temple, the only truly Jewish holy site in the world, the al-Aqsa mosque, and the Dome of the Rock, of great importance to Muslims, U.S. officials came up with several creative solutions. They proposed having the UN Security Council make the Palestinians custodians of the mosque area, giving them control and barring Israeli forces from entering, while Israel retained overall symbolic sovereignty. Since the Temple's ruins lay within the mount, Israel did not want to give total authority over it to the Palestinians but, for all practical purposes, they were ceding full control. The analogy used was that of a country's embassy, which is considered legally part of that state's territory though the land it is on formally remains that of the host country.[50]

Clinton very much wanted to produce a plan Arafat might accept and had tried to think of every possible concession to him that Barak, equally intent on success, might accept. And even then, the proposal was a framework which could be altered further as talks went forward, which meant Arafat would be able to obtain even more gains in that process. Clinton told Arafat that by taking the deal as a basis for further negotiations, he would achieve legitimacy and international recognition. There was no implication that Arafat must take it or leave it, but it was also clear that he could not merely "accept" Israeli concessions and then demand more without any commitments on his part. But, as Clinton told Arafat at the end of his presentation of the proposal, if Arafat walked away from this offer, "You will lose a Palestinian state of substantial size" and risk a slow slide into chaos.[51]

Arafat said he would discuss the plan with his delegation. Throughout the night, they sent out several questions to the Americans. Why was Israel asking for the equivalent of 9 percent of the West Bank? Why didn't the Palestinians get full control over all the East Jerusalem neighborhoods? How would cooperation in certain areas of East Jerusalem work? They also asked for a two-week adjournment to go around the Arab world to consult with other leaders there.

The United States refused the last request. Experience had shown that in previous such situations, when Arafat went to talk to Arab leaders, he would make what he was offered sound bad, plead for a hard line, get support for his position, and then tell the Americans that his hands were tied.[52]

Finally, the Palestinians responded that they rejected the proposal and had no counteroffer. On every point, Arafat was sticking to his traditional position: all the West Bank and Gaza, all East Jerusalem, and all refugees offered a right to live in Israel.

Enraged by Arafat's response to the peace proposal, Clinton banged on the table and said: "You are leading your people and the region to a catastrophe."[53]

Portraying himself as the representative of all Christians and Armenians, Arafat said he would not compromise on Jerusalem. "Who can accept this in all the world: Muslims or Christians?" he says he told Clinton. "Do you want me to betray the Christians and Muslims? If I will betray [them], no doubt [some]one will come to kill me." He also said he told Clinton, "My name is not Yasir Arafat, it is Yasir Arafatian," making his name sound Armenian.[54] "I will not betray my Armenian brothers," by leaving the Armenian quarter under Israeli rule.[55] Actually, Clinton's plan would have given Arafat sovereignty over all Christian holy sites and there was no reason to believe that the Armenians preferred his control.

As for the proposed solution for the Temple Mount/Haram al-Sharif area, Arafat countered, "Such arguments are like time bombs that will ignite raging fires in the entire region. Be careful—don't repeat such proposals! They are dangerous and destructive. Do you want to plunge the entire region into a new religious war?" Yet it would be Arafat himself who made the main effort to spark such a war after the summit ended.[56]

Finally, he indicated that he was not in such a hurry to make a deal: "If I'm not the one who liberates Jerusalem and raises the Palestinian flag there, another will come one day to liberate it."[57] According to one colleague, Arafat later said that he told Clinton, "Indeed we are weak now. But after two years or ten or fifty or a hundred, someone will come who will liberate [Jerusalem]. . . . Let us stay under occupation, for we know how to resist the occupation, but we are a people who do not betray trust; we are negotiating here in the name of the Arabs and Muslims, and Muslims and Christians, and not in our own name."[58]

The Israeli side had made a significant sacrifice on a very emotional issue, despite a near-unanimous desire of their people to keep all of Jerusalem and certainly full control over the Old City. Even Danny Yatom, a delegate who strongly supported Barak, remarked, "I was shocked and astonished when Barak said we needed to divide Jerusalem, but I realized this was something we had to accept."[59] But Israelis would accept it only in the context of a plan to let both sides control their own holy places. In contrast, Arafat would only accept full Palestinian control over all the holy places, allowing Jews to pray or even visit the wall of the Temple, the most important Jewish religious site in the world, only with Palestinian permission.

Indeed, Arafat denied that there were any Jewish holy sites at all in Jerusalem. He told Barak and Clinton, "I don't know why Israel demands the [area]. It's not a sacred place [to them], there's no evidence of the ruins of [any] temples."

Clinton cut him off and said, "I'm not a Jew. I'm a Christian. It's well known this is where the Temple is." But Arafat repeated this claim often in other places and times.[60]

Since the summit had apparently failed, the delegations prepared to leave Camp David, but both sides also let the Americans know that they wanted to stay and keep talking. Clinton then invited them to continue meeting under Albright's direction while he went to Japan. Everyone agreed, but no progress was made in his absence.

The Moment of Truth

When Clinton returned to Camp David on July 23, he tried a different technique to reach a solution. Both sides sent an appropriate person on each issue to discuss it with Clinton and one of his aides. Some progress was made on security guarantees. The Palestinians accepted the idea of Israeli early-warning stations in the West Bank, though Arafat flatly rejected the presence of any Israeli soldiers to staff them.[61]

Regarding refugees, the next issue discussed, absolutely no progress was made at all. The Palestinians demanded that Israel take responsibility for creating the refugee problem in 1948 and formally recognize that all refugees had a right to return to live in Israel. Yet if Israel did so, it would then be responsible for full compensation as well. Israel contended that the Arab side caused the refugee problem by refusing to accept Israel's creation, alongside a Palestinian state, in 1948 and by launching a war intended to destroy it. Moreover, Israel pointed out that a massive inflow of Palestinian refugees would lead to more violence, instability, and probably to its own ultimate destruction.

Instead, Israel was ready to offer compensation to Palestinian refugees for their losses of property in 1948 and proposed resettlement, if they wished, in the new Palestinian state. Barak, through his delegates, also offered to accept a symbolic seven thousand refugees over fifteen years for purposes of family reunification.[62]

The only qualification that the Palestinians would make to a full return was offering the possibility of making that option seem unattractive to the refugees and putting a high limit on how many could come back in any given year. Even this would only be discussed, however, after Israel agreed to take them all. More than any other issue, the Palestinian position demanding a total return persuaded the Israelis that they were not really interested in a deal and had not given up their hope of destroying Israel. Some Palestinian leaders were aware that their stance on this point would make peace impossible. Before the summit, several had told Israeli counterparts that they regarded the "right of return" demand as a "pain in the neck," and they wanted to find a way out.[63] Yet Arafat, Abu Mazin, the great majority of the leadership, and the masses did not feel that way and would denounce as traitors anyone contemplating the idea that the refugees should be repatriated to Palestine instead of Israel.

There was, however, an important development regarding the issue of borders that might have provided an opening for progress. Near the summit meeting's end, Abu Alaa suggested a deviation from the traditional Palestinian position by suggesting that the Palestinians might trade 2 percent of the West Bank for an equal amount of Israeli territory. This was endorsed by Arafat.[64] While Arafat and other Palestinian leaders frequently claimed that the Jewish settlements were taking huge amounts of West Bank land, privately Arafat repeatedly told the Americans that they only used 1.4 percent of the territory. Thus, a 2 percent trade would be more than adequate to accommodate them. This idea, however, does not seem to have been raised again.[65]

Later, Palestinians would claim that Clinton's proposal regarding borders was a plot to make any Palestinian state unviable by cutting the West Bank into small sections.[66] American and Israeli officials say that this claim was ridiculous.[67] First, there were no maps presented at Camp David and hence no specific borders were ever defined. Second, most of the land that Israel wanted to annex lay right along the border between the West Bank and Israel and thus did not split up the West Bank at all.[68]

Arguably, the proposed deal would make Israel's territory equally or more divided and vulnerable as that of Palestine. Palestinian corridors connecting Gaza to the West Bank would split Israel's land. According to Israel's plan for Jerusalem, the Jewish quarter and the Western Wall would be connected to other Israeli territory by a passage about the width of two automobiles, while Israeli West Jerusalem would be linked to the rest of the country only by a narrow neck of land, as it had been before 1967. Israel's aerial space, including that needed by planes to land at the country's sole international airport, would also have been constricted.

The truth was that any agreement on the terms offered would have created a tremendous incentive for Israel and Palestine to get along peacefully but, by the same token, would inevitably have left both sides vulnerable to violations of the accord. In this respect, Israel would have been no better off than the Palestinians. What if, as happened a few months later, Palestinian terrorists attacked Israel and an Arafat-led government denied responsibility and did nothing to stop them? What if, after independence, the Palestinian government rejected the demilitarization clause or even invited help from the army of some Arab state? Israel's only recourse would have been to go to war under very unfavorable security and international conditions.

In addition, if Arafat had accepted the plan as a basis for negotiation, he could then have presented a list of reasonable alterations. Consequently, as the summit came to an end and the Palestinian leader's unwillingness to bargain became clear, Clinton told Arafat: "If the Israelis can make compromises and you can't, I should go home. You have been here fourteen days and said 'No' to everything. These things have consequences; failure will mean the end of the peace process. . . . Let's let hell break loose and live with the consequences."[69]

Clinton tried one more gambit. He telephoned several Arab leaders, asking them whether they would encourage Arafat to accept an agreement. Clinton gave them some examples of the compromises suggested on Jerusalem. The basic response was friendly but non-committal. They would agree to whatever Arafat accepted. When asked to help persuade Arafat to make a deal, however, Saudi crown prince Abdallah refused, while Mubarak responded that he would see what he could do but then did nothing. Only Jordanian king Abdallah and Tunisian president Ben Ali called Arafat to encourage compromise.[70]

Throughout the summit Sha'th and other Palestinian delegates had regularly briefed a long list of people, including the foreign ministers of Egypt, Jordan, Morocco, and Tunisia, and Saudi, Algerian, Lebanese, Syrian, and Algerian diplomats.[71] In each case, they had tried to make the American and Israeli offers look as bad as possible, encouraging Arab leaders to reject the deal to give them an excuse for doing so as well.[72] Indeed, when later asked about Camp David, Mubarak claimed that Clinton wanted him to "tell Arafat to accept Israeli sovereignty over the holy places," a misstatement of what had been proposed. Mubarak said he replied, "I cannot dare to say this. Nobody in the Arab world would dare to say this. It could lead to terrorism."[73]

This was quite different from what had happened in private. While Mubarak was angry when he heard the Palestinian version of events, on being given a full briefing in Cairo on the offer by a high-ranking State Department official, Egypt's leaders had a different response. Foreign Minister Amr Musa turned to Mubarak and said, "There's more here than we understood." Afterward, the Egyptians tried to encourage Arafat to make a deal but could not budge him. Only privately would one of Mubarak's top lieutenants admit, "Arafat should have accepted the deal as a basis for negotiations. We Arabs have to learn how to compromise."[74]

Other Arab leaders agreed. Saudi Arabia's ambassador to Washington, Bandar bin Sultan, later said that to criticize Arafat publicly at the time would have damaged the Palestinian cause but claimed to have told him privately, "Since 1948, every time we've had something on the table we say no. Then we say yes. When we say yes, it's not on the table anymore. Then we have to deal with something less. Isn't it about time we say yes? . . . If we lose this opportunity, it is not going to be a tragedy. This is going to be a crime."[75]

On the summit's last night, Clinton and Ross sat with Israeli foreign minister Ben-Ami and Saeb Arikat of the Palestinian delegation for almost three hours, trying to come up with one last attempt to resolve the Jerusalem question. At one point, Arikat suggested deferring both Jerusalem and refugee issues. Israel rejected this idea since it would then be giving up the West Bank and Gaza to a new Palestinian state without any real peace agreement, almost guaranteeing that there would be continued conflict over these issues. Clinton then proposed another major concession to the Palestinians: they would have full sovereignty over the surface of the Temple Mount—and thus full control over the al-Aqsa mosque—while Israel would have sovereignty under it, where the remains of the Jewish Temple lay. Arikat made clear that even this was unacceptable to Arafat.

Then Clinton proposed still another unilateral concession to the Palestinians, giving them virtual full control of all East Jerusalem neighborhoods with the exception of the tiny Jewish and Armenian quarters in the Old City. Clinton asked Arikat to take these ideas back to Arafat, but Arikat explained that Arafat would not change his mind. "We were trying whatever we could," said Ross, "but what really emerged was that Arafat just wasn't going to decide. We could have said everything to him, and he would have come up with some other issue. He wasn't going to decide and that was all."[76]

By turning down a deal, Arafat not only denied his people a state and ensured prolonging the occupation and their refugee status, he also threw away an opportunity to gain huge material benefits for every Palestinian. American delegates estimated during the Camp David talks that the Palestinians could receive more than $20 billion in internationally raised refugee compensation money.[77] The United States proposed to lead a global fundraising campaign for money, which would then be administered by a special international committee.[78]

Arikat did read Clinton's proposals to Arafat and the Palestinian delegation. "Not much discussion was needed," a Palestinian negotiator later wrote. Abu Mazin would later call the entire proposal "humiliating."[79] Palestinian participants erroneously claimed that the United States had simply accepted the Israeli position on Jerusalem.

But if anyone was humiliated, it was the Americans. As the Palestinian response rejecting the proposal was being drafted, U.S. participants were begging the Palestinians to reconsider. "It's a good deal," they said. "Convince Arafat to accept it! You can limit the number of Jews who pray at the Wall. The proposal gives you huge gains!"[80] In this context came Arafat's reply to the U.S. official who made the final impassioned direct plea to him to help his people, get a state, and not lose the best opportunity for the Palestinians since 1948: "I can't."[81]

When Arikat and Dahlan went to Clinton's room at 1 A.M. to hand over the official response, President Clinton was standing in the wide hallway. He listened to the letter, which Arikat began translating aloud into English. It thanked President Clinton for his efforts, expressed hope that they would continue, and emphasized the Palestinian desire to continue negotiations. It ended by stating that international legality had to be the basis for any agreement and that the proposals on Jerusalem were in contradiction with this requirement. "I was expecting a response like this," Clinton said.[82]

All that was left was for the leaders to draft their press statements. Although Clinton said he did not want Arafat to feel like "the skunk at a picnic," he was more interested in helping Barak, who had gone so far to try to make a deal possible.[83]

"Barak had made a supreme effort and Arafat had given him nothing," Ross noted. The failure surprised Clinton, who knew only too well the difficulties all along but thought that there was a good chance of success. Arafat had frequently flattered him by stating that only Clinton could make peace, saying, "You're the only one we can do this with," "You're a historic figure," "My people can never thank you enough." Clinton felt that Arafat had let him down.[84]

But Clinton had promised Arafat that he would not be blamed if the meeting did not succeed, and the president also did not want to foreclose some future possibility of peace. So rather than speak of his anger, Clinton gave only a hint of his feelings toward Arafat at the postsummit press conference on July 25, 2000. "Prime Minister Barak," he told reporters, "showed particular courage, vision, and an understanding of the historical importance of this moment.... The prime minister moved forward more from his initial position than Chairman Arafat— particularly [on] the question of Jerusalem."[85]

At the end of the summit, Arafat urged that there be another such meeting. "He wanted a second summit or third before the first one was over," said an American official sarcastically.[86] Arafat then embarked on a tour of the Arab world and other countries, presenting the Israeli offer in the worst possible light to justify his rejection. To Palestinians, Arafat seemed a hero for rejecting a perceived attempt by the United States and Israel to force his surrender. Yasin, Hamas's leader, who would have condemned Arafat for any concession, instead now praised him "for his firm and principled stance."[87]

At first, the general Western reaction was that Arafat had missed a good opportunity and turned down a reasonable proposal. Meanwhile, the clock continued to tick away Clinton's remaining days in office. Barak's political position at home was worsened by exaggerated reports in Israel's media that he had made big concessions at Camp David with no reciprocity from Arafat. Popular concern grew that Barak might offer more and more without receiving anything in return.

Barak later said that he "had been educated at Camp David" and knew at the end of the summit that "we don't have a partner, at least for now." The failure was not only the inability to reach an agreement but that "there was no serious effort. Arafat wasn't willing to negotiate."

Clinton told Barak that even if they had made fifty mistakes, the important point was that Arafat was unwilling to make a deal.[88]

What would Arafat do next? On June 25, just before going to the summit, Arafat had told a Nablus rally that Palestinians were ready to start their struggle all over again from the beginning.[89] At Camp David, he predicted on many occasions that if he did not get everything he wanted, the Palestinians would erupt in violence.[90] This was no mere political analysis on his part but a threat to gain leverage over the other parties and an alternative if and when the talks broke down. Even before the summit ended, his Fatah movement announced a general call-up of young men for weapons' training.[91] Palestinian television stepped up the belligerent tone of its broadcasts, showing military parades and video clips of violence against Israeli soldiers.[92] The PLO Executive Committee issued a call "to exercise the maximum degree of vigilance and to be prepared for all eventualities."[93]

Palestinian communications minister Imad al-Faluji later said that Arafat ordered preparations for a new Intifada after returning from Camp David.[94] Sakhr Habash, the man in charge of Fatah's ideological and educational activities, explained that after the summit ended, Arafat warned, "The next phase requires us to prepare for conflict [with Israel], because Prime Minister Barak is not a partner capable of complying with our people's aspirations." Habash added that the Intifada

> did not break out in order to improve our bargaining ability in the negotiations, nor as a reaction to Sharon's provocative visit.... This was only the spark. It was accumulated in the depths of our people and was bound to explode...because of the political problem that was put off for more than a year and a half—the problem of independence.[95]

Mamduh Nofal, a political advisor to Arafat, explained that the new Intifada was

> not a mass movement separate from the [PA] nor did it break out in isolation from it. Rather, the opposite is true; it began on the basis of a central decision from the [PA] before it became a popular movement.... Arafat saw [Sharon's] visit to al-Aqsa as explosive enough not only to ignite the fire on Palestinian land but also to stir up the situation outside the borders of Palestine. Decisions were made regarding practical preparations.[96]

As had happened before, Arafat saw violence as an alternative to negotiations, as a way to get what he wanted either by intimidating or defeating his foe. In this effort, he used his old tactic of seeking international sympathy and the even older one of trying to wear down Israel through terrorism. In addition, Arafat's popularity had been at a low point for some time, with growing complaints about corruption, repression, and the failure of a state to materialize. Once the fighting began, however, all the Palestinians' anger was turned away from Arafat and toward Israel. After all, since Camp David had failed—and their leaders told them it was because Israel would never offer them either a state or East Jerusalem—a return to violence quite logically seemed the only option they had left.

Some informal contacts did continue since both sides wanted to show they were not responsible for any diplomatic breakdown.[97] On September 25, Barak even invited Arafat to his home. This was only Arafat's second trip to Israel, and the two leaders met alone for forty-five minutes. The atmosphere was friendly, but no progress was made. Barak again concluded, "Even in this 'four-eyes' meeting I couldn't say that I found a man ready to take decisions." But in order to show that he was doing his best, Barak told Clinton over the telephone, as Arafat stood next to him, "I'm going to be the partner of this man even more so than Rabin was."[98]

There were more meetings at New York's Waldorf Astoria Hotel and at the Ritz-Carlton Hotel near the Pentagon in Virginia during the last few days of September. But nothing new was said.[99] Meanwhile, the U.S. side was pulling together Clinton's follow-up peace proposal, which it planned to present on October 1.

But then, on September 28, the explosion that Clinton had prophesied and that Arafat had threatened at the summit's end began. Ariel Sharon, Israel's opposition leader, made a one-hour visit to the Haram al-Sharif/Temple Mount area in Jerusalem's Old City. Arafat later contended that he tried to stop Sharon's visit because he knew it would trigger clashes, though before the visit his security chief, Jibril Rajub, said the situation could be handled.[100] U.S. officials asked Barak if he could stop the visit. But as head of a democratic state, Barak could not find a way to bar the opposition leader from going to a public site.

With a heavy police guard, Sharon strolled around the compound for an hour, entered no buildings, and left. Thirty policemen and four Palestinians were lightly wounded in scuffles. Rumors spread in Palestinian neighborhoods—soon supplemented by incitement from the media under Arafat's control—that Sharon had defiled the Muslim holy sites and that al-Aqsa might be seized by Israel or even destroyed. Marwan Barghouti, Fatah's leader on the West Bank saw Sharon's visit as merely a pretext: "I knew that the end of September was the last period [of time] before the explosion, but when Sharon reached the al-Aqsa mosque, this was the most appropriate moment for the out-break of the Intifada." After Sharon left, Palestinian activists held a two-hour meeting on how to spread the battle to all PA-controlled areas. Barghouti recalled:

> The night prior to Sharon's visit, I participated in a panel on a local television station, and I seized the opportunity to call on the public to go to the al-Aqsa mosque in the morning, for it was not possible that Sharon would reach al-Haram al-Sharif... and walk away peacefully. I... went to al-Aqsa in the morning.... We tried to create clashes without success because of the differences of opinion that emerged with others in the al-Aqsa compound at the time.[101]

At al-Aqsa the next day, a large number of Palestinians demonstrated. Some threw stones, and Israeli police replied with rubber-coated metal bullets and live ammunition to disperse the demonstrators, killing four and injuring about two hundred of them. Fourteen Israeli policemen were also hurt. Violence spread quickly. By the end of the first week, more than sixty Palestinians and five Israelis were killed. Albright called Arafat and asked him to stop the violence. But he did nothing.[102]

The Palestinians called the new uprising the "al-Aqsa Intifada," a name inflaming religious passions. But few of those demonstrating in what they thought to be the defense of an endangered holy site knew that Arafat had already been offered sovereignty over al-Aqsa at the Camp David summit. For Arafat, the conflict was actually a Palestinian war to gain independence without compromise or negotiations.

Arafat encouraged the masses to fight through the media, speeches, and meetings, while ordering his security forces not to interfere. While not involved in the planning and details of the attacks, he clearly controlled the overall strategy and set guidelines for what was permitted. Sakhr Habash explained:

> Since brother Arafat is busy with many... missions, authority was delegated to leaders in the field.... However, the leadership of the PA remained the source of authority, and [led] the operations of the Intifada throughout the homeland. I can say for certain that [Arafat] is the ultimate authority for all operations, and whoever thinks otherwise, does not know what is going on.[103]

On October 4, after Arafat rejected the first American call for a ceasefire, Barak and Arafat met with Albright at the U.S. embassy in Paris with plans to continue talking in Egypt the following day. During the meeting, Arafat expressed reluctance to issue a public statement calling for an end to the uprising, and Barak refused to accept Arafat's demand for an international investigation on the origins of the violence without even getting a ceasefire in exchange.

At one point, Arafat said he would call some of his police commanders to make a truce. Barak responded, "But these are not the people organizing the violence. If you are serious, then call Marwan Barghouti and Hussein al-Sheikh," West Bank Fatah officials who were leading the insurgency. Arafat looked at Barak with an expression of innocence, Barak recounted, "as if I had mentioned the names of two polar bears, and said: 'Who?' So I repeated the names, this time with a pronounced, clear Arabic inflection . . . and Arafat again said, 'Who?' Some of his aides burst out laughing. Arafat finally agreed to call them later."[104] But nothing happened, and the shooting continued.

Arafat's attempts to escape from the pressure to stop the fighting turned into an actual flight. At one point that night, Albright was talking to Barak when Arafat decided to walk out. Suddenly, she heard people yelling, "He's leaving! He's leaving!" She ran across the cobblestone courtyard, stumbling in her high heels and shouting to the Marines guarding the exit, "Close the gates! Close the gates!" Just as his car was pulling out, the gates swung shut. Albright jumped into the seat next to Arafat and persuaded him to come back inside.[105]

After Arafat returned to the meeting, the Americans believed that they had hammered out an agreement with him to stop the violence. After all, he should have had every incentive to make a ceasefire since his people were being killed and Palestinian facilities were being destroyed. As Albright's staff typed up the notes indicating what steps each leader would take to stop the violence, Arafat and Barak went to see French prime minister Jacques Chirac. Chirac was so supportive of Arafat that the Palestinian leader, already reluctant to finalize an agreement, decided that he could do better by not continuing the talks. He simply did not show up for the scheduled signing.[106] The Americans, still eager to broker a deal, neither criticized his behavior nor gave up trying to mollify him.

Whether or not Arafat started the conflict, he quickly decided that he wanted it to continue. As a U.S. official put it, "He was not going to stand in the way of the tiger, so he rode it."[107] Unimpeded by Arafat, the violence intensified. In October, two Israeli army reservists who accidentally drove into Ramallah were brutally murdered by a mob as other Palestinians cheered. Israel retaliated with air raids on Ramallah, Gaza, Jericho, Nablus, and Hebron, the first military incursions into PA-ruled territory.

Two days later, Clinton joined Arafat at Sharm al-Sheikh, Egypt. Barak was so disgusted by Arafat's performance in Paris that he did not come to the meeting. Nevertheless, while no actual agreement was reached, Mubarak wanted a ceasefire declared and let Clinton announce that the two sides had reached an understanding on ending the violence. Arafat remained silent, not wanting to challenge the Egyptian president. Thus, Clinton was able to tell the world that the Israelis and Palestinians would take immediate measures to stop the violence and, as Arafat wanted, there would be a fact-finding committee on the violence.[108]

Although Clinton's new proposal had given him the international investigation he had been demanding, later known as the Mitchell Commission, Arafat still did not impose a ceasefire. Once again, he had pocketed a concession and not fulfilled his own obligation. He even blamed the United States for the continuing violence, saying Israel was "killing us with . . . American weapons."[109]

His vision, he told the Palestinians, was that

the embers of the Intifada will continue until Palestinian independence, the return of Jerusalem and al-Aqsa to Palestinian sovereignty, and the establishment of a sovereign Palestinian state with Jerusalem as its capital. The decision regarding the Intifada is in the hands of the brave Palestinian people, who decided to carry out this battle to achieve independence and to establish their state.[110]

Indifferent to the casualties and material damage, Arafat had returned to his classical conception of victory through violence.

At an emergency Arab League session in Cairo on November 5, Arafat spoke of his people's suffering and received the Arab leaders' verbal support. Asked by reporters whether he had any message for Israel, Arafat responded that the battle would go on until there was an independent Palestinian state. "If Israeli Prime Minister Ehud Barak doesn't like it," Arafat paused, perhaps planning to use some Arab proverb like "He can drink the Nile." Instead, Arafat blurted out a phrase that he knew would be more familiar to Western reporters: "He can go to Hell!"[111]

In political terms, that is precisely what happened to Barak. With his popularity plummeting and his coalition splintered, Barak resigned on December 10 and called for early elections, a desperate move apparently timed to give himself some slim chance of victory, since his opponent would be Sharon rather than the more popular Netanyahu.

That same month, Israeli and Palestinian negotiators met at Bolling Air Force Base near Washington for Clinton's last effort to make peace. On December 23, the president officially presented both sides with his proposal for a final agreement at a meeting in the White House cabinet room. He offered new concessions for the Palestinians, going beyond even what had been offered at the end of Camp David.[112]

According to the new offer, the Palestinian state would include between 94 and 96 percent of the West Bank plus a 1–3 percent land swap between Israel and Palestine. Thus, the Palestinians would get roughly the equivalent of the entire pre-1967 land area of the West Bank. The goal would be to incorporate 80 percent of the settlers into areas that would be part of Israel while also maximizing the territorial contiguity of the Palestinian state. In addition, there would be three Israeli early-warning stations on the West Bank to ensure that foreign armies were not moving to cross into that area, with Palestinian officials present to ensure the proper use of these places.

On Jerusalem, too, the offer was improved for the Palestinians. Now they would have total sovereignty over the Haram al-Sharif area and Israel would only have sovereignty over the Western Wall. Israel's only influence over the temple's site would be that its permission be required to excavate there, while the Palestinians would also be able to veto any Israeli digging behind the Western Wall.

Finally, regarding refugees, the U.S. offer tried to meet Palestinian demands. An international commission would be established to handle this issue. Two alternative ideas were offered, which might meet both parties' wishes. One idea was for both sides to recognize the right of Palestinian refugees to return to "historic Palestine" and "their homeland," which could be fulfilled by migration to the Palestinian state. Alternatively, the agreement could list a number of acceptable destinations for the refugees: the state of Palestine, areas of Israel transferred to Palestine in the land swap, Arab states where they now lived, another country, or Israel. Both Israel and Palestine would decide their own policies on admitting refugees.

The Clinton plan came close to giving the Palestinians 99 percent of their demands, aside from the return issue, while transcending any previous Israeli interpretation of its goals and security needs. Clearly, it was a package tailored to win Arafat's acceptance. "This is the best that I can do," Clinton told the group of Israeli and Palestinian negotiators. "Brief your leaders and tell me if they are prepared to come for discussions based on these ideas.... These are my ideas. If they are not accepted, they are not just off the table, they also go with me when I leave office."[113]

After Clinton left the room, Ross stayed behind to ensure that both sides understood the proposal and to tell them, "This is the culmination of the effort. If you don't accept [our proposal] as a framework for negotiation, that is the end of it, we withdraw it."[114]

The Israelis approved the plan despite reservations that Ben-Ami called "minor and dealing mainly with security arrangements." Specifically, Israel wanted to ensure its sovereignty over the Jewish and

Armenian quarters, clarify the proposed solution on the holy site, and gain a transitional period of some years when its forces could remain in the Jordan Valley as a line of defense against other Arab states. He recalled, "There was no doubt that our reply was positive." To make sure this was clear, Barak instructed Ben-Ami to telephone Arafat on December 29 and tell him that Israel accepted the plan as a basis for negotiation and was ready to discuss how to implement it.[115]

But it was clear that Arafat had grave concerns about the plan. As he was about to meet Clinton, the Palestinian press was already publishing his letter of rejection. It declared that the U.S. proposal was unacceptable because it would allegedly divide a Palestinian state into three sections, undermining its ability to survive; split Palestinian Jerusalem into disconnected islands; and constitute an unacceptable surrender of the right of return. The letter concluded, "The American proposals seem to respond to Israeli demands while ignoring the basic Palestinian requirement: a viable Palestinian state that can survive."[116]

On January 3, 2001, Arafat came to the White House. While he told Clinton he agreed to the plan, "he then added reservations that basically meant he rejected every single one of the things he was supposed to give," said Ross.[117] Rather than accepting the plan as a framework for negotiations, Arafat said it would first have to be totally changed. In fact, his responses merely amounted to a repetition of all his earlier claims, without even the one or two small compromises he had offered at Camp David.

Regarding the issue of territory, for example, the Palestinians again insisted that the starting point must be that they would get all the West Bank, East Jerusalem, and the Gaza Strip. On refugees, they repeated that all must be offered the choice of admission to Israel. On security, they rejected any Israeli military presence anywhere in the territory of a Palestinian state. Nor could there be any Israeli sovereignty over any place in East Jerusalem, including no special role in controlling the Jewish holy site. Arafat also rejected Israel's use of what would become Palestinian air space for civilian planes landing at Israel's main international airport, which could make use of that facility impossible.[118]

The Palestinians later maintained that Arafat did accept the agreement with reservations. A PA official insisted, "Unlike what had happened at Camp David, there was no Palestinian rejection." But many Palestinian accounts make clear that this was not so. At most, Arafat said that he viewed the agreement as containing interesting elements which the negotiators might study without being bound by them. Indeed, when asked later if he had accepted Clinton's proposal, Arafat told the Palestinian media that there was "no such thing as a Clinton plan."[119]

When, after two years of failed Intifada, an Arab reporter asked Arafat whether all the destruction to the Palestinians' lives, cause, and land did not make him think it was a mistake to have rejected the peace proposals, Arafat said, "No and I will tell you why. I approved the Mitchell report, accepted the Paris agreement, and approved Clinton's [plan] with two minor amendments. . . ."

"So why," asked the journalist, "did . . . Clinton accuse you of rejecting it?"

"For electoral reasons," Arafat replied, only because Clinton's wife, Hillary, was running for senator in New York and she needed Jewish votes there.[120]

Arafat never told his own people what he was offered. But his Fatah group's most comprehensive official analysis of the plan shows what he wanted them to believe about the proposal and the reasons they should reject it completely.[121] Fatah's argument begins by insisting that the peace process "was launched on the basis of international legitimacy," a phrase Arafat often used to imply that international law and world opinion supported his position and so there was nothing really to negotiate about except the details of implementing it. In addition, this formula implied that since the proper outcome of negotiations was already set, Israel had no right to bargain over the terms.

According to Arafat, the peace process was based on an agreement for the Palestinians to receive all the West Bank, the Gaza Strip, and East Jerusalem and that all Palestinian refugees were entitled to live in Israel. There was never, however, a single American or Israeli statement or international agreement that supported such an interpretation. Moreover, the Fatah analysis undermined this argument by admitting that the Oslo Agreement did not accept a right of return. And if UN Resolutions 242 and 338 so totally supported Arafat's position, why then had he rejected them for so many decades?

In its second point, the Fatah document denounces "the monopoly of the Zionist Clinton administration" as mediator, despite the fact that Arafat had constantly sought to increase the American role in the negotiations. Clinton's performance had proven, Arafat's group told its members, "that the Zionist group of the White House and the Zionist Lobby are controlling the future of the Palestinian people['s] cause." The position paper then rejected every basic point in Clinton's plan, including "any rights for Jews in the Western Wall" or any Israeli presence in East Jerusalem. Jews would only be able to visit or pray at the Western Wall with the permission of Palestinian authorities.

Equally telling was the Fatah paper's broader conclusion. Unless all Palestinian demands are met, states Point 9, the conflict will not end. Thus, even if compromises were made, these would not be truly binding on a Palestinian state. Moreover, according to Point 11, the peace process was wrongly "launched on the basis that the conflict is around the occupied territories in 1967 which is 23 percent of the Historical Palestine area. They are trying to ignore the historical and natural right of the Palestinian people on all of the Palestinian territories." In short, Arafat's own movement had not yet given up a claim to all of Israel.

What was most telling of all, however, was Arafat's perception of the right of return, ultimately the issue that really blocked any chance for an agreement. He always spoke as if UN Resolution 194 were a virtually sacred document which guaranteed a right of return, a total misstatement of that document's purpose and contents. The resolution was in fact a nonbinding set of instructions for a short-lived, abortive mediation effort, which the Arab side rejected shortly after the 1948 war. Indeed, while proclaiming that document to be the inviolable basis of his claim, Arafat ignored and rejected many of its other provisions, which included UN rule over Jerusalem and other areas he claimed for his state.[122]

In line with Arafat's viewpoint, the Fatah position paper argued, "The issue of the refugees is the core of the Arab-Israeli conflict," and the only acceptable solution is their return to Israel. Indeed, to make clear its determination to make Palestinian refugees go to Israel and nowhere else, Fatah insisted that all returnees, even if they regained their old property, receive the same compensation as those who did not go back. They were entitled to a large sum of money, Fatah argued, because of their sufferings and their property's use by others since 1948. In contrast, it declared any resettlement in Arab states—even for those living there for a half century and on the basis of full citizenship—to be "collective punishment." Unless the refugees all could go to Israel, Fatah warned, the conflict would continue forever.[123]

To leave nothing vague, the position paper explains that the purpose of demanding this return is to ensure the end of Israel as a Jewish state. Since having a right of return for Jews made Israel a Jewish state, Fatah pointed out, giving the same right to Palestinians would instantly make Israel a binational state. In language reminiscent of PLO positions in the 1970s, it explained that the huge number of refugees would change Israel's structure and "help Jews get rid of the racist Zionism that wants to impose their permanent isolation from the rest of the world."[124]

What was most shocking about Arafat's approach, however, was how irrational it was from the standpoint of a genuine Palestinian nationalism. Nationalists want their people to live in their own country in order to maintain a separate identity and to build its population, power, culture, and prosperity. If the goal was to create a strong, stable Palestinian state living in peace alongside Israel, everything would be done to discourage any notion of a return. Why should a Palestinian state apparently make a gift of these people, their money, and talents to Israel? Aside from any other consideration, Palestine would lose hundreds of thousands of its most educated and energetic citizens because they would seek jobs and better living standards in Israel. These bizarre contradictions seem to show Arafat's belief that a return would subvert Israel and put it under Palestinian rule. In that case, the returnees would not be lost to Palestine but would soon be making a real return to that state, while bringing all of Israel with them.

As Feisal al-Husseini explained, "If I tell the Palestinian refugees, I have reached an agreement with Israel that allows the return of three million Palestinian refugees, but excludes five hundred thousand, then ten years later the five hundred thousand will create another problem and another new plight."[125] Were all these people demanding a right they did not intend to use? The Palestinian leadership and media constantly equated any refusal of refugees to return to Israel with treason. Abu Mazin put it plainly: the refugees were the main Palestinian issue, and it could only be solved by ensuring they returned to their homes and property from 1948.[126] Qaddumi was also candid: "The Right of Return of the refugees to Haifa and Jaffa is more important than statehood."[127] In the end, Arafat agreed.

Fatah's explanation for Arafat's rejection of all the plans offered him gives one more reason that helps to explain his behavior: "Accepting these proposals... means moving the conflict into an internal Palestinian-Palestinian conflict that will destroy the Intifada and turn it into an Arab-Palestinian conflict." Arafat and his colleagues knew that making a deal would create conflicts with some Palestinians and Arab states who would oppose it as making too many concessions. Rather than face this problem—which would always be unavoidable since only total military victory would bring him a solution without compromise—Arafat decided it was safer for him to say no and go on demanding everything.

Finally, Arafat did not share the view of many observers that his interests lay with helping Clinton and Barak. He had reason to be happy to see Clinton leave office and Barak fall from power. After all, this would relieve the pressure on him to make a deal. When a right-wing Israeli government came to power, it could be portrayed as being responsible for the peace process's collapse. At times, Arafat implied that he preferred Clinton to not succeed in his peacemaking efforts so Bush would win the American presidential election, since he hoped the new president would be like his father, President George Bush, and favor the Arab side.[128]

After the Clinton plan was rejected, for all practical purposes the peace process was over. There was one last attempt at Taba, Egypt,

January 21–27, 2001, but neither Arafat nor Barak were there, and it was more of an exchange of opinions than a negotiation.[129] The difference between the two sides' stance was quite wide. Abu Alaa, the Palestinian team's head, stated, "There has never before been a clearer gap in the positions of the two sides."[130] Arikat added that the Taba talks "emphasized the size of the gap between the positions of the two sides and the depth of the disagreements...primarily on the subjects of Jerusalem and the refugees."[131]

Later, Palestinian leaders did a 180-degree turnaround and proclaimed that the Taba meeting had come close to success. Their motive was to consolidate Israel's new concessions as the starting point for future negotiations. On Jerusalem, Israel proposed a special regime for the whole city, but the Palestinians again demanded control over all East Jerusalem.[132] On borders, the Palestinians informally offered to swap 2 percent of the West Bank for an equal amount of land from Israel, an echo of Abu Alaa's idea at Camp David, and agreed to let three Israeli settlement blocs be incorporated into Israel.[133] But Arafat never confirmed such a plan and even this exchange would only include the actual land on which the buildings stood. All land adjacent to the settlement and the roads would remain in Palestinian hands, making them unviable and undefendable.[134]

But this was all an exercise in futility. "Arafat never seriously considered" the offers made at Camp David, in the Clinton plan, or at Taba, said an American official. "When the violence started, the Palestinian price tag went up It was the worst time to make concessions. There was never any chance of a political solution in an eleventh-hour fix."[135] Even if all of the details of the specific issues could have been solved, the real cause of the failure was that Arafat preferred to continue the conflict for years—even if this meant occupation and many more casualties—rather than make the necessary tough decisions and concessions to resolve it.

As Clinton was preparing to leave office in January 2001, Arafat called him and praised the president. "You are a great man," Arafat said in a flattering tone.

"The hell I am," Clinton said he responded. "I'm a colossal failure, and you made me one."[136] Clinton told his successor, George W. Bush, that he had misjudged Arafat and advised that Bush not make the same mistake.[137]

On January 28, 2001, less than twenty-four hours after the Taba talks ended, Arafat addressed the World Economic Forum in Davos, Switzerland. Former Israeli prime minister Shimon Peres, Arafat's long-time partner for peace and now Israel's regional cooperation minister, had just delivered a conciliatory address about the need to make peace.

Indeed, only seven years earlier, the two leaders had walked onto the same stage holding hands as a sign of their partnership. Now, as Peres listened with shock, Arafat delivered a blistering attack on Israel.

"The current [Barak] government of Israel is waging, for the last four months, a savage and barbaric war, as well as a blatant and fascist military aggression against our Palestinian people," said Arafat. Israel has

> la[id] against us total siege, indeed, worse than that, it is imposing this siege against every village and town. It is prohibiting the freedom of movement and travel of our people. It is jeopardizing the basic human rights of our Palestinian citizens, dismissing our workers, closing our factories, destroying a number of these, so much so that 90 percent of our workers are forcibly unemployed, destroying our farms and fruit trees and prohibiting export and import, indeed it is forbidding us to receive, from brothers and friends, donated provisions.[138]

He even made the wild and unsupported accusation that Israel was using radioactive uranium against Palestinian civilians.[139] One would hardly know that Arafat had been the one to refuse every opportunity for a ceasefire.

Ironically, Peres had been the main Israeli advocate of unilateral concessions to Arafat, repeatedly defending his intentions and the likelihood of a successful peace deal. He had argued, "The Palestinians have been 'Americanized' by the process. Arafat has had a sea change in how he views the United States, and the Palestinians are constantly courting the United States now."[140] Despite continuing to say that Arafat was a partner for peace publicly, even Peres began privately remarking after Davos that he no longer believed it.[141]

The outcome did not necessarily mean that Arafat went into the peace process knowing he would not reach an agreement in the end. But this point could mean that his failure to make a deal in 2000 was a logical consequence of his basic world view rather than a conscious design on his part.

If he expected to get an agreement with Israel without reining in terrorism, or thought that a peace treaty would grant Palestinian refugees a full right of return, or considered it possible to arrange things so that the door would remain open for destroying Israel in a later stage of conflict, or expected the United States and Europe to force Israel to make unilateral concessions to him without responding in kind, then he was taking notions into the peace process that doomed it to failure. Equally, Arafat had done virtually nothing to prepare Palestinians for compromise during the seven-year-long process and instead had led them to believe that they would get everything they wanted through negotiation or violence.

Thus, the peace process did not fail because Rabin was assassinated, or Netanyahu was intransigent, or Barak was insufficiently charming at Camp David, or Israel did not offer a percentage point or two more territory initially, or Clinton did not postpone the Camp David meeting for two weeks. The problems lay deeper, first and fundamentally, with Arafat himself. While Peres, Clinton, and many of their top lieutenants were "peace romantics," Arafat and his colleagues remained revolutionary romantics. He had trouble making decisions, but when he did so he almost always chose the radical alternative.

There was no contradiction between Arafat's militancy and his strategic passivity in this regard. Whatever mental reservations he had, Arafat's predominant attitude toward the process seemed to be that he would enter it and see what happened. After all, in the early 1990s, he had no better alternative, and Arafat was a man who always seemed to believe that things would turn out all right no matter what the short-term reasons were to think otherwise. In private, he told colleagues in 1993, "We entered Lebanon through a crack in the wall and we ended up controlling Beirut. We're entering Palestine through a crack in the wall and we'll see where it gets us."[142]

This fits with Arafat's tendency not to plan ahead or to develop grand strategies. "Arafat," the Palestinian political analyst Majdi Abd al-Hadi explained, "is the maestro of tactics. He abides by no specific holy strategy, jumps from one thing to another and reacts to events."[143] A UN official said Arafat had "a mind like a grasshopper," leaping from thought to thought, topic to topic, without going logically or systematically into anything.[144] Abu Ali Mustafa, head of the PFLP, made the same point more scornfully: "Arafat's policy is one of a man that thinks from day to day, like a day laborer."[145]

Ambiguity and keeping his options open were old patterns for Arafat. He never minded not making up his mind.[146] Yet apparent indecisiveness for Arafat was often, more accurately, a decision to stick with the harder-line approach. Most leaders usually operated on the principle that moderation was generally the safest course. But Arafat's reading of his role, history, and domestic constituency made him gravitate toward militancy.

One of Arafat's greatest skills was his ability to convince so many that he really wanted peace but had been cheated and victimized by others. The sheer audacity of his behavior helped promote this claim. Who could believe he would turn down a chance to get an independent state and rescue his people from occupation if made a good offer? But this is precisely what had happened.

The Moment of Truth

Arafat was no fool. He knew that the Clinton administration was leaving office soon; that the Barak government was going to fall because of its failure to achieve a peace settlement and end Palestinian violence against Israelis; and that consequently Ariel Sharon would replace Barak. By trying to postpone the Camp David summit, rejecting the offer made there, turning to violence, saying no to the Clinton plan, and refusing to implement any ceasefire, he was no longer just bargaining toughly, he was destroying any peace process altogether.

Certainly, he knew that no one on the Israeli side or among the U.S. mediators ever said or implied that the Palestinians would get everything they wanted. He was aware all along that Israel's interpretation of UN Resolution 242 was that it did not require a return to the 1967 borders and that Israel would never accept a right of return. If Arafat was going to stick to his full demands, he had to know that they could only be reached, if ever, through more years of warfare and additional rivers of blood.

By the same token, though, Arafat could not admit that in both the Camp David and Clinton plans, the ostensible gap between the two sides was over a tiny portion of the West Bank, small sections of East Jerusalem where no Arabs lived, and a right of return, which Israel would never grant. One cannot persuade people to fight and sacrifice so much on such a minimal basis. To justify all the suffering, casualties, and destruction, Arafat had to maintain that Israel and the United States had offered nothing to the Palestinians. Thus, he told his own people that there had never been a reasonable offer by the United States or Israel. "Was a real opportunity for peace lost? I think not," he told a major rally in March 2001. He claimed that since Israel had withdrawn the proposal, this proved that it never intended to implement a deal. This argument ignored the fact that the offers had been clearly made only on the basis of his acceptance. Moreover, Arafat's own rejection of the peace plans, his war against Israel, and his refusal to stop the attacks were the causes for Israel rethinking its offer to make concessions. But Arafat simply insisted to Palestinians, "There was no opportunity that was wasted."[147]

In turning down those very real opportunities, though, Arafat had once again made a choice in line with his life's work, self-image, and goals. In international terms, he had embraced one more in a long series of defeats, but in the context of Arafat's domestic politics, it was one more victory. That contradiction was simultaneously the secret of Arafat's success and of his failure. In his usual manner, Arafat was leading his people into another catastrophe.

9

Being Yasir Arafat

A s the twenty-first century began, Yasir Arafat had spent five decades as a revolutionary, forty years as chief of his own group, thirty-three years as leader of an entire people, and seven years as head of a government. Despite all this opportunity and responsibility, however, he had been unable to bring his people victory, peace, or an independent state. This was a record of political failure almost unparalleled in history.

He was brilliant at maintaining his personal position and preserving internal unity. But Arafat's devotion was to the Palestinian cause and not to the Palestinian people. Such goals as raising living standards; building a peaceful, stable society; and adjusting to the limits of the possible—along with many other aspects of political pragmatism— meant nothing to him. As a result, Arafat delayed the conflict's solution, leaving a legacy of avoidable disaster and unnecessary suffering.

But when Arafat defied the rules, it was others who paid the price. He was a captain who steered his ship into storms rather than away from them, refusing to head for a safe harbor if that meant ending his journey. As a result, his ship was constantly battered and often seemed on the verge of sinking, yet never did. Whatever their qualms, passengers and crew obeyed him, fearing mutiny would be even worse. Arafat felt secure in this disorder, heedless of the consequences of his own decisions.

He seemed neither to change nor learn much new over time. In 2003, he was still promoting the same basic ideas, often using the identical phrases, as he had in 1973. Those who persuaded themselves that Arafat had changed or believed they could reform him were ultimately surprised and disappointed. Those who ignored Arafat's history or patterns ended with broken hearts and careers. An official who studied Arafat longer than anyone else in the U.S. government concluded after decades of research, "Arafat is a mystery. I don't have a good sense of who he is and what he wants. If he is the embodiment of Palestinian aspirations, what does he want to achieve?"[1]

Yet whether or not Arafat and others were aware of it, he did demonstrate a consistent political philosophy based on tried and trusted principles: when you are losing is precisely the best time to act as if you were the victor; flexibility encourages pressure on yourself, but if you stand firm, conditions will eventually change in your favor; convince adversaries you are ready to make a deal and that one more concession by them will solve everything; denying responsibility for an action or claiming moderation, no matter how obviously untrue, will make some believe you while others suspend judgment; the man who causes crises is the one others must appease to end them; and few will notice if you say contradictory things to different audiences.

Arafat had also learned that a systematic strategy of terrorism does not inhibit diplomatic gains. After all, he was first invited to speak at the United Nations as he directed a campaign of bloody, anticivilian terrorism against Israel and a string of international atrocities. By responding to his deeds in this way, the world taught Arafat that terrorism can gain attention, sympathy, and support. What he did not learn, however, was that using terrorism does not win political struggles. It never defeated Israel and arguably delayed a Palestinian state's creation by many years.

Experience taught Arafat that militancy and refusal to compromise kept him popular among his own people and in the Arab world. When Arafat initiated violence, it stifled Palestinian criticism of the incompetence and corruption around him, his unfulfilled promises and failed prophecies. His intransigence was repeatedly rewarded with Western concessions, too. The revolution, he concluded, could go on forever.

In the end, Arafat had nothing to show for all the struggle and bloodshed except press clippings. Only Israel could give him a state, and no matter how his actions played in the Western media, no one could or would force that country to make suicidal concessions to him. By refusing to give up, he was never defeated, but by refusing to compromise, he never gained anything lasting either.

History taught Arafat that the merest pretext and boldest distortion can be widely accepted as truth. In the 1970s, Arafat denied he had any connection with his Black September terrorist group and got away without punishment or permanent damage. In Jordan and Lebanon, he insisted he had no control over groups that were part of his organization. He used the same tactic with equal effectiveness for the new Intifada that began in 2000. "I never approved the killing of civilians throughout my military career," Arafat claimed in August 2002. "Why? Because I am a military man and respect being so."[2]

As Arafat's own bodyguards carried out terrorist attacks, Westerners debated whether he had any responsibility for the violence. He rejected reasonable peace offers, and many excused him on the grounds that the proposals were insulting or that those making them had hurt his feelings. His broken promises of ceasefires were quickly forgotten. No sooner was one of his wild claims of conspiracies or Israeli atrocities disproved then the next would be treated credibly. Who but Arafat could launch a long terrorist campaign and then persuade the world to pity him as the victim?

But what he did not learn from history was Abraham Lincoln's maximum that it is possible to fool some of the people some of the time but not all of the people all of the time. Eventually, countries and leaders caught on to the deception. They might not fight against or even criticize Arafat, but they did nothing much to help him either. They ensured his survival but not his success.

Finally, history taught Arafat that any defeat could be portrayed as a glorious victory to Palestinians and Arabs in general. But what he failed to learn was that no matter what spin he succeeded in putting on events, his movement would still have to pay the costs of setbacks. Arafat could play the victim only as long as he ensured that he was the loser. Arafat's great ability was to get himself chance after chance, but his great weakness was the disaster that inevitably concluded each missed opportunity. Arafat's survival seemed almost miraculous, and he bounced back after every defeat. Yet starting over again also meant that he was not making progress, he was just repeating the process.

Many of Arafat's problems and those he caused others arose from the fact that his personality was both well adapted but very much at odds with his task. To become a leader almost always requires passing difficult tests. Those who inherit that position are groomed from childhood. Many rise to lead their people through military ranks, learning the martial virtues of discipline, order, and responsibility. Career politicians come up through political parties and elections by proving they can make decisions, win elections, and administer well. Finally, there are revolutionaries, who prove their fitness by choosing and implementing strategies that bring them to power. Those who do not achieve success are usually quickly replaced by rivals.

Arafat fit none of these categories. He had the ability to hold on to power but not the qualities needed to use it well. He had not built institutions, made decisions leading to victory, or solved problems. In a sense, Arafat's character and vision required that he not find a solution. He saw the establishment of a state without achieving his goal—eliminating Israel or advancing that process by the Palestinian refugees' return—as a betrayal. Since his main skill was survival, he focused on ensuring that the revolutionary stage itself survived permanently. Arafat was in love with revolution, and he never tired of this idealistic intoxication. "We are the flying carpet revolution, we are treading on burning coals," he once exulted. "Tonight I am seeing you in Baghdad. I don't know where I will see you tomorrow."[3]

Arafat's counterparts all over the world saw being a revolutionary as a specific phase in their careers, which they were ready—often eager—to trade in for new lives as their countries' presidents. In contrast, Arafat was an addict to the lifestyle. Boasting of sleeping in a different place each night, he was not eager to settle down in a state of his own and hang up his uniform forever. He changed none of these revolutionary habits during the peace process era.

Why did he find a strange glory in unstable prospects and flight caused by weakness and defeat? By losing, he proved he was not a sell-out like those pompous suit-wearing officials or practical-minded Arab rulers for whom he had such contempt. Arafat might consider himself the Middle Eastern version of Che Guevara but rather then end up a dead hero, Arafat wanted to go on being a live fighter in an immortal struggle. Ross remarked, "I've often thought that maybe he wants to be the last revolutionary on the Palestinian side."[4]

For a permanent revolutionary like Arafat, the worse things were, the better he liked it. Bad conditions inspired struggle; satisfied demands led to abandoning it. Crises and confrontations demonstrated heroism. "He is self-obsessed," explained a Palestinian, and he loved to "create a situation in which only he can deliver, a crisis only he can solve, . . . [one in which] he has to come in and save the day."[5]

In February 2002, just before being trapped in his Ramallah bunker, Arafat told one of his best foreign friends that Israeli prime minister Ariel Sharon was intent on killing every Palestinian one by one, "So it is better to bring on Sabra and Shatilla [a big massacre of Palestinians in Lebanon] now."[6] It was as if he preferred such an outcome as proof that he was correct and as a way to inspire even more conflict. In a sense, suicide bombing was a perfect metaphor for Arafat's deep-seated belief that it was better to die injuring one's enemy than to live making the compromises required by necessity.

A slogan dating from Arafat's early career urged Third World revolutionaries to create "two, three, many Vietnams" to strike at the United States. Arafat's unspoken byword seemed to be the creation of "two, three, many *nakbas* [catastrophes]" to prove the foe's evil ferocity and the revolution's enduring purity. Each phase of his life ended in a new *nakba*, a manifestation of his near–death wish. He was besieged and defeated in Amman in 1970, then in Beirut in 1982, and in Tripoli, Lebanon, in 1983. Next, Arafat shared Iraq's loss of the 1991 Kuwait war, and once again Palestinians had to flee into exile. At last, he maneuvered himself into being twice besieged in Ramallah in 2002.

An Arab writer explained, "Pressure increases his stature. Serious distress seems to calm him."[7] A veteran observer close to him explained:

> Arafat always prefers isolation in two rooms, with no electricity and his friends being killed or imprisoned rather than pay the price of giving up the struggle. Being engaged in battle is the peak of his life, far better than being the president of Palestine. Reporters flock to meet him, world leaders court him. Hamas and Islamic Jihad praise him rather than trying to kill him. Why should he become a traitor in the eyes of his own people by compromising?[8]

The business of plotting and strategizing, revolution and crisis, struggle and excitement was what truly galvanized him. Arafat had no personal interest in becoming ruler of a state largely because he did not care to handle the issues and problems required by that role. Economics bewildered him.[9] He only wanted to find enough money to meet his payroll so the battle could continue. Arafat never expressed any opinion on the dozens of issues that Third World countries must confront.

Even while serving as the PA's leader, he ignored day-to-day problems and made it hard for anyone else to deal with them effectively either. He had not been transformed into an administrator or statesman; he did not become someone who educated and prepared the masses or even his own hierarchy for the requirements of statehood. Arafat simply remained a revolutionary for whom the West Bank and Gaza was a better base of operations than Jordan or Lebanon had been.

The root of Arafat's problem was not that he did not have a state, but that he and his movement acted in a way that ensured they did not get one. In modern history, there have been more than a hundred individuals who led their people to a state or made a revolution so transforming as to, in effect, create a new one. They were diverse types: George Washington and Vladimir Lenin, Mao Zedong and Ruhollah Khomeini, Giuseppe Garibaldi and Nelson Mandela, Julius Nyerere and

Kwame Nkrumah, Mahatma Gandhi and Sukarno, Kemal Ataturk and David Ben-Gurion.

Some were democrats, some dictators. What they had in common, though, was a foundation of pragmatism, a willingness to compromise, a keen sense about the balance of forces, and a flexibility in fitting means with ends. Lenin, Ho Chi Minh, Eamon de Valera, and Ben-Gurion, for example, were quick to accept partition solutions, believing that once they had a state, they would either get more territory or at least be able to use what they had to fulfill their purpose. Rulers of small countries were sensible enough not to go to war with more powerful ones, which would inevitably defeat them. Despite many differences, they all knew that the delivery of material goods, peace, and security to their constituents was intimately connected with their ability to retain power.

In each of these categories, Arafat was sorely lacking. What distinguished Arafat from so many failed revolutionaries was that although he could not achieve victory, he was still able to stay atop his movement for a lifetime. He was unique: forever suspended between victory and defeat; able to keep his struggle going but not to resolve it. He could break the rules, commit terrorism in the midst of a global war against terrorism, and make statements sounding like those of a madman and still preserve his hold on his people, the Arab world's support, and often even his credibility with the West.

At the root of his world view and his popular support was the Palestinian belief that Israel's creation was both unjust and reversible. Consequently, it was right and proper to struggle for that entity's elimination by any means necessary. This battle must continue no matter how long it took or how much it cost. Even if total victory could not be attained, at least honor could be preserved, revenge could be extracted, and the possibility of future triumph kept alive.

It is easy to believe that the dominion of such views was inevitable, but that would overstate the case considerably. Even the most strongly held beliefs and fiercest hatreds have changed in the fullness of time if alternatives are made evident and someone leads in that direction. The post–World War II transformation of Germany and Japan, Communism's collapse, and the dissolution of centuries-old European rivalries offer examples of such dramatic alterations. Stability, peace, and a better life have a strong attraction for human beings. Even among the Palestinians, there were conflicting viewpoints. Many wanted something different, better, and more peaceful. A leader's duty is to draw his people toward realizable and beneficial goals. With proper guidance, moderation could have triumphed.

The continuation of hard-line attitudes, of course, might always be blamed on Israel. It can be claimed that Israel did not offer an attractive solution and instead maintained its presence in the West Bank and the Gaza Strip for many years. But no country would make risky concessions to a movement that openly proclaimed an intention to wipe it off the map and that used as its main tactic the deliberate murder of its citizens wherever they could be found. Even so, about half of Israel's population always supported turning over the West Bank and Gaza Strip to an Arab partner willing to make peace; most of the other half doubted such a partner would ever appear. When Arafat signed the Oslo Agreement, the dovish faction grew stronger; when Arafat rejected peace in 2000, many of its members switched sides.

Of course, Arafat's personality and preferences also had roles in his successes as a leader. He rose and remained in power because his talents were well adapted to the particular Palestinian condition. Spread over a dozen countries, often having limited contact with the Palestinian masses and no totally reliable base of support, the PLO faced nightmarish problems throughout its history. Arab states intervened in its affairs by sponsoring their own groups and repeatedly trying to seize control. Arafat was constantly constrained by having to please non-Fatah groups and unruly leaders inside Fatah, partly to ensure they did not become agents of Arab states against him. Arafat tried to convince them that the movement must remain independent, once explaining, "One can only scratch oneself with one's own fingers."[10]

Yet Arafat also perpetuated this anarchy by refusing to impose or enforce unity. Many nationalist movements built a united front to bring together an entire people behind a leadership that coordinated and controlled it. Instead, Arafat extolled decentralization as proving that the PLO was "a real democracy" and "a fusion of all the political currents of the Palestinian people."[11]

Arafat so often claimed to have only limited power that some of his colleagues made the mistake of believing it. Jamal al-Surani, the PLO Executive Committee's secretary, said in 1989 that Arafat "is not the head. He and we are partners. We are not his employees.... [Arafat] does not decide what is right and what is wrong on his own personal whim."[12] In fact, though, when he so desired, Arafat changed the PLO's rules, appointed whom he wanted to the Executive Committee or PNC, and generally did as he liked. He preferred to rule by a laissez-faire strategy, keeping his coalition intact by never challenging any member's ideology or behavior. But this did not mean that they could sway Arafat. When Arafat decided to sign the Oslo Agreement in 1993 and Surani tested his own theory by criticizing the move, Arafat simply fired him.

One special technique of Arafat was his habit of suspending his own authority. Arafat thought that voluntarily stepping aside to let the most militant forces make extreme statements and carry out unbridled violence strengthened his position without tarnishing his moderate credentials. By this method, he expected to inflict punishment on his foes while still being considered relatively moderate and thus gaining Western support, or at least toleration. This was the game he played with the PFLP in the 1970s and 1980s and with Hamas in the 1980s and 1990s. Yet Arafat always retained the option of stopping the anarchy that he himself had permitted.

Surely, no one in the world was a more thoroughgoing exemplar of politics-as-theater than Arafat. At times, he resembled Abbie Hoffman with an army. Most politicians only fill one role, which they employ for every audience. But Arafat was the play's entire cast, always on stage, doing a different part in each scene, and starring in a new play every few weeks. To the Western audience, he would often play Charlie Chaplin, the pitiful, homeless yet lovable outcast; to the Arab or Islamic audience, he would act the part of Salah al-Din, the all-conquering warrior.

Other political figures turned themselves into vehicles for causes, yet no one went so far as did Arafat in rewriting and acting out every detail of his life to further that end. He seemed to feel that reality was his to bend at will. If he said he was born in Jerusalem, then that was the truth. If Arafat claimed he could understand Israeli prime minister Barak because they were both generals, he apparently believed he did possess that military rank.[13] Even at the Camp David summit, he recounted mythical stories about how he had personally built Saudi Arabia's ports, a claim everyone present knew was false.[14]

In every respect, his existence revolved around politics alone. Having no personal or family life made such a fanatical focus easier. Even after he had a wife and child, he took no interest in them. A Palestinian joke claimed that when a group of children visited Arafat, he asked one of them, "What's your name, little girl?" She answered, "Zahwa. I'm your daughter." He did not drink alcohol, for religious reasons, but he also did not smoke and avoided red meat. Arafat was never much interested in women or at all in men, though he seems to have had secret girl-friends in Tunis and Beirut. The only diversions he ever admitted to were watching cartoons and riding horses, and Arafat quickly added that he had no time for those things. Even cartoon watching became integrated into his political world view. He professed that his favorite was "Tom and Jerry" because of "the way the mouse outsmarts the cat."[15]

Someone with no interest except the revolutionary cause cannot really respect others' concerns with anything else in life. If Arafat cared nothing for material goods, a decent house, personal security, raising children, or love, and was absolutely allergic to stability, he would not put a high priority on providing these things to his people either.

Not only did Arafat never allow himself to be diverted or broadened by anything outside his mission, he also never slowed in its pursuit. By the late 1990s, his health was declining though less than was generally thought. His lips, knees, and hands shook, and there was reason to believe he had Parkinson's disease, the medication for which can affect the patient's mental state.[16] But Arafat had always been a nervous man, his hands perpetually in motion. And he could still keep up his traditional intense schedule even into his seventies.

Usually, Arafat awoke at 10 A.M. or so, worked until 2 P.M., when he had one of his favorite lunches, corn sautéed with almonds, yogurt, or fish, with tea and honey to drink. Arafat was fanatical in preaching the therapeutic value of honey. He then took a nap until around 4:30, following which he worked until 2, 3, or even 4 A.M. For exercise, he would go for walks in his office, quickly marching back and forth with his hands behind his back.

He preferred important meetings to be in the middle of the night.[17] As a result of his nocturnal habits, he sometimes fell asleep during daytime meetings or simply tuned out—some called it his "thousand-miles stare"—especially when someone tried to tell him something he did not want to hear. On occasion, he greeted visitors by saying, "Nice of you to come," and then fell asleep. A half hour later he would awake, smile, and say, "That was a good meeting, thanks for coming," and escort them out the door.[18]

Arafat never wanted to build any institutions, which could only detract from his personal authority.[19] Unlike other Arab leaders, he created no family, party, or regional power center. Despite the trappings of government and all sorts of councils and committees, there was never any chain of command in the PA or in the PLO. A respected Palestinian intellectual put it this way: Egypt's political structure resembled a pyramid, with a wide base narrowing to Mubarak at the peak; Syria's political structure was like a television antenna, with a small, highly stratified hierarchy; and the Palestinian political structure had the shape of . . . Arafat.[20]

Like many dictators, Arafat simply could not understand democratic attitudes. Once, during a meeting with Arafat in Gaza, Rabin said, "I will give permission to [Israeli General] Uzi Dayan to give his opinion which is against my opinion." One of the Israeli officials present recounted, "You could see in Arafat's eyes that he thought this was the behavior of a lunatic."[21]

Despite his claim to be the cause's servant, Arafat was a great egoist. Obsessed with his own importance, he demanded that everyone show him the proper respect. He was quick to take offense and constantly looked for some slight to react against. He justified this attitude by claiming he represented the Palestinian people's collective honor. He had a permanent chip on his shoulder, an angry undertone that seemed to insist: we are weak, and you have injured us. We are thus entitled to do whatever we want. No one can judge or stop us. And you, for your sins, must pay and pay and pay forever.

As one U.S. official put it, "He thinks he is the most important guy, that the Palestinian conflict is the most important conflict in the Middle East—even in the world—and that he is the only one who can deliver peace." Arafat was convinced that the Middle East's stability depended on him because the masses supported his cause and would force Arab governments to back him, though this never happened. He thought, said a long-time observer, "I sit on a volcano. I can ride this tiger." If he did not get what he wanted, Arafat threatened to unleash the Palestinians' wrath, destabilize the Arab world, and bring American interests tumbling down.[22]

Yet this behavior was also motivated by a personal insecurity which inflated his hypersensitivity, arrogance, and constant need to prove his manly courage. Arafat's sense of power subverted his effectiveness. He would complain, "Would the French or Japanese put up with this?"[23] But he was not the leader of a great power. No Palestinian state could ever be big enough for him or more than an anticlimax to a mythological struggle. And as the unchallengeable leader, he did not seem to feel the need to produce material gains to justify or maintain that status.

The sum total of this mix of personality traits, attitudes, and ideas was that Arafat appeared to consider himself more prophet than politician on a mission to rid the holy land of those who polluted it by their presence. It did not matter how long the struggle took or how much it cost, victory—God willing—was inevitable. Why settle, then, for a smaller homeland to provide immediate relief for his people's suffering? Revolutions are not made, as his fellow insurgent Khomeini put it, to lower the price of watermelons.[24]

Arafat's genuine piety was also an essential element in his thinking. He did not see politics in simply secular terms. While Arafat was not a radical Islamist, he was more Islamist than secular nationalist. He was a believing Muslim who prayed the requisite five times a day and who did not eat pork or drink alcohol. Unlike any other Fatah or PLO leader, his speeches were studded with Qu'ranic quotations. This world view and lifestyle linked him to a large sector of the masses who were also practicing Muslims without being radical Islamists. Indeed, Arafat had more devout Palestinian Muslim supporters than did Hamas. Arafat fully believed that God would inevitably bring him victory despite the apparent odds. This gave him one more reason to carry on the struggle forever, to launch new battles even when there was every reason to expect defeat, and to stick to his basic thinking and strategy in the face of humiliating losses.

In pursuing his single-minded agenda, Arafat had many tools in his arsenal, some of which he forged himself. The first was his appearance, carefully constructed to make him a walking, breathing symbol of his cause. He dressed in a khaki military uniform to be seen as a soldier but, in contrast to grandiose dictators, Arafat wore no medal, gold braid, or rank because he was a man of the people, a general in a private's uniform.[25] Practically his sole adornment was a shoulder patch with the tricolor Palestinian flag and the word "Palestine," to show his national allegiance.

He wore a headscarf draped carefully to resemble the shape of a Palestine that included all of Israel. Since this checkered *kaffiya* had once been the common people's garb, Arafat wore one to show his devotion to tradition. Yet while he made it into a political symbol, no other PLO or PA leader was populist enough to imitate him. Arafat did not wear a suit and tie because that was the costume of the Westernized Arab bureaucrat, and expensive clothing would convey a love of luxury that also implied corruption. His beard stubble made him look like many poor or peasant Palestinian men of his age. It also showed him to be a soldier in the field who had no time for personal primping.

Arafat's next important asset, at least regarding the West, was his shortness and ugliness, which inspired pity rather than fear. Arafat radiated weakness, not power, and this was of paramount importance in his campaign to win global support for his suffering people and sympathy for their eternal victimhood. It was hard to believe this homely little man was responsible for so much violence and killing, easy to think he was not in control of events and in need of international assistance.

Khomeini, Asad, Saddam Hussein, or Usama bin Ladin were each, in their own ways, strong, handsome men who could be cast as supervillains intent on world conquest in some Hollywood thriller. They were credible as tough adversaries and aggressive tyrants. In contrast, Arafat seemed so much the opposite in appearance and manners as to lull others into doubting he could ever outsmart or outmaneuver them. Looking more like an unwanted puppy than a vicious doberman, Arafat made Western politicians want to help or housebreak him.

Important in this respect was what the UN diplomat Brian Urquhart described as Arafat's "feline charm," an apparent personal warmth and seeming concern for others, which overlay a colder, calculating nature and sharp claws.[26] This asset was largely reserved for Western or Israeli visitors. With his own people, he showed a rougher, bossier side. He could joke with them or act the patriarch distributing wealth and favors while always holding them at a distance. All Palestinians, no matter how high they rose, were subject to his whims. For Arafat, charm was a product strictly for export. In his own circles he was, as an Arab writer noted, "given to outbursts of bad temper, foul language and huge swings in mood and thinking."[27]

With Western journalists, politicians, diplomats, or intellectuals, however, he was determined to prove he was a nice guy who had been misunderstood and slandered. Every non-Arab who met Arafat tells stories of such performances: his warm personal greeting, hugs and kisses, flattery, the eagerness with which he plied visitors with food, and how he tried to please guests in small ways. When an American journalist brought his little daughter along for an interview with him, Arafat summoned his servant to bring refreshments by ringing a bell. The little girl giggled. Arafat then rang the bell again and again so that the servant had to keep coming back over and over again, just to win more laughter.[28]

His ability to make everyone he met feel important was tremendously effective. Arafat appealed directly to guests by using flattery. Only you, he told them, can solve the crisis and bring peace to the Middle East. How could anyone refuse to help or deny the great influence and marvelous skills Arafat imputed to them? Many found him a kind, gentle host who made them feel at ease and respected. He knew, Uri Savir recalled, how to "touch your ego." Arafat would take visitors by the arm, tell them how "honorable" they were, and listen to them raptly. He would never say no to any request but only "I'll think about it," "I'll see what I can do best," or "You're right. We have to make more efforts."[29]

The effect was only spoiled when he burst into displays of manic anger or wild exaggeration, which served as reminders that one was watching an act by a man who might not be entirely stable or honest. Some were put off by his strange behavior, rapid blinking, extreme mood swings, and what they described as a mad look that sometimes came into his eyes. "Whenever I came to meet him," said Ron Pundak, one of the Israeli authors of the Oslo Agreement, "I ask which Arafat I will find." And many concluded, as did another Israeli, Yakov Peri, who dealt with him often, "To uncover Arafat's feelings is something impossible."[30]

But most fell, at least temporarily, under the spell of his charm. Despite his lapses, Arafat was a fantastic manipulator of people, mixing manufactured emotions of sincerity, innocence, shock, anger, tears, and a dozen other emotions the way an artist wields colors. As one Israeli who met him frequently put it, "He makes you think that maybe you were wrong. I would say to him, 'We met two weeks ago and I asked you to help on this, and you promised me something.' He would reply. 'You are mistaken. What I told you was...' And by the time he finished, you'd think that perhaps he was right and you had forgotten what really happened."[31]

Arafat used extreme and cynical emotional reactions—including his willingness to cry and to humiliate himself—as a way to win sympathy. A *New York Times* editor traveled to Gaza after arranging an interview with Arafat. The meeting was canceled at the last minute by aides, who said Arafat was too sad, crying so much "you wouldn't recognize him" because he had met with the families of Palestinians killed in the conflict. The next day, Abu Alaa was asked about Arafat's mood. "I spoke to him yesterday and he was in a great mood!...Never better!"[32] French president Jacques Chirac said he felt compelled to give Arafat certain concessions because he cried when asking for them.[33]

This mastery of his emotional repertoire was Arafat's great skill. When pushed into a corner during negotiations, he would throw a tantrum, shouting, waving his arms, and claiming to have been insulted. At other times, Arafat would beg for concessions that he could not get by threats to walk out. Equally, when it suited his strategy, he would explode in mock anger, wave his hands above his head, insist that his dignity had been insulted, and threaten to walk out unless his demands were met. One who often negotiated with him observed, "When Arafat starts kissing up and flattering you, then you know you've got the upper hand."[34]

Yet as well as he was served by bluff and bluster, Arafat's style also rejected the give and take of normal negotiations. He did not like to make agreements and almost never saw the need to give—or at least implement—concessions to get one. "He's never happy with anything offered to him because it inevitably falls short of his expectations," was how one American diplomat who dealt frequently with him in such circumstances put it. "I never heard Arafat give a clean yes to an agreement. He never felt enthusiastic about an agreement. He doesn't like the idea of compromising, and at the last minutes of negotiations he's in a very bad mood."[35]

Still, everyone was impressed with his tenacity, skill, and inventiveness. Yoel Singer, an Israeli lawyer involved in many talks, called Arafat "one of the best negotiators I've seen." He was like the gambler in a Western film who, despite his bad cards, beats everyone by bluffing and shrewd tactics.[36] One technique Arafat used effectively was to escalate his demands when everyone else thought the deal was made and were eager to conclude it. "When the signing ceremony is tomorrow, that is for him the time to negotiate," said Singer.[37] This was how, for example, Arafat blew up the 1994 Cairo signing ceremony. His goals were both to seek more concessions and to show his people how hard he was fighting on their behalf and how he never gave away anything to their enemies.

Another useful tactic was his ability to make people feel they could get a deal by giving him just one more concession. After receiving it, however, he would request another one without giving anything himself. Arafat's negotiating style could be described as saying no until everyone else said yes. In this process, he was always able to find some reason to be aggrieved, some specific problem he could portray as showing the other side's hostility or bad faith. Thus, everyone was supposed to be constantly in his debt, forced to prove their credibility to him.

Yet despite his obsessive efforts to get every possible gain in negotiations, Arafat was largely indifferent to the substance of agreements. Rabin would go over each word of a document, proposing amendments and even changing punctuation. Arafat did not care about such details. He would focus on a particular symbolic issue and push very hard on it. A Palestinian negotiator said the only detail he cared about in the Oslo Agreement "was that there was a Palestinian flag and policemen in uniform" on the Egypt-Gaza border.[38] A U.S. official who worked closely with Arafat in the peace process remarked, "If you ask him what's in any of the peace plans, he wouldn't have a clue." But then again, Arafat did not need to worry about such matters since he knew he would later interpret the text as he wished and ignore any commitments he did not like.

There is a thin line, however, between playing hard to get and being impossible to deal with. Arafat acted as if he held all the winning cards, but when his bluff was called, he always had a losing hand. His technique worked only as long as others thought they could work with him. When they tired of doing so—as happened with Jordan in 1970, Lebanon in 1982, Syria in 1983, and Saudi Arabia and Kuwait in 1991—he was in real trouble. If his charm and appeals for help or pity made a good first impression, over time Arafat's inflexibility and unreliability discouraged or disgusted the other negotiators.

In short, despite all his skills, Arafat mistakenly ignored some key principles of international bargaining. One of them is knowing when to stop negotiating and close a deal. A second is to remember that the other side's concessions are ultimately contingent on one's own compromises. A third is that the weaker side must take into account the balance of forces. If Israel holds territory that Arafat wants, he must pay some price to get it. Finally, nations are inspired to make deals in order to gain clearly defined benefits. If they no longer believe in the other side's credibility, they will not believe that an agreement will improve their situation.

As a result, Arafat's techniques often sabotaged negotiations. Hanan Ashrawi's complaints about his management of talks in the early 1990s applied equally to the later peace process. They included "conflicting instructions, multiple channels, lack of a coherent strategy, inconsistent political decision making, total disregard for our structures, and lack of accountability and openness in our internal work." What she told Arafat in 1993 also applied to later events: "Never before in the history of negotiations had a government formed a delegation and given it all the elements of failure as you have."[39]

Arafat gave his negotiators no clear guidelines, making them guess what would please him. After negotiating sessions, they told him they had won big gains from opponents while minimizing anything they had promised in exchange. Palestinian officials frequently told Israeli and U.S. counterparts that they thought the demand for a full right of return to be a pain in the neck, a burden they sought to escape by finding some compromise.[40] But they certainly would not tell Arafat he was being unrealistic.

Some Palestinian leaders were ready for a deal, eager to achieve a real state and to help their people. They said so privately and sometimes made that point to their Israeli and American counterparts. Left on their own, they sometimes offered compromise ideas, which made Israelis or Americans think progress was being made so that they offered concessions of their own.

Yet Arafat thought it his right to take back anything his delegates said while holding Israel to all compromises its team tentatively proposed. He never offered a plan of his own, another way to get his adversary to offer more to gain his agreement. Arafat was, in Ross's words, "long on complaints but short on prescriptions."[41] This was how he successfully advanced from Camp David to the Clinton plan to the Taba talks without ever changing his own stance. But this was also how he lost the chance to make an agreement at all.

Arafat was unwilling and unable to reach a peace treaty with Israel for at least three main reasons: he felt that he could always improve on any deal ever offered him, his demands were beyond anything Israel could ever accept, and he knew that making any deal could well leave him worse off.[42] Arafat would never agree to a provision to end the conflict, concluded Ross. "Everything he has done as leader of the Palestinians is to always leave his options open, never close a door. For him, to end the conflict is to end himself."[43] Israeli foreign minister Shlomo Ben-Ami, at first convinced that if he kept giving up more that Arafat would make peace, finally concluded that Arafat preferred death to "signing an agreement that is less than every single one of his demands."[44]

Still, Arafat's behavior was not all due to calculation. His poor grasp of English might have led to misunderstandings. Many Western and Israeli negotiators concluded that he simply did not understand everything said to him. This was one reason for his stock repetition of certain phrases and his fear of engaging in a real substantive dialogue on major issues. The Americans usually used an interpreter with him but the Israelis did not, something several of them thought a mistake in retrospect.[45]

Yet disenchantment with Arafat was not merely the result of cultural miscommunication. Quite the contrary, his fellow Arab leaders had the fewest illusions about him. In public, they usually professed undying support, at least to his cause if not to Arafat himself. In private, they expressed contempt and mistrust. Even Mubarak, on whom Arafat depended so much that he met with him at least sixteen times between December 1994 and August 1997 alone, privately expressed frustration and anger at Arafat. Syrians did not conceal their contempt. Defense Minister Mustafa Tlas compared Arafat to a "striptease dancer" and called him the "son of sixty thousand whores." A Kuwaiti columnist urged Arafat to resign because of "the calamities of destruction" he brought on Palestinians.[46]

An Arab leader once asked Arafat why he lied so much. He replied, "I would kill for Palestine, so you don't want me to lie for Palestine?" Other Arab leaders took for granted that he could not be trusted and that he would not implement any agreements that he did make.[47] Over and over again one is told by Arabs in different countries, "I don't know a single Arab leader who has a good word to say about Arafat."[48] In a closed meeting in 2002, Lebanon's president spoke for forty minutes on how Israel had to make concessions to Arafat, then concluded, "Of course, I would never trust him myself."[49]

Fellow Palestinians often felt the same way. Even his colleagues rarely knew what he would do next. In many ways, the Arafat they saw was quite different from the figure who appeared to Westerners. As one Arab observer put it, the "Palestinian people respect him, but they don't like him."[50] In a November 1998 poll, less than 45 percent said they would vote for Arafat.[51] Even amidst the Intifada, a February 2001 poll showed Arafat receiving positive marks from only 47 percent as opposed to 43 percent who found him either a "mediocre" or "negative" leader. This was small backing for a charismatic national symbol at a time of intense patriotic crisis. Only 28 percent said they would definitely vote for Arafat in an election while another 31 percent claimed they would decide only when it came time to vote, either hiding discontent with Arafat or showing a lack of enthusiasm for him.[52]

Personal patronage and tolerance of corruption bought him popularity among some Palestinians while angering and disappointing others. Arafat liked to play traditional family patriarch or village mayor and to be called by a favorite nickname, "the Old Man." He constantly met all sorts of Palestinians from every walk of life who asked him for help or money. Arafat wrote down each favor in his notebook against the day when he might ask a favor in return. Often, he personally approved receipts for petty expenses, including payment for senior officials' vacations.[53]

A 2002 study ranked Arafat the world's sixth richest political leader, with an estimated $300 million in wealth. Even if Arafat was not using the money for himself, he also was not spending it to build up the Palestinian economy or benefit those under his rule. So tight was his personal control that Azmi Shuaibi, a PLC member, explained, "We are afraid if something happens to Arafat, we will not know where all the money is."[54]

If some Palestinian leaders or officials were eager to make or steal money, Arafat let them do so to ensure their future loyalty. Personally, Arafat was interested in money only as political operating capital. His close aide, Muhammad Rashid, a Kurd whom Arafat had met in Lebanon, handled Arafat's own political funds, which were taken from PA money, foreign aid, and siphoned profits from state monopolies. Rashid also managed a secret channel to former Israeli intelligence chief Yossi Ginossar, which seemed to involve covert payments and joint enterprises that swelled Arafat's coffers.[55]

While corruption became more open during the PA era, it was always part of Arafat's leadership style. Rashid Khalidi noted the riches, luxurious apartments, and expensive cars obtained by PLO officials in Beirut using movement funds. The pro-PLO French leftist author Jean Genet, himself a former thief, at about the same time voiced prim disapproval of the "sharks among the leaders who instead of hijacking aircraft hijacked the Resistance's funds." Palestinians gave him specific examples of such behavior "and were full of contempt for Arafat's entourage."[56]

As a result of using the PA's assets for political purposes or the leadership's enrichment, vast amounts of money disappeared while citizens had to pay off officials to get privileges or services. One of Arafat's most notoriously corrupt officials was Hisham Maki, head of Palestinian television, who pocketed a good portion of that institution's budget. Arafat reportedly gave him a large grant to buy a home for his mother-in-law. At a Ramadan 1999 reception in Gaza, in front of hundreds of people, Arafat patted the head of Maki's son and told him, "You're a nice kid but be careful not to become a criminal like your father."[57] Arafat kept Maki on long after his corruption was notorious, and his career ended only when he was gunned down by a mysterious Palestinian hit squad in 2001.

Arafat easily circumvented international efforts to stop corruption. "Not to reform is not an option," warned one author of a 1999 European Union–funded report which documented devastating corruption, over-staffing, incompetence, and misuse of funds. But anyone who thought Arafat could be compelled to do anything had not been following his life story. Donors cut back aid, but there was still enough money to continue running the struggle and that was all Arafat cared about. He also used another of his favorite techniques: wearing down opponents with prom-ises and stalling. Arafat appointed a committee—some of whose mem-bers had been personally accused of corruption by the PLC—to investigate the financial criticisms, and it was never heard from again.[58]

What did rank-and-file Palestinians feel about Arafat? Whatever they thought of him personally, they knew he was their sole leader who was recognized by the world and protecting them from civil war. Many saw him as saving them from an Islamist takeover, while traditionalist Muslims thought him preferable to either a secular leftist or Hamas leadership.

In private conversations among themselves and those they trusted, though, Palestinians often made clear their contempt for Arafat and misgivings about his strategy. One well-known leader remarked in private that Arafat's policy was headed for disaster and, since Israel would never accept a full right of return, was a recipe for endless conflict. Another famous Palestinian figure said privately that he should challenge Arafat for the leadership but would never do so because it would divide the movement. A well-known Palestinian intellectual and militant activist spent two hours in conversation, without a pause, complaining about mistake after mistake by Arafat. Yet, within hours of these interviews, all these people would uncritically defend and justify Arafat's positions and acts in public.[59]

Most Palestinians viewed Arafat as their struggle's symbol but hardly viewed him as a hero or role model. And so they grumbled and told jokes about him. Since Arafat had no son, went one of them, he decided to be cloned. The Americans and Germans tried, but they could only make a donkey. The Japanese, however, succeeded in producing a little Arafat, explaining, "We cloned a donkey and out came Arafat."[60] Another tale had Hebron's mayor planning a ceremony for Arafat's visit. He promised a red carpet, honor guard, and twenty-one-gun salute. An official asks, "Twenty-one? Do you really think they will miss him the first twenty times?" These jokes, and many others like them, reveal a hard edge of resentment.

Nor did his colleagues view Arafat with admiration or high regard. They knew they must be constantly on guard lest they displease him. He could be friendly one moment and brutal the next, ready to humiliate his closest comrades. At times, he affectionately squeezed Muhammad Dahlan's cheeks but also slapped him in front of others. He made colleagues the butt of nasty jokes. Once in 1995, Arafat turned to Sha'th and snarled, "You know why refugees aren't coming back? They don't want to see you."[61]

He kept all his colleagues off balance, pitting one against the other, giving subordinates conflicting instructions and rivals identical assignments. But they were always his to command and control. His colleagues were afraid to act too moderately or independently lest he then accuse them of treason or withdraw his protection if others did so. Arafat pushed people down if he decided they were becoming too strong or just to keep them in their place, and he brought them back when he needed them, perhaps to use against someone else. In this way, he shuffled Abu Alaa, Abu Mazin, Abd Rabbu, and Saeb Arikat as negotiators throughout the 1990s. After launching a new Intifada, he shoved them all aside to turn toward such PLO veterans as Abbas Zaki and Sakhr Habash, who had never supported the Oslo Agreement at all. Since most of the Palestinian leadership was dour to the point of blandness, Arafat's legendary mood swings between bleak pessimism and near-hysteria tired and sometimes frightened them.

While Arafat tolerated generalized complaints, anyone treading directly on his own dignity was treated harshly. When in 1984, the rebel Abu Musa circulated a book filled with claims of scandals involving Arafat in refugee camps, Arafat ordered every copy seized. The militant Palestinian nationalist cartoonist Najib Ali was killed in London, probably at Arafat's order, after making fun of the leader and his girlfriend too many times. *Al-Quds* editor Mahir al-Alami was arrested and intimidated for not putting an article about Arafat's goodness to Christians on his newspaper's front page. The West Bank bureau of al-Jazira television was closed down for a time after a preview of a program on Lebanon's civil war showed a demonstrator holding a pair of shoes over Arafat's picture, a terrible insult in Arab society.

Just as Arafat created different personal images—one for the West, another for Palestinians and Arabs—by the 1980s he also maintained two widely disparate policy messages to those audiences as well. Facing westward and speaking in English, he was usually the pitiable victim who only wanted a reasonable peace and had no control over violence. Once, he compared himself to ET, the lovable refugee extraterrestrial who only wanted to go home. To the East and speaking in Arabic, he was the fiery, powerful revolutionary full of hatred for a diabolical enemy which deserved no mercy. As one UN diplomat noted, "He was reasonable in Europe, but outrageous in the Arab world."[62]

In his interviews and statements directed at the West between 2000 and 2002, for example, he voiced support for ceasefires and claimed to be trying to stop Palestinian attacks against Israel. At the same time, in Arabic speeches—as well as in instructions to his movement, security forces, and the Palestinian media outlets he controlled—Arafat was whipping up fervor to justify, continue, and even escalate such attacks. At times, press releases were distributed in English to Western reporters announcing Arafat's call for a ceasefire—which were then reported as headline stories throughout the world—while not a word of such news appeared in any Palestinian media nor was echoed by other PA leaders.

Arafat's version of pragmatism and confidence in redefining reality was well illustrated in an April 2002 conversation with Secretary of State Colin Powell, who visited him in his bunker. Arafat made a long speech claiming that Israel was massacring the Palestinians, but people all over the world were demonstrating to support them. He was especially excited about a story that a Japanese citizen had committed suicide in solidarity with their cause. Powell replied:

> Let's be frank. You are a general, and I am a general. Generals must be clear, direct, and practical. The Japanese [person] who committed suicide is already dead. Demonstrations are demonstrations. I say to you frankly: If you do not move ahead, nothing will happen. But if you comply with the international desire to fight terror, many things will happen.[63]

After flattering Arafat by bestowing on him the military rank he coveted, Powell explained that only results count in political life. Rather than focusing on ultimately futile public relations gimmicks, Powell urged Arafat to achieve real triumphs by ending the violence and making a peace agreement. But Arafat ignored Powell's sound advice.

A decade earlier, he had exhibited the same pattern of self-delusion, proclaiming, "Among our masses we are at a peak, with the Arab masses, at a peak, with the Muslim nation, we are at a peak, and throughout the Third World.... I have gained credibility among my people and the entire Arab nation. Have you seen all the demonstrations...? My picture is being brandished everywhere."[64] But these claims were made in January 1991, as Arafat sided with Saddam Hussein. Within a few weeks, Iraq was defeated, and Arafat's international stock was at zero. In previous years, Arafat had made similar statements in Amman and Beirut, mistakenly prophesying victory based on propaganda triumphs.

This repetition was by no means unique in a career of remarkable continuity in his thought and behavior. Many of the same ideas that Arafat used and phrases he uttered in the 1970s remained and reappeared time after time into the twenty-first century. It could well be asked, despite the Oslo Agreement—or because of it, given its fate—whether Arafat's doctrine, goals, strategy, and tactics really changed all that much throughout his career.

Arafat's life as a leader can be divided into four crisis cycles, each characterized by his ambiguous course of action and each ending in what seemed to be a crushing defeat: Jordan, 1967–1971; Lebanon, 1971–1983; Tunisia, 1982–1991; and the West Bank and Gaza from 1994 onward.[65] Each time, Arafat refused to acknowledge mistakes so that he and his movement never really reexamined or amended their doctrine, strategy, goals, or leadership.

During the Jordan years, he did not decide whether he wanted to get along with King Hussein or to overthrow him. He did not restrain the most militant forces which provoked the Jordanians. Instead, he often supported them, sometimes joined them, and always hoped their actions would serve his interests. In the end, the Jordanians threw him out.

In Lebanon, too, Arafat rejected responsibility for his men's undisciplined behavior and tolerated the provocative acts of radical groups supposedly under his authority. Unable to decide whether he was avoiding Lebanese politics or trying to overthrow the regime, Arafat antagonized the Lebanese and contributed to the onset of civil war. Again, Arafat tended to break every agreement and subvert each commitment he made, ultimately destroying his credibility. Eventually, many of the same people who had welcomed Arafat came to demand that he leave.

At least in Tunisia, Arafat was able to get along with his host country, but the overall pattern was the same. In this case, Arafat broke his old pledge of staying out of inter-Arab disputes by siding with Iraq against his old benefactors in Saudi Arabia and Kuwait. Once more, he tried to overthrow governments that were supposedly his allies. Intoxicated with the prospect of Saddam conquering the Arab world, Arafat chose to join the losing side. And again, Arafat would not break decisively with terrorism nor discipline radical groups that ostensibly followed his leadership, thus sacrificing a promising new relationship with the United States.

Throughout each of the earlier cycles, Arafat had also pursued a useless strategy in regard to Israel. He continued to believe that a combination of terrorist violence and international backing for the Palestinians would defeat it. Arafat never firmly decided to abandon ambiguity and strive with all his might for a nation-state in exchange for ending the conflict altogether.

In many other ways, he treated Israel the same way he had behaved toward Jordan, Lebanon, Kuwait, and Saudi Arabia. Arafat alienated his new peace partner just as he had his old allies. He refused to choose between cooperation and confrontation until the latter inevitably gained the upper hand. He would not constrain the most militant forces, partly because he was using them to further his own ends. He did not keep commitments, nor would he decisively abandon violence. With Israel as with his previous Arab hosts, he made coexistence impossible.

Again and again, he made identical errors. He was arrogant when apparently winning and manically eager for more combat when losing. In either case, Arafat never knew when to stop. Violence was how the movement arose, and through violence he expected it to succeed. Violence brought unity, stilled criticism of incompetence and corruption, and created crises in which Arafat felt powerful. Palestinian casualties furnished fresh martyrs, proving his side's victimhood and the other side's bloodthirstiness, inspiring new sacrifices and battles. Oslo at first appeared the exception to this pattern but ended by confirming the rule. As Friedman wrote, "It is a constant struggle for Arafat to stay on this pragmatic track. He is like an alcoholic on the wagon and at moments he can fall off again in a drunken pursuit of politics, of symbols and illusions."[66]

Each time, Arafat was thrust back into his bunker and onto his flying carpet, largely due to his own performance. It was as if violence and flight were drugs he could not do without. Next to winning, for Arafat, the next best thing was losing. And defeat was far easier to attain than victory. He himself survived but kept doing things that made his survival seem a great accomplishment.

Aside from his own abilities, Arafat survived as an ineffective leader because there was no other candidate with the requisite ambition, skills, or charisma. In addition, Palestinians correctly saw rivals as either puppets of Arab states or as representing narrow ideological views.[67] Palestinians also continued to support him because they feared civil war and largely shared both his militant goals and profound misperceptions. Finally, despite the many problems Arab and Western states made for him, they gave Arafat enough support and recognition to keep him going.

Even given all these factors, however, Arafat's behavior would make no sense if his overriding priorities were to end the occupation, alleviate suffering and gather in the exiles. The idea of an independent Palestinian state consisting only of the West Bank, the Gaza Strip, and East

Jerusalem was, after all, an idea that came late in the movement's history and was never fully absorbed, expressed, or taught by it. For two decades or more, the PLO had viewed such a state at best as a stage, merely a way to ensure that no one else took permanent control of that territory, while seeing a West Bank/Gaza state as a solution was considered treason. Through the 1990s, there was no sharp break with the past but only a gradual, partial one. By the time of the Camp David summit, the idea of a compromise peace still competed with a continuing desire for revenge and hope of total victory, even if that had to be postponed to the indefinite future.

What did Arafat really think? Of course, that is impossible to know. Nevertheless, in 1968, 1977, and 1988, he had sworn never to commit the crime of accepting Israel's existence, asking, "Shall we pass on this blemish to our children?" Abu Iyad once explained that even if his and Arafat's own generation could not triumph, it had "no right to abandon the cause" or negotiate a settlement that would bind future generations. The highest duty was to preserve a future option to regain all Palestine "even if they cannot liberate a single inch." Otherwise, the Arabs would permanently lose Palestine as they had lost Spain in the fifteenth century.[68]

Most Palestinians basically thought along similar lines. But what did the Palestinians want Arafat to do? Like any people facing critical situations, they had mixed feelings, being unhappy about the situation but hoping or believing that Arafat knew how to deal with it. They wanted a compromise peace but hoped for victory. They simultaneously laughed at some of the absurd misconceptions Arafat passed on to them and passionately embraced them. In the same conversation, within a few minutes' time, individuals could convey their utter conviction that they would defeat Israel in the struggle and then admit that they saw no hope of winning.[69]

Palestinians held at least four diverse views of the situation, and most individuals accepted some or all of them simultaneously. Many wanted peace because they were tired of bad conditions, fighting, and the Israeli presence. Others thought violence would get them a better deal in negotiations. Still others believed that Israel could be militarily defeated and then forced to give the Palestinians everything they wanted. And a sizable number rejected any agreement, no matter on what terms, and still believed that armed struggle would eliminate Israel.

On top of that, whatever their idea of what should be done in the short term, a large proportion in each of these groups hoped for a long-term total victory. In a May–June 2002 poll of West Bank and Gaza Palestinians, 51 percent said the Intifada's purpose was to destroy

Israel, compared to only 43 percent who defined their goal as ending the Israeli occupation and creating a West Bank/Gaza state. In December 2001, the figures were 44 and 48 percent, respectively, still a remarkably high proportion. And many of those who put the priority on creating their own state still favored destroying Israel as the next step.[70] Arafat understood these factors and used his ambiguity to show he was supporting all groups and options at once.

Arafat's perception of Israel was prisoner to his political program as well as to public opinion. Believing that Israel should not exist made him underestimate the difficulty of wiping it from the map. True, he embraced some leftist Israeli peace advocates during the PA era and professed a love for Rabin, but on a political level he never distinguished in any real manner among Israeli political forces nor did he accurately evaluate Israel either as foe or as supposed peace partner.

From beginning to end, Arafat's misconception of Israel set his strategy. In 1968, giving his first interview ever to the Western media, he explained the theme that would guide his use of terror for more than three decades, "We are not trying to destroy the Israeli army, of course. But Israel is not just an army. It is a society that can only survive and prosper on peace and security. We aim to disrupt that society. Insecurity will make a mess of their agriculture and commerce. It will halt immigration and encourage emigration. We will even disrupt their tourist industry."[71]

So, Arafat made war on Israeli society by deliberately targeting and killing civilians whenever possible. This approach, of course, made Israel conclude that Arafat was not a partner for peace in the 1960s, 1970s, 1980s, and, after an all-too-brief pause, again in the year 2000. In this way, Arafat subverted his own struggle. By convincing Israelis that the only alternative to fighting and sacrifice was annihilation, Arafat ensured that Israel would never give up or make the kind of massive concessions he envisioned.

Similarly, Arafat ensured the failure of Israeli politicians most willing to work with him and the success of those most hostile. Peres, his most devoted ally, who once told Israelis that it was their duty to give and the Palestinians' task to take, lost the 1996 election largely due to a wave of Palestinian attacks which Arafat had not prevented. Arafat then had to deal with Netanyahu, who slowed the process and offered him less. Arafat's rejection of compromise in 2000 and his war against Israel ensured Barak's defeat and Sharon's victory in 2001.

Putting his emphasis on achieving propaganda "victories" over Israel, Arafat never campaigned for conciliation among Palestinians and permitted unbridled anti-Israel incitement in the media and schools he controlled. This behavior made sense if his goal was to continue the battle and win it by force but not if he wanted a negotiated deal.

One indication of how Arafat felt on these issues was his spreading of bizarre conspiracy stories about Israel. In many meetings and interviews he pulled press clippings from his pocket to "prove" some wild theory about his enemy's evil nature. This appalled Israelis and some in the West, making them question Arafat's hold on reality, but persuaded Palestinians to be more doubtful about peacemaking.

Arafat constantly found new twists on his theme of trying to prove Israel to be an illegitimate or criminal state. An early theory of his was that Israel's creation was the product of a secret 1907 conference of Western leaders, who decided to establish a "hostile alien nation" to ensure that the Middle East remained "disunited and backward."[72] He repeatedly claimed, including at a major UN speech in May 1990, that an irregularly shaped ancient coin depicted on the Israeli ten-agorot piece was actually a secret map showing Israel's claim to most of the Middle East.[73] He insisted that there was "no doubt" that an Israeli tear-gas canister fired at demonstrators had caused the death in 2001 of Feisal al-Husseini, who in fact died of a heart attack.[74]

In 1988, on the eve of making his first statement ever accepting Israel's existence, he still openly expressed his extremely hostile view of that country even to an American audience. He claimed that the proof that Israel did not want peace was based on the following false assertions:

> Look at the slogans they use: that the land of Israel is from the Euphrates to the Nile. This was written for many years over the entrance to the Knesset, the parliament. It shows their national ambition. . . . Do you know what the meaning of the Israeli flag is? . . . It is white with two blue lines. The two lines represent two rivers, and in between is Israel. The rivers are the Nile and the Euphrates.[75]

These are all myths with no historical basis.

Asked in the same interview if he respected Israelis, Arafat replied that he did not, "because they always behave like barbarians, there's never a drop of humanity in them."[76] Such a response, the epitome of dehumanization, let him justify any tactic or deed against Israel. Even at the Camp David summit, he could deny that there was any real Jewish connection with the Temple Mount in Jerusalem. In this context, it was easy to believe that peace with Israel was impossible or that terrorism would make Israel collapse.

Arafat accused Israeli government leaders of being involved in Rabin's assassination and committing mass murder of Palestinians.[77] He said that Israel was planning to bring a half million Jews from

Afghanistan to replace the Arabs in the West Bank and Gaza Strip. He showed his disbelief in genuine differences among Israeli leaders by saying that Barak and Sharon were in cahoots to bring to power a right-wing government in 2001 and thus block Palestinian aspirations. "Barak could have stayed in power for another two and a half years," he explained, but instead made a secret agreement with Sharon. The two of them had "preplanned" Sharon's visit to the al-Aqsa mosque, a massacre of Palestinians, the Intifada itself, and then Sharon's winning the election. What was especially noteworthy is that all these claims were contained in one interview alone. And such rhetoric was not atypical for him.[78]

For Arafat, Israel's survival was never taken for granted. Privately, he told high-level colleagues throughout the 1990s, "I can see the future," and that a combination of factors—the decadence of Israeli society, the high Palestinian birth rate, and emigration from Israel—would eventually lead to its collapse.[79] In the twenty-first century, Arafat made the same points he had put forward in the 1970s. After seven years of negotiating with Israel about peace, Arafat told an incredulous Indonesian president Abdurahman Wahid that the Palestinians were ready to wait, if necessary, for 150 years to "throw the Jews into the sea."[80]

Israeli foreign minister Shlomo Ben-Ami, who had begun his work convinced that peace was inevitable and that Arafat was a reliable partner, concluded at the end of the experience "that the Palestinians don't want a solution as much as they want to place Israel in the dock of the accused. They want to denounce our state more than they want their own state."[81]

If Israel was behind the terrorist attacks on itself, as Arafat charged on many specific occasions, then he had no responsibility for such operations and did not have to do anything to stop them. If the Israeli people were so monstrous, it was justified to target all of them. When he falsely accused Israel of mass murder or of using inhumane weapons like radioactive uranium, Arafat was stirring up more hatred among Palestinians and Arabs in general, raising further barriers to peace, and inciting violence. After all, if Israel were anywhere near as demonic and voraciously aggressive as described by Arafat, how would it ever be possible, sensible, or even morally acceptable to make peace with it?

What, then, was Arafat's goal for his movement? Clearly, from its inception until at least 1988 and probably until 1993, it was Israel's destruction and replacement by a Palestinian Arab state. After the Oslo Agreement, the picture becomes more complex. The most likely conclusion is that Arafat was open to an agreement with Israel but only if it was on his terms, letting him—or some successor—still carry on the struggle's next stage to win a Palestinian Arab state from the Jordan River to the Mediterranean Sea.

Equally important, he was very much aware that the kind of compromises necessary to get a deal with Israel would inevitably split his movement and people. This was a major paradox for Arafat. "My goal was, first, unite all Palestinians in the struggle for a homeland and then, second, get that homeland."[82] But what if there was a contradiction between these two objectives? Since actually getting the homeland proved the biggest threat to national unity, perhaps even the prelude to civil war, it became a far less attractive goal for Arafat.

As a result of these and other factors, Arafat was not desperately eager to make a deal leading to the quick creation of a Palestinian state, certainly if it was not completely on his terms. Because this distinction was so important to him, Arafat was ready to sacrifice thousands of lives, years of time, and the whole Palestinian infrastructure for this vision of total victory. Not all Palestinian leaders thought the same way, but only what Arafat thought mattered.

Arafat never spoke about what Palestine would be like. He saw his task as achieving victory and not creating a vision for the future or a solution for immediate problems. Arafat never said a word about a glorious day on which the exiles in Lebanon would live as free Palestinian citizens in Ramallah or how refugee camps would empty out to be replaced by new housing in Gaza. He did not paint an attractive picture of peace that would enthuse people but spoke only of the need for continued struggle. He did not talk of creating a great Palestinian university or a successful economy. He did not encourage young people to stay in school so their skills could build up Palestine some day.

To create a state purchased at the cost of a real, final peace would be the end of his purpose, the death of his mission. Indeed, Arafat admitted that after independence Palestinians might quickly dispense with him as the British got rid of Prime Minister Winston Churchill as soon as he won World War II for them.[83] Thus, after complaining for years that Israel was stalling and demanding faster progress, when the process did move toward a conclusion in 2000, Arafat suddenly decided things were going too fast. Similarly, after urging more U.S. involvement in negotiations, when this in fact happened, Arafat claimed that the Americans were against him.

Some Palestinians thought Arafat and his colleagues might well prefer the status quo to a concerted effort to attain a state through negotiations. Ghassan al-Khatib, a Palestinian political analyst, wrote that the status quo met the PA elite's needs far better than that of the Palestinian people. The leaders had their ranks and titles, had enriched themselves, and could travel freely. In contrast, most Palestinians suffered from restricted travel, economic deprivation, and poor services. "Palestinians see road signs leading to ministries and army barracks, but do not feel any stabilizing effect or authority from them.... Not only has the political elite been alienated from the public, but more ominously, there is now an internal Palestinian conflict of interests."[84]

There must have been times in the 1990s when, preoccupied by day-to-day events and intermediate negotiations, Arafat put a short-term view foremost in his mind and pushed aside anything else to the status of distant dream. As long as he did not have to make any final choice, Arafat need not decide his real intentions. But ultimately forced into a corner by demands, so that he could no longer postpone his choice, Arafat decided against a deal precisely because the moment of decision was at hand. Whatever Arafat thought during the 1990s, in the year 2000, the dream of total victory in the future returned to blow up the hope for peace in the here and now.

Rather than admit that the Intifada was waged solely over the demand for all refugees to live in Israel, or to gain a small bit more of East Jerusalem and perhaps a few acres more of the West Bank, Arafat had to argue that everything was at stake. He needed to convince his people that the only alternatives were between war and permanent occupation or even genocide. Many in the West seemed to think that throwing away such a good chance for peace was so illogical that the opportunity must not have been there in the first place. Arafat once more exploited his weakness as proof of his virtue: if he was the underdog, how could he possibly be the aggressor?

This was a man terrified at the prospect of being considered insufficiently revolutionary, a man who ultimately could not imagine a peaceful resolution of his mission. Asked by an interviewer in 1995, "Has the revolutionary era ended? Has the state era begun?" Arafat answered passionately, "The revolution will go on until an independent Palestinian state is established with Jerusalem as its capital.... We will struggle on all fronts to prove that this land is Arab, Arab, and Arab; we will defend every particle of Palestinian soil; and we will wage the battle of building a Palestinian state as we waged the liberation and peace battle."[85]

Along with Arafat's dream, there was Arafat's nightmare. He told associates that his worst fear was that one day, long after his death, there would be a question on the final examinations of Arab schools asking, "Who was Yasir Arafat?" And the correct answer will be: "The man who gave up Palestine to the Jews."[86] To say that Arafat got part of it back would not be an acceptable response. Arafat had learned that he was more likely to be followed for what he promised rather than for what he delivered.

Many outsiders thought Arafat had to make progress toward a state and raise his people's living standards in order to stay in power. But from the start of the PA, for example, Arafat's policy was that none of those living in Gaza or West Bank refugee camps would be moved out or given better housing. Keeping them in the camps would maintain their sense of grievance, their access to UN relief payments, and their case for repatriation to Israel or compensation.[87] Arafat knew he would be more popular and stronger if he did not get a deal but instead went to war and roused the masses to unite in battle against Israel.

By refusing to compromise, he kept Palestinians united and feeling they had saved their honor by not selling out their dream. Statehood involved inevitable disappointments, the death of enthusiasm in the face of routine and the grubby necessities of everyday life. To be a revolutionary forever was to be forever young, like the suicide bombers and other martyrs whose pictures adorn the peeling posters on walls wherever Palestinians live in the Middle East.

But while Arafat was deeply concerned that his own movement and people regarded compromise as treason, he never tried to convince them otherwise, even during the height of the peace process. His speeches merely exhorted the masses to fight in stock phrases used over and over. There were no briefings on the peace process nor any explanation of deals he accepted or rejected. Despite his revolutionary rhetoric, Arafat was of the profoundly traditional school, which saw the people's job as being to obey its leaders without question or complaint.

Arafat formed no peace lobby and made no critical reexamination of past PLO policies or practices. Throughout the 1990s, those living in refugee camps were constantly told by Arafat and other PA officials that they were definitely going "home" at the end of the process.[88] In the mosques, it was impossible to distinguish between the statements of Hamas and pro-Fatah clerics. The textbooks ignored Israel's existence except to condemn it. Fatah's own education and ideology department was a stronghold for hard-line indoctrination and never accepted a two-state solution.[89] The media it controlled glorified violence and martyrdom, often hinting that Palestinian goals basically remained the same. Israel was not portrayed just as a former or temporary enemy but as an eternal enemy, not only that it had done evil but that it was intrinsically evil.

Thus, Jarir al-Kidwa, an advisor to Arafat on educational matters, could proclaim on PA television, "This is our Palestine, from Metullah [Israel's northernmost town] to Rafia [on the Egypt-Gaza border] and to Aqaba [Israel's southernmost point], from the [Jordan] River to the [Mediterranean] Sea; whether they want it or not." Issam Sissalem, a history professor in Gaza, explained that Israel is "a cancer in our country," and the story of the Holocaust was "all lies and unfounded claims." The real "holocaust was against our people. . . . We were the victims, but we shall not remain victims forever."[90]

All these institutions and the messages they presented were under Arafat's control, as shown by his quick action when preachers, schools, or media did anything not in accord with his wishes. This framework conditioned a belief that terrorism was justified, that becoming a suicide bomber was noble, that compromises were treason, and that total victory was inevitable. Explicitly opposing views, as opposed to ambiguous ones, were rarely expressed.

In interpreting the meaning of Palestinian historical experience, Arafat set the tone and agenda. Was the lesson of a half-century of struggle that defeat required compromise, or was it that the heroes who fought with stones, guns, and bombs must be emulated in new battles? To those listening to Arafat in Arabic, there could be no doubt which view was foremost. When Arafat issued a condemnation of terrorism in response to American or Israeli demands, then told his people that those still fighting and becoming martyrs were the Palestinians' proper role models, the answer was not in doubt.[91]

Arafat once remarked to those complaining that they had no part in decision making: "Every Palestinian feels he or she should be leading."[92] Yet in fact only one man, Arafat, had any real power. Everyone else was almost equal in their exclusion. True, he preferred to build coalitions and win assent for his policies from key figures in Fatah, the PLO, and the PA. But whenever Arafat did choose to exert himself, he had overwhelming power and support. And when he chose to let chaos reign, it was because he was content with the direction that events took without his intervention.

Leaders can always excuse continuing a disastrous policy by insisting they must await the ideal solution or bow to the public's demands. French president Charles de Gaulle might have gone on fighting for Algeria; Soviet rulers could have kept Communism going; Ayatollah Khomeini might have fought the war with Iraq for a generation; and U.S. presidents could have gone on battling in Vietnam for ten or twenty more years. But a true leader must go beyond existing opinion and shape his people's thinking without losing touch with them. The mark of a great leader is someone who, when necessary, is willing and able to drag and persuade them toward change.

This path was open to Arafat. He had devised a system which kept challenges to a minimum. He ruled through his legitimacy, patronage, and power to punish; activists followed him out of patriotism, careerism, and personal loyalty. Everyone knew that he alone determined their rank and importance in the movement, and they believed that only he could hold together the struggle and lead it to victory.

While Arafat paid great attention to gaining Arab and Western support as well as to managing the Palestinian political elite, he was remarkably disinterested in reshaping Palestinian society, economy, and intellectual life. He also cared relatively little for the factors that would have made a different kind of leader eager to achieve a peace agreement: material benefits for his people, an end to violence, economic development, social progress, and the gathering in of exiled and refugee Palestinians before another generation was lost.

The Oslo Agreement did present Arafat with what literally was a once-in-a-lifetime opportunity if he only had chosen to prepare and mobilize his people for peace rather than repeat earlier, failed strategies and beliefs. After all, Arafat did not get back to Palestine in 1994 because of his victories. His return was made possible because Israel's leaders genuinely wanted peace and were willing to give up almost all the territories captured in 1967 and to accept a Palestinian state there. What they wanted in return was full peace and a real end to violence.

Yet Arafat did not seem to change his old view of his opponents, which he had so long purveyed to Palestinians. If Israel and the United States were the kind of countries Arafat claimed they were, he would have long since been dead or, at least, in permanent exile. This was a vital point often forgotten amid the claims by Arafat, his supporters, and Western sympathizers of his endless victimization. Over the course of his career, Arafat was less the victim of discrimination than the beneficiary of special treatment. Others using terrorism were shunned or hunted down while Arafat was invited to address the United Nations.

Now, however, Arafat was demanding that Israel stake its survival on an agreement with him yet he did little to build his credibility. After all, he wanted to be made head of a state which, once independent, could do anything it wanted. Palestinians would never seek, he said in a 1998 speech in Stockholm, "to enter into any military struggle or any arms race with Israel" or join any "military or political alliance" aimed at Israel or anyone else.[93] Only twenty months later, he was leading a military struggle against Israel. What might Arafat do if he ever did run a country, given his record of finding reasons why he could not stop terrorism?

In the end, it was not Israel that turned down Arafat but Arafat who turned down Israel. If Arafat did want an agreement, he badly overplayed his hand. Yet there was nothing new to this pattern. Historically, Arafat had dealt with the consequences of his behavior by starting over again at a new location every few years. He destroyed his credibility with Jordan and shifted to Lebanon. He was thrown out of Lebanon and fled to Tunisia. He antagonized the Saudis and Kuwaitis but then was allowed to return to the West Bank and Gaza. Finally, though, he burned Israel and the United States in 2000, bringing down the Israeli leader and humiliating the American one. There was no one left willing to put up with him.

To the world, he insisted that fighting was the only way to end an occupation that Israel allegedly refused to terminate and to obtain a state that Israel supposedly refused to give. But for Arafat, violence was still a substitute for compromise, a way of making gains without making concessions. He seemed to still believe what he had said in 1969, "Revolutionaries do not expect victory to come from a meeting. Victory only comes by struggle and by arms."[94]

Arafat's attitude on this point was close to Qaddumi's explanation that the Palestinian leadership wanted to combine talks with Israel and violence against it: "We are adopting the strategy of the Vietnamese, who negotiated and fought the Americans at the same time until [they] defeated them."[95] This was a revealing precedent to choose. The Vietnamese revolutionaries had taken control over part of the country and then used it to wage a war that won them the rest. They had maneuvered the United States into an unconditional withdrawal through a campaign combining armed force, international pressure, and domestic dissent. Finally, they violated their agreements and seized the entire country.

This is not to say that the Palestinians and Arafat did not have many real grievances over Israel's behavior in the process. The point was, however, that a peace agreement would have resolved these problems. By signing some variation on the offers made by Barak and Clinton, Arafat could have ended the occupation, removed all settlements from Palestinian-ruled territory, freed prisoners in Israeli hands, and controlled the al-Aqsa mosque. By refusing to do so he was ensuring that all these problems continued into the indefinite future.

To show why Arafat preferred this option and thought Palestinians would be pleased by his strategy, consider the words of one relative moderate, Iyad Sarraj, a human rights activist and critic of Arafat. In 1999, he wrote that Palestinians were better off without the peace process. Previously, they had many "winning cards...despite our weaknesses." Refusing to recognize Israel had been a "nuclear weapon," which they had "refused to surrender for 50 years." Now, he claimed, the peace process had taken away armed struggle, national unity, and the sympathy of the world's media. Palestinian refugees abroad were thinking of settling down in their places of exile, "as if everything were over!" Before serious negotiations could really begin, he concluded, the Palestinians "must regain our winning cards."[96]

This was precisely what Arafat tried to do. For many, it was unimaginable that he would prefer extremism, violence, and suffering to peace and statehood at the price of relatively small compromises. Arafat, however, was counting on this belief since under that assumption, Israel would have to be at fault for any continuing bloodshed and occupation.

Another element of Arafat's traditional strategy was to create a huge crisis, which would threaten the region's stability and U.S. interests there and force both the Arab states and the Americans to agree to his demands. Arafat thought his greatest asset was an ability to make the region "burn," to use his word. A high-ranking Fatah official, Mazin Izz al-Din, reflected this sense of power and leverage by claiming that the new Intifada was very costly to the United States—he cited bin Ladin's attack on the USS *Cole* as one action it inspired—and claiming that moderate regimes like Egypt and Jordan "have begun to feel violent powerful 'earthquakes'" and "massive demonstrations of rage," which might even overthrow them.[97]

What was especially remarkable was Arafat's ability to convince much of the world that he had nothing to do with the violence or the war he advocated.[98] To see the doubts about whether Arafat had any link to terrorism or extremism after 2000 would be to think this was a person whose sterling record and proven credibility were enough to render any such accusations absurd. Yet Arafat was completely consistent in this regard, simply repeating his false denials of any connection with Black September from decades earlier. Moreover, he maintained that Fatah and the PLO had never committed terrorism. In reviewing the movement's history in 2001, he declared, "Our revolutionary code of ethics has always won the admiration of the entire world. Our civilized, humane, and democratic options have always constituted one of the bright and shining faces of this people's march."[99]

Sakhr Habash, a close colleague who ran Fatah's educational and ideological activities, explained both aspects of Arafat's strategy: "When the Zionist society has suffered heavy losses, it will demand that its government achieve a peace based on international legitimacy [i.e., Arafat's terms]. The continuation of the struggle will also influence American interests" and make it pressure Israel's government for concessions. "Any damage we cause to the Zionist society and to American interests will bring us closer to our goal."[100] Any Israeli retaliation to Palestinian attacks would deepen the international criticism and pressure against it.

In the negotiations, the same factors prevailed. Arafat could raise the price so high and get away with so much precisely because "everyone" else wanted peace—Israel, Europe, the United States, and even many

Arab leaders. He could hold them all hostage by being the one who held up a deal as they offered him more and more precisely because they wanted one. The situation, then, was the precise opposite of how Arafat described it. Arafat was the person who blocked peace, and being able to do so was his main strength and strategy.

But no matter how many times Arafat appeared unreliable, he was given another chance. There were several reasons for this situation. Arafat's support was deemed indispensable for making peace, and the fact that he was the one remaining roadblock only made pleasing or persuading him seem more urgent. Other leaders kept working with him because they yearned for peace, or hoped he would change, or wanted to get the credit for solving the world's most unsolvable conflict, or hated Israel, or felt sorry for the Palestinians, or wanted to please the Arab states who backed him, or feared his threat of disrupting the Middle East.

This was why, for example, Clinton refused to criticize Arafat after he broke up the Camp David summit. Any conflict with Arafat was seen as making it harder to ease the problem. Asked about reports that he was "disappointed by Arafat," Clinton replied, "I don't think that anything I say that stirs this up is very helpful.... We need to stop people dying.... This is not the time to be assessing that. This is a time to ... end violence, to keep calm, to start the peace process again, and then they can establish some mechanism to evaluate what happened and why, and how to keep it from ever happening again."[101]

Albright voiced similar ideas. She would "hate to begin to think" he was not a partner for peace. This would be an admission of failure and the terrible difficulty of solving the conflict. "We were so close" to an agreement, and since Arafat "is respected [and] is obviously the leader of the Palestinian people," his cooperation was essential to reduce violence and return to the "peace track."[102]

Clinton's successors quickly rediscovered the same apparent paradox: Arafat was the key factor blocking progress toward peace yet they were reluctant to challenge the man whose cooperation was deemed essential for achieving peace and satisfying the Arab world. Secretary of State Colin Powell, who had hitherto been Arafat's biggest defender in the U.S. government, privately complained that Arafat was "devious," explaining, "The guy is lost. He blames everybody else, except for himself. Israel, Iran, the United States." Powell told Arafat that he must end the violence if he wanted the United States to help him or to restart negotiations, but he concluded that Arafat was incapable of comprehending this point.[103]

Still, Arafat could congratulate himself on a remarkable accomplishment. After rejecting peace offers and ceasefires, he had forced

Arab leaders to support him, mobilized Palestinian forces for a united war effort, persuaded most Europeans that he was a man of peace and that Israel was an aggressive state which should be criticized or even punished, and even kept the United States running after him, trying to think up some offer he might accept. It could even be argued that his actions in the year 2000, by setting off a new and bloody Arab-Israeli conflict, had pushed the Arab world from a period of unprecedented moderation to one of renewed militancy.

Yet there had always been a truly realizable alternative scenario. Certainly in the 1990s, probably in the 1980s, and possibly in the 1970s, Arafat could have become president of an independent Palestinian state if he had been ready to demonstrate his abandonment of terrorism and his readiness to accept Israel's existence. This required not appeasement but persuasion and a genuine commitment to change the Palestinian world view and his tactics.

Palestine might have evolved over the next two decades under Arafat's leadership. It would not have been a wealthy country, but it could have brought back hundreds of thousands of refugees and given them new, productive lives. Playing on the guilt and political competition of Arab oil-producing states—as well as the Cold War U.S.-Soviet competition—Arafat could have gathered a lot of money. A whole Palestinian generation could have been educated and an economy built on servicing the needs of wealthy Arab oil-exporting countries and by managing the compensation money wisely.

By the year 2000, Arafat could have looked back on his labors with satisfaction, having firmly laid the foundation for a state that had many problems but was relatively peaceful and democratic by Arab standards. The millennium's end would have found Palestine a fair, if modest, success, celebrated as a model for other Arab countries. Arafat would have been a statesman cited as an example of peaceful solutions to deep problems. He could have won the Nobel Peace Prize, too. Of course, he did that in the end, but in this scenario he would have fully merited the award.

Was Arafat then a successful leader or a disaster for his people? Surely, he took the Palestinians from the depths of defeat and humiliation to receiving extraordinary attention and often sympathy from the world. He almost single-handedly created Palestinian nationalism. He kept the movement going, mobilized Arab support, but ensured its independence. He took the Palestinians through many disasters and even back to part of the homeland they claimed. He attained international legitimacy and made the world forget time after time his previous reprehensible actions. It was a remarkable work of political art over an incredible length of time.

But if he often made his people feel good, he did not make their lives good. If the Palestinian people's goal was an independent, peaceful, prosperous Palestinian state, he did not attain it, and he threw away the best opportunity to do so. If the goal was to destroy Israel, he failed at that also.

There were, of course, many reasons which could be cited for Arafat's unwillingness and inability to make a deal. He never trusted either Israel or the United States. Of course, they did not trust him either, but that did not prevent them from offering him a deal. He still believed in a future total victory and did not want to foreclose that option, yet no one would make an agreement with him suspecting this was his intention. He wanted to appease Palestinian extremists to maintain national unity but ended by endorsing a program close to theirs.

In the end, then, while there was no substitute for Arafat, Arafat was no substitute for a leader who could make peace. He failed the tests that dozens of other nationalist and Third World leaders had met. In too many ways, he was largely the same person in 2002 as he had been in 1972, often using the same expressions and concepts, repeating the same cycles of failure. The terrible irony was that the very man who had made it possible for the Palestinians to revive their cause and pride was also apparently incapable of solving their problems.

Arafat told the Swedish parliament in December 1998 that he understood that "the era of peace is not the same as the era of war, and that the requirement[s] of violent struggle are not those of the struggle for peace, and that the bitter struggle for peace may be still harder and more difficult than the challenges of confrontation and war."[104] But ultimately Arafat did not understand this distinction at all. Unable to make the transition from revolution to compromise or from extremism to moderation, he never led his people from homelessness to statehood.

10

No End to the Struggle

2001–2003

As the sun broke the horizon, blazing across the Red Sea on January 3, 2002, Israeli commandos captured the freighter *Karine A* in a lightning-fast raid. Bound for Gaza, the vessel had aboard fifty tons of weapons they would later determine had been ordered by Yasir Arafat's forces, including Katyusha rockets, Sagger and LAW antitank missiles, mortars, mines, sophisticated explosives, sniper rifles, and bullets. If all of this equipment had arrived as planned, Arafat's troops could have greatly escalated their war on Israel.

Discovery of this ship's mission implicated Arafat as the one behind the violence that had been raging since September 2000 and the difficulty in ending it. But there was even more to the story that might discredit Arafat internationally. The weapons had been purchased through Hizballah and supplied by Iran. Just four months after the devastating September 11, 2001, terrorist attack on America, Arafat was aligning himself with a movement and country that the United States saw as principal elements in an "axis of evil," foes in its war against terrorism, and even allies to a degree with the forces of Usama bin Ladin.

There was still another—perhaps the most remarkable—element in the *Karine A* affair: if Arafat's plan had succeeded, it would have produced a far larger catastrophe for himself and his movement. Palestinian forces could have used these arms to raise the level of fighting high enough to impel an all-out Israeli attack to reconquer the West Bank and the Gaza Strip, resulting in the destruction of the PA and in Arafat's flight abroad.

The evidence linking Arafat to the ship was substantial. The ship's captain, Omar Akawi, a twenty-five-year veteran of Fatah, said he knew he was carrying arms to the PA. Adal Mugrabi, head of the PA's arms procurement department and a naval officer, was in radio contact with Akawi during the voyage.[1] The ship itself had been purchased by Fouad Shoubaki, one of Arafat's closest aides, who sat at a desk just a few steps away from Arafat's office in the Ramallah headquarters compound. Since Arafat was famous for micromanaging PA expenditures, the idea that he would not have been consulted on buying $15 million worth of weapons was ludicrous. And the *Karine A* had been preceded by two similar operations to supply the PA with arms, both intercepted by Israeli forces.[2] Yet Arafat still maintained to the Arab and Palestinian media that he had nothing to do with the *Karine A*.[3]

As always, though, Arafat felt secure that his survival skills made up for his penchant for making bad decisions. He and his lieutenants disclaimed any link to the shipment. He argued, rather unpersuasively, that he did not need to buy weapons because he had his own arms depots all over the world or because Arab countries would give him whatever he wanted.[4] Instead, he insisted it was all a plot by Israel to frame him.[5] Arafat even wrote President George W. Bush a personal letter denying he knew about the ship. An angry Bush declared that he did not believe this: "I am disappointed in Yasir Arafat. He must make a full effort to rout out terror."[6]

Generally speaking, though, Arafat's post–peace process circumstances were not all that different from the circumstances he had been facing throughout his career. Arafat's strategy against Israel had once more failed. He was making no progress toward a state. Contrary to his predictions, Israel did not collapse or retreat. Equally, the world did not send forces to take control of all the West Bank and Gaza Strip, expel Israel's presence, and simply create a Palestinian state without any negotiated agreement. Instead, much of the Palestinian gains from the peace process years were wiped out, amid heavy human losses, because of the war he had waged.

Still, he was a man who always saw glorious victory in the midst of what was actually a disastrous defeat and, as usual, there were also factors that helped him believe—and that persuaded most Palestinians— that this was an accurate assessment. On the positive side, for example, the West was still willing to deal with him or at least not treat him like an enemy. Despite his rejection of the Camp David and Clinton plans, broken promises of ceasefires, evidence of his direct involvement in terrorism, the post–September 11 war on terrorism, and the *Karine A* affair, Arafat was hardly treated as a pariah by the United States or Europe. Secretary of State Colin Powell floated one new scheme after another to restart talks without forcing Arafat to implement a real ceasefire. In March and September 2002, the U.S. government forced Israel to end sieges of Arafat in his office.

In Europe, Arafat's rejection of peace, conduct of a war against Israel, and involvement in terrorism had no effect on his standing. True, in February 2001, European Union foreign affairs commissioner Chris Patten warned that Europe would not bankroll Arafat's PA forever and that the money would be given only if it were used properly. But despite the *Karine A*, documents showing Arafat's direct role in sponsoring terrorist attacks on Israel, and evidence that European aid money had been used for promoting violence, almost eighteen months later Patten was calling Arafat an "indispensable partner" for peace, and the funds were still flowing into his coffers.[7]

Western leaders were still horrified at the prospect of the PA collapsing and Arab states being outraged at the Palestinians' fate, and they believed that shutting Arafat forever out of negotiations would doom all hopes for peace.

Not having to worry too much about such a popular revolt was Arafat's second asset. After the initial burst of popular enthusiasm for the uprising quickly faded, the fighting was conducted by armed Fatah members—activists operating through Fatah's Tanzim or al-Aqsa Martyrs Brigade groups, as well as some PA security officers—along with Hamas and Islamic Jihad warriors. Once again, the masses had returned to passivity, ready to cheer their leaders publicly whatever the costs of their strategy or their private misgivings about its efficacy.

Indeed, the renewed battle against Israel reinforced Arafat's popularity. Palestinians overwhelmingly backed his policy and the violent tactics being used. Instead of talking about mismanagement, corruption, and economic woes, Palestinians, convinced they had no choice, again rallied behind Arafat's leadership against an enemy portrayed as diabolical and intransigent. They believed that neither Israel nor the United States had ever made a reasonable or attractive offer for a peaceful resolution of the conflict. Since their leadership made it clear to them that negotiations had failed and the enemy was uninterested in ever ending the occupation and letting them have a state, most believed violence was the only alternative.

As the war continued in 2002 and 2003, as Israeli forces advanced periodically deep into the West Bank, Palestinian grumbling increased. It became clear that the war could not defeat Israel and was causing far larger losses for their own side. Palestinians increasingly expressed their sense of insecurity and complained about the lack of PA relief efforts, declining living standards, the loss of educational opportunities, and such maladies as stress, depression, and sleep deprivation.[8] The Intifada's first fifteen months cost the Palestinian economy an estimated $2.4 billion. Real income fell by 30 percent to a level lower than in the late 1980s; unemployment tripled. The PA could barely, and not always, pay employees.[9]

Still, from Arafat's standpoint, all these problems were secondary. He never put a priority on social or economic well-being, and the discontent never seriously threatened to overthrow him. If his popularity declined, it still remained far above any conceivable challengers or that of the PLC.[10] And how, Arafat implied, could anyone put mere economic well-being above the defense of Arab, Islamic, and Palestinian rights?

Finally, though Arab states would not do much to help him, most of them continued to give lip service to his leadership and cause, demanding that the West aid him and focusing their outrage against Israel. From the Atlantic Ocean to the Persian Gulf, there were articles, speeches, songs, and television programs supporting Arafat. Arab summits hailed Arafat's heroism. In Egypt, there was even a cheese puff snack food named in Arafat's honor, replete with his cartoon image.[11]

But as had happened in 1982, when Arafat was besieged in Beirut, and during the first Intifada, more substantial financial aid or diplomatic efforts from the Arab world did not come. Arafat complained that Saudi money went completely to Hamas and Islamic Jihad without him receiving any share.[12] The new Syrian president, Bashar al-Asad, continued his father's feud with Arafat and never invited him to Damascus. Mubarak, feeling that Arafat never listened to him anyway, dropped any pretense of being his patron. "Nobody is willing to burn their fingers for Arafat any more," one Arab official explained. "He has no credibility in any leading Arab capital. He burnt his bridges by playing both sides against the middle, too many times."[13] Except for the Lebanese Hizballah group and limited help from Iran and Iraq, Arafat was once again on his own.[14]

All these factors were typical of the balance among illusory successes, actual defeat, and—most important of all—political survival so common in Arafat's career.

Another constant for Arafat was his profound misperception or indifference to how his behavior affected Israel. He almost always severely misjudged that country and damaged his own interests by making life harder for the Israeli political forces friendly to his more moderate aspirations. No matter how much Arafat and his followers hated or mistrusted that country, they should have learned by this point that they could only free the West Bank and Gaza to gain a state through Israel's agreement. And, despite their desire for revenge, they should also have learned that terrorism would strengthen, not weaken, Israeli resolve and bring a hard-line response.

The landslide electoral victory of Ariel Sharon, Arafat's old nemesis, in early 2001 should have bothered Arafat. After all, Barak, who had offered Arafat more than any other Israeli leader and was probably ready for more concessions to reach an agreement, was now discredited. In contrast, Sharon had been responsible for Arafat's great defeat of 1982 in Lebanon, refused to shake his hand at the 1998 Wye meeting, and opposed Barak's peace plan as far too generous.

Yet there was every sign that Sharon's victory pleased Arafat, who preferred facing his military reprisals rather than Barak's diplomatic offensives. Arafat knew that Sharon would be unpopular with Western and Arab governments, media, and public opinion. He could easily portray Sharon as a war-loving reactionary opposed to peace or compromise. In addition, many PA leaders expected that if Sharon—whom they called the last bullet in Israel's gun—could not defeat the Intifada, Israel would have to surrender and withdraw unilaterally from the territories.

At first, even Egypt's top leaders thought Arafat's strategy might work and that a combined fear of terrorism and discontent with Sharon would bring the election of an Israeli leftist prime minister, who would make a deal on Arafat's terms. U.S. counterparts warned that Arafat could only get such a result if he stopped the violence and showed himself ready to make compromises. As the violence escalated, the Egyptians realized that Arafat had miscalculated. But Arafat did not seem to see the effect he was having on Israeli politics and public opinion.[15]

As further encouragement for the belief that he was succeeding, Arafat could note that the gap in casualties between the two sides was narrowing as Palestinian attacks, especially by suicide bombers, killed more Israelis than had ever died from terrorism in the pre–peace process era. Until about March 2002, Israeli reprisals within the PA-ruled territories were mainly air attacks against PA installations or individuals whom it accused of being responsible for terrorism. Despite the Palestinians' high casualties and economic losses up to that point, Arafat cited his historic argument that victory was inevitable since the enemy could take far fewer casualties and less suffering than his people.

Another reason victory was inevitable, Arafat thought, was that he enjoyed the support of virtually everyone in the world. And if anyone did criticize him, it was only due, Arafat said, to the fact that they had been misled by "the Zionist lobby [which] rules sensitive areas in the world and controls the media and elections."[16]

How, an al-Jazira television interviewer asked Arafat in December 2002, did he expect to gain victory? By helping dovish forces win power in Israel or getting U.S. or Arab aid? Arafat replied with Qu'ranic quotations about the virtue of steadfastness, the glory of martyrdom, and the certainty of victory. Compromise was not necessary. Anyone "who relinquishes a grain of the soil of holy Jerusalem . . . is not one of us, nor does he belong to the Palestinian people." Instead, they would fight, "Until doomsday, defending our Christian and Islamic holy places. . . . We will not stop demanding our rights, no matter how long this takes. We are like a mountain that no wind can shake. . . . If you are tired, I am not. We will see who gets the upper hand in the end."[17]

Among the stratagems Arafat used to control events while appearing uninvolved were ordering security forces not to interfere with Islamist groups attacking Israelis, giving a green light to security officers who wanted to participate in attacks, glorifying terrorism in his own speeches and the Palestinian media, releasing almost all imprisoned Hamas and Islamic Jihad terrorists in late 2000, and integrating Hamas into the Arafat-led committees running the Intifada.[18] A symbolic example of this new alliance was a November 29, 2001, joint suicide bombing in Israel in which two terrorists—a Palestinian policeman and an Islamist militant—blew themselves up together on a crowded Israeli bus near the city of Hadera.[19]

Meanwhile, the overwhelming majority of Palestinians, 70 percent according to one poll, believed that Arafat did have full control over the violence.[20] He also showed himself able to halt attacks when he wanted, for example, during Powell's February 2001 visit to Ramallah. To provide security for his American visitor, Arafat gave the job to Force 17, his elite service, which furnished his own bodyguards. But this was also the PA security agency most involved in previous operations against Israeli civilians. As soon as Powell left Ramallah, Fatah squads restarted their attacks.

The most detailed evidence of Arafat's direct involvement in terrorist attacks came from documents taken by Israel during its March 2002 siege of his Ramallah office compound. The al-Aqsa Martyrs Brigade, nominally an independent group ignoring Arafat's authority, was shown to be led by local Fatah leaders who were on Arafat's payroll and used official Fatah stationery to ask his personal approval to give money for gunmen, weapons, posters, and financial assistance to the families of its terrorists who had been captured or killed in action.[21]

When a Fatah leader in Tulkarm on April 5, 2001, asked Arafat to pay sixteen "fighting brothers" involved in many attacks on Israel, he agreed.[22] While Tanzim, Force 17, and the Iraqi-backed Palestine Liberation Front (which had carried out the *Achille Lauro* attack a decade earlier) were killing Israeli civilians despite his public requests for them to stop, Arafat wrote notes on his own personal stationery ordering payments to the gunmen. Some of this money was sent by Arafat in response to a personal request by Marwan Barghouti, leader of the Tanzim. Another of those he paid was Atef Abiat, a terrorist Arafat had said he could not find when Israel had requested his arrest.[23] But Arafat made some of the money back by having the PA serve as middleman in selling Iraqi oil abroad to circumvent UN-mandated sanctions against Saddam Hussein's regime.[24]

While these connections were handled in secret, Arafat publicly cheered suicide attacks and extolled a war whose main tactic was deliberate anti civilian terrorism. As he had done in other situations, the line he expressed to foreigners or in occasional television broadcasts made at Western request was different from what Arafat told Palestinians directly in his speeches or PA-controlled media coverage. Every time Arafat made a call to end the fighting in English, news was broadcast around the world that he opposed the violence. But his colleagues, officers, and the people in general knew which statements to take seriously and which were to be ignored. While for the West, Arafat played the man of peace, for the Palestinians and Arabs, he was clearly a man of war.

On June 1, 2001, a Saturday night bombing by Hamas outside a Tel Aviv disco killed twenty Israeli teenagers. After a direct appeal from German foreign minister Joschka Fischer, who was visiting him at the time, Arafat agreed to speak on Palestinian television, promising to "exert the utmost efforts to stop the bloodshed of our people and of the Israeli people."[25] But aside from this broadcast, he did nothing. A few days later, the suicide bomber's family received a letter from the PLO embassy in Jordan, over Arafat's signature, calling the bomber's act a "heroic martyrdom operation, . . . the model of manhood and sacrifice for the sake of Allah and the homeland."[26] When Israel identified the two men who ran the operation and, with U.S. support, asked the PA to arrest them, PA security agents interrogated them. They admitted their involvement. The security officers then told them to sign an agreement not to do it again and let them go home.[27]

In December 2001, under U.S. pressure, Arafat made another formal call to end the violence in a televised address marking the end of Ramadan. But a day later, speaking at a rally in Ramallah and with no Western media around, Arafat reiterated his support for attacks, extolling martyrs and summing up his political stance by concluding, "We shall fight on this blessed land. . . . This is our message."[28]

On another occasion, Arafat asked, "Do you know what a mother of a martyr does when she is informed of the martyrdom of her son? She goes out to the street with cheers of joy saying, 'Allah be praised, my son, that you married Palestine rather than your cousin.' This is the Palestinian people."[29] Even in his own home, that view clearly prevailed. In April 2002, his wife, Suha, said that if she had a son, there would be "no greater honor" than his being a suicide bomber. "Would you expect me and my children to be less patriotic and more eager to live than my countrymen and their father and leader [Yasir Arafat] who is seeking martyrdom?"[30]

It was one of Arafat's oldest techniques—which he had used in Jordan, Lebanon, and from Tunisia decades earlier—to unleash and encourage attacks from radical PLO groups, or even his own Fatah, while denying any responsibility or involvement. For example, the al-Aqsa Martyrs Brigade was simply a new version of the Black September group of the 1970s. Amazingly, many foreigners accepted the notion that Arafat, the Palestinian movement's leader for thirty-five years and commander of a dozen security agencies in a tiny territory, suddenly had no control or knowledge about the doings of terrorists even if they were members of Fatah or his own bodyguard. Having asserted his total personal control over the first Intifada from far-away Tunis a decade earlier, Arafat now presented himself as helpless though he was right on the scene. "Our people are not like chess pieces," he asserted.[31] The man known as the "Teflon terrorist" had not lost his skill.[32]

Cabinet secretary Ahmad Abd al-Rahman, Arafat's closest aide and the man most likely to express accurately his leader's personal views, predicted certain victory if the war continued: "2003 is the year of defeat...of Sharon's Zionist project in Palestine. Our inferiority complex must disappear. The true achievements of the intifada in the past two years will appear." Israel would collapse socially and militarily, forced to accept withdrawal on Palestinian terms. "If they fail to do so, they will enjoy no security" because the Palestinians would keep on fighting no matter what the cost to themselves.[33]

"I bow to all [those attacking Israelis] in admiration and respect.... Who else shall we glorify if we do not glorify those who defend freedom and the homeland?" And to make clear that terror attacks on Israeli territory were part of his leader's strategy, Abd al-Rahman added, "Israeli tanks reach the heart of Palestinian cities, but the Palestinians will reach wherever they want with simple technology to retaliate for Israeli crimes," precisely what the groups sending suicide bombers inside Israel said they were doing.[34]

Beyond all the details was a simple fact that in itself was both astonishing and yet typical of Arafat's career: Arafat viewed the continued fighting and the use of terrorism to be brilliant strategies that served Palestinian interests—even though this was obviously a mistake.

The Palestinians could not win the battle directly, and their society and government seemed far closer to collapse than did those of Israel. Equally, Arafat's tactics were not going to mobilize the type of Western or Arab support that would gain victory for them. Yet the disastrous strategy did serve some purposes: ensuring Arafat stayed in power, avoiding the type of peaceful compromise he saw as disgraceful, and proving the Palestinians to be heroic in their own and in Arab eyes.

On the political front, Arafat and many—though by no means all—of his colleagues seemed happy to return to the past. Arafat still argued, as he had in the 1960s and 1970s, that attacks on Israeli civilians would demoralize that country and lead to its collapse or surrender. In fact, as had happened earlier, it made the Israelis toughen their stance and fight all the harder, believing—unlike in the 1993–2000 era—that there was no alternative. The fragile trust built up at that time could not be reestablished as long as Arafat led the Palestinians.

Yossi Sarid, leader of the left-wing Israeli party Meretz and one of the peace process's main champions, advised Arafat in March 2001:

> Maybe it's time you stopped flitting from one country to another. Settle down in Gaza and Ramallah and start bringing order, because this anarchy is going to bring a terrible disaster upon our people as well as on yours.... Do not make us suspect that you ... care more for an armed and violent struggle for a Palestinian state than for the Palestinian state itself.[35]

But this is exactly what Israelis did suspect. Yossi Beilin, an architect of the Oslo Agreement and the most important Israeli politician still friendly toward him, told Arafat during an April 2001 visit that even the leftists now believed that "the Oslo Agreement was a plot and not a historic program of conciliation. At the critical moments of test—at Camp David, at Sharm al-Sheikh and at Taba—Arafat's true face was revealed. What he wanted was not a peace treaty but the implementation of the Palestinian 'plan of stages' for annihilating Israel."[36]

Arafat's ambiguity about his ultimate political goals, even to his own people, as well as the violence itself, produced this reaction. His refusal, observed Palestinian analyst Yezid Sayigh, "to discuss, publicly or internally what would constitute an acceptable deal [had] left the Palestinian public unprepared for necessary compromises and trade-offs," even though the people might well have supported them "if properly approached and as part of a package deal."[37]

Yet Arafat's incitement, the political atmosphere he created, and the tactics he justified were also pushing Palestinians in a radical direction. Inasmuch as Arafat was signaling Palestinians as to his goals, they were those of revolutionary armed struggle until victory. Public opinion polls in 2002 showed that half of all Palestinians saw the Intifada's goals as being "to liberate all of historic Palestine." The other half wanted a Palestinian state alongside Israel yet many of them also saw this as a first step toward total victory by future struggles and using the return of refugees to subvert Israel.[38] Emboldened by this atmosphere, Qaddumi stated that the PLO no longer recognized Israel and had reverted to the goal of destroying it.[39]

Yet whatever his own program and regardless of whether or not he sincerely desired to make peace, Arafat missed significant opportunities. Having proven his willingness to fight—and presumably having shown his people he was not surrendering—Arafat could then have accepted the Clinton plan or made last-minute compromises to make a deal before Barak fell from office. Throughout 2001 or 2002, he could have opted for a ceasefire and diplomatic breakthrough. If Sharon had rejected a serious offer coupled with an end to violence, Arafat could even have won a major international victory without having to make any real political concessions.

Two specific developments that year also offered Arafat a life preserver, which he refused to grab. In April 2001, an international commission—which originated with Arafat's own demand to look into the causes of the new Intifada—issued what was usually called the Mitchell report. Although it did not accept Arafat's request for an international force to be sent to the West Bank, there were many points favorable to Arafat's position. For example, it acceded to Arafat's demand for a freeze on settlements, a plan for returning to negotiations, and an analysis of the violence which avoided blaming Arafat.[40] Arafat could have ended the fighting and demanded that Israel implement the commission's provisions.[41] Instead, he merely complained about the sections he did not like and kept the fighting going.

The September 11 attacks on the United States offered him a combination of opportunity and threat. Unable to restrain their glee, several thousand Palestinians celebrated the terrorist operation that had killed three thousand Americans.[42] With U.S. policy now focused on the horrors of Middle Eastern terrorism—the precise strategy he was using against Israel—continuing his war would expose Arafat to Washington's wrath. Yet if Arafat had proclaimed he was joining the war against terror, suppressed radical forces, and implemented a quick ceasefire, he would have won U.S. gratitude. Since the Bush administration was eager to mobilize Arab support for its war on terrorism, bin Ladin, and the Afghani Taliban regime, Arafat could have traded support on these issues to get American backing and pressure on Israel.

Instead, though, he merely responded with a public relations campaign: criticizing the attacks on New York and Washington; personally donating blood for victims, though he knew it would never reach them; and ordering a candlelight vigil and a moment of silence in PA schools. Foreign reporters were barred from Gaza while his security agencies warned Palestinian journalists—at Arafat's direct request, they were told—not to report on pro–bin Ladin demonstrations. Arafat took firm measures to suppress the marches; his police opened fire on the demonstrators and killed at least two Palestinians.[43]

Once again, he had showed that he could intervene decisively and impose his will when he felt that to be in his interest. But the Americans overthrew the Taliban, hunted bin Ladin, and waged war on terrorism without Arafat's help. Instead of gaining something, Arafat seemed to prove himself part of the terrorist problem rather than part of the solution. Arafat's own deeds made the Bush administration hostile to him, doubt he was a partner for peace, and demand Palestinian political reform, including his departure from power.

Despite the opportunities offered by the Mitchell report and the September 11 crisis as well as the pleas of European leaders who wanted to help him, Arafat made no serious attempt to end the fighting as it dragged through 2001 and 2002. In August 2001, Israeli forces killed PFLP leader Abu Ali Mustafa, whom it accused of planning terrorist attacks. Two months later, the PFLP slew Israeli tourism minister Rehavam Zeevi at a Jerusalem hotel. Despite PFLP claims of responsibility for the latter shooting, Arafat denied that Palestinians were involved and suggested that Zeevi's death was an Israeli conspiracy. When Israel accused four Palestinians of culpability, Arafat protected them.[44]

Sensitive to international pressure and to his own reputation as an extremist, Sharon acted with relative restraint at first. He knew that Israeli ground forces could seize control of the West Bank, destroy the PA, and force Arafat into exile, but he refrained from such a strategy. Arafat had to be aware that Sharon always retained that option. As terrorist attacks escalated, there was no sign of a ceasefire, and Arafat lost Arab and Western support, Sharon had less incentive to hold back his full retaliation. On December 1, eleven Israelis were killed and about one hundred and eighty injured when explosive devices were detonated by two Hamas suicide bombers on a pedestrian mall in the center of Jerusalem. The next day, fifteen Israelis were killed and forty injured in a Hamas suicide bombing on a bus in Haifa. On December 4, as a warning to Arafat, Israeli missiles destroyed his three helicopters and tore up the landing strip at Gaza International Airport.

Arafat's critique of some of these terrorist operations was based on their timing, not their moral nature, costs, or political effects. By blowing up Israeli civilians at "the very moment when Sharon went to meet with President Bush with no cards in his hands," he complained after one such operation, those responsible "gave Sharon these operations as a present."[45] But these events were a direct result of Arafat's own strategy, and with each month of continued warfare the balance shifted even further against him, regardless of which particular day the attacks took place.

Still, the terrorist assaults on civilians within Israel continued and even accelerated, at times when Sharon was not meeting with Bush. On January 17, 2002, six Israelis were killed and dozens wounded in the northern city of Hadera, when a former PA policeman with the al-Aqsa Martyrs Brigade burst into a crowded banquet hall and opened fire with an M-16 assault rifle. On March 2, ten people were killed in a suicide bombing by the al-Aqsa Brigade at a bar mitzvah celebration in downtown Jerusalem. On March 9, eleven people were killed and fifty-four injured when a Hamas suicide bomber blew himself up at a popular Jerusalem café. On March 20, seven were killed and thirty wounded in an Islamic Jihad suicide bombing on a bus traveling from Tel Aviv to Nazareth. On March 21, three people were killed and eighty-six injured in a suicide bombing by the Fatah al-Aqsa Brigade in downtown Jerusalem.

Even after all this, the U.S. government was eager to give Arafat another chance, dispatching its envoy, retired general Anthony Zinni, to try to mediate a ceasefire. On March 21, 2002, just before Zinni arrived, Arafat called a secret meeting at his Ramallah headquarters of the umbrella group running the Intifada, which was supposedly completely independent of him and whose members included Hamas and Islamic Jihad. He claimed credit for "conducting this difficult war." It was succeeding, he insisted, and "everyone is on our side," including the United Nations and most of the world's countries. Even the Americans were backing down and accepting a Palestinian state, he claimed, due to the Palestinians' tough stance.[46]

But with Zinni on the way, Arafat said at the meeting, some of the latest operations were ill-timed, interfering with his strategy. The Hamas representative on the joint committee, Hassan Yousef, who headed that group in Ramallah, agreed with Arafat, remarking, "We are close to each other, and we can agree on everything." Under pressure from Zinni, Arafat made a speech on television opposing terrorism and ordered his security forces to close down Hamas and Islamic Jihad institutions in the Gaza Strip and West Bank. Supposedly, he also approved the arrests of Palestinian policemen involved in terrorism. In fact, however, those detained were told it was to protect them from Israeli raids, and they were kept in apartments, not jails. The offices of the radical groups continued to function, and the terrorist apparatus remained untouched.[47]

Then, on March 27, twenty-one people were killed by a suicide bomber at a Passover celebration in Netanya. This was the final straw for Sharon. Israel's army was ordered to advance into PA territory to damage facilities, kill or arrest terrorist leaders and planners, and destroy bomb and munitions factories. Arafat's compound in Ramallah was surrounded, and he was under siege. The specific quarry in the encirclement of Arafat was Zeevi's assassins, whom Arafat had moved into his headquarters for protection. Arafat claimed the real killers of Zeevi were Israeli agents.[48]

But Arafat and his people were also to be shown the high cost of continuing the war. Battles between Israeli soldiers and Palestinian security forces broke out, especially in Jenin, which attracted international attention. PA leaders, including Arafat, claimed that Israel had massacred many Palestinians. "What happened [in Jenin]," Arafat said, "was more than what happened in Stalingrad" by the Nazis during World War II. The Stalingrad siege lasted a year and one million Russians died. At Jenin, fighting took a few days and the Palestinian death toll was thirty-five."[49] While at first the Western media reported or accepted such exaggerations, it was soon shown that they were untrue. Despite inflicting casualties on Israeli forces, the Palestinians suffered far higher losses and a humiliating military defeat.[50]

By bringing home the dangers of Arafat's policy and the unlikelihood that the fighting would end soon or on favorable terms, these events had a devastating effect on Palestinian morale. Many argued in private that by failing to take into account the costs and conditions of his war strategy, Arafat was leading the Palestinians to disaster. But even if more Palestinians wanted the fighting to end, there was still a strong mood of militancy and support for Arafat, which was defined as a patriotic imperative. Nevertheless, just after the siege ended, Palestinians were split almost evenly on whether Arafat's performance during the crisis was adequate or disappointing.[51]

In public, the main criticisms were that reform was needed in the conduct of Palestinian affairs, that Arafat was too moderate by making any deal to end the siege, and that the PA had not effectively defended its people from the Israeli army. Privately, there were more complaints about the militant policy's high costs and negative effects on the people's lives. Despite Arafat's praise of Jenin for being the center of the heaviest fighting, he canceled a visit to the refugee camp there in May out of fear that the residents would heckle him.[52]

While Bush had saved Arafat from the siege, he was also disgusted with the Palestinian leader's performance. Parts of his administration, especially in the State Department, argued that the United States must engage Arafat in some new round of negotiations. But Bush's earlier anger over the *Karine A* affair was reinforced by credible documents captured by Israel from Arafat's headquarters, which showed, for example, that Arafat had authorized a $20,000 payment to a suicide bomber from the al-Aqsa Martyrs Brigade who had killed seven people at a crowded bus stop in Jerusalem.[53]

On June 25, Bush made a major shift in U.S. policy toward Arafat by publicly concluding that progress toward peace was impossible as long as Arafat was the Palestinians' leader or, at least, their exclusive decision maker. Bush said:

> I call on the Palestinian people to elect new leaders, leaders not compromised by terror. I call upon them to build a practicing democracy, based on tolerance and liberty. If the Palestinian people actively pursue these goals, America and the world will actively support their efforts. If the Palestinian people meet these goals, they will be able to reach agreement with Israel...on security and other arrangements for independence. And when the Palestinian people have new leaders, new institutions and new security arrangements with their neighbors, the United States of America will support the creation of a Palestinian state whose borders and certain aspects of its sovereignty will be provisional until resolved as part of a final settlement in the Middle East.[54]

Bush made clear that this type of change must go beyond minor alterations "or a veiled attempt to preserve the status quo." A large part of the problem was that Arafat's regime was "encouraging, not opposing terrorism. This is unacceptable. And the United States will not support the establishment of a Palestinian state until its leaders engage in a sustained fight against the terrorists and dismantle their infrastructure."[55] The intention was that rather than offer Arafat a big reward for meeting the commitments he had been making—and often violating—for a decade, the incentive of quickly receiving a state would be given to the Palestinian people if they chose a leadership ready for a real compromise peace.

Even Powell, Arafat's main advocate in the U.S. government, made clear his displeasure. Arafat, Powell complained, simply refused "to bring the violence under control" by using his "moral authority as leader of the Palestinian people" or political power with "the organizations he has under him. And so he missed all these opportunities, just as he missed the opportunity that President Clinton presented to him." The Palestinian people, then, should "consider whose leadership brought them to their bad situation [and realize] they are not going to be able to move forward toward a state with this kind of leadership unless it changes."[56]

Arafat, however, interpreted the new U.S. policy in his own way. He focused on Bush's promise of a state preceding a full peace agreement with Israel and tried to transform it into a major American concession to himself. Asked if Bush was referring to him in speaking about a change of Palestinian leadership, Arafat responded, "Definitely not."[57] Indeed, Arafat asked, "Who initiated the reforms? I did."[58]

Still, given the high levels of Palestinian criticism coupled with U.S. pressure for reform, Arafat knew he had to do something, but once again he put the emphasis on public relations measures by trying to show himself to be the leader of a good government movement. In part, this also functioned as a substitute to ending the war with Israel. Even in the face of the highest levels of domestic and American pressure he had seen in many years, Arafat seemed to believe that purely cosmetic gestures would suffice. As always, he expected the critics to give up or the situation to change dramatically in his favor.

He announced there would be presidential and PLC elections and a "100 Days Plan" for reform, including a separation of powers, consolidation and tightened discipline over security agencies, and a school curriculum that emphasized moderation and democratic values. In addition, all PA income would be turned over to a Palestinian investment fund with strict, independent auditing, and Arafat would implement "all laws that have been passed" by the PLC.[59] Once again, none of the promised reform measures were made. He did name a new cabinet, but a majority of its members were the old ministers, including all four of those the PLC had earlier demanded be investigated on corruption charges.[60]

As he had often done in similar circumstances in the past, Arafat also threatened to resign and suggested that anyone who thought they could do better could replace him. In September, when he made his first speech to the PLC in eighteen months, it included little about reform and no sign at all that he was ready to change his catastrophic warfare strategy.[61] In the ensuing debate, many PLC members—including those from Fatah—expressed skepticism about Arafat's leadership and promises. Abd al-Jawad Salah, a PLC member and one of his most respected critics, pointed out that Arafat had not implemented the pledges he had made the previous year.[62] Ziyad Abu Amr, head of the PLC political committee, said he doubted that Arafat would "engage in any serious process of accountability. We wanted a change in the whole style of leadership and not only to change names."[63]

A few of Arafat's closest comrades, especially Abu Mazin and Muhammad Dahlan, warned that his policy was seriously mistaken. Dahlan, who resigned as Arafat's national security advisor after concluding he had no intention of making reforms, urged Arafat to end the armed conflict and even the uprising altogether. "The Intifada," he said he reminded Arafat, "is the means, not the purpose." He also warned that Hamas was becoming too bold and that Arafat's refusal to rein in that group might be convincing it to try to overthrow the PA.[64] Equally outspoken was the veteran PLO official Interior Minister Abd al-Razak Yahiya, who had quit in September, and made it clear that Arafat had stopped him from reforming the security forces and replacing officers who participated in attacks on Israelis. Like Dahlan, he argued that armed struggle was a mistake, denounced suicide attacks on both moral and tactical grounds, and complained that Arafat let Hamas and Islamic Jihad sabotage ceasefire efforts. Yahiya's attitude toward armed struggle stood in sharp contrast to Arafat's by dint of its simple pragmatism: "I look at it in terms of profit and loss. This won't do us any good and we should stop it."[65]

Nabil Amr, a veteran PLO official and member of parliament, wrote an open letter asking Arafat, "What is to be done now . . . that Israeli tanks are in full control of the West Bank and surround Gaza? . . . Now . . . that every Palestinian militia on the streets acts without any central command and controls and defines the battle as [it sees] fit?"[66] The only response was that PA security forces opened fire on Amr's Ramallah home as an apparent warning to him to be quiet.

Even hardliners, like Abbas Zaki, a veteran Fatah official who specialized in relations with the Arab world, were increasingly critical, claiming Arafat now surrounded himself with worthless people, opportunists and murderers quite different from the strugglers and pioneers who built the movement. But, like many, Zaki thought that any reforms must not challenge Arafat's leadership, saying, "You may argue with the man, but not question the fact that he's the supreme commander of the people."[67]

Many others shared this last sentiment, supported Arafat's policies, or at least would not openly dissent from them. Even in the face of national disaster, the only step the PLC took was to reject Arafat's proposed new cabinet, which it had come close to doing on at least three previous occasions, in September 2002.[68] Even then, Arafat merely had to make some small alterations in the cabinet in order to win the PLC's overwhelming approval six weeks later.[69] When the real showdown might have come, at the October 2002 Fatah Central Committee meeting, the opposition collapsed. Abu Mazin and Abu Alaa did not even show up, and no one there would demand that Arafat name a powerful prime minister.[70]

After additional months of costly war, however, the level of internal and international opposition became high enough to force Arafat into a tactical retreat. For the first time, Arafat's critics won some limited victories. Arafat appointed Salam Fayyad, a professional banker, as finance minister, for the first time providing some independent oversight on his management of Palestinian finances.

In March 2003, Arafat appointed Abu Mazin as prime minister but tried to limit this office's power, making clear that the prime minister would be responsible to him—and not to parliament—and would have no role in foreign policy, negotiating with Israel, or directing the Palestinian security agencies. Abu Alaa called for a prime minister with real authority "and not just someone who would do secretarial work under Arafat," saying there was no need for Arafat to deal with the tiniest details.[71] Fatah members of parliament forced Arafat to accept that the prime minister would choose the cabinet.[72]

The growing internal criticism of Arafat was reinforced by U.S. efforts to push him aside. But he dealt with these seemingly overwhelming odds with his usual skill at evading pressure and surviving. Pushed into appointing Abu Mazin as prime minister, he did so in a way that won international applause while depriving this step of any practical meaning.

The forces aligned against him were impressive. Arafat was physically isolated in his half-destroyed headquarters building, unable to travel far. Arab states gave him no real support and even Egypt pressed him for concessions. Abu Mazin, Abu Alaa, and his former protégé Dahlan had concluded that Palestinians could never achieve a state or even stop the disastrous war as long as Arafat remained their total leader.

Bush, conqueror of Saddam Hussein and leader of the world's most powerful nation, was fed up with Arafat. "I saw what he did to President Clinton," Bush explained, and he had no intention of wasting his time on a man who was not going to make peace. [73] Even Powell, the American leader least hostile to him, declared, "We do not believe that Mr. Arafat has shown the kind of leadership that is needed to take us through this crisis."[74]

Yet once again Arafat outmaneuvered everyone. Abu Mazin's original proposed cabinet was full of new faces and reform-minded people. The United States demanded that the new prime minister appoint whomever he wanted. But by the time Arafat finished wearing him down, most cabinet members were reappointed Arafat loyalists.

Similarly, Abu Mazin, with U.S. backing, demanded full control over the security forces and negotiations with Israel. [75] Yet Arafat retained most of this power, too, through various means. One of his gimmicks was to create a National Security Council that would report to him, not Abu Mazin, and direct these key activities. Another was to continue appointing officials to the Interior Ministry, without Abu Mazin's approval.

Aside from his own bargaining skills, Arafat retained much support among the Palestinian public and activists. True, his popularity rating fell to a startlingly low 35 percent, but Abu Mazin's stood at only

3 percent.[76] He benefited from a Palestinian belief, which he himself had so long programmed, that anyone proposing compromise was a traitor, any leader able to work with Israel and the United States was immediately suspect for that reason alone, and anyone who concluded a peace agreement would be suspected of treason.

Arafat also enjoyed the support of many PLO, PA, and Fatah officials who had corruption to hide or were dependent on him for their careers, as well as Hamas and those militant forces in Fatah who wanted to keep on fighting. Most astonishing was the continued European help to him, with many countries demanding he retain power and not be subject to pressure. Their officials lined up to meet him in his besieged office. British Foreign Secretary Jack Straw expressed their consensus, saying, "Arafat is still the person who we are dealing with."[77]

This was precisely the message Arafat sought to convey. At his inauguration as prime minister on April 29, Abu Mazin told the PLC session that there was no military solution for the Palestinians' situation, demanded an end to the "armed chaos" in their own society that so threatened their welfare, insisted that only the PA security forces should have arms, and inveighed against corruption.[78] But Arafat sat next to him, subverting all these points and still holding the real power. In his own speech urging the new cabinet's confirmation, Arafat explained that it supported his positions and its appointment was only a tactical measure given the "sensitive and dangerous phase" the movement faced in the region due to enhanced U.S. power.[79]

Bush hoped that the offer of a state along with the encouragement of an alternative but legitimate Palestinian leadership would bring the actions needed to reach peace. "If the Palestinian people take concrete steps to crack down on terror, continue on a path of peace, reform and democracy," he said, "they and all the world will see the flag of Palestine raised over a free and independent nation."[80]

But Arafat preferred to forgo the prize rather than do what was necessary to attain it or, at least, believed he could get everything he wanted without giving up power or changing his strategy. It was very much in line with his old pattern. As a Western diplomat remarked, "Once again, efforts to write Arafat's [political] obituary have been grossly premature."[81] Not only was this true as it had so often been before but it also increasingly seemed as if the only thing that might break the roadblock to peace posed by Arafat was his actual, physical obituary.

Meanwhile, then, Arafat's traditional patterns of behavior continued to prevail in leading the Palestinians. For ten days, beginning on September 19, 2002, Israel's army had again besieged Arafat in Ramallah. Like the previous time earlier that year, the operation came after suicide bombings within Israel and was aimed at capturing men wanted for their involvement in planning attacks on Israelis. This time, few prisoners were taken, but the army brought in bulldozers and tore down most of the compound's buildings. Arafat's office was left surrounded by the empty shells of structures and piles of rubble.[82]

Once again saved by the Americans, Arafat emerged flashing his hand in a V-for-victory sign and blowing kisses to a crowd of chanting supporters.[83] To an American journalist, Arafat's situation seemed to have sadly declined: "Once the father of an emerging nation and now an aging pariah waiting for others to decide his fate." Yet Arafat himself seemed unbothered by his situation, saying, "It's hard, but I'm used to it."[84]

Perhaps more than ever before, Arafat seemed to descend into megalomania, which was punctuated by an increasing dependence on religious rhetoric. Asked if Israel planned to expel him, he responded:

To a remote area! . . . To the desert! They are most welcome. "Oh Mountain! the wind cannot shake you." Have you forgotten my motto? They will not take me captive or prisoner, or expel [me], but as a martyr, martyr, martyr. "Oh Allah, give me martyrdom." [Muhammad said:] "There still exists a group in my nation that preserves its religion, vanquishes its enemy, and is not harmed by anyone who attacks it, and its people are the victors, due to Allah's strength." It was said [to Muhammad], "Oh Messenger of Allah, where are they and who are [these people]?" The Prophet answered: "They are in Jerusalem and its surroundings, and they are at the forefront until Judgment Day."[85]

The ghastly scene of wreckage in contrast with the celebration by those just defeated seemed a fitting symbol for Arafat's career. It reflected the fact that his long march had been far too often a circular one, repeating mistakes and confusing foolish intransigence with courageous steadfastness.

Ramallah in 2002 and 2003 was a bizarre reenactment of Arafat's earlier days, living the life of the heroic guerrilla. "We are expecting a big Israeli attack," Arafat had said one day at his headquarters in Jordan in 1968. "His voice was almost gay, as if he welcomed the prospect," wrote a journalist standing next to him. "And his lips were parted in a smile."[86] Once again, Arafat felt comfortable repeating the type of losing fight he had conducted in Ramallah thirty years earlier and then later in Amman, Beirut, Tripoli, Tunis, and vicariously alongside Saddam Hussein in Baghdad in 1991.

Similarly, Arafat's rhetoric and analysis of events also seemed subject to his timeless world view. In his speech to the March 2003 Arab summit, he blamed the continuing violence exclusively on Israel which he accused of "cancerous settlement activity," "the Judaization of holy Jerusalem," "erection of the Berlin wall" around Palestinian towns, "desecration of our holy shrines," the use of U.S.-supplied "poisonous gases," and "a war of genocide and ethnic cleansing" intended to impose Israel's rule over all the Arabs "from the Nile to the Euphrates."

He also claimed that Israel had instigated a U.S. war against Iraq as an attack against the "entire Arab nation" to be used as a cover for expelling all Palestinians from the West Bank and Gaza by force.[87] Such a U.S. attack on Iraq, Arafat said a few days before the fighting began, would be an American imperialist war to partition the Middle East.[88]

His conclusion was that Israel sought "to return the situation another fifty years back so as to bring our people another setback, which is as grave as the first setback in 1948."[89] Yet that first catastrophe had taken place when Arafat's predecessors rejected partition and the establishment of a Palestinian state. Now Arafat himself was repeating the error. Even he could admit that "the [Palestinian] infrastructure had been completely destroyed."[90] But his decisions had been responsible for that destruction.

All his life, Arafat had before him two models of political behavior. The one he could not seem to escape was a doctrine he enunciated many times, but perhaps most clearly in remarks made in 1968, just as he was becoming leader of the Palestinians. "We have believed that the only way to return to our homes and land is the armed struggle," Arafat said. "We believe in this theory without any complications and with complete clarity, and this is our aim and our hope.... We understand that the political solution means surrender."[91]

In a sense, Arafat never abandoned that world view. As a result, despite his impressive services to his people's cause—unifying them, activating them, bringing their case to international attention, elevating their self-esteem—Arafat's infliction of unnecessary damage, sufferings, and delays in redressing their grievances may weigh far heavier in the historical balance.

Arafat himself laid out the alternative course in an interview he gave in 1990. "Politics," he explained, "remain[s] the art of the possible and must not be based on the spirit's preferences and chimerical dreams."[92] If Arafat had followed that advice, the history of the Middle East and indeed of the world would have been a much happier and ultimately a more just one for all concerned.

This was the ultimate irony of his life: Arafat, the man who did more than anyone else to champion and advance the Palestinian cause, also inflicted years of unnecessary suffering on his people, delaying any beneficial redress of their grievances or solutions to their problems.

NOTES

PROLOGUE

1. *Washington Post*, May 3, 2002.
2. *Washington Post*, March 29, 2002; *Los Angeles Times*, March 29, 2002; *Time*, April 8, 2002.
3. *Ha'aretz*, March 31, 2002.
4. *Washington Post*, March 29, 2002.
5. *Al-Jazira* and Palestinian Authority television, March 29, 2002. Translated in MEMRI No. 361, March 31, 2002.
6. Egyptian and Palestinian Authority television, March 29, 2002. Translated in MEMRI, No. 361, March 31, 2002.
7. *Al-Jazira* and Palestinian Authority television, March 29, 2002. Translated in MEMRI, No. 361, March 31, 2002.
8. Jordanian Television, cited in Associated Press, March 30, 2002.
9. *Washington Post*, March 31, 2002.
10. Associated Press, March 30, 2002.
11. Jibril Rajoub. See *Washington Post*, April 2–3, 2002.
12. *Jerusalem Post*, May 24, 2002.
13. *Al-Jazira* television, April 2, 2002.
14. Ibid.
15. *Ha'aretz*, April 30, 2002.
16. Wafa [PLO] news agency, April 10, 2002.
17. Text of Bush speech, White House transcript, April 4, 2002.
18. Ibid.
19. *Washington Post*, April 5, 2002.

20. Wafa, April 14, 2002.

21. *Washington Post*, April 15, 2002.

22. ABC television, *Nightline*, May 1, 2002.

CHAPTER 1

1. Dr. Salah Abdel-Jaber Issa, "The Arabs in Egypt According to the Censuses (1897–1986)," *Magazine for Arab Studies and Research*, Cairo, #219, 1991, pp. 73–102. As quoted in Abdel Qadir Yasin, "Palestinians in Egypt," downloaded from <http://www.badil.org/Publications/Majdal/1999/2i.htm>.

2. Muhammad Heikal, *Secret Channels: The Inside Story of Arab-Israeli Peace Negotiations* (London, 1996), p. 446.

3. He apparently used that name exclusively from around 1949.

4. Alan Hart, *Arafat: A Political Biography* (Bloomington, Ind., 1984), pp. 67–68.

5. Gowers and Walker, op. cit., p. 10.

6. Ibid., p. 5.

7. Yasin, op. cit.

8. Janet and John Wallach, *Arafat in the Eyes of the Beholder* (New York, 1990), p. 61.

9. On the conference and the Arab world's attitudes at the time, see Barry Rubin, *The Arab States & the Palestine Conflict* (Syracuse, N.Y., 1981), especially pp. 42–44.

10. Gowers and Walker, op. cit., p. 13, calls them minor aristocracy.

11. Interviews with family members cited in "My Little Brother Yasir," *Ma'ariv*, May 10, 1994. Arafat almost never mentioned his father and after returning to Gaza in 1994 never visited his grave.

12. In this context, European-influenced nationalism includes Pan-Arab nationalism which was shaped by European, especially Italian and German, experience.

13. Wallach and Wallach, op. cit., p. 27.

14. Ehud Yaari, *Strike Terror* (New York, 1970), pp. 14–15; Said K. Aburish, *Arafat: From Defender to Dictator* (New York, 1998), pp. 18–19; Gowers and Walker, op. cit., p. 12.

15. Wallach and Wallach, op. cit., pp. 73–75.

16. Speech in Ramallah, December 18, 2001, Wafa, December 18, 2001. He recounted a similar story to Hart, op. cit., p. 79. There is even a contradiction in this story. Egyptian forces did not enter Gaza until May 15, 1948, yet Arafat tells the story as if it happened in Gaza. In that case, he could not have arrived there in April as he told interviewers. It seems more likely that the incident happened when they tried to cross the frontier without any papers or permission of the Egyptian authorities.

17. Wallach and Wallach, op. cit., p. 73. The Jaffa Gate and Silwan were two of the most hotly contested places in all the fighting. By saying he was there, Arafat claims a share of the glory but by admitting that he was not involved in battle, he makes the story seem unlikely. What is worth noting here is that almost all journalists and most writers—with the exceptions of Gowers and Walker—simply accept Arafat's versions of various stories without seriously raising doubts. This

phenomenon both reflects Arafat's ability to get away with questionable assertions and the way the Western media taught him it was easy to do so.

18. Ibid.

19. Hart, op. cit., p. 78.

20. This is not to say that this factor was the only source of the refugee problem, but this situation was most clearly true for the specific place Arafat cites to prove his case.

21. Hart, op. cit., p. 78.

22. Ibid., p. 79.

23. Gamal Abdel Nasser, *Egypt's Liberation: The Philosophy of Revolution* (Washington, D.C., 1955), p. 22.

24. Hart, op. cit., p. 113.

25. Gowers and Walker, op. cit., p. 16.

26. Wallach and Wallach, op. cit., p. 85.

27. Gowers and Walker, op. cit., p. 17. It might also be pointed out that if Arafat presented himself to Doh as someone who had no military training or experience, this conflicts with all his claims about his activities in 1948, several years earlier.

28. Charles Saint-Prot, *Yasser Arafat: Biographie et Entretiens* (Paris, 1990), p. 81.

29. Interview with Arab intellectual.

30. Yasin, op. cit.; Gowers and Walker, op. cit., p. 17.

31. Abu Iyad, *My Home, My Land: A Narrative of the Palestinian Struggle* (New York, 1981), p. 20.

32. Ibid.

33. Aburish, op. cit., p. 17.

34. For a more detailed look at Nasser's early attitude toward the Palestinian question, see Barry Rubin, *The Arab States and the Palestine Conflict* (Syracuse, N.Y.: 1982).

35. Laurie A. Brand, *Palestinians in the Arab World: Institution Building and the Search for State* (New York, 1988), pp. 43, 55–56.

36. Yezid Sayigh, *Armed Struggle and the Search for State: The Palestinian National Movement, 1949–1993* (London, 1997), p. 87; Yaari, op. cit., p. 18.

37. Most of Arafat's generation, even among Palestinians, would become enthusiastic supporters of Nasser or other Pan-Arab nationalist movements. The fact that he stayed outside this mindset while also not becoming an Islamist is of the greatest importance for the future course of Fatah and the PLO.

38. Hart, op. cit., p. 108; Yaari, op. cit., p. 22.

39. John Amos, *Palestinian Resistance: Organization of a National Movement* (New York, 1980), p. 47. On the raid and its historical consequences in starting the chain of events leading to the 1956 Suez War, see Kenneth Love, *Suez, the Twice Fought War* (New York, McGraw-Hill, 1969), p. 85; Abdullah Schliefer, "The Emergence of Fatah," *The Arab World*, Vol. 15, No. 5 (May 1969), pp. 16–20.

40. Yaari, op. cit., p. 20; Zeev Schiff and Ralph Rothstein, *Fedayeen: Guerillas against Israel* (New York, 1972), p. 58; Hart, op. cit., pp. 115–117.

41. Aburish, op. cit., p. 31; Barry Rubin, *Revolution until Victory? The Politics and History of the PLO* (Cambridge, Mass., 1994), p. 6.

42. Yaari, op. cit., p. 23.

43. Gowers and Walker, op. cit., p. 21.

44. On the development of populist dictators, see Barry Rubin, *Modern Dictators: Third World Coupmakers, Strongmen, and Populist Tyrants* (New York, 1987).

45. Amos, op. cit., p. 53.

46. Saint-Prot, op. cit. (Paris, 1990), p. 78.

47. Yaari, op. cit., p. 21; Hart, op. cit., p. 119. He may have also explored then or slightly later, job possibilities in Saudi Arabia.

48. Hart, op. cit., pp. 119, 127; Aburish, op. cit., p. 51.

49. Abu Iyad, op. cit., p. 38.

50. Shafeeq Ghabra, *Palestinians in Kuwait* (Westport, Conn., 1987), p. 40; U.S. Embassy Kuwait to Department of State, February 6 and 13, 1964. All State Department documents cited below come from Record Group (RG) 59, U.S. Archives, and the relevant country files.

51. U.S. Embassy Kuwait to Department of State, February 27, 1964.

52. Ibid.

53. Although Arafat made no direct statement to that effect, some of his later remarks about having helped build Kuwait and faced ingratitude in response indicate such sentiments. See, for example, chapter 6, below.

54. Amos, op. cit., p. 54. Hasan was born in 1928 and Qaddumi about three years later. While Qaddumi was born in Nablus, he grew up in Jaffa. Hasan came from Haifa. For a discussion of the PLO's secondary leaders, see Barry Rubin, *Revolution Until Victory? The Politics and History of the PLO*, op. cit., pp. 153–158 and for an overview of the top cadre, see Barry Rubin, *The Transformation of Palestinian Politics* (New York, 1999), pp. 203–218.

55. *Al-Mussawar*, January 5, 1968, cited in Aryeh Yodfat and Yuval Arnon-Ohanna, *PLO Strategy and Politics* (New York, 1981), p. 23.

56. Abu Iyad, op. cit., pp. 29–30.

57. Amos, op. cit., p. 56; Gowers and Walker, op. cit., p. 30.

58. Amos, op. cit., pp. 141.

59. Fatah Political Platform, Fourth Fatah Congress, May 1980, text in Raphael Israeli, *PLO in Lebanon* (London, 1983), p. 12.

60. Arafat interview, *International Documents on Palestine* (hereafter *IDOP*) 1969 (Beirut, 1970), p. 695; *IDOP* 1968 (Beirut, 1969), p. 413; *New York Times*, October 29, 1969.

61. Interview, *Al-Usbu al Arabi*, January 22, 1968, *IDOP* 1968, op. cit., p. 298; August 1968 statement, *IDOP* 1968, op. cit., p. 413. Habash, July 25, 1970, *IDOP* 1970 (Beirut, 1971), pp. 878–882. Arafat interview, May 1969, *IDOP* 1969, op. cit., pp. 691–692.

62. It should be recalled that genocide does not merely mean mass murder but the destruction of a society, culture, and state.

63. *Filastin al-Thawra*, June 1968; Y. Harkabi, *The Palestinian Covenant and Its Meaning* (London, 1979), p. 9.

64. Amos, op. cit., pp. 136, 140.

65. Interview with Abbas Zaki, December 17, 2002.

66. PLO Charter, text in Walter Laqueur and Barry Rubin, *The Israel-Arab Reader*, Sixth Revised Edition (New York, 2001), p. 117.

67. *Arab World Weekly*, December 2, 1974; *al-Nahar Arab Report*, July 15, 1974, and August 2, 1974.

68. Shaul Mishal, *The PLO under Arafat: Between Gun and Olive Branch* (New Haven, Conn., 1986), pp. 38–39; Hani al-Hasan interview in *al-Aam*, April 23, 1970.

69. This is not to say that Arafat never established some money-making and social welfare activities but these were limited efforts focused on sustaining the struggle rather than providing the training or economic basis for the future.

70. Arafat interview in *al-Sayyad*, January 23, 1969.

71. Arafat interview in *Playboy*, September 1988; Gowers and Walker, op. cit., p. 33; interviews.

72. Ibid., *Playboy* interview. See also Saint-Prot, op. cit., p. 80.

73. Zaki interview.

74. Abu Iyad, op. cit., p. 43; Gowers, op. cit., p. 37; Amos, op. cit., p. 49.

75. Abu Iyad, op. cit., p. 41.

76. Ibid., p. 43.

77. Gowers and Walker, op. cit., p. 43.

78. See, for example, Amos, op. cit., p. 56. It is interesting to note that at a time when Syria was sponsoring Fatah, the U.S. embassy in Damascus insisted there was no proof of any connection between them. RG59, Box 2606, Paganelli to Secretary of State, August 20, 1965.

79. Moshe Shemesh, *The Palestinian Entity: 1959–1974: Arab Politics and the PLO* (London, 1988), p. 113; see also Patrick Seale, *Asad of Syria* (London, 1988), p. 124.

80. Intelligence Memorandum No. 2205/66, December 2, 1966, in U.S. Department of State, *Foreign Relations of the United States*, 1964–1968, Volume XVIII, Arab-Israeli Dispute, 1964–1967 (Washington, D.C., 2000), p. 699.

81. Zaki interview.

82. On the ineffectiveness of these attacks, see for example Stewart Steven, *The Spymasters of Israel* (New York, 1980), pp. 237–247.

83. Yaari, op. cit., p. 61; *Foreign Relations of the United States*, op. cit.

84. Ibid., Yaari.

85. British Public Records Office, Foreign and Colonial Office (hereafter FO) 371, A. C. Goodison to D. J. Roberts December 29, 1965. See also E10711/7 G, November 20, 1965 recording a conversation with Syrian Navy Captain Adnan Abdallah who told the British defense attaché on November 4, 1965 that Syria had no knowledge of Fatah or al-Asifa and believed they were Israeli front groups.

86. FO 371/180858 October 23, 1965.

87. Western governments and even intelligence services knew little about Fatah's aims, politics, and international connections. "We do not know very much about the origin of Fatah's weapons and explosives but they probably come from outside the Levant and are moved into and around it through established smuggling channels." Ibid.

88. Abu Iyad, op. cit., p. 44.

89. Ibid., pp. 46–47.

90. RG59 Box 2685 al-Asifa Communique Number 54, December 24, 1966 in U.S. Embassy Damascus to Secretary of State, December 30, 1966 and Asifa

memorandum published in *al-Ba'th*, December 28, 1966. By this time, al-Asifa was openly admitting it was an arm of Fatah.

91. Hart, op. cit., p. 177.

92. Gowers and Walker, op. cit., p. 47.

93. Ibid., p. 48; Seale, op. cit., p. 125; Amos, op. cit., p. 50; Abu Iyad, op. cit., p. 45; Hart, op. cit., p. 201; Yaari, op. cit., pp. 86–89. This incident is said to have taken place in February or May by different sources. The U.S. State Department at the time gave the date as early June. RG59, Box 2606, Amman to Secretary of State, August 12, 1966. To show Syria's resentment, Asad's biographer decades later recorded the Syrian claim that Arafat was thrown into jail because he had betrayed a Fatah operation, hinting that he was an Israeli agent.

94. Abu Iyad, op. cit., p. 46. Ghaleb Kayyali, Syria's charge d'affaires in Washington, told the State Department in October 1966 that Syria was no longer allowing Fatah operations from its territory and Syria had no connection with that group. RG59, Box 2406, Pol 23–9 Syr 32–1 Isr-Jordan, October 7, 1966.

95. From U.S. Embassy (hereafter AmEm) Amman to Department of State, "Joint Week #26, December 28, 1965." As early as 1965, Israeli intelligence officers predicted that Arafat would take over the PLO. From AmEm in Tel Aviv to Department of State, September 30, 1965.

96. From AmEm in Amman to Department of State, "King Hussein Clarifies GOJ position Vis-à-vis PLO and Extremist Palestinian Groups," October 7, 1965. It was impossible to deal with the PLO in its present form, Hussein complained, because its policies had become "boils in which strange germs breed nourishing Arab disputes and destroying Arab solidarity." From AmEm Amman to Secretary of State "King Hussein's Speech," July 15, 1966. Sa'id Dajani, a Palestinian member of Jordan's cabinet, explained that the king wanted to help the PLO but no one could expect him to let a second army operate outside his control into Jordan. He predicted that Shuqeiri would soon be ousted and Jordan would find the new PLO leadership easier to deal with. From AmEm Amman to Department of State, July 25, 1966.

97. From AmEm Algiers to Department of State, "Palestinian 'Student' demonstration at Jordanian Embassy," November 29, 1966.

98. From AmEm Amman to Department of State, "Joint Week #31, February 9–15," February 16, 1967.

99. From AmEm Amman to Department of State, "Joint Week #32, February 16–22," February 23, 1967.

100. From American Consul Jerusalem to Department of State, "Conversations on Current Topics with some Leading Jerusalem Residents," February 28, 1967.

101. Hart, op. cit., pp. 231–234.

102. Saint-Prot, op. cit., p. 117.

103. U.S. Embassy in Kuwait, "PLO Office Shakeup," May 19, 1968.

104. Hart, op. cit., p. 258.

CHAPTER 2

1. U.S. Embassy Amman 3683 7/31/70, July 31, 1970. Of course, the Greeks later united and defeated Persia but that was not the point of Arafat's story. For

an interesting parallel, see chapter 3 for Arafat's reaction to the story of the Alamo.

2. Saint-Prot, op. cit., pp. 87–88.

3. Arafat interviews, *IDOP* 1969 (Beirut, 1970), pp. 691–692.

4. Mohammed Heikal, *The Road to Ramadan* (New York, 1975), p. 63.

5. Ibid., pp. 63–64.

6. Text in Laqueur and Rubin, op. cit., p. 116.

7. Fatah rejection, December 12, 1967, *IDOP* 1967 (Beirut, 1968), op. cit., p. 723.

8. Abu Iyad, op. cit., p. 52.

9. Ibid., pp. 52–55; David Pryce-Jones, *The Face of Defeat: Palestinian Refugees and Guerrillas* (New York, 1973), p. 156.

10. Yaari, op. cit., p. 22.

11. Ibid., p. 137.

12. Amos, op. cit., p. 58; Yossi Mellman and Dan Raviv, *Imperfect Spies: History of Israeli Intelligence* (London, 1989), p. 173.

13. Ian Black and Benny Morris, *Israel's Secret Wars* (New York, 1991), p. 242; Yossi Melman and Dan Raviv, op. cit., p. 163.

14. Interview with Yakov Peri, July 1, 2001.

15. Quoted in *Time*, December 13, 1968.

16. *IDOP*, 1970, op. cit., pp. 945–948.

17. Ibid., pp. 692–95.

18. Of course, Arafat denied he was committing terrorism, defining any military act advancing his cause as legitimate armed struggle. To Arafat, terrorism meant "wanton acts of destruction" rather than the Western sense of being a deliberate attack on civilians. "Any armed resistance can be condemned as a terrorist activity," Arafat commented. "Yassir Arafat," *Third World Quarterly*, Vol. 7, October 1985; interview with Khalid al-Hasan, *al-Riyad*, December 5, 1978, translation in U.S. Department of Commerce, Joint Publications Research Service, No. 72836, February 16, 1979.

19. Ariel Merari and Shlomo Elad, *The International Dimension of Palestinian Terrorism* (Boulder: Colo., 1986), p. 5.

20. Interview with Arafat, January 22, 1968 in *IDOP* 1968, op. cit., p. 300.

21. "Yassir Arafat," *Third World Quarterly*, Vol. 8, No. 2 (April 1986), and also *South*, January, 1986, p. 18; *al-Anwar* symposium of March 8, 1970, cited in Harkabi, *Palestinian Covenant*, op. cit., p. 12; Arafat statement, May 1969, *IDOP* 1969, op. cit., pp. 691–692.

22. *Filastin al-Thawra*, January 1970. Compare this statement with a remarkably similar PLO document a dozen years later, "Guidelines for attacking civilian targets in Israel," text in Israeli, op. cit., p. 31: The enemy's "greatest weakness is his small population. Therefore, operations must be launched which will liquidate immigration into Israel" by attacking immigrant absorption centers, sabotaging water and electricity, "using weapons in terrifying ways against them where they live...attacking a tourist installation during the height of the tourist season." Holidays were said to be the best time for assaults since there were more human targets on the street.

23. Interview with Arafat, in *IDOP*, op. cit., p. 300.

24. U.S. Embassy report from Jordan, July 12, 1968.

25. Yaari, op. cit., p. 342; Shemesh, op. cit., p. 135.

26. Zaki interview.

27. Yodfat and Arnon-Ohanna, op. cit., p. 28; Yaari, op. cit., p. 244; Schiff and Rothstein, op. cit., p. 83; Moshe Dayan, *Story of My Life* (New York, 1976), p. 415.

28. Pryce-Jones, op. cit., p. 179.

29. From AmEm Amman to Department of State, "Reported Soviet Attitudes toward Fedayeen and Jordanian National Charter Group," May 9, 1968.

30. Anthony Nutting, *Nasser* (New York, 1972), p. 88; Shemesh, op. cit., p. 106.

31. Mohammed Heikal, *The Road to Ramadan* (New York, 1975), pp. 64–65.

32. Mishal, op. cit., pp. 6–7; The PLFP was a merger of the Palestine Liberation Front, the Heroes of the Return, and the Youth of Vengeance. *New York Times*, July 14, 1968; *Arab Report and Record*, October 1–15, 1968: p. 316; Bard E. O'Neill, *Armed Struggle in Palestine: A Political-Military Analysis* (Boulder, Colo., 1978), p. 127.

33. U.S. Department of State Archives, Thomas Hughes, "Jordan and the Fedayeen," April 4, 1969.

34. U.S. Embassy in Saudi Arabia to State Department, Discussion with Prince Sultan, 1123 9/5/70, September 5, 1970; AmEm Kuwait to Department of State. December 31, 1969.

35. From AmEm Kuwait to Department of State, "Fedayeen," March 29, 1969.

36. Shemesh, op. cit., pp. 116–117.

37. Gresh, op. cit., p. 12. The man was Isam Sartawi.

38. *Arab World*, March 3 and January 9, 1971. At the March 1971 PNC, Arafat did put forward a plan for unity of command within the PLO while the PFLP proposed that each group maintain its own ideological identity and military independence. He did not push very hard for this proposal, however, and rarely made such attempts thereafter.

39. Shemesh, op. cit., pp. 114–120. In 1969. Fatah men were prohibited from collecting money, wearing uniforms, or carrying weapons outside their camps there except when on missions with Syrian intelligence's permission. Most important of all, they could not cross into Israel or Jordan without written authorization from the defense minister, Asad himself.

40. Ibid. p. 122.

41. Ibid.; Amos, op. cit., p. 40; Gresh, op. cit., p. 13; *IDOP* 1970 (Beirut, 1971), p. 750 and 993. When colleagues urged him to act decisively Arafat responded that he preferred the Vietnamese model of revolution. As happened so often when Arafat used examples from history or elsewhere in the world, he got it wrong. The Vietnamese success was closely related to the strong unity imposed by North Vietnam's leaders.

42. For an interesting transcript of one such coffee house debate, see U.S. Embassy Beirut to Department of State, April 18, 1969.

43. FCO 17/69 J.A. Shepherd to Leonard Appleyard, British Embassy, Amman Jordan, October 3, 1969 "Embassy Contacts with Al-Fatah."

44. Ibid.

45. Ibid.; FCO 17/69, C. D. Lush to R. E. Evans, October 3, 1969.

46. Indeed, Azhari's direct boss as he assured the British of Fatah's opposition to terrorism was Kamal Adwan who within a few months would become a leader of the Fatah terrorist front, Black September.

47. *Time*, December 13, 1968.

48. Gowers and Walker, op. cit., p. 65.

49. Shafiq al-Hout, head of the PLO office in Beirut, insisted that if the king tried to suppress the PLO even his own officers would swear allegiance to Arafat. From AmEm Beirut to U.S. Department of State, "PLO view of Hussein's visit to US," April 11, 1969. But for the shrewd response to such assertions by a U.S. diplomat from Zaid al-Rifai, one of the king's main advisors, who explained why Hussein would win, see Symmes to Secretary of State, June 24, 1968.

50. Shemesh, op. cit., p. 133.

51. Ibid., p. 132.

52. Hughes, op. cit. A senior Fatah official in Amman claimed that the PLO's military plan was ahead of schedule, that Fatah would soon control the smaller groups, and that Israel would be eliminated in twelve to fifteen years of struggle. He concluded, "1970 will be a very difficult year for Israel." FCO 17/69 J. A. Shepherd to Appleyard, op. cit.

53. Shemesh, op. cit., p. 132.

54. Zaki interview.

55. Zaki interview.

56. U.S. Embassy report from Jordan, "Al-Fatah Propaganda Activity in Jordan," May 3, 1968.

57. U.S. Embassy in Amman 4642/9–25–69, September 25, 1969.

58. U.S. Embassy in Amman, September 4, 1969.

59. Ibid.

60. Joel Migdal, *Palestinian Society and Politics* (Princeton, N.J., 1980), pp. 118–119.

61. Ibid.

62. Norvell De Atkine, "Urban Warfare Lessons from the Middle East," *Special Warfare*, Fall 2001, pp. 20–29. See also Abdullah M. Lutfiyya, *Baytin, a Jordanian Village* (London, 1966), p. 87; James Lunt, *Hussein of Jordan* (New York, 1989), pp. 122–123. P. J. Vatikiotis, *Politics and Military in Jordan: A Study of the Arab Legion from 1921–1957* (London, 1967), p. 132, wrote that the Arab Legion virtually created the state of Jordan.

63. Yaari, op. cit., pp. 202 and 254; Gowers and Walker, op. cit., p. 71; Sobel, op. cit., p. 26.

64. Shemesh, op. cit., pp. 135–136.

65. Sobel, op. cit., p. 76.

66. Ibid.

67. Shemesh, op. cit., p. 138.

68. The murdered American officer lived near the PFLP headquarters and predicted to a colleague, shortly before his death, that they would assassinate him. Interview with a colleague.

69. Gowers and Walker, op. cit., p. 80; Sobel, op. cit., p. 80; Shemesh, op. cit., p. 139.

70. Ibid.

71. Edgar O'Ballance, *Arab Guerrilla Power* (Hamden, Conn., 1973), p. 134; Nutting, op. cit., pp. 467–468; Shemesh, op. cit., p. 109.

72. U.S. Embassy Amman 3683, July 31, 1970.

73. O'Ballance, op. cit., p. 134.

74. Shemesh, op. cit., p. 142.

75. Migdal, op. cit., p. 229; Shemesh, op. cit., p. 144; Sobel, op. cit., p. 82.

76. PREM 15/202, downloaded from <http://www.pro.gov.uk/releases/ny02001/hijack3.htm>, Telex Amman-London, September 13, 1970; Cab 128/47 "Conclusions of a Meeting of the Cabinet, September 21, 1970 at 10 Downing 10:30 A.M." It is interesting to note that if King Hussein had been plotting with the Americans all along, as Arafat had repeatedly charged, he would never have needed to turn to the British for help.

77. Ibid.

78. U.S. Embassy Beirut 7481 9/8/70, September 8, 1970. At the time, the PFLP's chief, George Habash was so popular among Palestinians that Hisham Sharabi, a Palestinian teaching at Georgetown University, remarked that Habash would already be the PLO's leader if he were a Muslim and not a Christian.

79. Ibid. Obviously, Arafat was confident of victory. Yusuf Sayegh, chairman of the PLO Planning Council, said that it was only a matter of time before King Hussein gave in to the Palestinians.

80. Sobel, op. cit., p. 84; Shemesh, op. cit., p. 141; Abu Iyad, op. cit., p. 82; Peter Snow, *Hussein* (Washington, D.C., 1972), p. 234. The PLO was so unpopular among Jordanians in the north that they burned PLO offices and ransacked their supply warehouses. U.S. Embassy in Amman, No. 451 1–25–71, January 25, 1971.

81. Abu Iyad, op. cit., p. 81.

82. U.S. Embassy Amman 4849/9–17–70, September 17, 1970.

83. De Atkine, op. cit.

84. Cab 128/47 "Conclusions of a Meeting of the Cabinet, September 21, 1970 at 10 Downing 10:30 A.M."

85. Gowers and Walker, op. cit., p. 85; Abu Iyad, op. cit., p. 80.

86. Nutting, op. cit., p. 471; Shemesh, op. cit., pp. 144, 175; Sobel, op. cit., p. 86; Abu Iyad, op. cit., p. 89.

87. Gowers and Walker, op. cit., p. 82; Nutting, op. cit., p. 472.

88. Lunt, op. cit., p. 144; Gowers and Walker, op. cit., p. 87; Nutting, op. cit., p. 475; Abu Iyad, op. cit., p. 90.

89. Heikal, *Road to Ramadan*, op. cit., p. 121.

90. On the roots of the Asad-Arafat feud, see chapter 1.

91. U.S. Embassy Amman 3352 7/19/71, July 19, 1971; Amman 3318 7/17/71, July 17, 187 U.S. Embassy Jidda 3405 9/16/71, September 16, 1971.

92. Gowers and Walker, op. cit., p. 84.

93. Ibid. The Jordanians took grim satisfaction when an Egyptian diplomat remarked privately that he "wouldn't like armed guerrillas running around his country either."

94. For example, see U.S. Embassy, Amman 5926 10/15/70, October 15, 1970.

95. Hart, op. cit., p. 320; O'Ballance, op. cit., pp. 87, 162, and 187; Yaari, op. cit., p. 59; Sobel, op. cit., p. 117. He was also involved in a serious car accident while traveling from Amman to Baghdad in January 1969. See Gowers and Walker, op. cit., p. 69; Amos, op. cit., p. 51.

96. On criticisms of Arafat see, for example, U.S. Embassy, Amman 5926 10/15/70, October 15, 1970.

97. *IDOP*, 1968, op. cit., pp. 298–300; *al-Usbu al-Arabi*, January 22, 1968.

CHAPTER 3

1. Ion Mihai Pacepa in *Wall Street Journal*, January 10, 2002.

2. David C. Martin and John C. Walcott, *Best Laid Plans* (New York, 1988). p. 161.

3. "The PLO Papers," *The Economist*, July 10, 1982, p. 48; James Adams, *The Financing of Terror* (Kent, 1986), pp. 86, 93–95, and 99.

4. Rashid Khalidi, "The Palestinians in Lebanon: Social Repercussions of Israel's Invasion," *Middle East Journal*, Vol. 38, No. 2 (Spring 1984), p. 258.

5. Migdal, op. cit., p. 231.

6. British Foreign and Colonial Office, 17/1107 June 5, 1970.

7. Hughes, op. cit.; AmEm Kuwait to Department of State, "The Kuwait Military and the Fedayeen," April 28, 1969; CIA Report, "Terrorism and the Fedayeen," September 1972, pp. 3–4; *Washington Post*, December 4, 1971.

8. Farid El-Khazen, *The Breakdown of the State in Lebanon, 1967–1976* (London, 2000), pp. 374–375.

9. Sobel, op. cit., pp. 362–365.

10. *Al Nahar*, May 9 and 10, 1969; Emile Boustany, *al-Safir*, March 15, 1997.

11. Sobel, op. cit., p. 148.

12. Downloaded from <http://www.arts.mcgill.ca/MEPP/PRRN/papers/sanctuary/ch2.html>.

13. *New York Times*, October 29, 1969.

14. Interview with Robert S. Dillon, U.S. Ambassador to Lebanon, April 23, 2002; FCO 17/1107, A. J. Sindall to C. W. Long, September 5, 1970.

15. In 1971 and 1972, Arafat made his only serious attempt to move toward unifying the PLO member groups under a Higher Military Council. But when smaller groups and even many in Fatah opposed him, Arafat backed down. John Amos, "The PLO: Millennium and Organization," in Peter Chelkowski and Robert Pranger, *Ideology and Power in the Middle East* (Durham, N.C., 1988), p. 373; Shemesh, op. cit., pp. 237–238; FCO 17/1107 Sindall to Long, November 7, 1970.

16. Amos, *Palestinian Resistance: Organization of a National Movement*, op. cit., p. 64.

17. Ibid., p. 63; Sobel, op. cit., p. 14.

18. CIA report in NSC files, Box 666, Sisco memo, March 13, 1973.

19. Sadiq al-Azm, "The Palestine Resistance Movement Reconsidered," in Edward Said, *The Arabs Today: Alternatives for Tomorrow* (Columbus, Ohio, 1973,), pp. 121–130; Paul Jureidini and William Hazen, *The Palestinian Movement in Politics* (Lexington, Mass., 1976), p. 16.

20. U.S. Department of State, dispatch of December 16, 1971, *Documents from the U.S. Espionage Den*, Vol. 42, p. 1; John Cooley, *Green March, Black September* (London, 1973), p. 26. An official U.S. government report stated that Fatah "used the name Black September Organization from 1971 to 1974," U.S. Department of Defense, *Terrorist Group Profiles* (Washington: 1988), p. 12.

21. At a January 1971 demonstration in Beirut, Muhammad Najjar, a Fatah leader, declared, "The Palestinian people will not tolerate [the] continued presence in Jordan of the regime which caused [the] September massacre. They

will work to topple this regime…and set up [a] national regime to liberate Palestine." He accused America of ordering the Jordanian army to kill Palestinian civilians. RG 59 Beirut 348 1–13–71, January 13, 1971.

22. See chapter 2.

23. "It is almost axiomatic that after [the] traumatic experience the fighting units have gone through there will be reactions against political leadership which could not deliver," wrote U.S. Ambassador to Jordan L. Dean Brown in October 1970. RG 59, Amman 5926 10/15/70, October 15, 1970.

24. RG 59, Beirut 8738 10–1–71, October 1, 1971; Jidda 4153 12/10/71, December 10, 1971; Jidda 4344 12/27/71, December 27, 1971.

25. See, for example, 2659 Beirut 8919 10–7–71, October 7, 1971.

26. Ibid.; RG 59 Pol 23.9 Jordan 4/16/71, April 16, 1971.

27. RG 59 Pol 23–8 Jordan, May 17, 1971.

28. See, for example, Amman 4543 10/17/72, October 17, 1972; Pol 23.9 Jordan 4/16/71, April 16, 1971. RG 59 Amman 1640 4/1/71, April 1, 1971. There is a remarkable parallel to the experience of the Druze leaders Kamal Junblatt and his son Walid, Nabulsi's counterparts, as Arafat's chief ally in Lebanon.

29. *New York Times*, September 6, 1972; Christopher Dobson, *Black September: Its Short Violent History* (London: 1975), pp. 11–12; U.S. Defense Intelligence Agency, *International Terrorism: A Compendium*, Vol. 2, *The Middle East* (1979), in *Documents from the U.S. Espionage Den*, Vol. 43.

30. U.S. Department of State, American Embassy Jidda 4153 12/10/71, December 10, 1971; Jidda 4344 12/27/71, December 27, 1971.

31. Amman 5647 12/16/71, December 16, 1971.

32. Text of testimony February 15, 1973, broadcast on Radio Amman March 24, 1973; *Washington Post*, March 15, 1973.

33. Dobson, op. cit., pp. 11–21; U.S. Defense Intelligence Agency, op. cit.

34. CIA Report on Black September, op. cit.; interviews.

35. Pacepa, op. cit., pp. 95–97. At the time Pacepa was director of Romanian intelligence.

36. Ibid.

37. The following account is taken from an interview with James Welsh, May 5, 2002; David Korn, *Assassination in Khartoum* (Bloomington, Ind., 1993); and the review of that book in *Middle East Quarterly*, June 1994, by Paul A. Jureidini who conducted an official investigation into the incident. It is supplemented by CIA and State Department documents cited in this chapter.

38. U.S. Department of State, Pol 13–10 Arab, March 1, 1973.

39. Eid was actually a Lebanese Christian. The German ambassador was also to be murdered but was escorting a delegation and could not attend the reception.

40. *London Times*, March 8, 1973; State Department telegram, Beirut March 5, 1973, and Khartoum cable, March 7 1973; *Ha'aretz*, December 14, 2001. The pattern was similar to the Achille Lauro hijacking of 1985.

41. NSC files, Box 666, CIA report, "The Black September Organization," attached to Secretary of State William Rogers message to U.S. embassies, March 13, 1973.

42. Text, Jaafer Numeiri speech, March 6, 1973; On Libyan connection, see *New York Times*, March 8, 1973; *London Observer*, March 4 and 11, 1973.

43. Interview with Harold Saunders, June 19, 2002.

44. NSC files, Box 666, Sisco memo, March 13, 1973. See also in the same file Macomber memo of March 1973 which details PLO involvement in the Khartoum attack.

45. Abu Iyad, op. cit., p. 121; Heikal, *Road to Ramadan*, op. cit., p. 178.

46. "The Way to Restoring the Violated Rights of the Palestinian People," *World Marxist Review*, February 1975, pp. 123–132.

47. Abu Iyad, op. cit., p. 126.

48. One of Abu Nidal's victims was Abu Iyad's bodyguard during an April 1979 ambush in Belgrade.

49. Abu Ubeid al-Qurashi, *al-Anssar*, February 27, 2002, translated in MEMRI No. 353, March 12, 2002.

50. For example, in the years after 2000, the use of the name al-Aqsa brigade for a group doing terrorist attacks, even though it acknowledged being part of Fatah, was sufficient to be taken as proof that Arafat had no control over these people or operations.

51. Arafat, May 1969, *IDOP* 1969, op. cit., pp. 695–696.

52. Arafat interview in Laqueur and Rubin, op. cit., p. 136; Fifth PNC, February 4, 1969, *IDOP* 1969, op. cit., pp. 589–590; DFLP, draft resolution for PNC, September 1, 1969, *IDOP* 1969, op. cit., p. 777; Arafat, October 1968, *IDOP* 1968, op. cit., pp. 453–454.

53. Ibid., Arafat interview.

54. Sobel, op. cit., p. 199. In Khalid al-Hasan's words, establishing a smaller Palestinian state would make possible "continuing the struggle [to establish] a state over the whole of Palestine." *IDOP* 1974 (Beirut, 1975), pp. 93–100, 104–108.

55. Abu Iyad explained the program clearly: "An independent state on the West Bank and Gaza is the beginning of the final solution. That solution is to establish a democratic state in the whole of Palestine." *IDOP* 1977 (Beirut, 1978), p. 347; *Los Angeles Times*, October 26, 1980.

56. Text of resolution, Laqueur and Rubin, op. cit., pp. 162–163; Jureidini and Hazen, op. cit., pp. 22–23. The plan, said the official PLO magazine, was an achievement, "On the road of continuous and unremitting struggle for the liberation of all the soil of the Palestinian homeland." *Filastin al-Thawra*, February 20, 1974.

57. Ibid.

58. Not surprisingly, the radicals bolted the PNC and even took a few disgruntled members of Fatah with them, forming what became known as the Rejectionist Front. Three years later, in 1977, most of them would return and sign an almost identical PNC resolution. Adam Garfinkle, "Sources of the al-Fatah Mutiny," *Orbis*, Vol. 27, Fall 1983.

59. Yodfat and Arnon-Ohanna, op. cit., p. 106. But equally significant, Arafat was not received by them on an equal basis as the leader of a country.

60. T. D. Allman, "On the Road with Arafat," *Vanity Fair*, February 1989.

61. Zaki interview.

62. For the full text of the speech, see Walter Laqueur and Barry Rubin, *The Israel-Arab Reader*, Sixth Revised Edition (New York, 2001), pp. 171–182.

63. It is hard to think of any nationalist or social revolutionary movement that actually won using a large element of anti-civilian terrorism. The main example

that comes to mind is Algeria, where the goal was to drive out the other community. In contrast, there are dozens of cases of failed groups for whom terrorism was ultimately counter-productive.

64. Qurashi, op. cit.

65. Isam Sartawi. Interview with Landrum Bolling, July 22, 2002.

66. Saunders interview.

67. Rogers to Nixon, April 13, 1973, "Memorandum for the President: Next Steps on the Middle East," Nixon archives.

68. Henry Kissinger, *Years of Upheaval* (New York, 1982), pp. 626–627.

69. Ibid.

70. Ibid., and U.S. embassy in Beirut to Secretary of State, March 25, 1973.

71. *Washington Post*, March 14, 1973.

72. White House, October 26, 1973, "Talking Points for Meeting with General Walters," in Palestinian folder, Kissinger files, Nixon papers, National Archives. Israel was informed of the contacts but the Jordanians were quite angry when they discovered the United States was holding secret meetings with the PLO without telling them. Pickering to Secretary of State, September 11, 1974, Nixon papers.

73. *Wall Street Journal*, February 10, 1983.

74. Eilts to Rogers, January 24, 1974, and February 10, 1974, Nixon papers.

75. Interview; Eilts to Kissinger, February 10, 1974; Godley to Kissinger and April 22, May 7 and 23, 1974, Nixon papers.

76. Ibid.

77. U.S. Department of State, "Guidelines for PLO at UN," October 1, 1974; Kissinger to UN Mission, October 1974; interview with U.S. official.

78. Saunders interview.

CHAPTER 4

1. Rashid Khalidi describes Arafat's basic tenets as: "The independence of Palestinian decisionmaking from external interference; a balance between those Arab states with the potential for interference in Palestinian affairs; the freedom to organize Palestinians throughout the Arab world; increased military and political strength; and the freedom to pursue a settlement when and if one becomes possible." Rashid Khalidi, "The Asad Regime and the Palestinian Resistance," *Arab Studies Quarterly*, Vol. 6, No. 4 (Fall 1984), p. 265.

2. *Washington Post*, December 26, 1982.

3. Downloaded from <http://www.arts.mcgill.ca/MEPP/PRRN/papers/sanctuary/ch2.html>.

4. Sami Farsoun, "How Revolutionary Is the Palestinian Resistance? A Marxist Interpretation," *Journal of Palestine Studies*, Vol. 2, No. 2 (Winter 1972), pp. 54–57.

5. "Under PLO Rule," *The Economist*, August 7, 1982, pp. 28–29; Israeli, op. cit., pp. 234–299; David Shipler, "Lebanese Tell of Anguish under the PLO," *New York Times*, July 25, 1982; William Haddad, "Divided Lebanon," *Current History*, January 1982; Rex Brynen, "PLO Policy in Lebanon: Legacies and Lessons," *Journal of Palestine Studies* Vol. 18, No. 2 (Winter 1989), pp. 59–60; Sobel, op. cit., p. 87.

6. *New York Times*, June 30, 1982.

7. *Washington Post*, December 26, 1982.

8. Rashid Khalidi, *Under Siege* (New York, 1986), p. 32.

9. Brynen, "PLO Policy in Lebanon," op. cit., pp. 55–56; Kamal Joumblatt and Phillippe Lapousterie, *I Speak for Lebanon* (London, 1982), p. 55. See also Rashid Khalidi, "Lebanon in the Context of Regional Politics: Palestinian and Syrian Involvement in the Lebanese Crisis," *Third World Quarterly*, Vol. 7, No. 3, July 1985, p. 500: The PLO's leading Lebanese ally, Kamal Junblatt, also complained that his friends brought "criticism and even hatred" on themselves from his countrymen. The founder of the Shia Muslims group, Amal, Musa al-Sadr, complained, "The other Arab states bought peace for themselves by indulging turmoil in Lebanon.... [The PLO] is a military machine that terrorizes the Arab world." *New York Times*, June 11, 1980, and January 29, 1981; *Monday Morning*, July 13, 1980; David Hirst, *The Observer*, June 22, 1980.

10. Thomas Friedman, *From Beirut to Jerusalem* (New York, 1989), p. 122.

11. Abu Iyad, op. cit., p. 166.

12. Ibid.; interview with Paul Jureidin, June 12, 2002.

13. John Bullock, *Death of a Country* (London, 1977), p. 88.

14. *New York Times*, June 21, 1982.

15. Itmar Rabinovich, *The War for Lebanon: 1970–1983* (Ithaca, N.Y., 1984), p. 86; Jimmy Carter, *Blood of Abraham* (Little Rock, Ark., 1983), p. 68.

16. Sobel, op. cit., p. 347; *New York Times*, June 21, 1982.

17. Adeed Dawisha, *Syria and the Lebanese Crisis* (New York, 1980), p. 139; *Guardian*, October 1, 1976; *The Times*, September 29, 1976. Sobel, op. cit., p. 347.

18. Dawisha, op. cit., p. 139; *The Times*, September 29, 1976; Sobel, op. cit., p. 348.

19. Amos, *Palestinian Resistance: Organization of a National Movement*, op. cit., p. 65.

20. Gresh, op. cit., p. 213.

21. Abu Iyad, op. cit., p. 205; Mohammed Heikal, *Autumn of Fury: The Assassination of Sadat* (London, 1983), p. 83.

22. Interview with Bolling.

23. Cable from U.S. Embassy in Damascus, "PLO Executive Committee Member says PLO should let US/Egyptian Style Autonomy Succeed," May 3, 1979.

24. Helena Cobban, *The Palestinian Liberation Organization: People, Power and Politics* (New York, 1984), p. 116.

25. For example, despite Arafat's strenuous opposition to Sadat's strategy, PFLP leader George Habash and others accused Arafat of secretly collaborating with Sadat's initiative. *IDOP 1977* (Beirut, 1978), pp. 508–510.

26. Among those involved in anti-Arafat criticisms or activities were Abu Yusif al-Kayid, a Fatah founder; Atallah Atallah (Abu Zaim); former Black September leader Abu Daoud; Fatah charter member Naji Allush; Abu Salih; and even for a time Abu Iyad.

27. Abu Iyad, op. cit., pp. 210–212.

28. Sobel, op. cit., p. 227.

29. Yodfat and Arnon-Ohana, op. cit., p. 121.

30. Cable from Secretary of State Warren Christopher, "PLO Threats to U.S. Interests," September 26, 1979.

31. Interview with Harold Saunders.

32. Dillon interview. As liaison with the embassy, Arafat chose Mahmoud Labidi, director of his foreign press department, perhaps because he had an American wife. Ironically, Labidi would later, in 1983, become spokesman for anti-Arafat rebels.

33. Gresh, op. cit., p. 218.

34. Christos Ioannides, "The PLO and the Iranian Revolution," *American-Arab Affairs* (Fall 1984), pp. 89 and 95.

35. Interview with Saunders.

36. Ibid.

37. Voice of Palestine, December 7, 1979, translation in *FBIS*, December 10, 1979, pp. A3–A5.

38. U.S. State Department, cable from Damascus, "PLO Executive Committee Member says PLO should let US/Egyptian Style Autonomy Succeed," May 3, 1979.

39. *Der Spiegel*, December 17, 1979, pp. 26–29.

40. RG59 Andrew I. Kilgore, "Gulf Foreign Ministers Uneasy about PLO Ties with Iranian Government," Doha, October 27, 1979.

41. Ibid.

42. Gowers and Walker, op. cit., p. 185; Bruce L. Laingen, Cable from Tehran, October 14, 1979.

43. Efraim Karsh, *Saddam Hussein: A Political Biography* (New York, 1991), p. 102.

44. Radio Monte Carlo, August 14, 1981, cited in Offer Yarimi, "Palestinian Issues," in Colin Legum et al., *MECS* (*Middle East Contemporary Survey*) 1980–1981 (New York, 1982), p. 313.

45. Yodfat and Arnon-Ohanna, op. cit., p. 122.

46. Yarimi, op. cit.

47. Jacob Goldberg, "The Saudi Arabian Kingdom," in Colin Legum et al., *MECS* VI 1981–1982, op. cit., p. 746.

48. Saudi policy also moved in this direction because the Saudis felt threatened by the Iran-Iraq war, feared the outbreak of another Arab-Israeli war, and missed Egypt's strong presence as an ally and moderating force in the Arab world.

49. The pro-Saudi Khalid al-Hasan pointed out that the plan "does not call for an official recognition of Israel." *Ukaz*, August 24, 1981: al-*Hawadith*, December 4, 1981; Khalid al-Hasan, al-*Anba*, August 31, 1981; al-*Sharq al-Awsat*, October 14, 1981. al-*Majalla*, August 1, 1981.

50. *Al-Hawadith*, December 4, 1981.

51. Twelfth Arab Summit Conference final statement, September 9, 1982, in Laqueur and Rubin, op. cit., pp. 263–264.

52. *New York Times*, June 21 and 30 and July 25, 1982; *London Times*, June 19, 1982.

53. Dillon interview.

54. Brian Urquhart, *A Life in Peace and War* (New York, 1987), p. 292.

55. On the deliberate targeting of towns see, for example, Israeli, op. cit., p. 214.

56. Melman and Raviv, op. cit., p. 276.

57. Bassam Abu Sharif and Uzi Mahnaimi, *Tried by Fire* (London, 1995), p. 180; Jonathan Randall, *Going All the Way* (New York, 1983), p. 257.

58. John Bulloch, *Final Conflict* (London, 1983), p. 132.

59. Arafat, *Playboy* interview, op. cit.

60. Interview, *Le Quotidien de Paris*, September 15, 1981.

61. Ibid. Though he also blamed the United States for stopping Arab states from intervening. *Liberation*, September 1, 1982.

62. *Al-Nuhur*, October 30, 1981.

63. Bulloch, *Final Conflict*, op. cit., p. 159.

64. Ibid.

65. Israeli, op. cit., p. 256; Gemayel interview with ABC News, June 27, 1982 and "20/20," July 8, 1982.

66. Dillon interview.

67. *Beirut Daily Star*, January 10, 1971.

68. This account is taken from Thomas Friedman, *From Beirut to Jerusalem* (London, 1998), p. 147.

69. Ibid., pp. 147–148.

70. *New York Times*, August 23, 1982; Associated Press, September 3, 1982. Friedman, op. cit., p. 153; Randall, op. cit., p. 270.

71. *New York Times*, August 31, 1982.

72. Voice of Palestine (Algiers) in *BBC Summary of World Broadcasts*, September 1, 1982.

73. Ibid.

74. Associated Press, August 30, 1982.

75. Lebanese radio, August 30, 1982, from *BBC Summary of World Broadcasts*, September 1, 1982.

76. Ibid.

77. Interview; Sharon interview in *Guardian*, April 30, 2001.

78. Associated Press, August 30, 1982.

79. Associated Press, September 1, 1982,

80. *Journal of Palestine Studies*, Vol. 11, No. 4/Vol. 12, No. 1 (Summer/Winter 1982), pp. 309–311.

81. *New York Times*, August 23, 1982.

82. Ibid.

83. *Washington Post*, August 22 and 31, 1982.

84. Dillon interview.

85. Associated Press, September 3, 1982; *New York Times*, September 4, 1982.

86. Interview with Arafat, *The Middle East*, May 1983; Interview with Khalid al-Hasan, *al-Madina*, August 31, 1982, in *FBIS*, September 9, 1982; Arafat speech, Voice of Palestine (Aden), September 8, 1982, BBC, *Survey of World Broadcasts*, September 11, 1982.

87. Downloaded from <http://www.arts.mcgill.ca/MEPP/PRRN/papers/sanctuary/ch2.html>.

88. Friedman, op. cit., p. 167.

89. *New York Times*, September 20, 1982.

90. Text in *New York Times*, September 2, 1982.

91. Asher Susser, "The Palestine Liberation Organization," Legum et al., *MECS*, 1981–1982, op. cit., p. 337; *New York Times*, October 12, 13, 14, and 15, 1982.

92. Jean-Francois Legrain, "The Successions of Yasir Arafat," *Journal of Palestine Studies*, Vol. 28, No. 4, Summer 1999, pp. 13–44.

93. Text, Laqueur and Rubin, op. cit., pp. 679–683. See also Barry Rubin, "United It Stalls: The PLO," in Laqueur and Rubin, op. cit., pp. 683–686; interview with Qadumi, *al-Dustur*, December 13, 1982.

94. Eric Rouleau, "The Future of the PLO," *Foreign Affairs*, Vol. 62 No. 1 (Fall 1983); *Filastin al-Thawra*, November 20, 1982. The first PLO official to hint at suggesting recognition of Israel was Sabri Jiryis, *Shu'un Filastiniyya*, May 1977. See *Journal of Palestine Studies* Vol. 6, No. 4 (Summer 1977), p. 150ff.

95. Muhammad Anis, "An Interview with 'Isam Sartawi," *al-Musawwar*, March 25, 1983; Avner Yaniv, "Phoenix of Phantom? The PLO after Beirut," *Terrorism*, Vol. 7, No. 3 (1984).

96. Ibid., Sartawi; "Sartawi: they prevented me from speaking in the Palestine National Council because I would demand a Palestinian commission of inquiry," *al-Hawadith*, March 4, 1983. Syria rewarded Abu Nidal for murdering Sartawi by bringing his headquarters to Damascus.

97. Text in Laqueur and Rubin, op. cit., pp. 274–276. See also text from Algiers radio, February 22, 1983 in *FBIS*, February 23, 1983, p. A19.

98. Karen House, *Wall Street Journal*, April 14 and 15, 1983.

99. Eric Rouleau, "Yasir Arafat Starts Difficult Rapprochement with Syria," *Le Monde*, May 5, 1983, translated in *FBIS*, May 6, 1983, pp. A2–A3.

100. Luyis Faris, "Asad avoids welcoming Arafat," *al-Majalla*, December 4, 1982; Damascus television, December 15, 1982 (BBC, *Survey of World Broadcasts*, December 17, 1982); Abu Musa, NIN (Belgrade), October 30, 1983, translation in U.S. Department of Commerce, *Joint Publications Research Service*, November 22, 1983.

101. Rouleau in *Foreign Affairs*, op. cit., p. 145.

102. See the coverage in *FBIS*, May 4, 1983, p. A1, and May 5, 1983 pp. A1–A2.

103. Kuwait News Agency, May 4, 1983, in *FBIS*, May 5, 1983.

104. The rebels' political leaders included PNC chairman Khalid al-Fahoum and Nimr Salah (Abu Salah), a Marxist founder of Fatah who had been the PLO's liaison and arms supplier to the Lebanese left.

105. *Al-Watan*, May 26, 1983; *al-Anba*, October 3, 1987; *JPS*, Vol. 27, No. 2 (Winter 1988).

106. *Al-Jazira*, November 4, 1983; *al-Khalij*, June 2, 1983.

107. Yezid Sayigh, "Fatah: The First Twenty Years," *Journal of Palestine Studies*, Vol. 13, No. 4 (Summer 1984), p. 115; *al-Anba*, October 3, 1987. See also the analysis of Moughrabi, op. cit., p. 211.

108. Garfinkle, op. cit., p. 637.

109. See the text of the statement in *FBIS*, May 17, 1983, p. A4.

110. In addition to their long-standing hatred of Arafat and clash of interests in Lebanon, the Syrians may have also wanted revenge for Arafat's help to Islamist revolutionaries within Syria, another possible example of his meddling in the politics of Arab states. Sahliyeh, op. cit., p. 156; *Tishrin*, June 25, 1983; *al-Thawra*, June 30, 1983.

111. Eric Rouleau, "The Future of the PLO," op. cit., pp. 142–143; Robert Baer, *See No Evil: The True Story of a Ground Soldier in the CIA's War on Terrorism* (New York, 2002), p. 124; *Washington Post*, June 14, 1983.

112. Abu Sharif and Mahnaimi, op. cit., p. 205.

113. Friedman, op. cit., p. 174.

114. Baer, op. cit., p 130.

115. Ibid., p. 229.

116. FBI Most Wanted List, October 10, 2001, in Barry Rubin and Judith Colp Rubin, *Anti-American Terrorism and the Middle East* (New York, 2002), p. 197; Baer, op. cit., pp. 129–130.

117. *Newsweek*, November 15, 1999.

118. William Harris, *Faces of Lebanon: Sects, Wars and Global Extensions* (Princeton, N.J., 1997), pp. 184–185.

119. Abu Iyad, Qatar News Agency, February 6, 1984, in *FBIS*, February 6, 1984; interview with Khalid al-Hasan, *al-Nahar al-Arabi wal-Duwali*, May 24, 1982; *al-Hadaf*, "Arafat's downfall is our main objective," February 20, 1984.

120. *Al-Hawadith*, March 1, 1985.

CHAPTER 5

1. Musa Sabri cited in Uri Kupferschmidt, "Egypt," in Ami Ayalon, *MECS*, 1991, Vol. 15 (Boulder, Colo., 1993), p. 361.

2. Radio Riyadh, February 6, 1991, in *FBIS*, February 7, 1991.

3. Interview with Robert Pelletreau, March 26, 2002; Visit to Tunisia and interviews with PLO leaders, 1989.

4. *The Guardian*, June 21, 1986.

5. Marie Colvin, "The Ambiguous Arafat," *New York Times Magazine*, December 18, 1988. Palestinian officials even said that his travels were intended to underline the Palestinians' homeless and "wandering" status.

6. Allman, op. cit.

7. *Washington Post*, December 27, 1982.

8. *Washington Post*, December 26, 1982.

9. Text, *Journal of Palestine Studies*, Vol. 14, No. 3 (Spring 1985), p. 201.

10. Asher Susser, "The Palestine Liberation Organization," in Itamar Rabinovich and Haim Shaked, *MECS* 1985, Vol. 9 (Boulder, Colo., 1987), p. 189.

11. Text in Laqueur and Rubin, op. cit., pp. 293–298.

12. Ibid.

13. Radio Monte Carlo, February 14, 1985, in *FBIS*, February 15, 1985.

14. Kuwait News Agency, February 2, 1985, in *FBIS*, February 4, 1985.

15. Arafat interview, *al-Hawadith*, February 21, 1985, in *FBIS*, March 1, 1985.

16. Hana Siniora and Fayiz Abu Rahmah. *Le Monde*, July 26, 1985.

17. Voice of Israel, September 14, 1985, in *FBIS*, September 15, 1985.

18. *Le Monde*, September 21, 1982.

19. International Policy Institute for Counter-Terrorism, "Force-17 Profile," downloaded from <http://www.ict.org.il>.

20. Ibid.; Arafat interview in *Playboy*, op. cit.; *Ha'aretz*, October 2 and 8, 1985; Colvin, op. cit. It was later discovered that satellite photographs of the Tunis headquarters used by Israel to plan the raid came from Jonathan Pollard, a U.S. Navy Intelligence analyst arrested in November for giving classified material to Israel.

21. *New York Times*, October 13, 1995.

22. Martin and Walcott, op. cit., p. 242.

23. *La Repubblica*, October 22, 1985; *La Stampa*, November 13, 1985.

24. L. Paul Bremer, Jr., "Countering Terrorism, U.S. Policy in the 1980s and 1990s," speech at George Washington University, November 22, 1988; Shultz, in *Washington Post*, January 5, 1989.

25. *Al-Akhbar*, October 20, 1985, in *FBIS*, October 24, 1985, pp. D-3 and 4.

26. *Al-Siyasa*, March 1, 1986; King Hussein's speech, Amman television, February 19, 1986, in *FBIS*, February 20, 1986. See also *New York Times* and *Washington Post*, February 20, 1986.

27. Interview.

28. *Sawt al-Sha'b*, March 12, 1986, in *FBIS*, March 12, 1986, p. F-1; Lamis Andoni, "Hussein stakes his claim," *Middle East International*, February 21, 1986, pp. 7–8.

29. Rubin, *Revolution until Victory*, op. cit., p. 80.

30. Palestine National Council Political Report, November 15, 1988; *Washington Post*, April 11, 1988.

31. Interviews; *Wall Street Journal*, July 21, 1986. James Adams, *The Financing of Terror* (Kent, 1986), pp. 83–127.

32. Ibid., *Wall Street Journal*, July 21, 1986.

33. *Washington Post*, April 21, 22, and 23, 1987. For text of the March 16, 1987, agreement, see *Journal of Palestine Studies*, Vol. XV, No. 4 (Summer 1987).

34. Gowers and Walker, op. cit., p. 369.

35. Radio Monte Carlo, in *FBIS*, December 1, 1987.

36. Rubin, *Revolution until Victory*, op. cit., p. 80.

37. *New York Times*, February 22, 1987. In fact, he would never shake hands with Asad but he would with Israeli Prime Minister Yitzhak Rabin.

38. Friedman, op. cit., p. 227.

39. Helena Cobban, "The PLO in the Mid-1980s: Between the Gun and the Olive Branch," *International Journal*, Vol. 38 (Autumn 1983), p. 649.

40. Yet it says something about the limits on the flexibility and prospects of PLO moderates to note that he expected that in the long run Israel and Palestine would merge into one state, and also that Qawasma—like Masri and Sartawi— would be murdered by fellow Palestinians and Arafat would leave them unrevenged. American Enterprise Institute, *A Conversation with the Exiled West Bank Mayors: A Palestinian Point of View* (Washington, D.C., 1981), pp. 3 and 5. See also p. 15.

41. Ibid., pp. 9–10.

42. Daoud Kuttab, "The PLO Must Not Forget the Palestinians," *Middle East International*, October 10, 1986.

43. Robert Satloff, *Islam in the Palestinian Uprising* (Washington, D.C., 1988); Zuhair Kashmeri, "Islamic Fervour Growing among PLO," *Manchester Guardian Weekly*, May 18, 1986.

44. Zeev Schiff and Ehud Yaari, *Intifada* (New York, 1990), p. 46.

45. Speech in *al-Ra'y al-Amm*, September 11, 1989, p. 16, in *FBIS*, September 14, 1989, pp. 6–7.

46. Ibid., p. 66.

47. *Al-Fajr*, August 14, 1988.

48. Arafat interview in *Playboy*, op. cit.

49. Allman, op. cit.

50. Colvin, op. cit.

51. Text in *FBIS* August 8, 1988, pp. 26–28. See also *Jerusalem Post*, August 12, 1988; Sari Nusseibah lecture, Oxford Arab Committee, *Middle East Mirror*, February 12, 1990.

52. Authors' interviews with Feisal al-Husseini, July 2, 1988; Khalid al-Hasan, interview in *Yediot Aharnot*, September 5, 1988, p. 17, in *FBIS*, September 7, 1988, p. 5. For the Husseini document, see *Jerusalem Post*, August 12, 1988, p. 10, and *FBIS*, August 12, 1988, pp. 30–32. Also see "A Critical Palestine National Council Session," *al-Fajr*, August 14, 1988, p. 5. Text of Call No. 27, *al-Ra'y al-Amm*, October 10, 1988, in *FBIS*, October 12, 1988, pp. 6–7.

53. *New York Times*, February 22, 1988; *Washington Post*, May 11, 1988.

54. Rubin, *Revolution until Victory*, op. cit., p. 97.

55. *Al-Thawra*, April 22, 1989, in *FBIS*, April 25, 1989, p. 3; *al-Quds al-Arabiyya*, February 7, 1990; *al-Majalla*, April 5–11, 1989, in *FBIS*, April 7, 1989, pp. 1–8; Agence-France Presse, April 18, 1989, in *FBIS*, April 18, 1989 p. 1; Interview, Middle East News Agency, August 12, 1988, in *FBIS*, August 15, 1988, p. 4; Interview, *al-Ahram*, in *FBIS* October 20, 1988, p. 14; Abu Iyad in *al-Muharrir*, November 25, 1989, in *FBIS*, November 29, 1989, p. 4; Khalid al-Hasan, *al-Watan*, October 13, 1989, in *FBIS*, October 17, 1989.

56. Rubin, *Revolution until Victory*, op. cit., p. 97.

57. *New York Times*, August 2 and 3, 1988.

58. Authors' interviews, Algiers, November 1988; Tunis, July–August 1989.

59. Text, "Palestinian Document Circulated At Arab Summit in Algeria, PLO View: Prospects of a Palestinian-Israeli Settlement."

60. Ibid.

61. Interview with Muhammad Rabie, April 10, 1990.

62. PFLP leader George Habash said he could accept a state or government only if it "does not offer concessions in its programs or hide the PLO role[,]..does not contradict the PLO Charter and rules, [and] includes all the Palestinian revolutionary factions." *Al-Anba*, September 19, 1988, pp. 1 and 30, in *FBIS*, September 22, 1988, p. 25. Hawatmeh rejected "establishing a government of the so-called moderates which will be accepted by the West and America's allies in the region." Reuters, October 11, 1988.

63. Voice of Lebanon, December 3, 1987, in *FBIS*, December 4, 1987, pp. 3–6; Voice of Palestine (Algiers), November 28, 1987, in *FBIS*, December 1, 1987, pp. 5–6; *al-Watan*, October 2, 1988. Yehoshafat Harkabi, *The Palestinian Covenant and Its Meaning* (London, 1979), p. 76; Interview, *al-Anba*, September 7, 1988, p. 23, in *FBIS*, September 9, 1988, pp. 3–5.

64. Kuwait News Agency, September 23, 1988, in *FBIS*, September 26, 1988, p. 6; *Der Spiegel*, August 29, 1988, op. cit., p. 5; Kuwait News Agency, September 1, 1988, in *FBIS*, September 2, 1988, p. 3; *al-Siyasa*, October 17, 1988, in *FBIS*, October 20, 1988, p. 5. As Nabil Sha'th, considered a moderate, put it, establishing a Palestinian state "on a part . . . and not on all the national soil" was only an interim step. The long-term goal remained Israel's replacement by a PLO-ruled Palestinian state. *Al-Majalla*, August 31–September 6, 1988, in *FBIS* September 2, 1988, p. 4.

65. *Times* (London), November 14, 1988.

66. Kuwait News Agency, September 1, 1988, in *FBIS*, September 2, 1988, p. 3; interview, *al-Siyasa*, October 17, 1988, in *FBIS*, October 20, 1988, p. 5.

67. Key sources for the PNC resolution were the September 1982 Fez Arab summit resolution, text in Laqueur and Rubin, op. cit., pp. 663–665, and Arafat's speech to the June 1988 Arab summit, text in *FBIS*, June 10, 1988, p. 6.

68. Author's observations at the meeting; Text downloaded from <http://www.palestinecenter.org/cpap/document.htm>.

69. *New York Times*, November 16, 1988.

70. Quotations are from the official translation. See also Abu Iyad's analysis in Kuwait News Agency, September 1, 1988, *FBIS*, September 2, 1988, p. 3.

71. Reuters, January 6, 1989; text of September 14, 1988, speech in *FBIS*, September 15, 1988. p. 6.

72. Text, *Washington Post* and *New York Times*, November 27, 1988, December 6 and 7, 1988; *Washington Post*, December 18, 1988; Menachem Rosensaft, "Meeting the PLO," *Reform Judaism*, Spring 1989.

73. George Shultz, *Turmoil and Triumph* (New York, 1993), p. 1038; Colvin, op. cit.

74. Text, Voice of the PLO (Baghdad), December 15, 1988, in *FBIS*, December 15, 1988, p. 3.

75. Interviews with U.S. officials; Shultz, op. cit., p. 1043; *New York Times*, December 14 and 16, 1988.

76. Text, Voice of the PLO (Baghdad), December 15, 1988, in *FBIS*, December 15, 1988, p. 3; *Washington Post*, December 15, 1988; *New York Times*, December 16, 1988.

77. Ibid., text.

78. Interview with Robert Pelletreau, March 26 and April 17, 2002.

79. Ibid.

80. Voice of the PLO (Baghdad), October 6, 1989, in *FBIS*, October 17, 1989, p. 6.

81. *Al-Ra'y al-Amm*, October 18, 1988, in *FBIS*, October 19, 1988.

82. *Al-Watan*, October 13, 1989, in *FBIS*, October 17, 1989. For the effect of the Cold War's end on the region, see Barry Rubin, "Reshaping the Middle East," *Foreign Affairs*, Summer 1990.

83. Interview with a U.S. official.

84. *FBIS*, January 25, 1989; *al-Musawwar*, January 19, 1990. Sadat's comment of February 17, 1977, is in *IDOP*, 1977, op. cit., p. 329.

85. Voice of Palestine (Algiers), March 9, 1989, *FBIS*, March 21, 1989, p. 11.

86. *Ma'ariv*, January 27, 1989; *New York Times*, January 28, 1989.

87. *Ha'aretz*, May 18, 1989.

88. *Ha'aretz*, May 2, 1989.

89. Agence-France Presse, May 3, 1989, in *FBIS*, May 4, 1989.

90. Balawi, quoted by Kuwait News Agency, May 6, 1989 in *FBIS*, May 8, 1989; interview with Abu Iyad, *al-Tadamun*, May 29, 1989. See also the explanation to readers in *Filastin al-Thawra*, September 3, 1989. This is not to say that the Charter itself was a text used in day-to-day PLO policy, but its basic ideas continued to govern the thinking of Arafat and the other leaders.

91. *New York Times*, December 5, 1989.

92. Ibid.; Youssef Ibrahim, "A Palestinian Revolution without the PLO," *New York Times*, February 14, 1988.

93. *Al-Ittihad*, March 17, 1989, in *FBIS* March 20, 1989, p. 18; *International Herald Tribune*, November 16, 1988; Abu Ahmad Fuad, PFLP Political Bureau and commander of its forces in Lebanon, *al-Qubus*, March 13, 1989, in *FBIS*, March 22, 1989, pp. 7–9; Hawatmeh, *al-Fajr*, December 18, 1989, in *FBIS*, December 19, 1989, p. 5.

94. Text, *FBIS*, August 10, 1989, pp. 11–14. *New York Times*, August 11 and 15, 1989; *Washington Times*, July 13 and August 11, 1989. Occasional PLO articles did advocate a two-state solution. For example, Hasan al-Batal, "Different Nationality, Different Zionism," *Filastin al-Thawra*, July 2, 1989.

95. *Al-Bayan*, August 6, in *FBIS*, August 8, 1989; *al-Anba*, August 21, 1989, in *FBIS*, August 25, 1989, p. 3.

96. *Al-Ra'y al-Amm*, September 11, 1989, in *FBIS*, September 14, 1989; *FBIS*, October 4, 1989, p. 4; *al-Sharq al-Awsat*, September 17, 1989, in *FBIS*, September 22, 1989, pp. 4–5.

97. *New York Times*, March 31 and April 7, May 24 and 28, and June 25 and 30, 1989; *Washington Post*, May 24 and June 29, 1989; *Washington Times*, June 8 and July 19, 1989.

98. *Washington Post*, November 9, 1989; *Wall Street Journal*, November 13, 1989; *al-Anba*, December 3, 1989, in *FBIS* December 5, 1989; *Jordan Times*, December 23, 1989.

99. See Israel Government Press Office report, March 22, 1990, in *FBIS*, March 23, 1990. A bomb was placed in the Mahane Yehuda market in Jerusalem by Arafat's Force-17 bodyguards on May 28, killing one man. *Ha'aretz*, July 11, 1990.

100. *Washington Post*, January 4 and 5, 1989.

101. Text of State Department report to Congress, March 19, 1990.

102. Abu Mazin to *al-Majalla*, March 13, 1990.

103. Sha'th to *al-Sha'b*, January 9, 1990.

104. *Al-Qabas*, December 23 1988, p. 19, in *FBIS*, December 27, 1988, p. 4; *al-Ahram*, February 14, 1989, in *FBIS*, February 22, 1989, p. 4.

105. Kelly testimony to House Foreign Affairs Subcommittee on Europe and the Middle East, May 24, 1990.

106. *Jerusalem Post* and *Ha'aretz*, June 6, 1990.

107. *Jerusalem Post*, June 1, 1990.

108. *Al-Qabas International*, May 10, 1990; Voice of Palestine (Baghdad), April 1, 1989 and Middle East News Agency, April 2, 1989, in *FBIS*, April 3, 1989.

109. Voice of Palestine (Baghdad), May 31 1990.

110. *Jerusalem Post*, June 6, 1990; *Ha'aretz*, June 22, 1990; Abbas to *al-Watan*, June 2, 1990.

111. Joshua Teitelbaum, "Saudi Arabia," in Ami Ayalon, *MECS* 1990, Vol. 14 (New York, 1991), p. 220.

112. Interview with a U.S. official.

113. For example, Arafat's monthly Intifada message, Voice of Palestine (Algiers), April 11, 1990, in *FBIS*, April 12, 1990.

114. Saint-Prot, op. cit., p. 232.

115. Associated Press, March 29, 1990.

116. *Al-Muharrir*, May 8, 1990; *Al-Hayat*, September 20, 1992.

117. Saudi Press Agency, 22 April 1990, cited in Teitelbaum, op. cit., p. 223.

118. Arafat's monthly Intifada message, Voice of Palestine (San'a), April 11, 1990, in *FBIS*, April 12, 1990.

119. *Le Figaro*, cited in *Ha'aretz*, April 1 and May 14, 1990; *al-Dustur*, May 7 and 9, 1990; *al-Anba*, May 10, 1990; *Jane's Defence Weekly*, September 29, 1990.

120. Gulf News Agency, June 3, 1990, in *FBIS*, June 4, 1990. The statement was made by the PLO ambassador in Baghdad, Azzam al-Ahmad. Nabil Sha'th declared that Iraq had paid out $35 million additional aid to the PLO.

121. Arafat to Amman television, April 25, 1990, in *FBIS*, April 27, 1990. See also Arafat to *al-Musawwar*, January 19, 1990, and his speech to the Baghdad summit, Radio Baghdad, May 29, 1990, in *FBIS*, May 29, 1990; *Jerusalem Post*, January 20, 1990; Abbas to Kuwait News Agency, January 14, 1990, in *FBIS*, January 16, 1990.

122. Arafat to *al-Ray*, February 12, 1990.

123. Middle East News Agency, August 10, 1990, in BBC, *Survey of World Broadcasts*, August 13, 1990; Bassam Abu Sharif to Independent Television, August 11, 1990, in *FBIS*, August 11, 1990.

124. Arafat claimed that he was the one who convinced Saddam to do this, although privately PLO aides confided to journalists that the PLO leaders had little influence with Saddam Hussein. *Washington Post*, January 8, 1991.

125. Teitelbaum, op. cit., p. 225.

126. Habash to *Arbeiderbladet*, August 27, 1990, in *FBIS*, August 30, 1990.

127. *New York Times*, March 15, 1991; *Le Figaro*, February 11, 1991.

128. *International Herald Tribune*, November 6, 1990.

129. *New York Times*, January 21, 1991.

130. *Jordan Times*, February 23, 1991. On the course of the war, see Barry Rubin, *Cauldron of Turmoil* (New York, 1992).

131. Pelletreau interview.

CHAPTER 6

1. The following story comes from interview with Yakov Peri, July 1, 2001 and confirmed by interviews with other officials involved in this matter.

2. Interviews; *Jerusalem Post*, July 13, 1994.

3. *New York Times*, December 11, 1991.

4. *Middle East International*, December 20, 1991.

5. Agence France-Presse, October 31, 1991; Hanan Ashrawi, *This Side of Peace: A Personal Account* (New York, 1995), p. 148; Associated Press, November 1, 1991; Pelletreau interview.

6. *New York Times*, October 27, 1991; Ashrawi, op. cit., p. 149; interview with Eytan Ben-Tsur, May 3, 2001.

7. *Jerusalem Post*, April 16 and June 19, 1992.

8. *La Repubblica*, March 12, 1991.

9. *New York Times*, October 23, 1991; Mahmoud Abbas, *Through Secret Channels: The Road to Oslo* (Reading, 1997), p. 87.

10. Mohammed Heikal, *Secret Channels: The Inside Story of Arab-Israeli Peace Negotiations* (London, 1996), p. 431.

11. Glenn Frankel, *Beyond the Promised Land: Jews and Arabs on the Hard Road to a New Israel* (New York, 1994), pp. 350–351.

12. Arafat to *al-Musawwar*, November 15, 1992, in *FBIS*, November 20, 1992.

13. Arafat to *Le Figaro*. February 11, 1991; see Abu Iyad cited in *al-Ray,* January 2, 1991. See also PNC Speaker Sa'ih's similar remark in *Akhbar al-Usbu,* September 5, 1991 in *FBIS*, September 6, 1991.

14. *Kurier*, April 19, 1991, in *FBIS*, April 22, 1991.

15. *Al-Watan al-Arabi*, February 14, 1992.

16. Associated Press, July 19, and 25, 1995; Author's interview with Suha Arafat, December 1, 1994.

17. Ibid.

18. *New York Times*, February 4, 1999; interview.

19. *Ha'aretz*, April 3, 2002.

20. Allman, op. cit.

21. *Jerusalem Post*, June 2, 1992.

22. Associated Press, July 19, 1995; *Financial Times*, April 9, 1992; *al-Majallah*, April 15, 1992; *Le Monde*, April 17, 1992; *Ha'aretz*, April 9 and May 28, 1992; *International Herald Tribune*, April 10, 1992; *al-Quds*, April 22, 1992; *al-Watan al-Arabi*, May 15, 1992.

23. *Jerusalem Post*, March 29, 1992; *Los Angeles Times*, April 14, 1992; *Le Monde*, April 17, 1992; *al-Hawadith*, May 8, 1992; *al-Usbu al-Arabi*, May 25, 1992.

24. Ibid.; *al-Hadaf,* May 31, 1992; *al-Usbu al-Arabi*, May 25, 1992.

25. Meir Litvak, "The Palestine Liberation Organization," in Ami Ayalon, *MECS* 1992, Vol. 16 (New York, 1995), pp. 252–253. Arafat had earlier declared that he was the Palestinian De Gaulle, waiting for an Israeli counterpart. Saint-Prot, op. cit., pp. 326–327.

26. Arafat to *Ha'aretz*, July 31, 1992, and to Reuters, August 10, 1992.

27. Ibid.; Arafat to Middle East Broadcasting Company, July 28, 1992 in *FBIS*, July 29, 1992.

28. *Al-Muharrir*, June 14, 1993; *Ha'aretz*, January 4, June 1, July 5, and August 24, 1993. *al-Safir*, March 22, 1993; *al-Hayat*, June 20, 1993; *al-Watan al-Arabi*, August 30, 1993.

29. Interview with Yusuf Sayegh, January 28, 2002.

30. Interview with Ron Pundak, April 15, 2001.

31. Abbas, op. cit., p. 118.

32. David Makovsky, *Making Peace with the PLO: The Rabin Government's Road to the Oslo Accords* (Boulder, Colo., 1996), p. 18.

33. Associated Press, September 1, 1993.

34. The other two members were Hasan Asfour and Maher al-Kurd. Asfour, the PLO's expert on negotiations had gone through the Communist party, imprisonment in Syria, and the PFLP before he joined Fatah. He represented a traditional PLO view, making long polemical speeches about his people's heroic struggle. Abbas, op. cit., pp. 114–115; Jane Corbin, *The Norway Channel* (New York, 1994), p. 50. Kurd, an economics advisor, served as translator.

35. Uri Savir, *The Process* (New York, 1998), p. 6; *New York Times*, June 14, 2002.

36. Interview with Oren Shachor, June 19, 2001; interviews; Makovsky, op. cit., p. 23; Savir, op. cit., p. 81; interview with Pundak.

37. Peri Interview.

38. Interview with Amnon Lipkin-Shahak, July 3, 2001.

39. Savir, op. cit., pp. 4–6; interviews with Pundak and others.

40. Pundak interview; Makovsky, op. cit., p. 23.

41. Pundak interview; interview with Yoel Singer, June 30, 2002.

42. Interview with Yair Hirschfeld, June 3, 2001; Singer interview.

43. Hirschfeld interview. See also *Al-Manar*, June 7, 1993; *Ha'aretz*, June 8, 1993; *Filastin al-Thawra*, June 13, 1993; *al-Wasat*, June 14, 1993; Voice of Palestine (Algiers), June 19, 1993 in *FBIS*, June 21, 1993.

44. *Ha'aretz*, June 6 and 11, 1993.

45. Makovsky, op. cit., p. 59.

46. Savir, op. cit., p. 38; Corbin, op. cit., p. 116; Singer interview.

47. Corbin, op. cit., pp. 119–121.

48. Interview with Uri Savir, July 1, 2001.

49. Singer interview; Abbas, op. cit., pp. 175–177; Corbin, op. cit., pp. 153–159.

50. Interviews.

51. Laqueur and Rubin, op. cit., pp. 424–425.

52. Text in *International Herald Tribune*, September 10, 1993; Israel-PLO Agreement, Declaration of Principles (Jerusalem, 1993), pp. 38–39. For the Arabic text, see *Filastin al-Thawra*, September 19, 1993.

53. Ami Ayalon, *MECS*, 1993, Vol. 17 (Boulder, Colo., 1995), p. 166.

54. Author's interviews with Abd al-Shafi, September 30, 1994, and Husseini; Ashrawi, op. cit., pp. 249–58. During the 1990s, Arafat repeatedly harassed Husseini and cut the budget for his operation in Jerusalem which was trying to promote PA and Fatah influence there. See Yezid Sayigh, "Arafat and the Anatomy of Revolt," *Survival*, Vol. 43, No. 3 (Autumn 2001), pp. 47–60. For Abd al-Shafi's criticisms of Arafat, see *Middle East Mirror*, July 15, 1993.

55. *Ha'aretz*, August 24, 25, and 29, 1993; *al-Nahar*, August 25, 1993.

56. Agence France-Presse, August 24, 1993, in *FBIS*, August 24, 1993; *New York Times*, August 25, 1993.

57. *New York Times*; August 25, 1993.

58. Agence France-Presse, August 22, 1993, in *FBIS*, August 23, 1993; *al-Hayat* , August 24, 1993.

59. Voice of Palestine (Algiers) and Middle East News Agency, August 29, 1993 in *FBIS*, August 30, 1993; *al-Ray*, September 1, 1993; *Filastin al-Thawra*, September 5, 1993; *al-Usbu al-Arabi*, September 6, 1993.

60. *Al-Hayat, September* 4, 5, and 6,1993.

61. *Al-Hayat*, September 10, and 11, 1993. For a complete list of how each member voted, see Rubin, *Revolution until Victory*, op. cit., p. 245, note 43.

62. *Al-Ray*, September 13, 1993; *al-Hurriyya*, September 19, 1993.

63. Makovsky op. cit., p. 180; interview with Eitan Haber, May 2, 2001.

64. *New York Times*, September 13, 1993.

65. Abbas, op. cit., pp. 210–213; Corbin, op. cit., pp. 200–201; Laqueur and Rubin, op. cit., p. 413. The preamble reads: "The Government of the State of Israel and the PLO team (in the Jordanian-Palestinian delegation to the Middle East Peace Conference)(the 'Palestinian delegation'), representing the Palestinian

people...." In Article 7 it says, "The Israel and Palestinian delegations will negotiate...." And so on.

66. Associated Press, April 25, 2001.

67. Ibid.

68. Interview with Haber.

69. Interview with Carmi Gillon, June 11, 2001.

70. Interview with Haber.

71. *Jerusalem Post*, September 14, 1993.

72. Laqueur and Rubin, op. cit., p. 427.

73. Ibid.

74. An anecdote recounted by several other U.S. officials in interviews.

75. Interviews with U.S. officials.

76. Laqueur and Rubin, op. cit., pp. 629–642.

77. Israel Foreign Ministry, *Israel-Palestinian Interim Agreement on the West Bank and Gaza Strip, September 28, 1995* (Jerusalem, 1995). Annex 2, "Protocol Concerning Elections."

78. U.S. Information Service, Official Text of the Wye River Memorandum, October 23, 1998. The complex arrangements included: the transfer of 12 percent from Area C to Area B, 1 percent from Area C to Area A, and 14.2 percent from Area B to Area A. This would leave the following division of territory: Area A, 18.2 percent; Area B, 24.8 percent; and Area C, 57 percent.

79. Interview with U.S. official.

80. Middle East News Agency, October 11, 1993, in *FBIS*, October 12, 1993; *al-Hurriyya*, October 17, 1993; *al-Hawadith*, October 22, 1993; Radio Monte Carlo, October 12, 1993 in *FBIS*, October 13, 1993.

81. *New York Times*, October 13, 1993; *Ha'aretz*, October 17, 1993.

82. Hart, op. cit., p. 400.

83. *Jordan Times*, November 14, 1993; *Ha'aretz*, November 14 and December 2, 1993; *al-Ray*, November 18 and 29, 1993.

84. *Sawt al-Sha'b*, December 4, 1993; *Jordan Times* and *Jerusalem Post*, December 6, 1993; *al-Ray*, December 28, 1993.

85. *Jordan Times*, November 18–19, 1993.

86. *Al-Sharq al-Awsat*, November 5, 1993.

87. Good examples of this phenomenon were Haydar Abd al-Shafi and Husam Khadar, perhaps Arafat's two most courageously persistent critics, both of whom urged him toward harder-line policies in the peace process.

88. *New York Times*, December 13, 1993; *Davar*, December 17, 1993.

89. Interview with Uri Savir; Savir, op. cit., p. 125.

90. Ibid.

91. Ibid., p. 127.

92. Ibid., p. 131.

93. Allman, op. cit.

94. The following account is taken from Savir, op. cit., p. 140; Savir interview and Pelletreau interview; interviews with U.S. officials.

95. Savir, op. cit., p. 140.

96. Pelletreau interview.

97. Interviews.

98. *New York Times*, May 5, 1994.

99. Laqueur and Rubin, op. cit., pp. 457–459.

100. The Oslo agreement defined Arafat's title as "chairman," not president.

101. When the Palestinian Legislative Council (PLC) was elected in 1996, its members' oath pledged them "to be faithful to the nation of Palestine." Article 3, "Standing Orders of the Palestinian Legislative Council," *Palestine Report*, August 9, 1996. As the PA issued identity cards, Deputy Interior Minister Ahmad Said Tamimi said this was intended to "reinforce Palestinian sovereignty." The PA's Interior Ministry also issued Palestinian passports. *Palestine Report*, July 5, 1996. The al-Hakawati Theater in Jerusalem was designated the Palestinian National Theater and a Palestinian team took part in the 1996 Olympics, marching behind the Palestinian flag, despite Israel's complaint, and the PLO's previous armed participation in the 1972 games. *Palestine Report*, June 28 and July 26, 1996. Later, this was reinforced by his frequent warnings that he would declare independence unilaterally unless he was given concessions, legitimizing the bypassing or destruction of the process. Since, in effect, Palestine was already independent, it could implement this status completely whenever it wished.

102. *Palestine Report*, November 22, 1996.

103. Arafat's speech at the signing of the 1994 Cairo Agreement in Laqueur and Rubin, op. cit., p. 645. Given the continuing strength of Pan-Arab nationalism, Arab states' claims to rule the Palestinian cause, and Islamism, the justification for a specifically Palestinian nationalism could not be taken for granted in the Arab world. At the same time, by appropriating the ancient Jewish role in creating monotheism and in the origins of Christianity, Arafat was denying any historical connection of Jews to the holy land or at least claiming they should be a subordinate part of his Palestinian people.

104. Eytan ben-Tsur interview.

105. *Jerusalem Post*, May 18, 1994.

106. Agence France-Presse, July 1, 1994.

107. United Press International, July 2, 1994.

108. Author's observations at the scene.

109. Associated Press, July 1, 1994.

110. Voice of Palestine radio, January 1, 1995, *FBIS*, January 6, 1995.

111. Sayegh interview.

112. *Al-Wasat*, January 9–15, 1995, *FBIS*, January 13, 1995.

113. *Financial Times* and *Wall Street Journal*, May 25, 1994; *New York Times* and *Washington Post*, July 3, 1994. For discussion of complaints about aid funds being misused, see *Arbeiderbladet* (Norway), August 29, 1995, in *FBIS*, August 30, 1995.

114. *Star,* January 26–February 1, 1995, in *FBIS*, January 26, 1995.

115. Adil Samara in *Palestine Report* January 3, 1997. See also *New York Times*, April 30, 1994; Hisham Awartani et al., *Evaluation of Paris Agreement: Economic Relations between Israel and the PLO*, November 1994 (Arabic with English text of the agreement).

116. Ibid.

117. Saint-Prot, op. cit., p. 166.

118. Numerous interviews; conversations with Palestinian officials and engineers; authors' observations.

119. Ibid.

120. Interview.

121. Voice of Palestine, February 6, 1995, in *FBIS*, February 7, 1995.

122. Dajani, op. cit.; *Palestine Report*, November 15, 1996.

123. *Palestine Report*, February 18, 1998.

124. *Palestine Report*, August 30 and October 4, 1996. On economic issues, see also Palestinian Economic Research Institute, *Poverty in the West Bank and Gaza Strip*, November 1995; Jamal Hilal, "Features of Poverty in Palestine," [Arabic], *al-Siyasa al-Filastiniyya*, Vol. 3, No. 12 (Fall 1996).

125. Palestinian National Authority Official Website, Special Reports, Donor Assistance Report, June 30, 1998, downloaded from <http://nmopic.pna.net/reports/aid_reports/150898/index.htm>.

126. Interviews with Toni Verstandig, May 14, 2002, and Dennis Ross, May 1, 2002.

127. Ibid.

128. *Ha'aretz*, November 19, 1996; *Washington Post*, June 13, 1994; *al-Hayat*, February 21, 1995. *Palestine Report*, August 9 and 23 and November 22, 1996, and February 13, 1998; Agence France-Presse, May 25, 1998.

129. Numerous interviews.

130. Interview with Pelletreau.

131. Interviews with those involved. *Palestine Report*, October 18, 1996 and February 7, 1997.

132. Ibid.; cited in *Palestine Report*, September 25, 1998; Dajani, op. cit.; *al-Quds*, November 15, 1996. See chapter 7.

133. *New York Times* and *Washington Post*, May 21, 1994.

134. Savir interview.

135. Shachor interview.

136. *Al-Sharq al-Awsat*, January 8, 1995, in *FBIS*, January 10, 1995; Radio Monte Carlo, January 12, 1995, in *FBIS* January 13, 1995; Voice of Palestine, February 6, 1995, in *FBIS*, February 7, 1995.

137. *Al-Hayat*, February 21, 1995, in *FBIS*, February 23, 1995.

138. Interviews.

139. Text of the decree, Voice of Palestine, February 8, 1995, in *FBIS*, February 9, 1995. See also *Kol Israel*, February 8, 1995, in *FBIS*, February 9, 1995. For text of the order to establish the security courts, see *al-Siyasa al-Filastiniyya* [Arabic] (Winter 1995), pp. 183–186. For criticisms of the courts, see *Middle East Mirror*, February 13, April 5, and May 25, 1995. For PA defenses, see *al-Sharq al-Awsat*, February 18, 1995; *al-Hayat al-Jadida*, February 20, 1995; *al-Majalla*, November 11, 1995.

140. *Kol Israel*, January 30, 1995, in *FBIS*, January 31, 1995; *Kol Israel*, January 31, 1995, in *FBIS*, February 1, 1995; *New York Times*, August 30 and September 13 and 14, 1995; *Kol Israel*, April 24, 1995, in *FBIS*, April 25, 1995; Voice of Palestine August 26, 1995, in *FBIS*, August 28, 1995; *New York Times*, August 27, 1995.

141. *Yediot Aharnot*, August 22, 1997.

142. Interview.

143. Interview with Gillon.

144. Other interviews.

145. Interview with Carmi Gillon, June 11, 2001.

146. Interview with Arafat, *Uqtabar*, March 19, 1995, in *FBIS*, March 21, 1995.

147. On the economic, educational, and medical impact of the closure and curfew imposed by Israel after the February–March 1996 attacks, see LAW press releases of March 11, 1996 "Statement on the Current Human Rights Situation in the West Bank" and March 13, 1996, "Update on the Human Rights Situation in the West Bank."

148. *Kol Israel*, February 6, 1995, in *FBIS*, February 7, 1995.

149. *Al-Hayat*, April 11, 1995; *al-Ra'i*, April 12 and 13, 1995.

150. Israel had not repressed the Islamic groups that preceded Hamas before its creation in 1987 because they had never engaged in violence.

151. Shachor interview.

152. Interview with Hirshfeld.

153. Savir, op. cit., p. 237.

154. Pundak interview.

155. *Newsday*, May 4, 1994.

156. Singer and other interviews.

157. Sayegh interview.

158. Laqueur and Rubin, op. cit., pp. 492–495.

159. *Ha'aretz*, March 20, 1995.

160. Savir interview.

161. Reuters, September 28, 1995.

CHAPTER 7

1. LAW, "Report of the Monitoring Unit on the Elections for the PLC," January 23, 1996; LAW, press release, January 9, 1996.

2. This is not to say the election was completely fair. In addition to media bias, Arafat or his men intimidated some PLC candidates and a few ballot boxes disappeared. For analyses of the election, see Khalil Shikaki, *Transition to Liberal Democracy in Palestine: The Peace Process, the National Reconstruction, and Elections* (Nablus, 1996); Jamal Hilal, "The Elections of the Palestinian Legislative Council: A Preliminary Reading of the Results of the Election," and Islah Jad, "Palestinian Women's Movement and the Elections" [Arabic], *al-Siyasa al-Filastiniyya*, Vol. 3, No. 10 (Spring 1996); Khalil Shiqaqi (editor), *Palestinian Elections: Political Environment, Electoral Behavior, Results* [Arabic] (Nablus: 1997), see pp. 12–15 for a discussion of the advantages provided by the elections. For a list of all PLC members and an analysis of their views see Barry Rubin, *Transformation*, op. cit., pp. 206–215.

3. Interview with Samiha Khalil, January 2, 1996. For a more detailed look at the Palestinian Authority and the peace process in this period, see Rubin, *Transformation*, op. cit.

4. *Jerusalem Post*, January 22, 1996.

5. On the Palestinian election law see *al-Quds*, December 9–12, 1995, in *FBIS*, December 19, 1995 Supplement.

6. *Palestine Times*, December 1997.

7. *New York Times*, June 29, 1999.

8. Ziad Abu-Amr, "The Palestinian Legislative Council: A Critical Assessment," *Journal of Palestine Studies*, Vol. 26, No. 4 (Summer 1997), p. 94.

9. *Al Sharq al Awsat*, February 1, 1995; *Jerusalem Times*, November 24, 1995

10. *Yediot Aharnot*, January 27, 1995 in *FBIS*, January 30, 1995.

11. The PBC's Gaza office, with one hundred and twenty workers, broadcast one channel of imported Arab programs and one with local entertainment and news. The Ramallah office had one hundred and eighty workers and broadcast six hours a day. *Ha'aretz*, February 2, 1996.

12. *New York Times*, December 28, 1995, and January 1, 1996; *Washington Post*, January 1, 1996.

13. Interview with *Kol Israel*, December 31, 1995, in *FBIS*, January 2, 1996.

14. Associated Press, November 28, 1994; *Washington Post*, July 29, 1994; *New York Times*, July 30 and September 6, 1994.

15. Roni Ben Efrat, "The Telltale Silence of the Post-Oslo Palestinian Press," Lecture for the conference: "A 21st century Dialogue: Media's Dark Age?" Athens, May 24–28, 1998.

16. *Al-Hayat al-Jadida*, December 8, 1997; *al-Ayyam*, October 29, 1997; *Yediot Aharnot*, June 25, 1997. For a discussion of the PA's and Arafat's attitudes toward Israel during the peace process, see Rubin, *Transformation*, op. cit., pp. 162–168.

17. *Al-Hayat al-Jadida*, September 1, 1997, August 6, 1997. See also October 26 and November 5, 1997.

18. See, for example, *Palestine Report*, July 5, 1996; Radio Monte Carlo, November 3, 1995 in *FBIS*, November 3, 1995; *Ha'aretz*, November 5, 1995 in *FBIS*, November 7, 1995.

19. *New York Times*, May 6, 22, 27, and 28, 1996. He was released shortly after his family wrote a note saying he had been misquoted. Later, though, Sarraj confirmed that the quotes were correct.

20. Interview.

21. *New York Times*, June 11, 1996; *Palestine Report*, June 14 and 28, 1996; LAW, press release, June 12, 14, 16, 17, and 27, 1996; *Washington Post*, June 27, 1996.

22. Palestinian Society for the Protection of Human Rights and the Environment (LAW). LAW, press release, March 12, 1998. The Palestinian police also abducted and held for a day an Israeli Arab citizen, Bassam Id of the B'tzelem human rights organization on January 3, 1996, after he had helped write reports critical of the PA. *New York Times*, January 4 and 19, 1996. Jibril Rajub responded to Id's human rights' work by accusing him of being an "Israeli police agent." *Jerusalem Post*, August 27, 1995.

23. *New York Times*, July 31, 1996; *Washington Post*, August 20, 1996.

24. *New York Times*, August 4 and 5, 1996; Human Rights Monitoring Group, "Deaths in Detention: A Pattern of Abuse, Illegality and Impunity," cited in *Ha'aretz*, December 18, 1997. Voice of Palestine, August 1, 1996 in *FBIS*, August 2, 1996; *New York Times*, August 2, 1996; *Washington Post*, August 20, 1996.

25. *Middle East Mirror* August 15, 1996.

26. Amin Hindi, head of the PA Intelligence Service, told reporters that the riot was organized by the Hamas political leadership in Jordan.

27. *Palestine Report*, August 9, 1996. Included on this committee were ministers Muhammad Nashashibi, Frayh Abu Midayn, Jamal Tarifi, and Sa'ib Arikat, as well as PA Secretary-General Tayyib Abd al-Rahim.

28. Abu-Amr, op. cit., p. 91.

29. As the PLO official and cabinet minister Nabil Amr put it, Reuters, August 5, 1998.

30. A list of those elected can be found in *Middle East Mirror*, January 22, 1996. For a full list and analysis, see Rubin, *Transformation of Palestinian Politics*, op. cit., Appendix 2, pp. 206–212. See also *Palestine Report*, January 17, 1997; *Ma'ariv*, May 12, 1996.

31. *Palestine Report*, January 17, 1997.

32. Abu-Amr, "Palestinian Legislative Council: A Critical Assessment," op. cit., p. 91.

33. Ibid., p. 95.

34. *Palestine Report*, January 17, 1997.

35. Ibid., June 28, 1996.

36. Ibid., June 14, 1996.

37. Ibid., October 25, 1996.

38. Ibid., July 12, 1996.

39. Ibid., July 12, 1996.

40. Mustafa Bargouti, "Post-Euphoria in Palestine," *Journal of Palestine Studies*, Vol. 25, No. 2 (Winter 1996), p. 161.

41. *Palestine Report*, November 7, 1997.

42. Ibid., November 15, 1996. For an independent evaluation of this period, see CPRS Parliamentary Research Unit, *Evaluation of the Palestinian Legislative Council's First Year, 1996* (Nablus, 1997).

43. *Jerusalem Post*, December 31, 1997.

44. *Journal of Palestine Studies*, Vol. 29, No. 2 (Winter 2000), p. 125.

45. *Al-Ayyam*, June 14, 1999.

46. *Al-Istiqlal*, July 9, 1999.

47. Reuters, May 23, 1996.

48. *Jerusalem Post*, April 25–26, 1996.

49. Author's observations. There were one hundred and eleven other delegates who either abstained or did not participate. Among those opposing the change were Ashrawi and Abd al-Shafi, an important reminder that those who were seen as moderates when it came to democracy were often extremists when it came to the peace process.

50. International Policy Institute for Counterterrorism Chronology, downloaded from <http://www.ict.org.il>.

51. Author's observations at the scene.

52. Ibid.

53. Interview with Jewish Telegraphic Agency, November 10, 1995.

54. *Jerusalem Post*, November 2, 2000.

55. Interviews with Eitan Haber and others.

56. Interview with Carmi Gillon.

57. Voice of Palestine, February 28, 1996 in *FBIS*, February 29, 1996.

58. Voice of Palestine, January 6, 1996, in *FBIS*, January 7, 1996; *New York Times*, January 6 and 7, 1996; *Middle East Mirror*, January 8, 1996; *Filastin al-Muslima*, February 1996; and *al-Hayat al-Jadida*, July 21, 1996.

59. *Washington Post*, February 25 and March 3, 1996; *New York Times*, February 26 and March 4 and 5, 1996; *Kol Israel*, March 2, 1996, in *FBIS*, March 4, 1996. Authors' observations of the Tel Aviv attack.

60. He added, "It is also binding on any PLO Executive Committee and any Palestinian National Authority." *Al-Sharq al-Awsat*, January 8, 1995, in *FBIS*, January 10, 1995. For another perspective on the election's effects, see Marwan Bishara, "The Defeat of Peres-A Defeat for Oslo" [Arabic], *al-Siyasa al-Filastiniyya*, Vol. 3, No. 11 (Summer 1996). Despite the title, Bishara concludes that if Peres had won the election Israeli policy would have been the same.

61. Barry Rubin, "External Influences on Israel's 1996 Election," in Dan Elazar and Shmuel Sandler, *Israel's 1996 Election* (Frank Cass, 1998).

62. *Washington Post*, June 1, 1996.

63. Dajani, op. cit; *al-Quds*, November 15, 1996.

64. *Palestine Report*, November 8, 1996.

65. *Palestine Report*, July 5, 1996, and November 28, 1997.

66. Ibid.

67. Jerusalem Media and Communication Center (JMCC) poll, December 13–14, 1996, in *Palestine Report*, January 3, 1997.

68. JMCC and Tami Steinmetz Center for Peace Research, November–December 1997, in *Palestine Report*, December 15, 1997.

69. Raji Sourani, "Human Rights in the Palestinian Authority: A Status Report," *Peacewatch*, No. 168 (Washington, D.C., June 10, 1998).

70. See, for example, on Palestinian police training in Germany, *Ha'aretz*, April 4, 1998.

71. Interview with former CIA official.

72. Interview with former CIA official; "How the CIA Operates in Israel." *Kol Ha-Ir*, November 24, 2000, pp. 54–60.

73. Ibid.

74. *Jerusalem Post*, March 14, 1996.

75. Interview with former Assistant Secretary of State Edward Walker, April 29, 2002, and confirmed by Ross interview.

76. *Ha'aretz*, April 1, 1998.

77. *Ma'ariv*, March 1, 1998; *Yediot Aharnot*, March 25, 1998.

78. *Jerusalem Post*, June 7 and 10, 1994.

79. Ibid.

80. Voice of Palestine, July 17, 1995, in *FBIS*, July 21, 1995.

81. Channel 2 television documentary, June 7, 1997. Text in *Mid-East Dispatch*, July 28, 1998.

82. *Yediot Aharnot*, March 6, 1998.

83. *Al-Dustur*, May 24 and 31, 1997.

84. Text of Arafat speech, March 15, 1997, Palestinian National Authority official Web site, downloaded from <http://www.pna.net/speeches/0397/1501e.html>.

85. *Palestine Report*, September 13, 1996.

86. Interview with Benjamin Netanyahu, May 31, 2001.

87. Interviews.

88. The following account is taken from interviews with Dore Gold, May 31, 2002, and others present.

89. Gold interview.

90. Ibid.

91. Transcript of Press Conference after Netanyahu-Arafat meeting, September 4, 1996.

92. *Palestine Report*, October 4, 1996.

93. Interview with Israeli official; interview with Netanyahu.

94. Arafat's speech in Gaza, March 15, 1997, downloaded from PNA Official Website: <http://www.pna.net/speeches/0397/1501e.html>.

95. *Palestine Report*, October 18, 1996.

96. Author's observations.

97. *New York Times*, March 14, 1997.

98. *Washington Post* and *New York Times*, October 7, 1996.

99. *Los Angeles Times*, March 4, 1997.

100. Gold interview.

101. Nidal Ismail, "Is Corruption the Problem?" *Palestine Report*, November 28, 1997.

102. Reuters, March 23, 1997; interviews.

103. *Jerusalem Post*, August 3, 1997.

104. *Washington Post*, January 31, 1997.

105. Yasin was released following a botched Israeli attempt to assassinate a high-ranking Hamas official in Jordan.

106. *Jerusalem Report*, October 30, 1997.

107. *Financial Times*, September 5, 1997; *Journal of Palestine Studies*, Vol. 27, No. 2 (Winter 1998), pp. 113–125.

108. Nidal Ismail, "Is Coruption the Problem?" *Palestine Report*, November 28, 1997; Ziyad Abu-Amr, "The Palestinian Legislative Council," *Guardian*, July 15, 1997.

109. *Al-Hayat al-Jadida*, May 24, 1999; *Haaretz*, May 26, 1999; *al-Ayyam*, February 13, 1999, *FBIS*; *al-Quds*. January 6, 1999, *FBIS*.

110. *Jerusalem Post*, January 7, 1998.

111. *International Herald Tribune*, June 25, 1998; *Ha'aretz*, March 8 and July 14, 1998; *Jerusalem Post* and *al-Quds*, August 6, 1998. For a full list of the cabinets, see Rubin, *Transformation*, op. cit., pp. 203–205.

112. Center for Palestine Research and Studies (CPRS) Poll No. 33, June 3–6, 1998. See also JMCC, Public Opinion Poll No. 19, April 1997 and CPRS Public Opinion Poll No. 27, April 1997, which found that 33.8 percent considered the PLC's performance to be good, 27.7 percent believed it to be average, and 24.1 percent found it to be bad. See also *Palestine Report*, January 3, 1997; JMCC poll, December 13–14, 1996.

113. Center for Palestine Research and Study poll, June 3–5, 1999.

114. Ibid.

115. *Jerusalem Post*, April 19, 1998.

116. *Al-Quds,* September 28, 1998, in *FBIS.*

117. *Jerusalem Post,* October 22, 1998

118. Interview on NBC-TV "Today" show, February 8, 1999.

119. For the text of the agreement, see Laqueur and Rubin, op. cit., pp. 529–534.

120. *Jerusalem Post,* October 25, 1997.

121. *Middle East Monitor,* January 4, 1999.

122. *Jerusalem Post,* November 12, 1999.

123. For the text of Clinton's speech, see Laqueur and Rubin, op. cit., pp. 535–541.

124. Interview with Ross, May 1, 2002.

125. *Jerusalem Post,* September 17, 1999.

126. Hani al-Masri, *al-Ayyam,* December 11, 1999, in *FBIS.*

127. CPRS poll, June 3–5, 1999.

128. Ibid.

CHAPTER 8

1. Interview with Barak in Benny Morris, "Camp David and After: An Exchange, Part 1," *New York Review of Books,* June 13, 2002.

2. Interview.

3. Interview with Ehud Barak, June 18, 2002.

4. Interview with Gilad Sher, May 3, 2001.

5. Ibid.; interview with Ross and others.

6. Interview with Ross.

7. Interview with Sher and others.

8. Ibid.

9. Interview with Ross.

10. Ibid.

11. Interview with Sher.

12. Interview with Martin Indyk, May 9, 2002, and Ross interview.

13. Interview with Toni Verstandig, May 14, 2002.

14. Ross interview.

15. Ibid.; interview with U.S. official.

16. Akram Hanieh, "The Camp David Papers," *Journal of Palestine Studies,* Vol. 30, No. 2, Winter 2001. Hanieh was editor of the Palestinian daily *al-Ayyam,* a close adviser of Arafat, and a member of the Palestinian team. Consequently, this can be regarded as an official Palestinian version of the summit.

17. *New York Times,* July 26, 2001.

18. Interview with Barak.

19. *Al-Ayyam,* July 28, 2001, translation in MEMRI No. 249, August 1, 2001.

20. Ross interview.

21. Agha and Malley, op. cit., *New York Review of Books,* June 13, 2002.

22. Ross interview.

23. Interview with American Middle East official and Camp David participant, May 30, 2002; Malley and Agha, op. cit., August 9, 2001.

24. Ross interview.

25. Ibid.

26. Interview with Danny Yatom, July 2, 2001.

27. Benny Morris, op. cit.

28. Interviews with those present.

29. Hanieh, op. cit.; Ross interview.

30. Interview with Ross.

31. Ibid.

32. Ibid. Ross stated that accounts in Israeli newspapers "bore no relationship to what was put on the table. They were so far beyond anything that was ever discussed in private at every stage."

33. Ibid.

34. Verstandig interview.

35. *New York Times*, March 25, 2001.

36. Interview with Shlomo Ben Ami, May 29, 2001.

37. American official interview.

38. Interview with Ross.

39. Interview with Barak; Morris, op. cit.; *New York Times*, July 26, 2001; Ross interview.

40. Interview with U.S. official.

41. Interview; Hanieh, op. cit.; Ross interview.

42. Ross interview.

43. Interviews, including U.S. officials and Shlomo Ben Ami, May 29, 2001.

44. Interviews with U.S. and Israeli officials. Some Israelis thought Abu Mazin was pushing Arafat toward a tougher line. Yatom interview.

45. Interview with Abu Mazin, "Had Camp David Convened Again, We Would Take the Same Positions." *Al-Ayyam* July 28 and 29, 2001. MEMRI, Nos. 249 and 250, August 1 and 2, 2001.

46. *Washington Post*, July 24, 2001; *Ma'ariv*, April 6, 2001.

47. Quoted in Hanieh, op. cit., p. 80.

48. Ross interview.

49. This account is taken from numerous interviews. It is interesting to note that where Palestinian accounts vary from those of Israel and American participants, they often claim Barak offered more, rather than less, regarding borders.

50. This was also referred to as giving "functional sovereignty" to the Palestinians and "residual sovereignty" to Israel.

51. *New York Times*, July 26, 2001.

52. Ross interview.

53. Barak in Morris, op. cit.

54. The ending to a family name "ian," meaning "son of" in Armenian, is a common one among that people.

55. Stated in an interview with *La Repubblica*, February 13, 2002.

56. Hanieh, op. cit.

57. Ibid.

58. *Al-Hayat al-Jadida*, September 20, 2000.

59. Yatom interview.

60. *Newsweek*, July 24–25, 2001. Confirmed by interviews. Asked why they would say such things, a Palestinian delegate suggested that to admit otherwise would be to "say that Islam is wrong."

61. Ross interview.

62. Interviews.

63. Ben Ami interview.

64. Abu Alaa later said, "We agreed in Camp David to land swaps equal in size and quality, but we did not recognize" the principle of Israeli settlement blocs. *Al-Ayyam*, January 29, 2001.

65. Ross interview.

66. *New York Times*, July 26, 2001.

67. Interview with American official; interview with Ross, and other interviews.

68. Interview with Barak; Morris, op. cit.

69. Malley and Agha, op. cit.

70. Ross interview.

71. Hanieh, op. cit.

72. Interviews with U.S. officials

73. *Newsweek*, March 31, 2001.

74. Interviews.

75. "The Prince: How the Saudi Ambassador Became Washington's Indispensable Operator," *New Yorker*, March 24, 2003, pp. 45, 55–56.

76. Ross interview.

77. *Palestine Report*, July 15, 2000; Verstandig interview. Rashid was said to be preparing a $40 billion claim which included refugee compensation, infrastructure projects, development assistance, and even a pension fund.

78. Verstandig, Ross, and other interviews.

79. Abu Mazin, op. cit.

80. Hanieh, op. cit.

81. Interview with U.S. official.

82. Hanieh, op. cit.

83. Ross interview.

84. Ibid.

85. White House, Statement on the Middle East Peace Talks at Camp David, Washington, D.C., July 25, 2000.

86. Interview with U.S. official.

87. Voice of Palestine, July 26, 2000, in BBC Survey of World Broadcasts, July 27, 2000.

88. Interview with Barak.

89. *Al-Hayat al-Jadida*, June 26, 2000.

90. Interview with U.S. official.

91. *Al-Hayat al-Jedida*, July 20, 2000.

92. Author's observations.

93. *Al-Quds*, September 17, 2000.

94. *Al-Ayyam*, December 6, 2000, in MEMRI, No. 194, March 9, 2001. He made similar remarks in *al-Safir*, March 3, 2001, in MEMRI, No. 194, March 9, 2001. See also *al-Ayyam*, December 6, 2000.

95. *Al-Hayat al-Jadida*, December 7, 2001. Translation in MEMRI, No. 165, December 13, 2001.

96. His statement was made on April 12, 2001, "Viewpoints Regarding the Development of the Intifada and Its Goals," in *al-Dirasat al-filistiniyya*, No. 47 (Summer 2001), p. 44.

97. *New York Times*, July 26, 2001.

98. Ibid.; Barak interview.

99. Interview with a U.S. official.

100. "60 Minutes," November 2000; *The Guardian*, April 30, 2001; *Der Spiegel*, *FBIS*.

101. *Al-Hayat*, September 29, 2001.

102. Dennis Ross, Margaret Warner, and Jim Hoagland, "From Oslo to Camp David to Taba: Setting the Record Straight," *Peacewatch*, Number 340, August 14, 2001.

103. *Al-Hayat al-Jadida*, December 7, 2001. Translation in MEMRI, No. 165, December 13, 2001.

104. Morris, op. cit.

105. Interview, ABC-TV, January 15, 2001.

106. *Time*, October 16, 2000.

107. Interview.

108. Transcript of "Clinton-Mubarak Statement at End of Mideast Summit," October 17, 2000; interviews with U.S. officials.

109. Interview, "60 Minutes," November 1, 2000.

110. *Al-Sharq al-Awsat*, November 26, 2000.

111. Observed by authors.

112. For the text of the Clinton plan, see Laqueur and Rubin, op. cit., pp. 562–564.

113. White House statement, December 23, 2000.

114. Interview with Ross, Fox News, April 21, 2002.

115. Ibid.

116. *Al-Ayyam*, January 2, 2000, in MEMRI, No. 170, January 3, 2001.

117. Interview with Ross.

118. Interview with U.S. official.

119. Hussein Agha and Robert Malley, "Camp David and After: An Exchange, Part 2, A Reply to Ehud Barak," *New York Review of Books*, June 13, 2002. Exchange, Wafa News Agency, June 21, 2000.

120. *Al-Sharq al-Awsat*, August 1, 2002. Translation in *FBIS*.

121. "44 reasons why Fateh Movement rejects the Proposals made by U.S. President Clinton," in Fatah Movement Central Publication, *Our Opinion*, January 1–7, 2001, downloaded at the PA's official Web site <http://www.pna.gov.ps/peace/44_reasons.htm>.

122. Text in Laqueur and Rubin, op. cit., pp. 83–86.

123. Fatah Movement, "44 reasons," op. cit.

124. Ibid.

125. Press conference, Palestine Media Center, April 9, 2001.

126. *Al-Ayyam*, January 26, 2001.

127. *Wall Street Journal*, March 29, 2002.

128. Verstandig interview.

129. Barak interview.

130. *Al-Ayyam*, January 28, 2001. Translated in MEMRI, No. 184, February 1, 2001.

131. *Al-Quds*, January 28, 2001. Translated in MEMRI, No. 184, February 1, 2001.

132. *Al-Ayyam*, January 29, 2001; *al-Hayat*, January 28, 2001.

133. Barak in Morris, op. cit.

134. *Al-Ayyam*, January 26, 2001. Translated in MEMRI, No. 184, February 1, 2001; *al-Quds*, January 26, 2001.

135. Interview.

136. *Newsweek*, July 24–25, 2001.

137. *New York Times*, May 31, 2001.

138. Text of speech, downloaded from <http://palestineaffairscouncil.org/arafat_economic.htm>.

139. *Al-Ayyam*, January 29, 2001; Associated Press, March 27, 2001.

140. Interview with Shimon Peres, in Scott Lasensky, "Underwriting Peace in the Middle East: U.S. Foreign Policy and the Limits of Economic Inducements," *MERIA Journal*, Vol. 6, No. 1 (March 2002), p. 97. Downloaded from <http://meria.idc.ac.il/journal/2002/issue1/lasensky.pdf>.

141. Interviews.

142. Interview with Palestinian official.

143. *New York Times*, April 4, 2001.

144. Urqhart, op. cit., p. 270.

145. *Palestine Report*, July 12, 2000.

146. Quoted in *New York Times*, November 20, 1984.

147. *New York Times*, March 11, 2001.

CHAPTER 9

1. Interview with U.S. official.

2. *Al-Sharq al-Awsat*, August 1, 2002. Translation in *FBIS*. He based this claim on his questionable assertion that he had been "since 1956 a reserve soldier in the Egyptian army's Engineers Corps. I am still in the army reserves till now."

3. *Al-Qabas*, May 10, 1990.

4. Interview with Ross.

5. Interview with Yusuf Sayegh, January 28, 2002.

6. Quoted from a close friend of Arafat, confirmed in an interview with Indyk.

7. Aburish, op. cit., p. 193.

8. Interviews with Palestinians.

9. This point is discussed in chapters 7 and 8, as well as in Barry Rubin, *The Transformation of Palestinian Politics*, op. cit.

10. *New York Times*, December 25, 1969.

11. Arafat interview in *Playboy*, op. cit., September 1988.

12. Jamal al-Surani, *al Majallah*, November 21, 1989.

13. Reuters, February 25, 2001. Arafat did not fight in the 1948, 1967, or 1973 Arab-Israeli wars, nor did he even direct PLO forces during the September 1970 battles in Jordan.

14. Interviews with U.S. officials.

15. Robert O. Freedman, "A Talk with Arafat," *New York Review of Books*, April 13, 1989.

16. This is according to a doctor who had first-hand knowledge of Arafat's health, interview.

17. Abu Sharif and Mahnaimi, op. cit., p. 219.

18. Interviews with Palestinians, other Arabs, and U.S. officials. But Arafat's stare was something dating from his childhood. See chapter 1.

19. See, for example, the Palestinian political scientist Ali Jarbawi, quoted in *Jerusalem Post*, June 29, 1999.

20. Interview with Palestinian intellectual.

21. Interview.

22. Interviews.

23. Interview with U.S. official.

24. Cited in Shahram Chubin, "Iran's Strategic Predicament," *Middle East Journal*, Vol. 54, Issue 1 (Winter 2000).

25. Oren Shachor recounted, "I asked him why he was wearing a uniform if it was peace time and he said, 'It's not the right time, I will wear it until there is a Palestinian state.'" Interview with Shachor.

26. Urqhart, op. cit., p. 270.

27. Aburish, op. cit., 193. Confirmed by interviews with Palestinians.

28. Interviews with many officials, journalists, and others.

29. Interview with Uri Savir.

30. Interviews with Pundak, Peri, and others.

31. Interview with Peri.

32. *New York Times*, March 11, 2001.

33. Interview.

34. Interview.

35. Interview.

36. Singer interview.

37. Ibid.

38. Interview. The issue of the maps at the 1994 Cairo signing was another example.

39. Ashrawi, op. cit., pp. 256–258.

40. Interviews with Palestinian, American, and Israeli negotiators.

41. Interview with Ross.

42. Even Hirschfeld, one of the architects and main champions of the Oslo agreement, concluded that Arafat wanted to "keep [his] options open against the logic of Oslo." Hirschfeld interview.

43. *New York Times*, January 28, 2002.

44. Interview with Ben-Ami, Maariv, April 3, 2001. Translation in MEMRI, No. 209, April 24, 2001.

45. Interviews with American and Israeli negotiators.

46. Interviews. For two examples of Mubarak's anger toward Arafat during the 1994 Cairo negotiations, see chapter 5. Tlas statement, BBC, August 4, 1000; Zayd bin Ghayam in *al-Watan*, May 10, 2002 in MEMRI, No. 380, May 15, 2002.

47. Interview.

48. Numerous interviews.

49. Numerous interviews with Arabs from several countries, Palestinians, and U.S. officials.

50. Interview.

51. CPRS Poll # 37, November 19, 1998. For a detailed study of Palestinian public opinion, see Khalil Shikaki, "The Peace Process and Political Violence,"

MERIA Journal, Vol. 2, No. 1 (March 1998), downloaded from <http://www.biu.ac.il/SOC/besa/meria/journal/1998/issue1/jv2n1a2.html>. Candidates of the Islamists (Yasin) and forces demanding more democracy on the left (Abd al-Shafi) usually received less than 10 percent support each.

52. Birzeit University Development Studies Program Poll, February 8 10, 2001, pp. 8–11.

53. Interviews; *New York Times*, June 29, 1999.

54. "Billionaire Kings, Queens & Despots," *Forbes*, March 17, 2003; Nathan Vardi, "Auditing Arafat," *Forbes*, March 17, 2003. See chapter 5 for an identical remark by a Jordanian official in 1986.

55. Interviews.

56. Rashid Khalidi, *Under Siege* (New York, 1986), p. 32; Jean Genet, *Prisoner of Love* (London, 1989), p. 120.

57. Interviews with Palestinian officials and journalists.

58. *New York Times*, June 29, 1999; *Palestine Report*, August 18, 1999.

59. Author's conversations with Palestinians.

60. Told in various versions to author by Palestinians.

61. Interview with eyewitness.

62. Urqhart, op. cit., p. 270.

63. *Al-Sharq al-Awsat*, April 18, 2002, translation in MEMRI, No. 92, April 26, 2002.

64. *MECS* 1991, op. cit., pp. 213 and 219.

65. Many events within each cycle, discussed in previous chapters, also illustrate these points, including PLO subversion in Sudan in 1973, the loss of the U.S.-PLO dialogue in 1990, and the bombing campaign of 1996.

66. Friedman, op. cit., p. 556.

67. Hamas and Islamic Jihad only appealed to those who were Islamists, while the PFLP, DFLP, or Communist party were supported by small groups who were attracted to secular leftist views. Most of those who opposed Arafat, including al-Saiqa, the Arab Liberation Front, Abu Nidal, and many others, were in the pay of the Syrians, Iraqis, Libyans, or Jordanians.

68. Interview with Arafat, August 1968, in *IDOP* 1968, op. cit., p. 413; interview with Abu Iyad, January 9, 1971, *IDOP* 1971, op. cit., p. 352. Arafat used almost precisely the same words in December 1977—*IDOP* 1977, op. cit., p. 458—and again in 1988, "Knowing the Enemy," *Time*, November 11, 1988, pp. 47–48.

69. Interview.

70. Text of JMCC report on May-June 2002 poll; cited in Reuters, June 11, 2002.

71. *Observer*, October 27, 1968.

72. *IDOP* 1968, op. cit., pp. 301, 379. When Senator Robert Kennedy was assassinated by a Palestinian in 1968, Fatah claimed that the killer "must undoubtedly have been a tool employed by world Zionism, by persons having political, personal or capitalistic interests, and by the American CIA."

73. See, for example, Algiers television, March 22, 1990; *FBIS*, March 23, 1990, pp. 4 and 6.

74. *Jerusalem Post*, June 1, 2001.

75. Arafat interview in *Playboy*, op. cit., p. 35.

76. Ibid.

77. Arafat had also falsely accused the Jordanians of massacres in 1970. See chapter 2.

78. *Al-Rai al-Am*, December 12, 2001.

79. Interview with Palestinians.

80. *The Australian*, April 13–14, 2002.

81. *Ha'aretz*, September 13, 2001.

82. Allman, op. cit.

83. *Playboy* interview, op. cit., September 1988.

84. Ghassan Khatib, "An Internal Conflict of Interests," *Palestine Report*, August 18, 1999. But it is typical of Arafat's ability to coopt people that Khatib, one of his most cogent critics, joined Arafat's cabinet in 2002 as minister of labor.

85. *Al-Wasat*, January 9–15, 1995, translation in *FBIS*, January 13, 1995.

86. Interviews. Sometimes he refers specifically to exams in Kuwait as his example.

87. Interviews with Palestinian officials and journalists.

88. Interviews with Gaza residents.

89. See for example, Thomas Kleine-Brockhoff and Bruno Schirra, "Arafat Bombs, Europe Pays," *Die Zeit*, June 7, 2002.

90. PA television, November 29, 2000, transcript in *Palestinian Media Watch Bulletin*, December 3, 2000.

91. Fouad Ajami, *Wall Street Journal*, March 29, 2002.

92. Ashrawi, op. cit., p. 249.

93. Text, Arafat's speech at the Swedish Parliament building, December 5, 1998.

94. *New York Times*, December 25, 1969.

95. *Al-Hayat al-Jadida*, November 25, 2000.

96. Iyad Sarraj, "Oslo, Democracy and the Return of al-Hakeem," *Palestine Report*, August 18, 1999.

97. *Al-Hayat al-Jadida*, November 27, 2000. Translation in MEMRI, No. 160, November 30, 2000.

98. The groups carrying out terrorist attacks during the 2000 intifada never criticized Arafat—in contrast to their complaints about him when he stopped them at times in the 1990s—precisely because he was helping and encouraging the violence. Fatah joined Hamas and Islamic Jihad in a joint declaration of support for Arafat, praising him for continuing the intifada and not falling into the trap of making a negotiated agreement. Armed struggle, they affirmed, was the only way "to force the Israeli enemy, regardless of who rules it, and the U.S. administration, regardless of who leads it, to withdraw and recognize the rights of our people." Letter to Yasir Arafat from all major Palestinian political groups, January 13, 2001, downloaded from <http://www.jmcc.org/new/01/factionlet.htm>.

99. Palestine Satellite Channel Television, December 31, 2001, "37th Palestinian 'Revolution' Anniversary, i.e., first armed attack on Israel," *FBIS*.

100. *Al-Hayat al-Jadida*, December 7, 2001. Translation in MEMRI, No. 165, December 13, 2000.

101. White House transcript, October 11, 2000.

102. Interview with CNN, October 8, 2000.

103. Telex from German Ambassador Juergen Chrobog to German Foreign Ministry, No. 596, March 31, 2001, describing Powell's conversations with Chancellor Gerhard Schroeder, published in *Der Spiegel*, May 21, 2001.

104. Text, Arafat's speech at the Swedish Parliament building, op. cit., December 5, 1990.

CHAPTER 10

1. *Ha'aretz*, January 7, 2002.

2. *New York Times*, March 24, 2002; Gal Luft, "The Karine-A Affair: A Strategic Watershed in the Middle East?" *Peacewatch*, No. 361, January 30, 2002.

3. *Al-Sharq al-Awsat*, August 1, 2002. Translation in *FBIS*.

4. Ibid.

5. Itim news agency, January 25, 2002.

6. *New York Times*, January 26, 2992.

7. *Guardian*, February 24, 2001; *Jerusalem Post*, February 25, 2001; Washington Institute for Near East Policy, "Accounting and Accountability: Defining Donor Requirements for Palestinian Reform," Policywatch #638, July 18, 2002.

8. See chapter 8 and the poll series by the Birzeit University Development Studies Program and the JMCC, op. cit.

9. World Bank, "Fifteen Months—Intifada, Closures and Palestinian Economic Crisis: An Assessment," downloaded from <http://lnweb18.worldbank.org/mna/mena.nsf/61abe956d3c23df38525680b00775b5e/81299af1b1220c528525680e0071d721?OpenDocument>. See also *al-Sharq al-Awsat*, August 1, 2002. Translation in *FBIS*.

10. See, for example, JMCC Poll no. 45, May 29–31 and June 1–2, 2002.

11. Reuters, May 28, 2002.

12. Mustapha Dib to Emir Salman Bo Abed al-Aziz, December 30, 2000, and Yasir Arafat to Mustapha Dib, January 7, 2001, texts in Israel Defense Force (IDF), "Large Sums of Money Transferred by Saudi Arabia to the Palestinians," Captured Document E2, pp. 50–54.

13. *Al-Ahram Weekly*, July 25–31, 2002.

14. Even the Saudi peace plan of March 2002, which Arafat endorsed, had some negative implications for him. Historically, the Arab states had generally maintained that they would accept any peace agreement that Arafat found satisfactory, thus leaving considerable autonomy in his own hands. Now, however, they had set out specific conditions for an agreement. Even though these coincided with Arafat's terms—all the West Bank, Gaza Strip, and east Jerusalem plus a complete right of return—this plan would forever after tie the hands of Arafat or any Palestinian leader who, by accepting less, could be condemned as a sell-out.

15. Interview with U.S. officials.

16. *Al-Sharq al-Awsat*, August 1, 2002. Translation in *FBIS*.

17. *Al-Jazirah* television, December 28, 2002, interviewed by Ghassan Bin-Jiddu.

18. Interviews with Palestinians, Israelis, and American officials and analysts.

19. Gal Luft, "The Palestinian H-Bomb: Terror's Winning Strategy," *Foreign Affairs*, July-August 2002.

20. JMCC Poll No. 41, June 2001.

21. See for example, Al-Aqsa Martyrs Brigades, Southern Area to Yasir Arafat, Text in IDF, "The 'al-Aqsa Martyrs Brigades' and the Fatah Organization," May 3, 2002, TRI 319–02, Document 2, pp. 9 and 11.

22. Fa'ak Kana'an to Yasir Arafat, April 5, 2001, text in IDF, "The Involvement of Arafat, PA Senior Officials and Apparatuses in Terrorism Against Israel and Corruption," Document No. 3.

23. Hussein al-Sheikh to Yasir Arafat, September 19, 2001; Marwan al-Barghouti to Yasir Arafat, January 7, 2002; texts in IDF, "Arafat's and the PA's Involvement in Terrorism (According to Captured Documents)," April 22, 2002, Appendix A, pp. 7–10. Fatah Bethlehem District to Yasir Arafat, July 9, 2001, text in IDF, "Palestinian Authority Captured Documents and their Implications," Appendix A. See also Appendix C, pp. 6 and 12.

24. CBS-TV, "60 Minutes," "The Arafat Papers," September 28, 2002.

25. *New York Times*, June 2, 2001.

26. The letter's text was shown on the German television station Westdeutscher Rundfunk on June 24, 2001, in the scrapbook of a suicide bomber's family. It was sent by the Palestinian Embassy in Jordan under Arafat's signature. *Al-Ayyam*, June 24, 2001, translated in MEMRI, No. 237. July 8, 2001.

27. *Ha'aretz*, June 22, 2001.

28. Wafa press agency, December 18, 2001. Translation in MEMRI, No. 317, December 20, 2001. See also *al-Sharq al-Awsat*, August 1, 2002. Translation in *FBIS*.

29. *Al-Rai Al-am*, December 12, 2001, translated in MEMRI No. 317, December 20, 2001.

30. From an interview in *Al-Majalla*, April 12, 2002, quoted in *New York Times*, April 15, 2002. See also her interview with the Saudi women's magazine, *Sayidaty*, May 3, 2001, as quoted in the Associated Press.

31. *Washington Post*, May 7, 2001.

32. See chapter 3, as well as Arafat's use of deniable terrorism and deliberate "lapses" of control in chapters 4, 5, and 6.

33. *Al-Hayat al-Jadida*, January 4, 2003. Translation in *FBIS*.

34. Ibid.

35. *Ha'aretz*, March 29, 2001.

36. *Ha'aretz*, April 12, 2001.

37. Yezid Sayigh, "Arafat and the Anatomy of Revolt," *Survival*, Vol. 43, No. 3, Autumn 2001, pp. 47–60.

38. JMCC Public Opinion polls. In March 2002 (Poll No. 44) 48.1 percent viewed the goal as establishing a separate state compared to 43.9 percent who wanted to conquer Israel. In the May/June 2002 poll the division was 42.8 percent to 51.1 percent. In the September 2002 poll, the numbers were almost exactly the same as they had been in March. Those accepting a separate Palestinian state also presumably supported this in the context of a total "right of return" for refugees as part of this outcome, though this point was not included in the polling question.

39. Interview with *al-Bayan*, October 7, 2002, translated in *FBIS*.

40. For the full text of the report see <http://usinfo.state.gov/regional/nea/mitchell.htm>.

41. Sayigh, op. cit.

42. Associated Press, September 12, 2001.

43. Associated Press, October 8, 2001; *New York Times*, October 11, 2001.

44. *Al-Sharq al-Awsat*, August 1, 2002, translation in *FBIS*.

45. *Al-Ra'i al-Am*, December 12, 2001, translated in MEMRI No. 317, December 20, 2001.

46. Abu Mahmud Rakkad to Abu Hassan, March 24, 2002, text in "The 'al-Aqsa Martyrs Brigades," op. cit., Appendix B, pp. 32–35.

47. *Jerusalem Report*, February 25, 2002.

48. *Al-Sharq al-Awsat*, August 1, 2002. Translation in *FBIS*.

49. Ibid.

50. On these events, see the prologue.

51. JMCC Poll no. 45, May 29–31 and June 1–2, 2002.

52. *Al-Ahram Weekly*, May 16–22, 2002.

53. *New York Times*, June 26, 2002; *Washington Post*, June 30, 2002.

54. Text downloaded from <http://www.whitehouse.gov/news/releases/2002/06/20020624-3.html>.

55. Ibid.

56. CBS-TV, "Face the Nation," June 30, 2002.

57. Associated Press, June 25, 2002.

58. *Al-Sharq al-Awsat*, August 1, 2002. Translation in *FBIS*.

59. *New York Times*, June 27, 2002.

60. Sh'ath, Abd Rabbu, Ali Qawasma, and Jamal Tarifi. The main novelty in the cabinet was the appointment of a respected professional economist as finance minister and of a former general as the first person to hold the interior ministry other than Arafat himself.

61. Arafat's speech to the PLC on September 9, 2002. Text in JMCC site, downloaded from <http://www.jmcc.org/new/02/sep/arafatspeech.htm>.

62. *New York Times*, May 16, 2002.

63. Associated Press, June 10, 2002.

64. *Al-Hayat*, October 16, 2002, translated in MEMRI, No. 430, October 18, 2002.

65. *Toronto Globe and Mail*, November 12, 2002.

66. Text of Amr's September 3, 2002 letter.

67. Zaki interview.

68. *New York Times*, September 12, 2002.

69. *New York Times*, October 29, 2002.

70. *Jerusalem Post*, October 2, 2002.

71. *New York Times*, March 7, 2003.

72. *New York Times*, March 18, 19, and 20, 2003.

73. Text, interview with NBC News, April 25, 2003; *New York Times*, April 26, 2003.

74. Associated Press, April 24, 2003.

75. For example, State Department spokesman Richard Boucher explained, "You don't have an empowered prime minister; you don't have a leadership that's capable of establishing the institutions of a state unless [he gets] to choose the members of their cabinet." Text, State Department briefing, April 22, 2003.

76. Palestinian Center for Policy and Survey Research (PSR) poll #7, April 3–7, 2003, downloaded from http://www.pcpsr.org/survey/polls/2003/p7a.html.

77. *Al-Sharq al-Awsat*, May 1, 2003.

78. Text of speech, April 29, 2003, downloaded from Palestine Media Center, http://www.palestine-pmc.com/details.asp?cat=2&id=177. See coverage in the *New York Times* and *Washington Post*, April 30, 2003.

79. *Boston Globe*, May 4, 2003.

80. Text of Bush commencement address at the University of South Carolina, Office of the White House Press Secretary, May 9, 2003.

81. *Boston Globe*, May 4, 2003.

82. Ibid., September 22 and 23, 2002. For Arafat's version, see his interview in *al-Hayat*, September 29, 2002, translation in *FBIS*.

83. *New York Times*, September 30, 2002.

84. *New York Times*, January 12, 2003.

85. *Al-Hayat*, October 5, 2002. Translated by MEMRI, No. 428, October 11, 2002.

86. *New York Times*, December 3, 1968.

87. Gaza Television, speech to Arab summit, March 1, 2003. Translation in *FBIS*.

88. Interview with Dubai television, broadcast on Gaza Palestine Television, March 16, 2003. Translation in *FBIS*.

89. Gaza Television, speech to Arab summit, op. cit.

90. Interview with Dubai television, op. cit.

91. *New York Times*, December 3, 1968.

92. Saint-Prot, op. cit., p. 66.

GLOSSARY

Abu Alaa (Qurei, Ahmad): PLO economics expert, Oslo accord negotiator, PA negotiator, and Palestinian Legislative Council speaker.

Abu Iyad (Khalaf, Salah): Cofounder of Fatah, PLO intelligence chief, ally of Arafat, he was assassinated by the Abu Nidal group in 1991.

Abu Jihad (al-Wazir, Khalil): Top Fatah and PLO leader, personally the closest one to Arafat, who was assassinated by Israel in 1988 in Tunis.

Abu Mazin (Abbas, Mahmoud): Veteran member of the PLO Executive Committee, its secretary-general from 1996, and a key architect of the Oslo Agreement. Although often viewed as Arafat's number-two man, he was often neglected by Arafat and increasingly critical of him after 2000. Named prime minister by Arafat in 2003.

Arikat, Saeb: Palestinian leader in Jericho and member of PA negotiating teams. One of the closest indigenous West Bankers to Arafat.

Al-Asad, Hafiz: Leader of Syria from 1970 until his death in 2000. He was generally hostile toward Arafat.

Barak, Ehud: Prime minister of Israel 1999–2001.

Barghouti, Marwan: Leader of the Fatah grassroots movement Tanzim on the West Bank and a key leader of the 2000 Intifada. Loyal to Arafat though not always in agreement with him.

Habash, George: Head of the Popular Front for the Liberation of Palestine (PFLP). Both a rival and an ally of Arafat, he favored revolution throughout the Arab world.

Habash, Sakhr: Head of Fatah's ideology and education department.

Hawatmeh, Naif: Secretary-general of the Democratic Front for the Liberation of Palestine (DFLP).

Hussein, King: Leader of Jordan from 1953 until his death in 1999.

Hussein, Saddam: Leader of Iraq from 1968 and president from 1979.

Al-Husseini, Feisal: Leading Fatah figure in West Bank, PA minister for Jerusalem affairs. Perhaps the man who might best have challenged Arafat for leadership in the 1990s, he died of a heart attack in 2000.

Khomeini, Ayatollah Ruhollah: Iranian cleric who led the 1979 Islamist revolution. Arafat courted him, but Khomeini distrusted the Palestinian leader.

Mubarak, Husni: President of Egypt from 1981 and Arafat's patron though increasingly disenchanted with him by 2000.

Nasser, Gamal Abdel: Egypt's leader between 1952 and his death in 1970. The most influential figure in the Arab world and an advocate of Pan-Arab nationalism, he became Arafat's patron after the 1967 war.

Netanyahu, Benjamin: Prime minister of Israel 1996–1999.

Peres, Shimon: Prime minister of Israel 1984–1986 and 1995–1996 and, at other times, foreign minister.

Qaddumi, Faruq (Abu al-Lutuf): PLO foreign minister, opposed to Oslo Agreement.

Al-Qadhafi, Muammar: President of Libya since 1969.

Rabbu, Yasir Abd: DFLP representative to the PLO Executive Committee, formed his own group in 1991, PA negotiator and cabinet member, junior ally of Arafat.

Rabin, Yitzhak: Prime minister of Israel 1974–1977 and 1992–1995. Assassinated by an Israeli right-wing extremist.

Al-Sadat, Anwar: President of Egypt from 1970, negotiated Camp David peace deal with Israel, assassinated by Islamist extremists in 1981.

Sharon, Ariel: Israeli minister of defense 1981–1983, elected prime minister in 2001.

Sha'th, Nabil: Member of Palestinian negotiating teams, PA minister of planning and international cooperation, an important Arafat advisor.

Shuqeiri, Ahmad: Head of the PLO from its founding in 1964 to 1967, client of Nasser and Egypt.

Yasin, Ahmad: Spiritual head of Hamas, arrested by Israel in 1989, released in 1997.

For a detailed study of the Palestinian political elite, see Barry Rubin, *Transformation of Palestinian Politics*, esp. pp. 203–219.

Al-Aqsa Martyrs Brigade: A terrorist group which served as a cover for Fatah operations in the 2000 Intifada.

Black September: A terrorist group which served as a cover for Fatah operations in the early 1970s.

DFLP (Democratic Front for the Liberation of Palestine): Led by Naif Hawatmeh, a self-styled Marxist-Leninist group which often cooperated with and sometimes opposed Arafat. A split created the Palestine Democratic party, led by Yasir Abd Rabbu, which was a junior ally of Fatah.

Fatah: The main group in the PLO, cofounded and led by Arafat.

Fatah Revolutionary Council: Abu Nidal's group, supported at various times by Syria, Iraq, and Libya. Periodically one of Arafat's most deadly Palestinian adversaries.

Force 17: Fatah's internal police and special operations group, which furnished Arafat's personal bodyguards and carried out terrorist attacks.

Hamas: The main radical Palestinian Islamist group, founded in 1987, often in conflict with Arafat but worked closely with him during the 2000 Intifada.

Islamic Jihad: A radical Palestinian Islamist group backed by Iran and Syria.

Muslim Brotherhood: An Islamist revolutionary group established in Egypt in the 1930s.

PA (Palestinian Authority): The governing body headed by Arafat which ruled much of the West Bank and the Gaza Strip from 1994 on.

PFLP (Popular Front for the Liberation of Palestine): A group with strong Pan-Arab nationalist overtones, which favored revolution in most Arab states. Led by George Habash, backed by Syria, often cooperated with and sometimes opposed Arafat.

PLA (Palestine Liberation Army): The regular armed forces of the PLO, some of whose units have been controlled by Arab states.

PLC (Palestinian Legislative Council): Legislative branch of the Palestinian Authority.

PNC (Palestine National Council): The PLO's parliament.

Al-Sa'iqa: The Syrian-controlled Palestinian group which was once the second-largest PLO member but went into sharp decline after the Syria-PLO fighting in Lebanon during the mid-1970s.

Tanzim: Local groups of Fatah on the West Bank, which played a leading role in the 2000 Intifada.

CHRONOLOGY

August 24, 1929: Yasir Arafat is born in Cairo, Egypt.

November 1947: Arab states reject UN partition plan to establish an Israeli and a Palestinian state; Palestinian forces launch guerrilla warfare.

April 1948: Arafat tries to enter Palestine to fight.

May 1948: British army leaves; state of Israel declared; Arab armies cross borders to begin war.

Fall 1949: Arafat enters King Fuad University in Cairo to study engineering.

1950: Arafat takes military training with Muslim Brotherhood.

1952: Arafat elected to student government; Arafat and others take over Palestinian Student Union; officers overthrow Egypt's monarchy and take power, with Gamal Abdel al-Nasser their key leader.

1956: Nasser nationalizes Suez Canal company; Suez War begins; Arafat takes job with Egyptian Cement Corporation.

1957: Arafat leaves Cairo for Kuwait to work for Ministry of Public Works.

October 10, 1959: Arafat and other Palestinians in Kuwait form Fatah; Arafat begins full-time political career.

May 1964: The Palestine Liberation Organization is founded in East Jerusalem under Egyptian patronage and led by Ahmad Shuqeiri.

December 1964: Arafat moves to Lebanon to begin military operations.

January 1, 1965: Fatah launches guerrilla war on Israel.

1966: Arafat becomes a client of Syria though due to internal factional fighting is briefly imprisoned in Damascus.

June 1967: Israel defeats Egypt, Syria, and Jordan in a six-day-long war; captures the Sinai peninsula, Gaza Strip, West Bank, and Golan Heights.

September–December 1967: Arafat becomes a client of Nasser and moves to West Bank to organize a guerrilla war against Israel, which was ultimately unsuccessful.

1968: Arafat and the PLO move to Jordan to set up military base to fight Israel.

March 1968: Battle of Karama in which Israeli forces defeat Arafat's forces, but Arafat turns it into a public relations victory; volunteers flow into the PLO and Fatah.

February 1969: Arafat becomes chairman of the PLO.

November 3, 1969: Arafat signs Cairo agreement with Lebanon, which allows PLO military units to move into south Lebanon near the Israeli border.

September 1970: Civil war erupts in Jordan between PLO and Jordanian forces; Arafat is driven out of Amman.

April 1971: Defeated in the civil war, Arafat leaves Jordan for Lebanon, which now becomes his headquarters.

1971: Arafat creates a covert international terrorist group within Fatah called Black September.

1973: Egypt and Syria attack Israel without notifying or involving Arafat.

February 1974: A resolution formulated by Arafat at the Palestine National Council proposes taking control of territory in the West Bank and Gaza Strip to use as a base for destroying Israel.

November 13, 1974: Arafat addresses the United Nations in New York.

April 1975: Civil war begins in Lebanon.

June 1976: Syria invades Lebanon to ensure that Arafat and his Lebanese allies do not take over the country.

March 26, 1979: Egypt and Israel sign Camp David agreements establishing peace between their countries.

1980: Iraqi forces invade Iran; Arafat supports Iraq.

June 6, 1982: Israeli forces invade Lebanon; PLO forces are quickly defeated and flee northward.

August 30, 1982: Arafat leaves Beirut at the Lebanese government's request; soon moves to Tunis as his new headquarters.

May 1983: Arafat returns to Lebanon to quell internal Syrian-backed PLO revolt.

December 1983: Arafat expelled from Lebanon again after defeats by Syrian army and its Lebanese allies.

December 1987: The Intifada (Palestinian uprising) begins in the West Bank and Gaza.

November 15, 1988: Arafat declares an independent Palestinian state at the Palestine National Council conference, the PLO parliament, in Algiers.

December 14, 1988: Arafat renounces terrorism against Israel and says he recognizes that country; beginning of U.S.-PLO dialogue.

May 1990: United States breaks off dialogue after Arafat refuses to condemn terrorism by PLO groups.

August 1990: Iraq invades Kuwait; Arafat supports Iraqi leader Saddam Hussein.

January–March 1991: U.S.-led international coalition defeats Iraq; Kuwait and other Gulf states expel Palestinians in anger at Arafat's policy.

November 1991: International peace conference, with participation by Palestinians under PLO control, meets in Madrid, Spain.

January 1992: Arafat announces marriage to Suha Tawil.

April 1992: Arafat is almost killed in a plane crash en route from Khartoum, Sudan, to Tripoli, Libya.

January 1993: Beginning of secret meetings between Israelis and Palestinians, which will result in the Oslo Agreement.

September 1993: Signing of the Oslo Agreement on the White House lawn.

May 1994: Agreement signed in Cairo for Israel to withdraw from most of the Gaza Strip and Jericho, which will be turned over to Arafat to rule under the Palestinian Authority.

July 1, 1994: Arafat enters the Gaza Strip for the first time in twenty-seven years to begin governing there.

August 27, 1995: Birth of Yasir and Suha Arafat's daughter, Zahwa, at the American Hospital near Paris.

September 28, 1995: Signing of Oslo-2 Agreement, which provided for Israeli withdrawal from West Bank towns and their turnover to Arafat.

November 4, 1995: Assassination of Israeli prime minister Yitzhak Rabin by an Israeli right-wing extremist.

January 20, 1996: First Palestinian elections ever held elect Arafat as PA leader and most of his slate to the Palestinian Legislative Council.

February–March 1996: Hamas and Islamic Jihad stage a wave of terrorist attacks in Israel.

April 22, 1996: Arafat leads a Palestine National Council meeting in Gaza to revoke clauses in the PLO Charter calling for the liquidation of Israel.

May 31, 1996: Benjamin Netanyahu is elected prime minister.

1997: Arafat takes over most of Hebron.

October 1998: Arafat, Netanyahu, and U.S. president Bill Clinton hold a summit meeting at the Wye Plantation conference center in Maryland.

May 17, 1999: Israelis elect Ehud Barak as prime minister.

July 11–25, 2000: Peace negotiations are held between Arafat and Barak with Clinton's help at Camp David; Arafat rejects the peace plan offered there.

September 28, 2000: Israeli opposition leader Ariel Sharon visits the Temple Mount/Haram al-Sharif area; riots erupt the next day; the second Intifada begins.

December 23, 2000: President Clinton presents his peace plan at a meeting in the White House cabinet room; Arafat rejects the plan.

February 6, 2001: Election of Ariel Sharon as Israeli prime minister.

January 3, 2002: Israeli commandos capture the freighter *Karine A* with arms shipment for Arafat's forces; Arafat's denial of involvement angers U.S. government.

March 2002: After continuing Palestinian terrorist attacks, Sharon orders Israeli army into PA territory; it besieges Arafat in his Ramallah headquarters for thirty-one days.

June 25, 2002: U.S. president George W. Bush calls for Palestinians to elect new leaders.

September 19, 2002: Terrorist attacks provoke Israel to launch its second siege of Arafat in Ramallah, which lasts for ten days.

March 2003: Arafat names Abu Mazin as the PA's first prime minister.

SELECTED BIBLIOGRAPHY

All documents from U.S. State Department records come from Record Group 59, U.S. Department of State records, National Archives, Washington National Reco'rds Center, Suitland, Md. Documents from Nixon papers come from the same archive.

All documents from British Foreign Ministry records come from FO 371, British Archives, Kew Gardens, England.

PERIODICALS

Al-Aam
Al-Akhbar
Amnesty International Reports
Al-Anwar
Arab Report and Record
Arab World
Arab World Weekly
Associated Press
Al-Ayyam
Al-Ba'th
Beirut Daily Star
Al-Bilad
Birzeit University home page, http://www.birzeit.edu
Center for Palestine Research and Studies (CPRS), public opinion polls
Christian Science Monitor

Davar
Der Spiegel
Economist
Federal Broadcast Information Service (FBIS), Daily Report
Filastin al-Muslima
Filastin al-Thawra
Financial Times
Globes
Guardian
Ha'aretz
Al-Hawadith
Al-Hayat
Al-Hayat al-Jadida
International Herald Tribune
Jane's Defence Weekly
Jerusalem Media Communications Center (JMCC) public opinion polls
Jerusalem Post
Jerusalem Report
Joint Publications Research Service
Jordan Times
Journal of Palestine Studies
Kol Israel
LAW (Palestinian Society for the Protection of Human Rights and the Environment), news releases and annual reports
London Observer
Los Angeles Times
Ma'ariv
Manchester Guardian Weekly
MEMRI (Middle East Media Research Institute)
Middle East
Middle East Mirror
Middle East Quarterly
Middle East Review for International Affairs (MERIA) Journal
Mideast Dispatch
Le Monde
Al-Mussawar
Al-Nahar Arab Report
Newsweek
New York Times
Palestine Human Rights Monitor
Palestine Report
Palestine Times
Palestinian Independent Commission for Citizens' Rights Newsletter
Palestinian National Authority Website
PeaceWatch, reports
Playboy
Al-Quds

Reuters
al-Safir
al-Sayyad
Al-Sharq al-Awsat
Shu'un Filastiniyya
Al-Siyasa al-Filastiniyya
al-Thawra
Third World Quarterly
Time
Times (London)
al-Usbu al-Arabi
Wall Street Journal
Washington Post
Washington Times
World Marxist Review
Yediot Aharnot

ARTICLES

Abu Amr, Ziyad. "The Palestinian Legislative Council: A Critical Assessment." *Journal of Palestine Studies* 26, no. 4 (Summer 1997): 90–97.

——. "Pluralism and the Palestinians." *Journal of Democracy* 7, no. 3 (1996): 83–93.

——. "Hamas: A Historical and Political Background." *Journal of Palestine Studies* 22, no. 4 (1993): 5–19.

Abu Khalil, As'ad. "Internal Contradictions in the PFLP: Decision Making and Policy Orientation." *Middle East Journal* 41, no. 3 (Summer 1987): 361–378.

Abu Nizar, Sakher. "The Role of Fatah Movement in Shaping the Palestinian Future." April 1994. Downloaded from http://www.fateh.org.

Agha, Hussein, and Malley, Robert. "Camp David and After: An Exchange. Part 2. A Reply to Ehud Barak." *New York Review of Books*, June 13, 2002.

——. "The Truth about Camp David." *New York Review of Books*, August 9, 2001.

"Agreement between the Hashemite Kingdom of Jordan and the Palestine Liberation Organization, January 7, 1994." *Palestine-Israel Journal* (Spring 1994).

Ajami, Fouad. "Lebanon and Its Inheritors." *Foreign Affairs* 63 (Spring 1985): 778–99.

——. "The End of the Affair: An American Tragedy in the Arab World." *Harper's Magazine* 268 (June 1984): 53–59.

——. "The Shadows of Hell." *Foreign Policy* 48 (Fall 1982): 94–110.

——. "The Arab Road." *Foreign Policy* 47 (Summer 1982).

——. "The Fate of Nonalignment." *Foreign Affairs* 59, no. 2 (Winter 1980–1981).

——. "The Struggle for Egypt's Soul." *Foreign Policy* 35 (Summer 1979).

——. "Stress in the Arab Triangle." *Foreign Policy* 29 (Winter 1977–1978).

——. "Between Cairo and Damascus." *Foreign Affairs* 54, no. 2 (April 1976): 444–61.

Allman, T. D. "On the Road with Arafat." *Vanity Fair*, February 1989.

Amos, John. "The PLO: Millennium and Organization." In *Ideology and Power in the Middle East: Studies in Honor of George Lenczowski*, edited by Peter Chelkowski and Robert Pranger. Durham, N.C., 1988.

Arafat, Yasir. "The Desirable, the Possible, the Acceptable." *Middle East* 103 (May 1983): 20–23.

———. "Interview." *Journal of Palestine Studies* 11, no. 2 (Winter 1982).

Aruri, Naseer. "The PLO and the Jordan Option." *Third World Quarterly* 7 (October 1985): 882–906.

———. "Palestinian Nationalism after Lebanon: The Current Impasse." *American-Arab Affairs* 8 (Spring 1984): 54–65.

Bahatia, Shiham. "Arafat's Torturers Shock Palestinians." *Guardian Weekly*, September 24, 1995.

Barakat, Halim. "Social Factors Influencing Attitudes of University Students in Lebanon towards the Palestinian Resistance Movement." *Journal of Palestine Studies* 1, no. 1: 87–112.

Bargouti, Mustafa. "Post-Euphoria in Palestine." *Journal of Palestine Studies* 25, no. 2 (Winter 1996): 161.

Beer, Eliezer. "The Emergence of Palestinian Arab Leadership: Husaini, Shuqairy, and Arafat." In *The Palestinians and the Middle East Conflict*, edited by Gabriel Ben-Dor. Ramat Gan, 1978.

Ben-Efrat, Roni. "The Telltale Silence of the Post-Oslo Palestinian Press." Lecture presented at the conference "A Twenty-First-Century Dialogue: Media's Dark Age?" in Athens, Greece, May 24–28, 1998.

Bishara, Marwan. "The Defeat of Peres: A Defeat for Oslo." *Al-Siyasa al-Filastiniyya* 13, no. 11 (Summer 1996).

Black, Ian. "Tunis Dilemma as PLO Lies Low." *Guardian*, June 21, 1986.

Brand, Laurie A. "Palestinians in Syria: The Politics of Integration." *Middle East Journal* 42, no. 44 (Autumn 1988): 621–637.

Browne, Donald R. "The Voices of Palestine: A Broadcasting House Divided." *Middle East Journal* 29, no. 2 (1975): 133–150.

Brynen, Rex. "PLO Policy in Lebanon: Legacies and Lessons." *Journal of Palestine Studies* 18, no. 2 (Winter 1989): 59–60.

Center for Palestine Research and Studies. "Special Poll Voting Behavior of al-Najah University Students: Election Day Poll." Nablus, July 19, 1996.

Chubin, Shahram. "Iran's Strategic Predicament." *Middle East Journal* 54, no. 1 (Winter 2000).

Cobban, Helena. "The PLO in the Mid-1980s: Between the Gun and the Olive Branch." *International Journal* 38 (Autumn 1983): 635–651.

Colvin, Marie. "The Ambiguous Yasir Arafat." *New York Times Magazine*, December 18, 1988, pp. 33–36, 60, 63, 66.

Cooley, John K. "China and the Palestinians." *Journal of Palestine Studies* 1, no. 2 (1972): 19–34.

———. "Iran, the Palestinians, and the Gulf." *Foreign Affairs* 57 (Summer 1979): 1018–34.

Corbin, Jane. "The Norway Channel." *Atlantic Monthly*, 1995.

Craig Harris, Lillian. "China's Relations with the PLO." *Journal of Palestine Studies* 7 (Autumn 1977): 123–154.

Dajani, Mohammed S. "The Palestinian Authority and Citizenship in the Palestinian Territories." Palestinian National Authority official Website, http://www.pna.net/reports/mcitizen.htm.

Darboub, Leila. "Palestinian Public Opinion and the Peace Process." *Palestine-Israel Journal* 3, nos. 3 4 (1996): 109 117.

———. "Palestinian Public Opinion Polls on the Peace Process." *Palestine-Israel Journal* 5 (1995): 60–63.

Dawisha, Adeed. "Saudi Arabia and the Arab-Israeli Conflict: The Ups and Downs of Pragmatic Moderation." *International Journal* 38, no. 4 (Autumn 1983): 674–689.

De Atkine, Norvell. "Urban Warfare Lessons from the Middle East." *Special Warfare* (Fall 2001): 20–29.

Dhaher, Ahmad J. "Changing Cultural Perspectives of the Palestinians." *Journal of South Asian and Middle Eastern Studies* 4 (Spring 1981): 38–64.

Diskin, Abraham. "Trends in Intensity Variation of Palestinian Military Activity: 1967–1978." *Canadian Journal of Political Science* 16 (June 1983): 335–348.

Farsoun, Samir. "How Revolutionary Is the Palestinian Resistance? A Marxist Interpretation." *Journal of Palestine Studies* 1, no. 2 (Summer 1972): 52–60.

Foley, Michael. "Democracy Courtesy Thomas Cook." *Index on Censorship* (1996).

Freedman, Robert O. "A Talk with Arafat." *New York Review of Books*, April 13, 1989, pp. 8, 10.

Ghosheh, Ibrahim. "The 1948 Nakba: Facts and Lessons." *Palestine Times*, May 1998.

Golan, Galia. "The Soviet Union and the PLO since the War in Lebanon." *Middle East Journal* 40 (Spring 1986): 285–305.

Haddad, William. "Divided Lebanon." *Current History* (January 1982).

Al-Hajj, Majid. "The Day after the Palestinian State: Arab and Jewish Attitudes in Israel." *Middle East Focus* 13, no. 4 (1991): 23–26.

———. "State, Territory and Boundaries: Attitudes and Positions in the Palestine National Movement." Israeli-Palestinian Peace Research Project, Working Paper Series 2, no. 12 (1991).

Hamid, Rashid. "What Is the PLO?" *Journal of Palestine Studies* 4, no. 4 (Summer 1975): 90–109.

Hanieh, Akram. "The Camp David Papers." *Journal of Palestine Studies* 30, no. 2 (Winter 2001).

Harkabi, Yehoshafat. "The Palestinians in the Fifties and Their Awakening as Reflected in Their Literature." In *Palestinian Arab Politics*, edited by Moshe Maoz. Jerusalem, 1975.

———. "The Revised Palestine National Covenant (1968) and an Israeli Commentary Thereon." *New York University Journal of International Law and Politics* 3, no. 1 (1970): 209–243.

Hechiche, Abdelwahab. "Renaissance et Declin De La Resistance Palestinienne." *Politique Etrangere* 38, no. 5 (1973): 597–620.

Hilal, Jamal. "Features of Poverty in Palestine." *Al-Siyasa al-Filastiniyya* 3, no. 12 (Fall 1996).

———. "The Elections of the Palestinian Legislative Council: A Preliminary Reading of the Results of the Election." *Al-Siyasa al-Filastiniyya* 3, no. 10 (Spring 1996).

Hoffman, Bruce. "The Plight of the Phoenix: The PLO since Lebanon." *Conflict Quarterly* 5 (Spring 1985): 5–17.

Hudson, Michael C. "The Palestinians after Lebanon." *Current History* 84 (January 1985): 16–20, 38–39.

———. "The Palestinians after Lebanon." *Current History* 82 (January 1983): 5–9, 34.

———. "Developments and Setbacks in the Palestinian Resistance Movement, 1967–1971." *Journal of Palestine Studies* 1, no. 3 (Spring 1972): 64–84.

Hummami, Rema. "NGOs: The Professionalization of Politics." *Journal of Race and Class* (1995).

Hussari, Ruba. "Arafat's Law." *Index on Censorship* (March 21, 1996).

———. "The Position of Palestine Islamists on the Palestine-Israel Accord." *Muslim World* 84, nos. 1–2 (1994): 127–154.

Ibrahim, Youssef M. "A Palestinian Revolution without the PLO." *New York Times*, February 14, 1988.

"Inside Al Sharpton's Controversial Meeting with the Palestinian Leader: Lunch with Arafat." *Village Voice*, November 7–13, 2001.

Ioannides, Christos P. "The PLO and the Iranian Revolution." *American-Arab Affairs* 10 (Fall 1984): 89–105.

Jiryis, Sabri. "On Political Settlement in the Middle East: The Palestinian Dimension." *Journal of Palestine Studies* 7, no. 1 (Autumn 1977).

Kelman, Herbert C. "Conversations with Arafat." *American Psychologist* (February 1983): 203–216.

———. "Talk with Arafat." *Foreign Policy* 49 (Winter 1982–1983): 119–139.

Khalidi, Rashid. "The Resolutions of the 19th Palestine National Council." *Journal of Palestine Studies* (Winter 1990).

———. "Palestinian Politics after the Exodus from Beirut." In *The Middle East after the Israeli Invasion of Lebanon*, edited by Robert O. Freedman, 233–53. Syracuse, N.Y., 1986.

———. "Lebanon in the Context of Regional Politics: Palestinians and Syrian Involvement in the Lebanese Crisis." *Third World Quarterly* 7 (July 1985): 495–514.

———. "The Asad Regime and the Palestinian Resistance." *Arab Studies Quarterly* 6, no. 4 (Fall 1984).

———. "The Palestinians in Lebanon: Social Repercussions of Israel's Invasion." *Middle East Journal* 38 (Spring 1984): 255–266.

Khalidi, Walid. "Regiopolitics: Toward a U.S. Policy on the Palestine Problem." *Foreign Affairs* 59 (Summer 1981): 1050–1063.

———. "Thinking the Unthinkable: A Sovereign Palestinian State." *Foreign Affairs* (July 1978): 695–713.

El-Khazen, Farid. "The Rise and Fall of the PLO." *National Interest* 10 (Winter 1987–1988): 39–47.

Khouri, Rami. "A View from the Arab World." June 16, 1998. Downloaded from http://msanews.mynet.net/Scholars/Khouri.

King Hussein. "Throne Speech, November 1, 1967." *American-Arab Affairs* 25 (Summer 1988): 194–198.

Kuttab, Daoud. "A Profile of the Stonethrowers." *Journal of Palestine Studies* 17, no. 3 (Spring 1988).

Lasensky, Scott. "Underwriting Peace in the Middle East: U.S. Foreign Policy and the Limits of Economic Inducements." *MERIA Journal* 6, no. 1 (March 2002): 97.

LAW (Palestinian Society for the Protection of Human Rights and the Environment). "Human Rights Annual Report 1997." March 29, 1998.

———. "Palestinian Legislative Council Basic Law Draft Resolution, Third Reading, Passed October 2, 1997."

———. "Report of the Monitoring Unit on the Elections for the PLC, January 23, 1996."

Legrain, Jean-Francois. "The Successions of Yasir Arafat." *Journal of Palestine Studies* 28, no. 4 (Summer 1999): 13–44.

Malki, Riad. "The Palestinian Opposition and Final-Status Negotiations." *Palestine-Israel Journal* 3, nos. 3–4 (1996): 95–99.

Miller, Aaron David. "Changing Arab Attitudes toward Israel." *Orbis* 32 (Winter 1988): 69–81.

———. "The Palestinians: The Past as Prologue." *Current History* 87 (February 1988): 73–76, 83–85.

———. "The PLO and the Peace Process: The Organizational Imperative." *SAIS Review* 7 (Winter–Spring 1987): 647–675.

———. "The PLO after Tripoli: The Arab Dimension." *American-Arab Affairs* 8 (Spring 1984): 66–73.

———. "Palestinians in the 1980s." *Current History* 83 (January 1984): 17–20, 34–36.

———. "The PLO: What Next?" *Washington Quarterly* 6, no. 1 (Winter 1983): 116–25.

———. "Lebanon: One Year After." *Washington Quarterly* 6 (Summer 1983): 129–141.

Miller, Judith. "The PLO in Exile." *New York Times Magazine*, August 18, 1985, pp. 26–30, 63, 66, 71–72, 76.

Mishal, Shaul. "'Paper War'—Words behind Stones: The Intifada Leaflets." *Jerusalem Quarterly* 51 (Autumn 1989).

Morris, Benny. "Camp David and After: An Exchange. Part 1. An Interview with Ehud Barak." *New York Review of Books*, June 13, 2002.

Moughrabi, Fouad. "The Palestinians after Lebanon." *Arab Studies Quarterly* 5, no. 3 (Summer 1983): 211–219.

Moughrabi, Fouad, and Zurayiq, Elia. "Palestinians on the Peace Process." *Journal of Palestine Studies* 21, no. 1 (1991): 36–53.

Muslih, Muhammad Y. "Moderates and Rejectionists within the Palestine Liberation Organization." *Middle East Journal* 30 (Spring 1976): 127–140.

O'Neill, Bard E. "Towards a Typology of Political Terrorism: The Palestinian Resistance Movement." *Journal of International Affairs* 32, no. 1 (1978): 17–42.

Palestinian Independent Commission for Citizens Rights. *Third Annual Report*. 1998. Downloaded from http://msanews.mynet.net/gateway/piccr/reports.html.

Palestinian Legislative Council. "Self-Evaluation Report." October 30–31, 1996.

Palestinian National Authority. "1998 Second Quarterly Monitoring Report of Donors' Assistance." June 30, 1998. Downloaded from http://www.pna.net/reports/mcitizen.htm.

"Periodicals and Pamphlets Published by the Palestinian Commando Organizations." *Journal of Palestine Studies* 1, no. 1: 136–151.

"Interview: Yasir Arafat." *Playboy*, September 1988, pp. 51–52, 56–59, 62–64, 66.

Qaddumi, Faruq. "Arabs in a Jewish State: Images vs. Realities." *Middle East Insight* (January–February 1990).

——. "Farouk Kaddoumi: An Interview." *Third World Quarterly* 8 (April 1986): 411–424.

——. "Qaddoumi: A West Bank State within Five Years." *Middle East* 71 (1980): 41–43.

Robinson, Glenn E. "The Growing Authoritarianism of the Arafat Regime." *Survival* 39, no. 2 (Summer 1997): 42–56.

Rosen, Jane. "The PLO's Influential Voice at the U.N." *New York Times Magazine*, September 16, 1984, pp. 59–60, 62, 70, 72, 74.

Rosensaft, Menachem. "Meeting the PLO." *Reform Judaism* (Spring 1989).

Rosewicz, Barbara, and Seib, Gerald F. "Aside from Being a Movement, the PLO is a Financial Giant." *Wall Street Journal*, July 21, 1986, pp. 1, 8.

Ross, Dennis, Margaret Warner, and Jim Hoagland. "From Oslo to Camp David to Taba: Setting the Record Straight." *Peacewatch* 340 (August 14, 2001).

Ross, Lauren G. "Palestinians: Yes to Negotiations, Yes to Violence." *Middle East Quarterly* 2, no. 2 (1995): 15–24.

Rouleau, Eric. "The Future of the PLO." *Foreign Affairs* 62 (Fall 1983): 138–156.

——. "The Palestinian Quest." *Foreign Affairs* 53, no. 2 (1975): 264–283.

Roy, Sara. "U.S. Economic Aid to the West Bank and Gaza Strip: The Politics of Peace." *Middle East Policy* 4, no. 4 (October 1996).

Rubenberg, Cheryl. "The Civilian Infrastructure of the Palestine Liberation Organization." *Journal of Palestine Studies* 12 (Spring 1983): 54–78.

——. "The PLO Response to the Reagan Initiative: The PNC at Algiers, February 1983." *American-Arab Affairs* 4 (Spring 1983): 53–69.

Rubin, Barry. "External Influences on Israel's 1996 Election." In *Israel's 1996 Election*, edited by Dan Elazar and Shmuel Sandler. London, 1998.

——. "Reshaping the Middle East." *Foreign Affairs* (Summer 1990).

Rubinstein, Danny. "Bio Sketch: Faruq Qaddumi, the PLO's #2." *Middle East Quarterly* (March 1996): 29–32.

Sahliyeh, Emile F. "Jordan and the Palestinians." In *In the Middle East: Ten Years after Camp David*, edited by William B. Quandt, 279–318. Washington, D.C., 1988.

Satloff, Robert. "Islam in the Palestinian Uprising." *Orbis* 33, no. 3 (Summer 1989).

Sayigh, Yezid. "Arafat and the Anatomy of Revolt." *Survival* 43, no. 3 (Autumn 2001): 47–60.

——. "Palestinian Armed Struggle: Means and Ends." *Journal of Palestine Studies* 16, no. 1 (Autumn 1986).

——. "Fatah: The First Twenty Years." *Journal of Palestine Studies* 13, no. 4 (Summer 1984).

Schliefer, Abdullah. "The Emergence of Fatah." *Arab World* 15, no. 5 (May 1969): 16–20.

Schiller, David Th. "A Battlegroup Divided: The Palestinian Fedayeen." *Strategic Studies* 10 (December 1987): 90–108.

Shadid, Mohammed, and Seltzer, Rick. "Political Attitudes of Palestinians in the West Bank and Gaza Strip." *Middle East Journal* 42 (Winter 1988): 16–32.

Shikaki, Khalil. "The Peace Process and Political Violence." *MERIA Journal* 2, no. 1 (March 1998).

Shipler, David K. "Since Jordan: The Palestine Fedayeen." *Conflict Studies* (September 1973): 18.

al-Shiqaqi, Khalil. "The Peace Process, National Reconstruction, and the Transition to Democracy in Palestine." *Journal of Palestine Studies* 25, no. 2 (Winter 1996).

Siniora, Hanna. "On the Palestinian Struggle." *World Policy* 3 (Fall 1986): 723–738.

Sourani, Raji. "Human Rights in the Palestinian Authority: A Status Report." *Peacewatch* 168 (June 1998).

Stanley, Bruce. "Fragmentation and National Liberation Movements: The PLO." *Orbis* 22 (Winter 1979): 1033–1055.

Supplement on the PLO, *al-Fajr*, May 30, 1986.

Talhami, Ali. "How a Satirist Saw the PLO." *Middle East* (October 1987): 16–18.

Tamimi, Azzam S. "The Legitimacy of Palestinian Resistance: An Islamist Perspective." Paper presented to the Seventh Annual Conference of the Center for Policy Analysis on Palestine, Washington, D.C., September 11, 1998.

Tarbush, Susannah. "Palestinian Groups: The Divided Front." *Middle East Economic Digest* 22 (September 1976): 8–9.

Tully, Shawn. "The Big Moneymen of Palestine Inc." *Fortune*, July 31, 1989.

UNSColo. "Report on Economic and Social Conditions in the West Bank and Gaza Strip." Spring 1998. Downloaded from http://www.arts.mcgill.ca/mepp/unsco/unfront.html.

———. "Report on Economic and Social Conditions in the West Bank and Gaza Strip." October 1997. Downloaded from http://www.arts.mcgill.ca/mepp/unsco/unfront.html.

———. "Report on Economic and Social Conditions in the West Bank and Gaza Strip." April 1997. Downloaded from http://www.arts.mcgill.ca/mepp/unsco/unfront.html.

———. "Report on Economic and Social Conditions in the West Bank and Gaza Strip." Fall 1996. Downloaded from http://www.arts.mcgill.ca/mepp/unsco/unfront.html.

U.S. Department of State. "Abu Nidal Organization." February 1989.

U.S. Information Service. "The Wye River Memorandum Signed at the White House." Washington, D.C., October 23, 1998.

"The Way to Restoring the Violated Rights of the Palestinian People." *World Marxist Review* (1975): 123–132.

Yaniv, Avner. "Phoenix or Phantom? The PLO after Beirut." *Terrorism* 7, no. 3 (1984).

"Yasir Arafat: An Interview." *Third World Quarterly* 7 (October 1985): 882–906.

BOOKS

Abbas, Mahmoud. *Through Secret Channels: The Road to Oslo.* Reading, Mass., 1997.

Abdallah, Samir. *Palestinian Economic Council for Development and Construction.* Nablus, 1994.

Abu Iyad. *My Home, My Land: A Narrative of the Palestinian Struggle.* New York, 1981.

Aburish, Said. *Arafat: From Defender to Dictator.* New York, 1998.

Adams, James. *The Financing of Terror.* New York, 1986.

Ajami, Fouad. *The Arab Predicament: Arab Political Thought and Practice since 1967.* London, 1992.

American Enterprise Institute. *A Conversation with the Exiled West Bank Mayors: A Palestinian Point of View.* Washington, D.C., 1981.

Amnesty International, *Report, 1995.* London, 1995.

Amos, John. *Palestinian Resistance: Organization of a National Movement.* New York, 1980.

Aruri, Naseer, ed. *The Palestinian Resistance to Israeli Occupation.* Wilmette, Ill., 1970.

Ashrawi, Hanan. *This Side of Peace: A Personal Account.* New York, 1995.

Baer, Robert. *See No Evil: The True Story of a Ground Soldier in the CIA's War on Terrorism.* New York, 2002.

Bailey, Clinton. *Jordan's Palestine Challenge, 1948–1983: A Political History.* Boulder, Colo., 1984.

Barghouthi, Mustafa. *Palestinian NGOs and Their Role in Building Civil Society.* Jerusalem, 1994.

Barghuti, Bashir. *The Development of the Palestinian National Movement.* Nablus, 1996.

Bar-Zohar, Michael, and Haber, Eitan. *The Quest for the Red Prince.* New York, 1983.

Beilin, Yossi. *Touching Peace.* London, 1999.

Ben-Tsur, Eytan. *Making Peace.* New York, 2001.

Black, Ian, and Morris, Benny. *Israel's Secret Wars.* New York, 1991.

Borowiec, Andrew. *Modern Tunisia.* Westport, Conn., 1998.

Brand, Laurie A. *Palestinians in the Arab World: Institution Building and the Search for a State.* New York, 1985.

Brynen, Rex. *Sanctuary and Survival.* Boulder, Colo., 1990.

Brzezinski, Zbigniew. *Power and Principle.* New York, 1983.

Buehrig, Edward Henry. *The U.N. and Palestinian Refugees: A Study in Non-Territorial Administration.* Bloomington, Ind., 1971.

Bulloch, John. *Final Conflict.* London, 1983.

———. *Death of a Country.* London, 1977.

Carre, Olivier. *Le Mouvement national Palestinien.* Paris, 1977.

———. *L'Ideologie Palestinienne de resistance.* Paris, 1972.

Carter, Jimmy. *The Blood of Abraham.* Arkansas, 1993.

Center for Palestine Research and Studies. *Comparative Analytical Study of Presidential Veto Power.* Nablus, 1997.

———. *Evaluation of the Palestinian Legislative Council's First Year, 1996.* Nablus, 1997.

———. *Parliamentary Research Unit, Committees in the Palestinian Legislative Council: Proposals for Their Development and Restructuring.* Nablus, 1997.

———. *Palestinians inside Israel and the Peace Process.* Nablus, 1994.

Chaliand, Gerard. *The Palestinian Resistance.* Harmondsworth, U.K., 1972.

Christopher, Warren. *American Hostages in Iran: The Conduct of a Crisis.* New Haven, Conn., 1985.

Cobban, Helena. *The Palestinian Liberation Organization: People, Power and Politics.* New York, 1984.

Cooley, John K., and March, Green. *Black September: The Story of the Palestinian Arabs.* London, 1973.

Corbin, Jane. *The Norway Channel.* New York, 1994.

Dawisha, Adeed. *Syria and the Lebanese Crisis.* New York, 1980.

Dayan, Moshe. *Story of My Life.* New York, 1976.

Deeb, Maurice. *The Lebanese Civil War.* New York, 1980.

Dobson, Christopher. *Black September: Its Short, Violent History.* London, 1975.

Dobson, Christopher, and Payne, Ronald. *The Never-Ending War: Terrorism in the 80s.* New York, 1987.

El-Edross, S. A. *The Hashmite Arab Army 1908–1979: An Appreciation and Analysis of Military Operations.* Amman, 1980.

Evron, Yair. *War and Intervention in Lebanon.* London, 1987.

Fallaci, Oriana. *Interview with History.* New York, 1976.

Farid, Abdel Magid. *Nasser: The Final Years.* New York, 1994.

Fathah. *La Revolution Palestinienne et les Juifs.* Paris, 1970.

Frangi, Abdallah. *The PLO and Palestine.* London, 1983.

Frankel, Glenn. *Beyond the Promised Land: Jews and Arabs on the Hard Road to a New Israel.* New York, 1994.

Friedman, Thomas. *From Beirut to Jerusalem.* New York, 1989.

Gabriel, Richard A. *Operation Peace for Galilee: The Israeli-PLO War in Lebanon.* New York, 1985.

Genet, Jean. *Prisoner of Love.* London, 1989.

Ghabra, Shafeeq. *Palestinians in Kuwait.* Westview, Conn., 1987.

Golan, Galia. *The Soviet Union and the Palestine Liberation Organization.* New York, 1980.

Gowers, Andrew, and Walker, Tony. *Behind the Myth: Yasser Arafat and the Palestinian Revolution.* London, 1990.

Gresh, Alain. *The PLO: The Struggle Within.* London, 1983.

Hamami, Jamil. *Islamists and the Next Phase.* Nablus, 1994.

Abd el-Hamid, Dina. *Duet for Freedom.* London, 1988.

Hareven, Alouph. *Retrospect and Prospects: Full and Equal Citizenship?* Tel Aviv, 1998.

Harkabi, Yehoshafat. *The Palestinian Covenant and Its Meaning.* London, 1979.

———. *Palestinians and Israel.* Jerusalem, 1974.

———. *Fedayeen Action and Arab Strategy.* London, 1968.

Harris, William. *Faces of Lebanon: Sects, Wars and Global Extensions.* Princeton, N.J., 1997.

Hart, Alan. *Arafat: A Political Biography.* Bloomington, Ind., 1989.

Al-Hasan, Hani. *The Relations between PLO and PA Institutions.* Nablus, 1996.

Heikal, Mohammed. *Secret Channels: The Inside Story of Arab-Israeli Peace Negotiations.* London, 1996.

———. *Autumn of Fury: The Assassination of Sadat.* London, 1983.

———. *The Road to Ramadan.* New York, 1975.

Abu Hilal, Ali, and Salim, Walid. *National Opposition and National Elections.* Nablus, 1995.

Hirst, David. *The Gun and the Olive Branch.* London, 1977.

Hourani, Albert. *Political Society in Lebanon: A Historical Introduction.* Cambridge, Mass., 1985.

Ignatius, D. *Agents of Innocence.* London, 1991.

Institute for Palestine Studies. *The Resistance of the Western Bank of Jordan to Israeli Occupation.* Beirut, 1967.

International Documents on Palestine (IDOP), 1967–1982.

International Symposium on Palestine. *Palestine Discussion Papers.* Kuwait, 1971.

Israel Foreign Ministry. *Israel-Palestinian Interim Agreement on the West Bank and Gaza Strip, September 28, 1995.* Jerusalem, 1995.

Israeli, Raphael, ed. *PLO in Lebanon: Selected Documents.* London, 1983.

Jadallah, Muhammad. *Opposition and the Palestinian National Authority.* Nablus, 1994.

Ja'fari, Mahmoud. *The Palestinian-Jordanian Trade Agreement.* Nablus, 1997.

Jansen, Michael E. *The United States and the Palestinian People.* Beirut, 1970.

Jarbawi, Ali, et al. *Palestinian Opposition: Where To?* Nablus, 1994.

Joumblatt, Kamal, and Lapousterie, Philippe. *I Speak for Lebanon.* London, 1982.

Jumblatt, K. *This Is My Legacy.* Paris, 1978.

Jureidini, Paul, and Hazen, William. *The Palestinian Movement in Politics.* Lexington, Mass., 1976.

Kadi, Leila S. *The Arab-Israeli Conflict.* Beirut, 1973.

———. *Basic Political Documents of the Armed Palestinian Resistance Movement.* Beirut, 1969.

———. *Arab Summit Conferences and the Palestinian Problem.* Beirut, 1966.

Karsh, Efraim. *Saddam Hussein: A Political Biography.* New York, 1991.

Kazziha, Walid. *Palestine in the Arab Dilemma.* London, 1979.

Kerr, Malcolm. *Arab Cold War, 1958–1970: Gamal Abd al-Nasir and His Rivals,* 2d ed. London, 1971.

Khaled, Leila. *My People Shall Live.* London, 1973.

Khalidi, Rashid. *Palestinian Identity.* New York, 1997.

———. *Under Siege.* New York, 1986.

Khamaysa, Rasim, Basim Makhul, and Adnan Awda, eds. *Conference on Palestinian-Egyptian Economic Relations.* Nablus, 1995.

El-Khazen, Farid. *The Breakdown of the State in Lebanon.* London, 2000.

Kiernan, Thomas. *Arafat: The Man and the Myth.* New York, 1976.

Kimmerling, Baruch, and Migdal, Joel. *Palestinians: The Making of a People.* New York, 1993.

King, John. *Handshake in Washington: The Beginning of Middle East Peace?* Reading, Mass., 1994.

Kirisci, Kemal. *The PLO and World Politics: A Study of the Mobilization and Support for the Palestinian Cause.* New York, 1986.

Kissinger, Henry. *Years of Upheaval.* New York, 1982.

———. *White House Years.* New York, 1979.

Korn, David. *Assassination in Khartoum.* Bloomington, Ind., 1993.

Laqueur, Walter. *The Age of Terrorism.* Boston, 1987.

Selected Bibliography

————. *Confrontation: The Middle East and World Politics.* New York, 1974.

Laqueur, Walter, and Rubin, Barry. *The Israel-Arab Reader,* 5th ed. New York, 2001.

————. *The Israel-Arab Reader.* New York, 1984.

Love, Kenneth. *Suez. The Twice Fought War.* New York, 1969.

Lunt, James. *Hussein of Jordan: A Political Biography.* London, 1989.

Lutfiyya, Abdullah M. *Baytin: A Jordanian Village.* London, 1966.

McDowell, D. *Palestine and Israel: The Uprising and Beyond.* London, 1989.

Makhoul, Basim. *Cement Trade in the West Bank: A Preliminary Evaluation.* Nablus, 1997.

Makovsky, David. *Making Peace with the PLO: The Rabin Government's Road to the Oslo Accords.* Boulder, Colo., 1996.

Al-Malki, Riyad. *Palestinian Opposition. Analysis of Alternatives.* Nablus, 1993.

Mansour, Jamal, and Jamal Salim. *Islamists and Elections.* Nablus, 1995.

Maoz, Moshe. *Palestinian Leadership on the West Bank: The Changing Role of the Mayors under Jordan and Israel.* London, 1984.

Martin, David C., and Walcott, John. *Best Laid Plans: The Inside Story of America's War against Terrorism.* New York, 1988.

Melman, Yossi, and Raviv, Dan. *Behind the Uprising: Israelis, Jordanians, and Palestinians.* New York, 1989.

————. *Imperfect Spies: History of Israeli Intelligence.* London, 1989.

————. *The Master Terrorist: The True Story behind Abu Nidal.* New York, 1986.

Merari, Ariel, and Shlomo, Elad. *The International Dimension of Palestinian Terrorism.* Boulder, Colo., 1986.

Mickolus, Edward F. *Transnational Terrorism: A Chronology of Events, 1968–1979.* Westport, Conn., 1980.

Middle East Contemporary Survey (MECS). Volumes VI–XXIII (1981–1999).

Migdal, Joel. *Palestinian Society and Politics.* Princeton, N.J., 1980.

Miller, Aaron David. *The Arab States and the Palestine Question: Between Ideology and Self-Interest.* New York, 1986.

————. *The PLO and the Politics of Survival.* Washington, D.C., 1983.

Mishal, Shaul. *The PLO under Arafat: Between Gun and Olive Branch.* New Haven, Conn., 1986.

————. *West Bank/East Bank: The Palestinians in Jordan, 1949–1967.* New Haven, Conn., 1978.

Moaz, Moshe. *Asad, the Sphinx of Damascus: A Political Biography.* London, 1988.

Norton Moore, John. *The Arab-Israeli Conflict.* 3 vols. Princeton, N.J., 1977.

Muslih, Muhammad Y. *The Origins of Palestinian Nationalism.* New York, 1988.

Nasser, Gamal Abdel. *Egypt's Liberation: The Philosophy of Revolution.* Washington, D.C., 1955.

Nasser, Jamal. *Palestinian Liberation Organization.* Tunis, n.d.

Norton, Augustus Richard. *International Relations of the PLO.* Carbondale, Ill., 1989.

Nutting, Anthony. *Nasser.* New York, 1972.

O'Ballance, Edgar. *Arab Guerrilla Power, 1967–1972.* Hamden, Conn., 1974.

O'Neill, Bard E. *Armed Struggle in Palestine: An Analysis of the Palestinian Guerrilla Movement.* Boulder, Colo., 1978.

———. *Revolutionary Warfare in the Middle East: The Israelis vs. the Fedayeen.* Boulder, Colo., 1974.

Pacepa, Ion Mihai. *Red Horizons.* Washington, D.C., 1987.

Palestine Liberation Organization Research Center. *Palestine Lives.* Beirut, 1973.

———. *Black September.* Beirut, 1971.

Palestinian Economic Research Institute. *Poverty in the West Bank and Gaza Strip.* Jerusalem, 1995.

Peres, Shimon. *Battling for Peace.* New York, 1995.

Porath, Y. *The Emergence of the Palestinian Arab National Movement, 1918–1929.* London, 1977.

———. *The Palestinian Arab National Movement, 1929–1939.* London, 1977.

Pryce-Jones, David. *The Face of Defeat: Palestinian Refugees and Guerrillas.* New York, 1973.

Rabie, Mohammed. *U.S.-PLO Dialogue: Secret Diplomacy and Conflict Resolution.* Gainesville, Fla., 1995.

———. *Conflict Resolution and the Middle East Peace Process.* Hamburg, Germany, 1993.

Quandt, William B. *Palestinian Nationalism: Its Political and Military Dimensions.* Santa Monica, Calif., 1971.

Quandt, William B., Jabber, Fuad, and Mosely Lesch, Ann. *The Politics of Palestinian Nationalism.* Berkeley, Calif., 1974.

Abd Rabbu, Yasir. *Analytical Review of the Reality and Nature of the Palestinian National Authority.* Nablus, 1995.

Rabinovich, Itmar. *The War for Lebanon: 1970–1983.* Ithaca, N.Y., 1984.

Abd al-Rahman, Asad. *Relations between Palestinians and Jordan after the Palestinian-Israeli Declaration of Principles Agreement.* Nablus, 1994.

Randall, Jonathan. *Going All the Way.* New York, 1983.

Raviv, Dan, and Melman, Yossi. *Every Spy a Prince: The Complete History of Israel's Intelligence Community.* Boston, Mass., 1990.

Rayyis, Riyad Najib. *Guerrillas for Palestine.* New York, 1976.

Robinson, Glenn E. *Building a Palestinian State: The Incomplete Revolution.* Bloomington, Ind., 1997.

Roth, Stephen J., ed. *The Impact of the Six-Day War.* New York, 1988.

Rubenberg, Cheryl. *The Palestine Liberation Organization: Its Institutional Infrastructure.* Belmont, Mass., 1983.

Rubin, Barry. *The Transformation of Palestinian Politics.* New York, 1999.

———. *Revolution until Victory? The Politics and History of the PLO.* Cambridge, Mass., 1994.

———. *Cauldron of Turmoil.* New York, 1992.

———. *Modern Dictators.* New York, 1987.

———. *The Arab States and the Palestine Conflict.* Syracuse, N.Y., 1981.

Rubin, Barry, and Judith Colp Rubin. *Anti-American Terrorism and the Middle East.* New York, 2002.

Rubinstein, Danny. *The Mystery of Arafat.* South Royalton, U.K., 1995.

Sahliyeh, Emile F. *In Search of Leadership: West Bank Politics since 1967.* Washington, D.C., 1988.

———. *The PLO after the Lebanon War.* Boulder, Colo., 1986.

Said, Edward. *The Question of Palestine*. New York, 1987.

———. *The Palestine Question and the American Context*. Beirut, 1979.

Said, Edward, ed. *The Arabs Today: Alternatives for Tomorrow*. Columbus, Ohio, 1973.

Izat Said, Nazir, and Hamami, Rima. *Research Into the Political and Social Trends in Palestine*. Nablus, 1997.

Saint-Prot, Charles. *Yasser Arafat: Biographie et entretiens*. Paris, 1990.

Sakhnini, Isam. *PLO: The Representative of the Palestinians*. Beirut, 1974.

Samir, Yusuf. *Abu Jihad*. Cairo, 1989.

Abd al-Sattar, Qasim. *The Islamic Movement and the Future of Opposition*. Nablus, 1996.

Savir, Uri. *The Process*. New York, 1998.

Sayigh, Rosemary. *Too Many Enemies: The Palestinian Experience in Lebanon*. London, 1994.

Sayigh, Yezid. *Armed Struggle and the Search for State*. Oxford, 1997.

Schiff, Zeev, and Rothstein, Ralph. *Fedayeen: Guerillas against Israel*. New York, 1972.

Schiff, Zeev, and Yaari, Ehud. *Intifada*. New York, 1990.

Seale, Patrick. *Asad of Syria*. London, 1988.

Sela, Abraham. *The Decline of the Arab-Israeli Conflict: Middle East Politics and the Quest for Regional Order*. Albany, N.Y., 1997.

Sharabi, Hisham. *Palestine Guerrillas: Their Credibility and Effectiveness*. Washington, D.C., 1970.

Abu Sharif, Bassam, and Mahnaimi, Uzi. *Tried by Fire: The Searing True Story of Two Men at the Heart of the Struggle between the Arabs and the Jews*. London, 1995.

Al-Sharq al-Awsat. *Palestinian Elections*. Cairo, 1996.

Shehadeh, Raja. *The Declaration of Principles and the Legal System in the West Bank*. Jerusalem, 1994.

Shemesh, Moshe. *The Palestinian Entity, 1959–1974: Arab Politics and the PLO*. London, 1988.

Shiqaqi, Khalil, ed. *Palestinian Elections: Political Environment, Electoral Behavior, Results*. Nablus, 1997.

———. *Transition to Liberal Democracy in Palestine: The Peace Process, the National Reconstruction, and Elections*. Nablus, 1996.

Shuqayri, Ahmad. *Liberation, Not Negotiation*. Beirut, 1966.

Shultz, George. *Turmoil and Triumph*. New York, 1993.

Snow, Peter. *Hussein*. Washington, D.C., 1972.

Sobel, Lester, ed. *Palestinian Impasse*. New York, 1997.

Steven, Stewart. *The Spymasters of Israel*. New York, 1980.

Sullivan, Denis J. *NGOs and Freedom of Association: Palestine and Egypt: A Comparative Analysis*. Jerusalem, 1995.

Tamari, Salim. *Political, Economic, and Social Dimensions of the Reintegration of Refugees*. Nablus, 1995.

Urquhart, Brian. *A Life in Peace and War*. New York, 1987.

U.S. Department of Defense. *Terrorist Group Profiles*. Washington, D.C., 1988.

U.S. Department of State. *Foreign Relations of the United States, 1964–1968*. Vol. 18, *Arab-Israeli Dispute, 1964–1967*. Washington, D.C., 2000.

———. *Abu Nidal Organization*. Washington, D.C., 1988.

Vatikiotis, P. J. *Politics and Military in Jordan: A Study of the Arab Legion from 1921–1957*. London, 1967.

Wallach, Janet, and Wallach, John. *Arafat in the Eyes of the Beholder*. New York, 1990.

Walters, Vernon. *Silent Missions*. New York, 1978.

Winslow, Charles. *Lebanon: War and Politics in a Fragmented Society*. New York, 1996.

Yaari, Ehud. *Strike Terror*. New York, 1970.

Yodfat, Aryeh Y., and Arnon-Ohanna, Yuval. *PLO Strategy and Politics*. New York, 1981.

INDEX

Index

Tibi, Ahmad, 137
Tlas, Mustafa, 232
Tunisian headquarters (PLO), 92, 102, 105
Turkman, Fakhri, 166

United Nations
    General Assembly, 70–73, 75, 115, 218
    on Palestinian economy, 171
    partition plan (1947), 16, 17
    refugee camp schools, 58
    Relief and Works Agency (UNRWA), 151
    Saudi Arabian peace plan and, 86
    Security Council, 6, 110, 195
    Security Council Resolution 194, 211
    Security Council Resolution 242, 38, 75,
        104, 108, 113–16, 136, 210, 216
    Security Council Resolution 338, 116,
        136, 210
United States. *See also* anti-Americanism
    Camp David agreement and (*see* Camp
        David agreement)
    Camp David summit and (*see* Camp
        David summit)
    Egypt-Israel peace and, 81
    Khartoum (Sudan) terrorist attack and,
        65
    Lebanon-Israeli ceasefire and, 86
    Oslo Agreement and (*see* Oslo Agreement)
    PA and, 178–79
    PLO, dialogue with, 113–17, 119–22, 172
    PLO secret agreement (Morocco 1973),
        73–75, 83
    Suez War and, 21–22
al-Urabi, Yusuf, 34
Urquhart, Brian, 227
U.S. embassy (Beirut) bombing, 97
U.S. embassy (Paris) negotiations, 205
U.S. marine barracks attack (Beirut), 97

Verstandig, Toni, 152
violence. *See also* terrorism
    Arafat's rejection of, 182
    Arafat's use of, 62, 153, 156–57, 162, 187–
        88, 203–5, 207, 236, 255
    Arafat's views on, 40–41, 67–68, 148,
        160, 179
    glorification of, 28, 258
Voice of Palestine, 62, 64, 122

Wachsman, Nachshon, 154–55
Walters, Vernon, 74
Washington, George, 140, 221
Washington talks (1991), 128–29, 132, 136
water system, Israeli, 32
al-Wazir, Khalil. *See* Abu Jihad
al-Wazzan, Shafiq, 89, 90
Weinberger, Caspar, 87
Weizman, Ezer, 105, 147
Welsh, James J., 64
West Bank. *See also* PA (Palestinian
        Authority)
    in Camp David agreement (*see* Camp
        David agreement)
    in Camp David summit (*see* Camp
        David summit)
    Intifada and (*see* Intifada)
    Jordan and, 26, 30, 107, 112
    in Oslo Agreement (*see* Oslo Agreement)
    PLO headquarters in, 39, 39–40, 172
    in Reagan peace plan, 92
    in Saudi Arabian peace plan, 85–86
Western media, 52, 58, 67, 218, 265
Western Wall, 13, 177, 195, 208, 210
women's rights, 129–30
World Economic Forum (Davos,
        Switzerland), 213–14
World Trade Center terrorist attack, 67, 97
Wye Plantation Agreement, 140, 181–83,
        191, 257

Yahiya, Abd al-Razak, 268
Yasin, Adnan, 143
Yasin, Ahmad, 149, 154, 180, 202
Yatom, Danny, 190, 197
Yusuf, Muhammad Ahmad al-Hamadi, 121
Yusuf, Nasir, 173–74

al-Za'nun, 168
Zabin, Abd al-Rahman, 174
Zaki, Abbas, 46, 142, 160, 235, 268
Zeevi, Rehavam, 4, 7, 8, 263, 265
Zinni, Anthony, 5, 264
Zionism
    Arafat's views on, 40–41, 68–69, 71, 84, 87
    Fatah's views on, 26, 211
    PLO and, 78
    UN General Assembly on, 72–73